Latin-English / English-Latin

Concise Dictionary

Latin-English / English-Latin

Concise Dictionary

Judith Lynn Sebesta

Hippocrene Books, Inc.
New York

INTRODUCTION

Latin has been in use as a language for over 2,500 years, since the beginning of Rome as a small settlement on the bank of the Tiber River. As Rome increased her control over the lands surrounding the Mediterranean and the areas of much of what is today northwestern Europe and much of Britain, the Latin language, the official language of the Roman government, became widely spoken by citizens and inhabitants of the Roman Empire. Following the fall of Rome, regional variations of Latin developed into the Romance languages and dialects which include Portuguese, Spanish, French, Italian, Romansh, Romanian, Sardinian, Catalan, and Occitan (Provençal). The western Christian church continued to use classical Latin, with some changes in pronunciation and grammar, as its liturgical language until the 1960s. Classical Latin served as a *lingua franca* for international affairs and correspondence by politicians, scientists, and scholars down to the seventeenth century. Nevertheless, some poets and authors have continued to write in Latin. In the past ten years or so, classical Latin as a medium for communication has experienced something of a small renaissance. For several years, for example, there has been a Finnish news program in Latin, and a number of classic children's stories (e.g. *Winnie the Pooh*, *The Wizard of Oz*) have been translated into Latin.

The English word list in this dictionary is based on the standard Hippocrene list, with some additional words peculiar to the Roman culture, such as titles of magistrates, terms used in the Roman calendar, and the like. The Latin word list is based on this amplified English word list and has been crosschecked with several Latin frequency word lists.

As in the case of all languages, exact equivalencies to English words sometimes do not exist. Latin *fābula*, for example, means any kind of a story, true or not, e.g. "narrative," "tale," "myth," as well as "conversation," and "play." While this dictionary focuses on classical Latin, it does suggest some more-modern expansions of Latin to English words, for example, "muffle up" is linked to *involvere*.

In translating English to Latin, the writer must keep in mind that Latin users were more concrete in their expression than users of English. That is, Latin users used concrete nouns in preference to abstract ones and more frequently used verbs rather than abstract nouns. For example, "The President has entered his second year of office," is expressed in Latin by "He began to preside over his second year of office" (*secundo anno officii praesse coepit*) in which *praesse* expresses the abstract noun "president." Another important difference between English and Latin expression, and hence vocabulary, is that some English transitive verbs are used intransitively in Latin. For example, "I obey you" is intransitive in Latin: *tibi pāreō*. In other instances, the intransitive English verb is expressed by a different verb ("the soldiers collected their weapons" *mīlitēs arma collēgērunt*, "a crowd was collecting" *multitūdō cōnveniēbat*). In a number of instances, where English uses a preposition, Latin may not: "to wait on" is equivalent in Latin to *servīre*.

PRONUNCIATION OF LATIN

SOUNDS OF VOWELS AND CONSONANTS

Latin vowels exist as long vowels marked by a macron or "long mark" (ā, ē, ī, ō, ū, ȳ and as short vowels that are unmarked. These vowels are pronounced as follows:

ā = *a* in *father*	**a** = *a* in *idea*
ē = *e* in *they*	**e** = *e* in *end*
ī = *i* in *machine*	**i** = *i* in *sit*
ō = *o* in *hole*	**o** = *o* in *not*
ū = *u* in *pool*	**u** = *u* in *full*
y or **ȳ** = *French u*	

Latin has six diphthongs, pronounced as follows:

ae = *i* in *like*
au = *ou* in *pout*
ei = *ei* in *eight*
eu = short *e* + *oo* in *pool*
oe = *oi* in *coil*
ui almost = *ui* in *ruin*

Latin consonants generally are pronounced like English consonants, with these exceptions:

bs is pronounced *ps*
bt is pronounced *pt*
c is always pronounced like *k*
ch is pronounced as *c* in *can*
g is always pronounced as in *get*
consonantal **i** is pronounced as *y* in *yes*
ph is pronounced like *p* in *put*
qu is pronounced as in *quick*
th is pronounced like *t* in *ten*
x is pronounced like *ks*
v is pronounced like *w*

SYLLABLES AND ACCENT

A word has as many syllables as it has vowels or diphthongs:

lau dant **ha be ō** **prō fi cīs cor**

All two-syllable words are accented on the first syllable:

<u>lau</u> dant **<u>pu</u> er**

If a word has more than two syllables, the accent falls on the next to last syllable (penult), if that syllable is long, i.e. if it contains a long vowel or diphthong or if it ends in a consonant:

au <u>dī</u> mus **a <u>moe</u> nus** **pu <u>el</u> la**

If the penult is not long, then the accent falls on the second to the last syllable (antepenult):

re <u>lū</u> ce ō **re <u>li</u> gi ō** **auc <u>tōr</u> i tās**

Words with an enclitic attached push their accent ahead by one syllable.

pu <u>el</u> la que

Compounded Words

Many verbs, and some nouns and adjectives, are formed by prefixing a preposition or other article:

Prefix	Meaning	Assimilation	Example
ā, ab, abs	away	au-	aufugiō
ad	to, towards	ac-, af-, ag-, an-, ap-, as-, at-	accēdō appōrtō
amb	around, both	---	ambigō
ante	before	---	anteferō
bī	both, two	---	bīduum
circum	around	---	circumdūcō
contrā	against	contrō-	contrārius
cum	together, with force	com-, col-, cōn-, cor-, cō-	cōnstō
dē	down, utterly	---	dēcēdō
dis	apart, asunder	dī-, dif-, dir-	dispār
ē, ex	out (of)	ef-	ēdō
in	in, on, against	il-, im-, ir-	illūstris
in	not	il-, im-, ir-	incertus
inter	between, to pieces	---	intersum
mult	many	multi-	multiplicō
ob	towards, to meet	oc-, of-, og-, op-	occāsiō

Prefix	Meaning	Assimilation	Example
per	across, very thoroughly, perfectly, completely	---	**permultus**
post	after, behind, following	**pō-**	**postquam**
prae	before, very	---	**praesum**
prō	forward, in front	**por-**	**prōdeō**
re	back, again	**red-**	**reddō**
sē	apart	---	**sēdūcō**
sub	towards, to meet, under, somewhat, secretly	**suc-, suf-, sug- sum-, sup-, sur-**	**sufficiō**
super	upon, over and above	---	**superstes**
trāns	across, over, beyond	**trān-, trā**	**trādō**

FORMAT OF ENTRIES

Alternate spellings of a principal part are given in parentheses:

abeō, -īre, -īvī (-iī), -itum
honōs (honor), -ōris
ubi (ubī)

VERBS

For transitive and intransitive verbs, the principal parts are given, as follows: present 1st person singular active, present active infinitive, perfect 1st person singular active, supine: **acuō, -ere, acuī, acūtum**

If a principal part is missing, it is indicated by three dashes: **ahorrēo, horrēre, horruī, ---**

For deponent verbs, the principal parts are present 1st person singular, present infinitive, perfect 1st person (masculine) singular: **abōminor, abōminārī, abōminā-tus sum**

For semi-deponent verbs, the principal parts are present 1st person singular, present infinitive, perfect 1st person (masculine) singular: **audeo, -ēre, ausus sum**

Because many Latin verbs exist as compounds with prepositional prefixes (e.g. **volvō, -ere, volvī, volūtum**), the verbal base is indicated in such entries (e.g. **involvō, -volvere, -volvī, -volūtum**) to enable users of this dictionary to see more easily this connection.

Nouns

For nouns, the nominative singular and genitive singular are generally given: **audītus, -ūs**

In some instances the genitive form is written out in full, or in abbreviated form so that the base of the noun is clearly identifiable: **arx, arcis; artifex, -ficis**

Adjectives

For first and second declension adjectives, the masculine, feminine, and neuter singular nominative forms are given; the base of the adjective can be determined from the masculine nominative form: **artificiōsus, -a, -um**

In the case of first and second declension adjectives for which the masculine nominative does not end in *-us*, the adjective base can be determined from the feminine nominative form: **asper, aspera, asperum**

For third declension adjectives of three terminations, the masculine, feminine, and neuter singular nominative forms are given; the base of the adjective can be determined from the feminine nominative form: **ācer, ācris, ācre**

For third declension adjectives of two terminations, the masculine, feminine, and neuter nominative forms are given; the base of the adjective can be determined from the masculine nominative form: **anīlis, -is, -e**
For third declension adjectives of one termination, the nominative form is given; the base of the adjective is given in parentheses: **absēns (absent-)**

ABBREVIATIONS

abb. abbreviation
abl. ablative
absol. absolute(ly) (transitive verb used without direct object)
acc. accusative
act. active
adj. adjective
adj. nt. neuter adjective
adj./pl. adjective plural
adv. adverb
anat. anatomical
arch. architectural
art. article
aux. auxiliary
bot. botanical
comp. comparative
conj. conjunction
dat. dative
def. defective
dem. pron. demonstrative pronoun
exp. expletive
f. feminine
f./pl. feminine plural
gen. genitive
ger. gerund
gerv. gerundive
imp. impersonal
impv. imperative
indecl. indeclinable
indv. indicative
infv. infinitive
interj. interjection
interr. interrogative
irreg. irregular
m. masculine
m./f. masculine and feminine
m./nt. masculine and neuter

m./pl. masculine plural
mid. middle
n. noun
neg. negative
nf. noun feminine
nm. noun masculine
nm/f. noun masculine and feminine
nnt. noun neuter
nt. neuter
nt./pl. neuter plural
num. numeral
opp. opposite of
pass. passive
pers. person
pl. plural
poss. possessive
postpos. postpositive
pref. prefix
prep. preposition
pron. pronoun
ref. reference
rel. pron. relative pronoun
sc. scilicet (i.e., understood without being expressed)
sg. singular
subjv. subjunctive
sup. superlative
usu. usually
v.d.i. deponent verb (intransitive)
v.d.i.t. deponent verb (intransitive and transitive)
v.d.t. deponent verb (transitive)
v.i. intransitive verb
voc. vocative
v.t. transitive verb
w. with
zool. zoological

Latin–English Dictionary

A

ā (*before consonants*), **ab** (*before vowels and consonants, esp. h, l, n, r, s*), **abs** (*only before c, q, and t, esp. before* **tē**) *prep.* (+ abl.) from, away from, out of (*of motion*); at (*of the direction from which an object is viewed*); by (*of agency*); since, after (*of time*)

abacus, -ī *nm.* abacus, counting board; gaming board; square board

abaliēnō, -aliēnāre, -aliēnāvī, -aliēnātum *v.t.* convey away; sell, transfer ownership; remove; estrange

abdicātiō, -ōnis *nf.* disowning (*of children*); resignation (*from public office*)

abdicō, -dicāre, -dicāvī, -dicātum *v.t.* resign (*from public office*); renounce (*a child*)

abditus, -a, -um (w. comp. + sup.) *adj.* hidden, concealed; secluded, remote (*of places*)

abdō, -dere, -didī, -ditum *v.t.* hide; put away

abdōmen, -inis *nnt.* abdomen, paunch; gluttony; sensuality

abeō, -īre, -īvī (-iī), -itum *v.i.* go away, leave; pass away, disappear

abhinc *adv.* hereafter; ago

abhorrēo, -horrēre, -horruī, --- *v.t., v.i.* shrink back from; shudder at; be inconsistent with, be averse to, be unconnected with (+ **ab** + abl.)

abiciō (abjic-), -icere, -iēcī, -iectum *v.t.* throw away, cast away; abandon, give up

abiectus (abject-), -a, -um (w. comp. + sup.) *adj.* downcast, overwhelmed; low, worthless

abigō, -igere, -ēgī, -āctum *v.t.* drive away; banish, get rid of

abnegō, -negāre, -negāvī, -negātum *v.t.* refuse; (+ infv.) refuse (*to do something*); deny

abōminor, abōmināri, abōminātus sum *v.d.t.* deprecate; abhor, detest

abortiō, -ōnis *nf.* miscarriage, premature birth

abrogō, -rogāre, -rogāvī, -rogātum *v.t.* annul, repeal (*of laws*); revoke, take away, remove (*of public office; w. acc. of office* + *dat. of person*)

abrumpō, -rumpere, -rūpī, -ruptum *v.t.* break off tear, burst

abruptus, -a, -um (w. comp. + sup.) *adj.* sheer, steep (*of places*)

abs *See* **ā**.

abscēdō, -cēdere, -cessī, -cessum *v.i.* give way, withdraw, march away (*of armies*); disappear; abandon, desist from (+ **ab** + abl., *or* + abl. alone)

absconditus, -a, -um *adj.* hidden, secret

absēns (absent-) (w. sup.) *adj.* absent, not present, away
absentia, -ae *nf.* absence
absolūtiō, -ōnis *nf.* acquittal (*in law*); completeness (*of rhetorical expression*)
absolūtus, -a, -um (w. comp. + sup.) *adj.* complete; unconditional, absolute (*of rhetorical expression*)
absolvō, -solvere, -solvī, -solūtum *v.t.* set free; acquit, absolve from a charge (+ abl. or gen. *or* + **dē** + abl.); pay off, satisfy; complete, finish
absque *prep.* (+ abl.) without
abstergeō, -tergēre, -tersī, -tersum *v.t.* wipe off; break off; banish, expel
abstinentia, -ae *nf.* abstinence, temperance; starvation
abstineō, -tinēre, -tinuī, -tentum *v.t., v.i.* hold back, keep away from; abstain from (+ abl., *or* **ab** + abl., *or* infv., *or* **quīn** or **quōminus** + subjv.; *or* gen.)
abstrahō, -trahere, -trāxī, -tractum *v.t.* drag away; exclude, divert, cut off (+ **ab** + abl.)
absum, abesse, āfuī, āfutūrus *v.i.* be absent, be far, be away
absūmō, -sūmere, -sūmpsī, -sūmptum *v.t.* take away; diminish, spend, consume; destroy, kill
absurdus, -a, -um *adj.* out of tune, harsh; incongruous, absurd; stupid, unreasonable
abundantia, -ae *nf.* abundance, plenty
abundō, -undāre, -undāvī, -undātum *v.i.* overflow, be rich in, abound with (+ abl.)
abūtor, abūtī, abūsus sum *v.t.* use up; abuse (+ abl.)
āc *conj. See* **atque**.
accēdō, -cēdere, -cessī, -cessum *v.i.* come near, approach (+ **ad** or **in** + acc.)
accelerō, -celerāre, -celerāvī, -celerātum *v.i.* hasten, hurry; make haste
accendō, -cendere, -cendī, -cēnsum *v.t.* ignite, kindle; inflame, arouse; encourage; embitter, exasperate
acceptiō, -iōnis *nf.* acceptance, reception
acceptus, -a, -um *adj.* welcome, pleasing (*of persons,* + dat.); popular
accessus, -ūs *nm.* approach to, access, entrance
accido, -cidere, -cidī, --- *v.i.* fall upon; reach; come to pass, take place
accipiō, -cipere, -cēpī, -ceptum *v.t.* receive, accept; take into possession; receive a guest; learn; meet with, experience; undertake
accipiter, -cipitris *nm.* hawk
acclīvitās, -ātis *nf.* inclination, upward slope

accommodātus, -a, -um (w. comp. + sup.) *adj.* adapted, suited, appropriate (+ dat. *or* + **ad** + acc.)

accommodō, -commodāre, -commodāvī, -commodātum *v.t.* adapt, fit, adjust to (+ **ad** or **in** + acc.)

accubō, -cubāre, -cubuī, -cubitum *v.i.* lie near; recline (+ dat.)

accūrātus, -a, -um (w. comp. + sup.) *adj.* careful, precise, exact

accūsātiō, -ōnis *nf.* accusation; indictment

accūsātor, -ōris *nm.* accuser, prosecutor, plaintiff

accūsō, -āre, -āvī, -ātum *v.t.* find fault with, blame; charge, accuse, prosecute (+ acc. of the person charged + **dē** + abl. *or* **propter** + acc. *or* gen. of the charge or punishment)

ācer, ācris, ācre (comp. **ācrior**, sup. **ācerrimus**) *adj.* sharp, piercing; harsh, bitter; keen, passionate; violent, fierce; severe

acerbitās, -ātis *nf.* bitterness; harshness; **acerbitātēs, -ātum** *or* **-atium** *nf./pl.* sorrows, affliction; calamities

acerbus, -a, -um *adj.* tart, sharp; harsh, cruel; rigorous

acervus, -ī *nm.* pile, heap; great quantity, mass

acētāria, -ōrum (*sc.* **olera**) *nnt./pl.* salad prepared with vinegar

acētum, -ī *nnt.* vinegar, sour wine; sense, shrewdness

acidus, -a, -um *adj.* sour, disagreeable

aciēs, -ēī *nf.* sharp point, sharp edge; sharpness of vision; line of battle; battle; force

acinus *or* **-um, -ī** *nm.* berry; grape; pit of a berry

acquiēscō (**adq-**), **-quiēscere, -quiēvī, -quiētum** *v.i.* become quiet; be at rest; be content; be resigned

acquīrō (**adq-**), **-quīrere, -quīsīvī, -quīsītum** *v.t.* gain in addition; add, obtain

āctiō, -ōnis *nf.* driving, doing; lawsuit; prosecution, trial; **āctiōnēs, -ōnum** *nf./pl.* public measures

āctum, -ī *nnt.* act, deed; method of procedure; **acta, -ōrum** *nnt./pl.* proceedings; register of public acts (*published by the Roman Senate*)

āctus, -ūs *nm.* driving, doing; act, achievement; act of a play

aculeus, -ī *nm.* sting; point; cutting remarks

acūmen, -inis *nnt.* point, tip; sharpness, keenness, intelligence

acuō, -ere, acuī, acūtum *v.t.* sharpen

acus, -ūs *nf.* needle

acūtus, -a, -um (w. comp. + sup.) *adj.* sharp, finely pointed; pungent; violent; keen

ad *prep.* (+ acc.) to, towards, near, at, near to, among, according to; up to, until; for; in order to (+ ger. *or* + gerv.); in regard to, according to

adaequō, -aequāre, -aequāvī, -aequātum *v.t., v.i.* make equal to (+ **cum** + abl.); match, keep up with

adamas, -antis *nm.* hardest iron; durable substance; diamond

adamō, -amāre, -amāvī, -amātum *v.t.* fall in love with

addīscō, -dīscere, -didicī, --- *v.t.* learn in addition, continue to learn, gain knowledge of

additīcius, -a, -um *adj.* additional, annexed

addō, -dere, didī, -ditum *v.t.* put to, bring to; add, increase; consider also

addūcō, -dūcere, -dūxī, -ductum *v.t.* lead to, conduct, persuade, prevail upon; draw tight

adeō *adv.* thus far, so much, so long; in fact, really

adeō, -īre, -īvī (-iī), -itum *v.i.* go to, approach; undertake; encounter; submit to (+ **ad** + acc.)

adeps, -ipis *nm/f.* fat, lard; obesity

adfīgō (aff-), -fīgere, -fīxī, -fīxum *v.t.* fasten to; annex; impress on

adfīnis (affīnis), -is, -e *adj.* neighboring, adjoining; connected with (+ dat.); **adfīnis (affīnis), -is** *nm/f.* relation or relative by marriage

adfīnitās (affīnitās), -ātis *nf.* relationship through marriage

adhaereō, -haerēre, -haesī, -haesum *v.i.* cling to, stick to; border on, be near to (+ dat.)

adhaerēscō, -haerēscere, -haesī, -haesum *v.i.* cling to, adhere; be devoted to; fit, suit (+ dat.)

adhibeō, -hibēre, -hibuī, -hibitum *v.t.* hold to, apply; furnish; employ, use

adhortor, adhortārī, adhortātus sum *v.t.* encourage, urge, exhort (+ **ut** or **nē** + subjv.)

adhūc *adv.* heretofar; so far, as yet; still

adiaceō (adj-), -iacēre, -iacuī, --- *v.i.* adjoin, lie by the side of, be adjacent (+ dat.)

adiciō (adj-), -icere, -iēcī, -iectum *v.t.* throw to, set near; turn; increase; do in addition

adiectiō, -ōnis *nf.* addition, adding to

adigō, -igere, -ēgī, -āctum *v.t.* drive; take; thrust, drive home; compel

adimō, -imere, -ēmī, -ēmptum *v.t.* take away; deprive of, free from

adipīscor, adipīscī, adeptus sum *v.t.* arrive at; obtain, get, acquire; win, secure

aditus, -ūs *nm.* a going to, approach; way in, entrance; access; arrival

adiūdicō (adj-), -iūdicāre, -iūdicāvī, -iūdicātum *v.t.* award, adjudge; assign

adiūmentum (adj-), -ī *nnt.* assistance, aid

adiungō (adj-), -iungere, -iūnxī, -iūnctum *v.t.* join to, attach to; annex, unite to; win; apply

adiūtor (adj-), -ōris *nm.* assistant, helper, deputy

adiūtrīx (adj-), -icis *nf.* helper, assistant

adiuvō (adj-), -iuvāre, -iūvī, -iūtum *v.t.* aid, assist, support, sustain

adloquor (all-), adloquī, adlocūtus sum *v.t.* address, speak to; encourage

administer, administrī *nm.* attendant, helper; tool

administra, -ae *nf.* female attendant, helper; tool

administrātiō, -ōnis *nf.* giving of help; administration, management

administrō, -ministrāre, -ministrāvī, -ministrātum *v.t.* manage, superintend; direct, conduct

admīrābilis, -is, -e *adj.* admirable, wonderful; strange; astonishing

admīrandus, -a, -um *adj.* worthy of being admired, wonderful; strange; astonishing

admīrātiō, -ōnis *nf.* admiration; wonder, surprise, astonishment

admīror, admīrārī, admīrātus sum *v.d.i.t.* admire, view with approval; wonder at, be astonished

admisceō, -miscēre, -miscuī, -mixtum *or* **-mīstum** *v.t.* mix with, mingle with; join; involve, implicate

admissiō, -ōnis *nf.* audience, formal interview

admittō, -mittere, -mīsī, -missum *v.t.* send to; admit, give access; permit; perpetrate

admodum *adv.* to full measure; quite, at least, no less than; no more than; fully, very; at all; considerably

admoneō, -monēre, -monuī, -monitum *v.t.* remind, suggest; advise, warn

admonitiō, -ōnis *nf.* suggestion, reminding

admoveō, -movēre, -mōvī, -mōtum *v.t.* move to; carry; drive; apply to

admurmurātiō, -ōnis *nf.* murmuring

adnumerō, -numerāre, -numerāvī, -numerātum *v.t.* count out, pay; include, reckon among

adnuō (ann-), -nuere, -nuī, -nutum *v.i.* nod to; nod assent, give assent (+ dat. *or* + acc.)

adoptiō, -ōnis *nf.* adoption

adoptō, -optāre, -optāvī, -optātum *v.t.* choose for oneself; adopt a child

adorior, adorīrī, adortus sum *v.t.* rise up; attack, assault; attempt

adōrnō, -ōrnāre, -ōrnāvī, -ōrnātum *v.t.* provide, equip; embellish, adorn

adsentior (ass-), adsentīrī, adsēnsus sum *v.i.* subscribe to, agree to (+ dat.)

adsum, adesse, adfuī, adfutūrus *v.i.* attend, be present; stand by, support; impend; be near at hand (+ dat. *or* + absol.)

adulēscēns (adol-), -entis *adj.* young, adolescent; **adulēscēns (adol-), -entis** *nm/f.* young person

adulēscentia (adol-), -ae *nf.* youth *(the age between fifteen and twenty-five or so)*

adūlor, adūlārī, adūlātus sum *v.t.* flatter; *v.d.t.* fawn on

adulter, adultera, adulterum *adj.* adulterous, unchaste

adulterium, -ī *nnt.* adultery

adultus, -a, -um (w. comp.) *adj.* fully grown, mature, adult

adumbrō, -umbrāre, -umbrāvī, -umbrātum *v.t.* sketch, shade in

advena, -ae *nm/f.* stranger, foreigner; immigrant; visitor

adveniō, -venīre, -vēnī, -ventum *v.i., v.t.* arrive, reach, come to (+ **in** + acc. *or* + acc. alone)

adventus, -ūs *nm.* appearance, arrival, approach

adverbium, -ī *nnt.* adverb

adversārius, -a, -um *adj.* opposed to; hostile, contrary (+ dat.)

adversor, adversārī, adversātus sum *v.t.* resist (+ dat.); *v.d.i.t.* oppose

adversum (adversus) *adv.* opposite to, against, toward; *prep.* (+ acc.) before, facing; in the presence of; in answer to; in comparison with; in respect of; against, contrary to

adversus, -a, -um *adj.* opposite, towards, facing, placed in front of; unsuccessful; adverse, hostile, opposed

advesperāscit, advesperāscere, advesperāvit *v.i.* (imp.) it is getting dark, evening is approaching

advocātiō, -ōnis *nf.* attendance in response to summons; consultation; counsel; legal aid

advocātus, -ī *nm.* one called in to help; advisor in a lawsuit, advocate

advolō, -volāre, -volāvī, -volātum *v.i.* fly to; hasten to (+ **ad** + acc.)

adytum, -ī *nnt.* sanctuary, shrine; inmost holiest place in a temple

aedicula, -ae *nf.* small building; small temple, shrine, chapel

aedificātiō, -ōnis *nf.* the process of construction; building, structure; site

aedificium, -ī *nnt.* structure, building

aedificō, -ficāre, -ficāvī, -ficātum *v.t.* build, erect, construct

aedīlis, -is *nm.* aedile *(the magistrate in charge of public works and records, buildings, and spectacles)*

aedis (aedēs), -is *nf.* temple, sanctuary; **aedēs, -ium** *nf./pl.* house, dwelling

aeger, aegra, aegrum *adj.* ill, sick; feeble; distressed, suffering

aegrē (comp. **aegrius**; sup. **aegerrimē**) *adv.* painfully; with distress, with difficulty; hardly; reluctantly

aegrōtō, -āre, -āvī, -ātum *v.i.* be ill, be sick; languish

aemulātiō, -ōnis *nf.* rivalry, emulation; jealousy, ill-natured rivalry

aemulor, aemulārī, aemulātus sum *v.d.i.t.* rival, emulate (+ acc.); envy (+ dat.)

aemulus, -a, -um *adj.* rivaling in, emulous; zealous (+ gen. *or* + dat.)

aēneus (ahēn-), -a, -um *adj.* made of bronze or copper; bronze in color

aenigma, -matis *nnt.* riddle, mystery

aequābilis, -is, -e *adj.* like, similar, uniform; impartial, fair

aequālis, -is, -e *adj.* like, equal; equal in age, contemporary (+ dat.)

aequātus, -a, -um *adj.* equalized, level, even

aequitās, -ātis *nf.* evenness, fairness, equity; calmness, contentment

aequō, -āre, -āvī, -ātum *v.t.* make level, make equal; equal, come up to

aequus, -a, -um (w. comp. + sup.) *adj.* even, level; equitable, reasonable, fair; calm, patient; favorable; **aequē** *adv.* equally; just as, in like manner

āēr, āeris *nm.* air, atmosphere; sky; mist, vapor; weather

aerārium, -ī *nnt.* the public treasury; finances

aerūginōsus, -a, -um *adj.* rusty, covered with rust

aerumna, -ae *nf.* hardship, trouble

aes, aeris *nnt.* bronze, copper; bronze coinage; **aes aliēnum, aeris aliēnī** *nnt.* debt

aestās, -ātis *nf.* summer; **aestāte** *adv.* in summer

aestimātiō, -ōnis *nf.* appraisal, valuation; worth, value

aestimō, -āre, -āvī, -ātum *v.t.* value, set a price on (+ abl. or gen. of value)

aestīvus, -a, -um *adj.* pertaining to summer

aestuō, -āre, -āvī, -ātum *v.i.* burn, be warm, glow; be excited, be inflamed; waver, hesitate; boil, seethe

aestuōsus, -a, -um (w. sup.) *adj.* hot; agitated

aestus, -ūs *nm.* violent agitation; heat, glow; swell, wave; ardor; doubt

aetās, -ātis *nf.* age, period of time; lifetime; generation; old age

aeternitās, -ātis *nf.* eternity; immortality; enduring renown

aeternus, -a, -um (w. comp.) *adj.* eternal, lasting, endless, unbroken, perpetual

aethēr, -eris *nm.* the upper air

aethereus, -a, -um *adj.* belonging to the upper air; heavenly

aevum, -ī *nnt.* eternity; period of life, lifetime; old age; age, generation

affectus (adf-), -a, -um *adj.* provided with, gifted; disposed; weakened; nearly at an end; **affectus (adf-), -ūs** *nm.* disposition, mood; desire, affection

afferō (adf-), afferre, attulī, allātum *v.t.* bring to, carry to; introduce; report, announce; contribute, offer

afficiō (adf-), -ficere, -fēcī, -fectum *v.t.* do something to, use; affect, influence; afflict, weaken, impair

affirmātiō (adf-), -ōnis *nf.* confirmation, asseveration

affirmō (adf-), -firmāre, -firmāvī, -firmātum *v.t.* strengthen; confirm, encourage; maintain, aver

afflātus (adf-), -ūs *nm.* blowing on, breathing on; inspiration

afflīctō (adf-), -flīctāre, -flīctāvī, -flīctātum *v.t.* break to pieces; curse; afflict, harass

afflīctus (adf-), -a, -um *adj.* downcast, dejected, distressed

affluēns (adf-) (affluent-, adfluent-) *adj.* abounding, overflowing

agellus, -ī *nm.* lot, section of land, small field

ager, agrī *nm.* field; land; territory, district

agger, aggeris *nm.* heap, pile dam, mole, barrier

aggravō (adg-), -gravāre, -gravāvī, -gravātum *v.t.* increase; aggravate, make worse

aggredior (adg-), aggredī, agressus sum *v.d.* approach, advance; address; attack; assume, begin; try

aggregō (adg-), -gregāre, -gregāvī, -gregātum *v.t.* add to a flock; attach; collect, gather together

agilis, -is, -e *adj.* easily moved, light; quick, active, nimble, prompt

agitātiō, -ōnis *nf.* movement; activity in; flourishing, quick movement; pursuit

agitātor, -ōris *nm.* driver of cattle or horses; charioteer

agitō, -āre, -āvī, -ātum *v.t.* set in motion; brandish, agitate, stir up, vex; consider, discuss

agmen, -minis *nnt.* a collection moving forward; retinue; stream; army; band; army on the march

agnoscō, -noscere, -nōvī, -nitum *v.t.* identify, recognize; acknowledge; perceive; understand

āgnus, -ī *nm.* lamb

agō, agere, ēgī, āctum *v.t., v.i.* set in motion, drive; lead, guide; incite; pursue; rob; do, transact; manage; accomplish; spend time, live; deal with confer; plead

agrestis, -is, -e *adj.* of the country, rural; rude, uncultivated

agricola, -ae *nm.* farmer; peasant; a rustic
agricultūra, -ae *nf.* agriculture
āiō *v.i.* (*def.*) say, assert *(used parenthetically)*
āla, -ae *nf.* wing of a bird; armpit; military squadron, wing of an army
alacer, alacris, alacre (w. comp.) *adj.* lively, quick, eager, enthusiastic,
cheerful
alapa, -ae *nf.* cuff, slap
albus, -a, -um *adj.* white, dead white; pale; bright
alea, -ae *nf.* dice; playing with dice, gambling; chance, risk; uncertainty
aleātor, -ōris *nm.* dice player, gambler
alga, -ae *nf.* seaweed
algor, -ōris *nm.* cold
aliās *adv.* at another time; sometimes
alibī *adv.* at another place, elsewhere; otherwise, in other respects
alicubī *adv.* somewhere, anywhere
aliēnus, -a, um (w. comp. + sup.) *adj.* of another, another's; alien, strange;
out-of-place, unsuitable; unfriendly; **aliēnum, -ī** *nnt.* the property of
another
alimenta, -ōrum *nnt./pl.* nourishment, food; support, maintenance
alipta, -ae and **aliptēs, -is** *nm.* trainer *or* manager of wrestlers; wrestling
master
aliquamdiū *adv.* for a while, for some time
aliquandō *adv.* occasionally, from time to time; formerly; hereafter; finally
aliquantum, -ī *nnt.* small amount; something
aliquantus, -a, -um *adj.* moderate, not small; **aliquantō** *adv.* somewhat,
rather
aliquī, aliqua, aliquod *adj.* some, any, some other
aliquis, aliqua, aliquid *pron.* someone; anyone, anybody
aliquō *adv.* to some place, somewhere; elsewhere
aliquot *adj.* (*indecl.*) several, some
aliter *adv.* otherwise; in another manner
ālium *or* **allium, -ī** *nnt.* garlic
alius *or* **alis, alia, aliud** *or* **alid** (gen. **alterīus**) *adj.* other, another; different; else
alliciō (adl-), -licere, -lexī, -lectum *v.t.* allure, attract, persuade (+ **ad** + acc.)
alligō (adl-), -āre, -āvī, -ātum *v.t.* fasten, tie down, tie to; hold fast,
detain, hinder; oblige; accuse
alō, -ere, aluī, altum *or* **alitum** *v.t.* feed, maintain, support, nourish;
cherish

altāria, -ium *nnt./pl.* altar

altē (w. comp. and sup.) *adv.* high, from above; deeply; far, remotely

alter, altera, alterum (gen. **alterīus**, dat. **alterī**) *adj.* the other of two, second, next; **alter (altera, alterum) . . . alter (altera, alterum)** *pron.* the one . . . the other

altercātiō, -ōnis *nf.* debate, discussion; altercation

alternus, -a, -um *adj.* one after the other; by turns

alteruter, alterutra, alterutrum (gen. **alterutrīus** *or* **alterīus utrīus**; dat. **alterutri** *or* **alterī utrī**) *adj.* one or the other, either

altitūdō, -inis *nf.* height, altitude; depth; secrecy

altum, -ī *nnt.* height; depth; sea; sky

altus, -a, -um (w. comp. + sup.) *adj.* grown great; high; deep; secret; ancient

alumna, -ae *nf.* foster daughter

alumnus, -ī *nm.* foster child, foster son

alveus, -ī *nm.* hollow, cavity; trough, tub; bathtub; riverbed; beehive

amābilis, -is, -e (w. comp. + sup.) *adj.* lovable; lovely, attractive

amārus, -a, -um (w. comp. + sup.) *adj.* bitter, sour, pungent; shrill; disagreeable, unpleasant; irritable, biting, acrimonious

ambigō, -igere, ---, -āctum *v.i.* be busy with two things at the same time; go about; avoid; hesitate, doubt; argue, debate

ambitiō, -ōnis *nf.* going around; canvassing for votes; flattery

ambitiōsus, -a, -um (w. comp.) *adj.* surrounding, entwining; ambitious; eager for favor or honor

ambitus, -ūs *nm.* going around; revolution, circuit; border, circumference; canvassing for votes

ambō, ambae, ambō *adj.* both *(of two together)*

ambulātiō, -ōnis *nf.* walk, stroll; place for walking

ambulō, -āre, -āvī, -ātum *v.i.* walk, take a walk

ambūrō, -ūrere, -ussī, -ustum *v.t.* burn around, singe; consume; be numb; be nipped

āmēns (āment-) (w. comp. + sup.) *adj.* out of one's senses, frantic; foolish

āmentia, -ae *nf.* madness; stupidity

amiciō, -īre, amixī *or* **amicuī, amictum** *v.t.* throw around, wrap around; clothe; surround, enclose

amīcitia, -ae *nf.* friendship, alliance

amīcus, -a, -um (w. comp. + sup.) *adj.* friendly, dear, kind, pleasing; **amīcus, -ī** *nm. or* **amīca, -ae** *nf.* friend

amita, -ae *nf.* paternal aunt

āmittō, -mittere, -mīsī, -missum *v.t.* send away, let go; lose

amnis, -is *nm.* stream, river

amō, -āre, -āvī, -ātum *v.t.* love, like; be fond of; take pleasure in; (+ infv.) like to, be wont to

amoenitās, -ātis *nf.* beauty, pleasantness, charm (*usu. of places*)

amoenus, -a, -um (w. sup.) *adj.* beautiful, pleasant, delightful to look at, charming

amor, -ōris *nm.* love, affection; devotion; passion

āmoveō, -movēre, -mōvī, -mōtum *v.t.* move away, take away, eliminate, remove, banish, get rid of

amplector, amplectī, amplexus sum *v.d.t.* hug, embrace; love, esteem

amplexus, -ūs *nm.* embrace, caress; confining circuit, limits, confines

amplificō, -ficāre, -ficāvī, -ficātum *v.t.* enlarge, broaden, extend, enhance

amplius *adv.* further; besides; more

amplus, -a, -um (w. comp. + sup.) *adj.* ample, large, considerable; magnificent; renowned, honorable

ampulla, -ae *nf.* vial, flask, bottle

amputō, -āre, -āvī, -ātum *v.t.* cut off, amputate; diminish

amygdala, -ae *nf. and* **amygdalum, -ī** *nnt.* almond

amylum *or* **amulum, -ī** *nnt.* starch

an *conj.* or, or rather, or indeed (*introduces the second item of an alternative question*)

anas, anatis *nf.* (gen. pl. **anatum** *or* **anatium**) duck

anatomia, -ae *nf.* anatomy

anceps (ancipit-) (*abl. sg. always* **ancipitī**) *adj.* two-headed; two-fold; uncertain, undecided

ancilla, -ae *nf.* maid, female servant

ancora, -ae *nf.* anchor

ancorāle, -is *nnt.* cable

andrōn, -ōnis *nm.* corridor

anfrāctus *or* **amfrāctus, -ī, -a, -um** *adj.* bending, turning, winding, crooked

angelus, -ī *nm.* messenger; angel

angiportus, -ūs *nm.* alley, narrow street

angō, angere, anxī, actum *or* **anxum** *v.t.* draw tight, squeeze; choke; distress, vex

angor, -ōris *nm.* throttling, strangling; anguish, torment

anguilla, -ae *nf.* eel

anguis, -is *nm/f.* snake, serpent

angulus, -ī *nm.* angle, corner

angustiae, -ārum *nf./pl.* narrowness; defile, strait; brevity; scarcity; distress

angustus, -a, -um (w. comp. + sup.) *adj.* narrow; short; pinching; critical; difficult; petty

anhēlitus, -ūs *nm.* wheezing, puffing, panting; vapor

anhēlō, -āre, -āvī, -ātum *v.i., v.t.* pant, puff, wheeze; pant for, desire eagerly

anīlis, -is, -e *adj.* of an old woman; silly

anima, -ae *nf.* air, air current; breath of life, soul

animadversiō, -ōnis *nf.* observation, inquiry; censure, punishment

animadvertō, -vertere, -vertī, -versum *v.t.* attend to, pay attention to; regard, perceive; censure, punish

animal, -ālis *nnt.* animal (*any living thing including mankind*)

animāns (animant-) *adj.* imparting life, animating; **animāns, animantis** *nm/f.* living being, animal

animus, -ī *nm.* soul, life; intellect, reason; heart, affection, passion; courage; frame of mind, mood; arrogance; resolution, design

annālis, -is, -e *adj.* yearly

annītor (adn-), annītī, annīsus *or* **annīxus sum** *v.d.i.t.* lean on; exert oneself; make an effort (+ **ut** or **nē** + subjv.)

anniversārius, -a, -um *adj.* annual, yearly

annōna, -ae *nf.* the year's crop; grain; price of grain; the grain supply

annotō (adn-), -notāre, -notāvī, -notātum *v.t.* observe; note down

annus, -ī *nm.* year

annuus, -a, -um *adj.* annual, for a year; lasting a year

ānsa, -ae *nf.* handle

ānser, ānseris *nm.* goose

ante *adv.* before, in front of, previously, earlier; *prep.* (+ acc.) before, previous to; superior to; in comparison with

anteā *adv.* before, previously, formerly

antecapiō, -capere, -cēpī, -ceptum *v.t.* take before, receive before; preoccupy; anticipate

antecēdō, -cēdere, -cessī, -cessum *v.t., v.i.* go before, precede; excel, be eminent

antecellō, -cellere, ---, --- *v.i.* rise beyond, surpass

anteferō, -ferre, -tulī, -lātum *v.t.* carry before; prefer

antelūcānus, -a, -um *adj.* before daylight, before light

antenna, -ae *nf.* sailyard
antepōnō, -pōnere, -posuī, -positum *v.t.* set before; prefer
antequam *adv.* sooner than, before
antevertō, -vertere, -vertī, -versum *v.t.* go before, precede; anticipate; prefer
antīquitās, -ātis *nf.* antiquity; the past
antīquus, -a, -um (w. comp. + sup.) *adj.* old, ancient; aged; former, old-fashioned; venerable
antlia, -ae *nm.* pump
ānulus, -ī *nm.* ring, signet ring
anus, -ūs *nf.* old woman
anxius, -a, -um *adj.* anxious, troubled; troublesome; cautious, uneasy
aper, aprī *nm.* wild boar
aperiō, -īre, aperuī, apertum *v.t.* open, reveal, uncover; make accessible; make known, explain
apertus, -a, -um (w. comp. + sup.) *adj.* uncovered, open, unobstructed; plain, clear; accessible, undefended
apex, apicis *nm.* peak, point, summit; helmet; crown, tiara; top of the flamen's conical cap; highest honor
apis (apēs), apis *nf.* bee
apium, -ī *nnt.* parsley; celery
apparātus, -ūs *nm.* preparing, getting ready; apparatus; supplies; splendor, pomp; display
appāreō, -pārēre, -pāruī, -pāritum *v.i.* appear, be evident; attend, serve
appāritor, -ōris *nm.* servant; attendant on a magistrate
apparō, -parāre, -parāvī, -parātum *v.t.* prepare, make ready for; provide; add
appellō, -pellāre, -pellāvī, -pellātum *v.t.* address, call, name, call upon; request, beg
appendix, -icis *nf.* appendix, appendage
appetēns (appetent-) *adj.* desirous of, eager for; greedy (+ gen.)
appetō, -petere, -petīvī (-petiī), -petītum *v.t., v.i.* strive for, long for, seek; attack
applicātiō, -ōnis *nf.* applying; inclination
applicō, -plicāre, -plicāvī, -plicātum *v.t.* join, add to; direct; bring; arrive
apportō, -portāre, -portāvī, -portātum *v.t.* carry; bring in, bring to
appositus, -a, -um *adj.* contiguous, bordering on (+ dat.); fit, proper, adapted (+ **ad** + acc.)
approbātiō, -ōnis *nf.* approval, assent

approbō, -probāre, -probāvī, -probātum *v.t.* assent to, favor

appropinquō, -propinquāre, -propinquāvī, -propinquātum *v.i.* approach, come near to (+ dat. *or* + **ad** + acc.)

aprīcus, -a, -um (w. comp. + sup.) *adj.* sunny; loving the sun

Aprīlis, -is, -e *adj.* April, belonging to April (*usu. w.* **mēnsis**); **Aprīlis, -is** *nm.* April

aptō, -āre, -āvī, -ātum *v.t.* fit, adapt, adjust; prepare

aptus, -a, -um (w. comp. + sup.) *adj.* fitted, joined (+ abl.); proper, suitable (+ **ad** or **in** + acc.)

apud *prep.* (+ acc.) at, by, near; at the house of; in the presence of; in the time of

aqua, -ae *nf.* water

aquaeductus, -ūs *nm.* aqueduct; conveying of water

aquārius, -a, -um *adj.* watery, belonging to water

aquātilis, -is, -e *adj.* aquatic, living or growing in water

aquila, -ae *nf.* eagle; the legionary eagle standard

aquilifer, aquiliferī *nm.* legionary standard bearer

āra, -ae *nf.* altar

arānea, -ae *nf.* spider; spider web

arātrum, -ī *nnt.* plow

arbitrium, -ī *nnt.* judgment, opinion; dominion; power; choice, will

arbitror, arbitrārī, arbitrātus sum *v.d.i.t.* declare one's judgment; believe, think

arbor, -oris *nf.* tree

arca, -ae *nf.* box, chest

arcānus, -a, -um *adj.* secret

arceō, -ēre, arcuī, --- *v.t.* keep away; hinder, prevent

accessō (accersō), -ere, -īvī, -ītum *v.t.* send for, summon

architectonicus, -a, -um *adj.* architectural, relating to architecture

architectūra, -ae *nf.* architecture

architectus, -ī *nm.* architect, master builder

arcus, -ūs *nm.* bow; rainbow; arch, vault

ardea, -ae *nf.* heron

ārdeō, -ēre, ārsī, ārsum *v.i.* be on fire, be aflame, burn; flash, shine

ārdēscō, -ere, arsī, --- *v.i.* ignite, take fire

ārdor, -ōris *nm.* glow

arduus, -a, -um (w. comp. + sup.) *adj.* steep, high, erect; difficult

ārea, -ae *nf.* threshing floor; building-site; open space, courtyard

argentāria, -ae *nf.* bank for exchanging money; silver mine

argentārius, -ī *nm.* banker, money-changer

argenteus, -a, -um *adj.* silver

argentum, -ī *nnt.* silver; silver coinage; object made of silver

argilla, -ae *nf.* clay, potter's clay

argūmentum, -ī *nnt.* argument; proof, evidence, sign, token; subject; plot of a play

arguō, -ere, arguī, argūtum *v.t.* show, prove; betray; accuse, inform, allege against; find guilty

arithmētica, -ae *or* **-ē, - ēs** *nf.* arithmetic

arma, -ōrum *nt./pl.* arms, weapons; armor; tools; war; soldiers; defense

armārium, -ī *nnt.* cupboard, chest

armō, -āre, -āvī, -ātum *v.t.* furnish with weapons; equip

arō, -āre, -āvī, -ātum *v.t.* plow, cultivate

arripiō (adr-), -ripere, -ripuī, -reptum *v.t.* catch hurriedly; grasp; take; seize upon; attack; ridicule

arrogantia (adr-), -ae *nf.* assumption; pride, conceit

ars, artis *nf.* skill, art; science, learning, knowledge; trait, virtue

artēria, -ae *nf.* wind pipe (*anat.*); blood vessel, artery

articulus, -ī *nm.* small joint; knob; division of a discourse; moment in time, crisis; part, division

artifex, -ficis *nm/f.* artist, craftsman

artificiōsus, -a, -um *adj.* skillful; skillfully made, ingenious

artificium, -ī *nnt.* practice of a craft; profession, trade; workmanship, skill; trick, artifice; work of art

artūs, -uum *nm./pl.* limbs, joints (*anat.*)

arx, arcis *nf.* citadel, stronghold; refuge, protection

as, assis *nm.* the lowest coin denomination; a unit of weight or area

ascendō, -scendere, -scendī, -scēnsum *v.t.* climb, go up; board ship

ascēnsus, -ūs *nm.* climbing up, ascent

ascīscō, -ere, ascīvī, ascītum *v.t.* receive; adopt; win over

ascrībō, -scrībere, -scrīpsī, -scrīptum *v.t.* write in addition, enroll, add; appoint; impute

aspectus, -ūs *nm.* sight; look, view, aspect, appearance

asper, aspera, asperum (w. comp. + sup.) *adj.* rough, rugged, uneven; harsh; adverse, dangerous; wild, fierce

aspergō, -spergere, -spersī, -spersum *v.t.* sprinkle; **aspergō, -inis** *nf.* spray

asperitās, -ātis *nf.* roughness, harshness; adversity; austerity; difficulty; inhumanity; rudeness

aspernor, aspernārī, aspernātus sum *v.d.t.* despise, disdain
aspiciō (adsp-), -spicere, -spexī, -spectum *v.t., v.i.* see, look upon, behold, observe, consider
asportō, -portāre, -portāvī, -portātum *v.t.* carry away, remove
assēnsus (ads-), -ūs *nm.* agreement; approval
assentātiō (ads-), -ōnis *nf.* assenting, approval; flattery
assentiō (ads-), -sentīre, -sēnsī, -sēnsum *v.t.* agree with, assent to
assentor (ads-), assentārī, assentātus sum *v.d.i.* agree with always; flatter
assequor (ads-), assequī, assecūtus sum *v.d.t.* follow up; accomplish; obtain
asser, asseris *nm.* pole, staff
asservō (ads-), -servāre, -servāvī, -servātum *v.t.* watch over, preserve, guard
assideō (ads-), -sidēre, -sēdī, -sessum *v.t.* sit by; attend; nurse, care for the ill; be busy
assīdō (ads-), -sidere, -sēdī, --- *v.i.* sit down
assiduitās (ads-), -ātis *nf.* constant attendance, devotion; continuance
assiduus (ads-), -a, -um *adj.* settled, having landed property; constantly in attendance, diligent, devoted, persevering, industrious; continual, frequent
assistō (ads-), -sistere, astitī, --- *v.i.* stand near, stand before, attend; take a station
assuēfaciō (ads-), -facere, -fēcī, -factum *v.t.* make accustomed to
assuēscō (ads-), -ere, assuēvī, assuētum *v.t.* accustom; become accustomed to
assula, -ae *nf.* chip, shaving
assurgō (ads-), -surgere, -surrēxī, -surrēctum *v.i.* rise up, stand up
assus, -a, -um *adj.* roasted
asthmaticus, -a, -um *adj.* asthmatic, short of breath
astō (ads-), -stāre, -stitī, --- *v.i.* stand near (+ dat.); stand up
astrictōrius, -a, -um *adj.* astringent, binding
astrologia, -ae *nf.* knowledge of the stars, astrology, astronomy
astūtia, -ae *nf.* shrewdness, cunning; dexterity; **astūtiae, -ārum** *nf./pl.* cunning, tricks
astūtus, -a, -um *adj.* subtle, clever, crafty
ast *or* **at** *conj.* but on the other hand, yet, nevertheless, however, but on the contrary
āter, ātra, ātrum *adj.* dead black; gloomy, sad; malicious

āthlēta, -ae *nmf.* athlete; wrestler

atomus, -ī *nm.* atom, thing incapable of being divided

atque (*before vowels and consonants*), **āc** (*only before consonants*) *conj.* and also, as well as, and too; as, than

atquī *conj.* and yet, but yet; but nevertheless, however

ātrāmentum, -ī *nnt.* black fluid; ink

ātrium, -ī *nnt.* atrium; hall

atrōx *or* **ātrōx (atrōc-)** (w. comp. + sup.) *adj.* fierce, savage, severe, horrible, violent; **atrōciter** *adv.* terribly, cruelly

attendō, -tendere, attendī, attentum *v.t.* direct to; consider, listen, pay attention to

attentus, -a, -um (w. comp. + sup.) *adj.* attentive, careful; frugal

attenuō, -tenuāre, -tenuāvī, -tenuātum *v.t.* make thin, lessen, weaken

attingō, -tingere, -tigī, -tāctum *v.t., v.i.* touch; seize; attack; approach; concern, relate to, refer to

attrahō, -trahere, -trāxī, -trāctum *v.t.* draw, pull, drag before; attract, allure

attribuō, -tribuere, -tribuī, -tribūtum *v.t.* assign, allot; entrust; attribute

auctiō, -ōnis *nf.* increasing; auction

auctor, -ōris *nm.* author, originator, father, founder; counselor, leader, adviser

auctōritās, -ātis *nf.* supremacy, authority; decision, opinion, decree; warrant; influence; dignity; reputation; importance, consequence

auctus, -ūs *nm.* development, growth, increase

audācia, -ae *nf.* nerve, boldness, daring, impudence, insolence; daring deed

audāx (audāc-) (w. comp. + sup.) *adj.* bold, daring; foolhardy, rash

audeō, -ēre, ausus sum *v.t., v.i.* dare, risk

audientia, -ae *nf.* hearing; attention; audience

audiō, -ire, -īvī, -ītum *v.t.* hear, hear of, listen to; learn from; assent

audītiō, -ōnis *nf.* hearing, listening; report

audītor, -ōris *nm.* listener, hearer

audītōrium, -ī *nnt.* lecture room

audītus, -ūs *nm.* hearing, sense of hearing

auferō, -ferre, abstulī, ablātum *v.t.* carry off, rob, steal, take away, remove; destroy

aufugiō, -fugere, -fūgī, --- *v.i.* flee away, escape

augeō, -ēre, auxī, auctum *v.t.* increase, enlarge, extend, enrich; praise

augur, auguris *nm.* augur, diviner

augurium, -ī *nnt.* augury; observance of omens; omen, sign; prediction

augurō, augurāre, augurāvī, augurātum *v.t., v.i.* act as an augur; predict, interpret omens; conjecture, imagine

Augustus, -a, -um *adj.* pertaining to the emperor Augustus; pertaining to the month of August (*usu. w.* **mēnsis**)

augustus, -a, -um (w. comp. + sup.) *adj.* majestic, venerable, sacred

aulaeum, -ī *nnt.* tapestry, elaborate hanging; curtain of a theater

aura, -ae *nf.* breath; draft, breeze

aureus, -a, -um *adj.* golden, of gold

auris, -is *nf.* ear

aurum, -ī *nnt.* gold

auspicium, -ī *nnt.* augury from birds; divination; omen

aut *conj.* or; or at least; **aut ... aut** *conj.* either ... or

autem *conj. (usu. postpositive)* however, but, on the contrary

autumnus, -a, -um *adj.* autumn; *nm.* autumn

auxilium, -ī *nnt.* assistance, help, support; **auxilia, -ōrum** *nnt./pl.* auxiliary units of the army

avāritia, -ae *nf.* greed

avārus, -a, -um (w. comp. + sup.) *adj.* greedy, covetous

avēna, -ae *nf.* oats; stalk, straw

aveō, -ēre, ---, --- *v.i.* wish for, long for

aversus, -a, -um *adj.* turned away, turned back; withdrawn; averse, hostile

āvertō, -vertere, -vertī, -versum *v.t.* turn away, turn aside; remove; ward off

avia, -ae *nf.* grandmother

avidus, -a, -um *adj.* eager; desirous, covetous, greedy; jealous (*w. gen. or dat.*)

avis, avis *nf.* fowl, bird

āvocō, -vocāre, -vocāvī, -vocātum *v.t.* call away; withdraw; divert, turn aside

avunculus, -ī *nm.* maternal uncle

avus, -ī *nm.* grandfather

axis, -is *nm.* axle of a wheel; axis of the earth; open air, the heavens; region

B

bāca *or* **bacca, -ae** *nf.* berry (*or anything berry-shaped*); olive; pearl
bacchor, bacchārī, bacchātus sum *v.d.i.t.* celebrate the festival of Bacchus; revel
baculum, -ī *nnt.* staff, cane
bālaena, -ae *nf.* whale
balbūtiō, -īre, ---, --- *v.i.* stammer, stutter
balineum *or* **balneum, -ī** *nnt.* bath; bathing establishment
ballista *or* **bālista, -ae** *nf.* ballista (*a military machine that threw huge stones*)
balneum, -ī *nf. See* **balineum**.
balteus, -ī *nm.* girdle, belt, sword belt
baptīsma, -atis *nnt.* washing, dipping in water; baptism
baptīzō, -āre, -āvī, -ātum *v.t.* baptize
barba, -ae *nf.* beard
barbarus, -a, -um *adj.* unintelligible; foreign, strange; of barbarians, of foreigners; barbarous, savage, uncivilized
barbātus, -a, -um *adj.* having a beard, bearded
basilica, -ae *nf.* basilica (*a double-colonnaded public building for law courts and merchants*)
basis, -is *nf.* base, foundation, support, pedestal
beātus, -a, -um (w. comp. + sup.) *adj.* happy, fortunate; prosperous, wealthy
bellāria, -ōrum *nnt./pl.* dessert
bellicōsus, -a, -um (w. comp. + sup.) *adj.* warlike, martial
bellicus, -a, -um *adj.* warlike, martial; of the army
bellō, -āre, -āvī, -ātum *v.i.* make war; fight (+ **cum** + abl. *or* + **adversus** + acc.)
bellum, ī *nnt.* war
bellus, -a, -um (+ sup.) *adj.* pretty, charming, handsome
bēlua, -ae *nf.* (large) beast, monster, wild beast
bene *or* **benē** (w. sup.) *adv.* well, successfully, prosperously; very, quite
benedictiō, -ōnis *nf.* praising, lauding; sacred object; blessing
beneficium, -ī *nnt.* kindness, favor, service, benefit; honor
beneficus, -a, -um (comp. **beneficentior**; sup. **beneficentissimus**) *adj.* generous, liberal; serviceable
benevolentia, -ae *nf.* kindness, goodwill; friendship
benevolus, -a, -um (w. comp. + sup.) *adj.* kind, obliging, well-disposed

benignitās, -ātis *nf.* kindness, courtesy; liberality; favor
benignus, -a, -um (w. comp. + sup.) *adj.* kind, friendly, generous, gracious, welcoming
beō, -āre, -āvī, -ātum *v.t.* bless, make happy
bēstia, -ae *nf.* beast, wild beast, animal
bēta, -ae *nf.* beet
biblia, bibliōrum *nnt./pl.* bible
bibliopōla, -ae *nm.* bookseller
bibliothēca, -ae *nf.* library, collection of books
bibō, -ere, bibī, bibitum *v.t.* drink
biduum, -ī *nnt.* period of two days
biennium, -ī *nnt.* period of two years
bīnī, -ae, -a *adv.* two by two, two at a time; double
bipertītō *or* **bipartītō** *adv.* in two divisions, in two parts
bis *adv.* twice, on two occasions; doubly, twofold
bivium, -ī *nnt.* fork of a road; crossroad
blandīmentum, -ī *nnt.* flattery, compliment; pleasure, delight
blandior, blandīrī, blandītus sum *v.d.i.* flatter, caress; compliment; please, allure, invite
blanditia, -ae *nf.* caressing; fondness; flattery; **blanditiae, -ārum** *nf./pl.* fascination, captivation
blatta -ae *nf.* insect that avoids the light; moth; cockroach
bonitās, -ātis *nf.* goodness, kindness, friendliness; excellence
bonum, -ī *nnt.* a good thing; profit, advantage; **bona, -ōrum** *nnt./pl.* property, goods
bonus, -a, -um (comp. **melior**; sup. **optimus**) *adj.* good worthy, excellent; kind; loyal
bōs, bovis *nm/f.* ox, bullock, cow; **bovēs, bovum** *or* **boum** *nm/f./pl.* oxen, cattle
brāchium *or* **bracchium, -ī** *nnt.* forearm, arm; the limb of an animal, claw; thigh, leg; arm of the sea; spur of a mountain chain
branchiae, -ārum *nf./pl.* gills
brassica, -ae *nf.* cabbage
brevis, -is, -e (w. comp. + sup.) *adj.* short, brief, concise, little; **brevī** (*sc.* tempore) *adv.* shortly (*in a short time*); **breviter** (w. comp. + sup.) *adv.* shortly (*in a few words*)
brevitās, -ātis *nf.* shortness, brevity, conciseness
būbō, būbōnis *nm.* owl
būbula, -ae *nf.* beef

bucca, -ae *nf.* cheek; trumpeteer
buccellātum, -ī *nnt.* biscuit (*especially that of soldiers*)
būcula, -ae *nf.* young cow, heifer
būfō, -ōnis *nm.* toad
bulbus, -ī *nm.* bulb; onion
bulla, -ae *nf.* bubble; knob; metal stud; bulla (*the amulet of Roman boys*)
būstum, -ī *nnt.* place for burning bodies, funeral pyre; place for burying
 bodies, mound, tomb, grave

C

cacūmen, -inis *nnt.* summit, top; zenith; end
cadāver, -eris *nnt.* corpse, dead body
cadō, -ere, cecidī, cāsum *v.i.* fall, fall down; fall dead, perish; be subject
 to; befall, happen
cadūcus, -a, -um *adj.* inclined to fall; perishable, transitory
caecitās, -ātis *nf.* blindness
caecus, -a, -um (w. comp.) *adj.* devoid of light; blind, blinded
caedēs, -is *nf.* slaughter, murder
caedo, -ere, cecīdī, caesum *v.t.* cut, cut down, hew; cut off; cut to pieces;
 strike; kill, murder; destroy
caelebs (caelib-) *adj.* single, unmarried
caelestis *or* **coelestis, -is, -e** *adj.* of heaven, celestial; *nmf.* deity;
 caelestia, -ium *nt/pl.* heavenly bodies
caelum, -ī *nnt.* heaven, sky; air, climate, weather, atmosphere; tempera-
 ture; height; summit of honor; vault, arch
caepa, -ae *nf.* or **caepe, -is** *nnt.* onion
caerimōnium, -ī *nnt.* sacredness; veneration; religious ceremony
caeruleus *or* **caerulus, -a, -um** *adj.* dark blue, dark green
Caesar, Caesaris *nm.* title of the Roman emperor
calamitās, -ātis *nf.* loss, hurt; calamity, ruin, disaster
calamitōsus, -a, -um (w. comp. + sup.) *adj.* causing loss; destructive;
 disastrous; suffering loss; unfortunate, unhappy
calcar, -āris *nnt.* spur, stimulus
calceus, -ī *nm.* shoe, half-boot
calcitrō, -āre, ---, --- *v.t., v.i.* kick
calefaciō *or* **calfaciō, -facere, -fēcī, -factum** *v.t.* heat, make warm; vex
calidus *or* **caldus, -a, -um** (w. comp. + sup.) *adj.* warm, hot; fiery, fierce,
 impassioned

caliga, -ae *nf.* leather shoe; soldier's boot

cālīginōsus *or* **cālīgōsus, -a, -um** (w. sup.) *adj.* foggy, misty; gloomy

cālīgō, -inis *nf.* fog, thick air, mist; darkness, gloom; confusion, ignorance; calamity

callidus, -a, -um (w. comp. + sup.) *adj.* skillful, shrewd, astute, crafty, artful

callis, -is *nm/f.* trail, path, footpath; declivity, mountain pass

calor, -ōris *nm.* heat, warmth; glow

calumnia, -ae *nf.* cunning, trickery; pretense, misrepresentation; false accusation, libel, malicious charge

calumnior, calumniārī, calumniātus sum *v.d.i.t.* accuse falsely, practice trickery; misrepresent, calumniate

calvāria, -ae *nf.* human skull; the Hill of Calvary

calvus, -a, -um *adj.* bald

calx, calcis *nf.* heel; limestone, chalk; goal of the race track

camēlus, -ī *nm/f.* camel

camera *or* **camara, -ae** *nf.* vault, arch, arched ceiling

campester, campestris, campestre *adj.* flat, level

campus, -ī *nm.* field, plain, open country

canālis, -is *nm.* pipe; groove, channel; splint

cancer, cancrī *nm.* crab; cancer; ulcer

candēla, -ae *nf.* candle, wax taper

candeō, -ēre, canduī, --- *v.i.* glitter, glisten, glow

candidātus, -ī *nm.* one clothed in a very white toga; candidate for office

candidus, -a, -um (w. comp. + sup.) *adj.* shining, white, clear, bright, splendid; clothed in white; guileless, honest, candid; prosperous

canis, -is *nm/f.* dog, bitch; shameless person; the worst throw of the dice

canō, -ere, cecinī, cantum *v.t., v.i.* sing, make music; sing of; foretell

canōrus, -a, -um *adj.* tuneful

canto, -āre, -āvī, -ātum *v.t., v.i.* sing; play (+ abl. of instrument)

cantor, -ōris *nm.* singer

cantus, -ūs *nm.* singing, song, music

cānus, -a, -um *adj.* white; hoary, gray; old; **cānī, -ōrum** *nt/pl.* gray hair

capāx (capāc-) (w. sup.) *adj.* able to hold (+ gen.); roomy, spacious; capable of, fit for (+ **ad** + acc.)

caper, caprī *nm.* he-goat

capessō, -ere, -īvī (-iī),-ītum *v.t.* lay hold of; repair to; undertake eagerly; manage

capillāmentum, -ī *nnt.* wig, false hair

capillus, -ī *nm.* hair

capiō, -ere, cēpī, captum *v.t.* seize, take, lay hold of, take possession of, capture; win, captivate; deceive, betray; harm; deprive of; suffer; experience; entertain; undertake; accept, gain; comprehend; be large enough to hold

capitālis, -is, -e *adj.* of the head; foremost; involving life; capital; dangerous

capra, -ae *nf.* she-goat

captīvus, -a, -um *adj.* taken prisoner, captive, captured, plundered

captō, -āre, -āvī, -ātum *v.t.* snatch; strive after; lay in wait for, try to trap, allure

captus, -ūs *nm.* seizing; capacity of mind, power of comprehension

caput, capitis *nnt.* head; person; life, soul; top, summit; source; citizenship; chapter, passage; point; principal thing

carbasus, -ī *nf.* linen canvas, sail cloth

carbō, -ōnis *nm.* coal, charcoal

carbunculus, ī *nm.* small coal; red precious stone, ruby; tumor

carcer, carceris *nm.* prison, place of confinement

cardō, -inis *nm.* hinge; astronomical pole; critical turn of events

careō, -ēre, -caruī, caritūrum *v.t.* be without, do without, keep from, lack, be deprived of (+ abl.)

carīna, -ae *nf.* keel of boat; boat, ship

cāritās, -ātis *nf.* dearness, love, affection; high price

carmen, -inis *nnt.* song, hymn; poem; form of prayer; prophecy, spell; metrical inscription

carō, carnis *nf.* flesh, meat; pulp

carpō, -ere, carpsī, carptum *v.t.* pull, pluck; browse; gnaw; tear off; carp at; wear away; harass; cut to pieces

cārus, -a, -um (w. comp. + sup.) *adj.* dear, beloved; affectionate; expensive

casa, -ae *nf.* cottage, hut, simple house

cāseus *or* **cāseum, -ī** *nmnt.* cheese

cassis, -idis *nf.* helmet

castellum, -ī *nnt.* fort, citadel, stronghold; refuge

cāstīgātōrius, -a, -um *adj.* relating to reproof; implying reproof

castitās, -ātis *nf.* purity, chastity

castra, castrōrum *nnt./pl.* camp, fort

castus, -a, -um (w. comp. + sup.) *adj.* pure, chaste, morally pure; holy, sacred

cāsus, -ūs *nm.* falling; happening; accident; emergency; destruction, misfortune, calamity

catasta, -ae *nf.* scaffold, stage

catēna, -ae *nf.* chain, shackle, fetter

caterva, -ae *nf.* crowd, troop, gang, armed group

catulus, -ī *nm.* young of an animal; puppy

cauda, -ae *nf.* tail

caulis, -is *nm.* stem of a plant; cabbage stalk, cabbage

caupō, -ōnis *nm.* landlord of an inn; tradesman

caupōna, -ae *nf.* inn; shop; female shopkeeper

causa, -ae *nf.* cause, reason; pretext, motive; condition, case, situation; lawsuit; side, faction

cautiō, -ōnis *nf.* watchfulness, precaution; safety

cautus, -a, -um (w. comp. + sup.) *adj.* cautious, circumspect, wary

cavea, -ae *nf.* hollow, cavity; cage, enclosure; seating area of a theater

caveō, -ēre, cāvī, cautum *v.t.* beware, be on guard; provide against; order; protect

cavum, -ī *nnt.* hole, cavity

-ce enclitic. *Demonstrative particle joined to prons. and advs.*

cēdō, -ere, cessī, cessum *v.i.* go away, retreat, yield, submit, surrender; comply; be inferior to; conform to (+ dat.)

cedrus, -ī *nf.* cedar; juniper

celeber, celebris, celebre (comp. **celebrior**; sup. **celeberrimus**) *adj.* crowded, thronged; honored, famous

celebrātiō, -ōnis *nf.* large gathering, crowd; celebration

celebritās, -ātis *nf.* crowd, throng; fame, publicity

celebrō, -āre, -āvī, -ātum *v.t.* crowd, throng; engage in; celebrate; make famous, make known

celer, celeris, celere (comp. **celerior**; sup. **celerrimus**) *adj.* quick, swift, hasty, rash; **celeriter** (comp. **celerius**; sup. **celerrimē**) *adv.* speedily, quickly, in haste, immediately

celeritās, -ātis *nf.* speed, quickness

cella, -ae *nf.* room; storeroom; sanctuary inside of a temple

cēlō, -āre, -āvī, -ātum *v.t.* conceal, hide, elude; keep ignorant of, keep secret

cēna, -ae *nf.* dinner (*which Romans ate in the late afternoon*); banquet; course of the meal

cēnāculum, -ī *nnt.* loft, room under a roof

cēnō, -āre, -āvī, -ātum *v.t., v.i.* dine, eat dinner

cēnseō, -ēre, cēnsuī, cēnsum *v.t.* assess, estimate; be of the opinion that; propose; vote (+ **ut** or **nē** + subjv.); suppose, think; decide

cēnsor, -ōris *nm.* censor, magistrate in charge of the census; registration lists, assessment of property and awarding of public contracts

cēnsus, -ūs *nm.* registration of citizens and of property; appraisement; census

centēsimus, -a, -um *adj.* hundredth

centrum, -ī *nnt.* center, middle point of a circle

centum *num. (indecl.)* hundred

centuria, -ae *nf.* division of one hundred; century (*the military unit of a legion*); the division of the Roman people in an assembly

centuriō, -āre, -āvī, -ātum *v.t.* divide into centuries; organize into companies; **centuriō, -ōnis** *nm.* officer of a century, centurion

cēra, -ae *nf.* wax; wax writing tablet; seal

cernō, -ere, crēvī, crētum *v.t.* distinguish, discern; perceive, see, understand; decide, resolve (+ **ut** or **nē** + subjv.)

cērō, -āre, -āvī, -ātum *v.t.* wax, smear with wax

certāmen, -inis *nnt.* contest, conflict, battle, dispute, match, rivalry, competition

certātim *adv.* zealously, competitively, earnestly

certē *adv.* of course

certō *adv.* surely, certainly; at least, yet surely; **certō, -āre, -āvī, -ātum** *v.i.* compete with; fight, contend; strive (+ **cum** + abl. *or* + **inter** + acc.)

certus, -a, -um (w. comp. + sup.) *adj.* certain, fixed, settled; special; definite; confident; trustworthy; unerring

cerva, -ae *nf.* deer

cervīcal, -ālis *nnt.* pillow, cushion

cervisia *or* **cervesia** *or* **cerevisia, -ae** *nf.* ale, beer

cervīx, -icis *nf.* neck; throat

cervus, -ī *nm.* stag

cessō, -āre, -āvī, -ātum *v.i.* loiter, delay, cease from doing, be unemployed, be idle; be null and void

cēterus *or* **caeterus, -a, -um** *adj.* the other, rest, remainder; **cēterī** *or* **caeterī, -ōrum** *pron. m./pl.* the rest, the others

charta, -ae *nf.* piece of papyrus, paper; that which is written on paper

chirūrgia, -ae *nf.* surgery

chorus, -ī *nm.* dance in a ring, choral dance; troop of dancers and singers, chorus; multitude, crowd

Christiānus, -a, -um *adj.* Christian

Christus, Christī *nm.* Christ (Jesus)

cibāria, -ōrum *nnt./pl.* rations, provisions; fodder

cibus, -ī *nm.* food, nourishment

cicāda, -ae *nf.* tree cricket

cicātrīx, -trīcis *nf.* scar

cicōnia, -ae *nf.* stork

cieō, -ēre, cīvī, citum *v.t.* cause to move, drive; disturb; summon, appeal to; enliven; produce, beget

cincinnus, -ī *nm.* hair curl, lock of hair

cingō, -ere, cīnxī, cīnctum *v.t.* surround, enclose, gird, wreathe; beseige

cingulum, -ī *nm.* or **cingulus, -ī** *nnt.* belt; zone

cinis, cineris *nm.* ashes, embers

cinnamōmum or **cinnamon** or **cinnamum, -ī** *nnt.* cinnamon

circā *adv.* around, about; near; *prep.* (+ acc.) about, around, surrounding, among, near to; nearly, almost; on both sides

circiter *adv.*, *prep.* (+ acc.) about, near

circitor, -ōris *nm.* guard, watchman

circuitō, -ōnis *nf.* patrol; patrolling; circuit

circuitus, -ūs *nm.* circling, circuit; compass; circumlocution

circulātor, -ōris *nm.* quack; pedlar

circum *adv.* about, around; *prep.* (+ acc.) around, about, among, near, near to

circumagō, -āgere, -ēgī, -āctum *v.t.* drive in a circle, turn about, turn round, wheel

circumclūdō, -clūdere, -clūsī, -clūsum *v.t.* enclose, surround

circumdō, -dare, -dedī, -datum *v.t.* put around, surround, encircle, beseige

circumeō, -īre, -iī (-īvī), -itum *v.t.* go around, travel around; solicit; surround, enclose; deceive

circumiectus or **circumjectus, -a, -um** *adj.* surrounding; lying around

circummittō, -mittere, -mīsī, -missum *v.t.* send around

circumscrībō, -scrībere, -scrīpsī, -scrīptum *v.t.* limit, restrict; cheat; cancel; set aside

circumscrīptor, -ōris *nm.* cheat, defrauder

circumstō, -stāre, -stetī, --- *v.t., v.i.* stand around, surround; threaten; besiege

circumveniō, -venīre, -vēnī, -ventum *v.t.* encircle, surround; beset, oppress, afflict; overthrow; deceive, entrap; attack

cis *prep.* (+ acc.) on this side of

cista, -ae *nf.* trunk, box

citerior (citeriōr-) *adj.* on this side, on the nearer side, nearer, next; **citimus, -a, -um** *adj.* on the nearest side, nearest

cithera, -ae *nf.* cithara, lyre

citō *adv.* quickly; **citius** *adv.* more quickly; **citissimē** *adv.* most quickly

citrā *prep.* (+ acc.) on this side of; nearer; short of, without

cīvīlis, -is, -e *adj.* relating to a citizen, civil, civic; political; public

cīvis, -is *nm/f.* citizen

cīvitās, -ātis *nf.* citizenship, inhabitants of a city; state, commonwealth; city, town

clādēs, -is *nf.* destruction, harm, misfortune, disaster, calamity; slaughter; defeat, reverse

clām *adv.* secretly, in secret

clāmitō, -āre, -āvī, -ātum *v.t., v.i.* cry out loud; proclaim, reveal; betray

clāmō, -āre, -āvī, -ātum *v.t.* cry out, shout, exclaim. proclaim; invoke

clāmor, -ōris *nm.* loud cry, shout, din, noise; applause, acclamation; war-shout

clandestīnus, -a, -um *adj.* secret, concealed

clāritās, -ātis *nf.* brightness, clearness; fame; splendor

clārus, -a, -um (w. comp. + sup.) *adj.* bright, shining, clear; manifest, renowned, honored, noble, illustrious; **clārē** (w. comp. + sup.) *adv.* brightly; distinctly, plainly, honorably, splendidly; aloud, loudly

classis, -is *nf.* division, class, rank; army; fleet; navy

claudicō, -āre, ---, --- *v.i.* limp, be lame; be deflected; halt; be defective

claudō, -ere, clausī, clausum *v.t.* close, shut; finish, end; shut in; besiege

claudus *or* **clūdus** *or* **clōdus, -a, -um** *adj.* crippled, lame; defective

claustra, -ōrum *nnt./pl.* bar, lock, bolt; barrier, dam, dike; barricade, defence

clāva, -ae *nf.* bat, club, staff

clāvis, -is *nf.* key

clāvulus, -ī *nm.* tack, small nail

clāvus, -ī *nm.* nail; rudder; purple stripe on clothing

clēmēns (clēment-) (w. comp. + sup.) *adj.* mild, calm; gentle; forebearing

clēmentia, -ae *nf.* mildness, forbearance; clemency

clēricus, -ī *nm.* clergyman

cliēns, clientis *nm.* client; personal dependent; retainer; companion; ally

clientēla, -ae *nf.* relationship of patron and client, patronage, clientship

clīvōsus, -a, -um *adj.* hilly, full of hills

clīvus, -ī *nm.* incline, slope, hill

cloāca, -ae *nf.* drain, sewer

coaedificō, -ficāre, ---, -ficātum *v.t.* build up, build upon; build together, join

coartō *or* **coarctō, -artāre, -artāvī, -artātum** *v.t.* press together, compress, contract; abridge, sum up, summarize

coccinus, -a, -um *adj.* scarlet

coclea *or* **cochlea, -ae** *nf.* snail; water screw

coclear *or* **cochlear, -āris** *nnt.* spoon; spoonful

cōdicillī, -ōrum *nm./pl.* writing tablet; anything written on a tablet

coemō, -emere, -ēmī, -ēmptum *v.t.* purchase, buy up

coeō, -īre, -īvī (-iī), -itum *v.i.* come together, meet, gather, unite, agree; join in battle; ally oneself; conspire

coepiō, -ere, coepī, coeptum *v.t., v.i.* begin, commence

coerceō, -ercēre, -ercuī, -ercitum *v.t.* confine, shut in; restrain, repress, curb

coetus *or* **coitus, -ūs** *nm.* assembly, meeting; crowd

cōgitātē *adv.* thoughtfully, with reflection

cōgitātiō, -ōnis *nf.* reflection, meditation, thought, imagination, reasoning

cōgitō, -āre, -āvī, -ātum *v.i.* think, ponder (+ **dē** + abl.); meditate; design, plan; plot (+ acc. *or* + acc. + infv.)

cōgnātus, -a, -um *adj.* related by blood, sprung from the same kin

cognitiō, -ōnis *nf.* knowledge; investigation; trial

cognitor, -ōris *nm.* attorney, advocate, defender, protector, supporter

cognitus, -a, -um (w. comp. + sup.) *adj.* known; proved (+ dat.)

cognōmen, -inis *nnt.* surname; name; name of the family

cōgnōscō, -gnōscere, -gnōvī, -gnitum *v.t.* hear of, learn; know; examine, investigate; recognize, acknowledge; appreciate

cōgō, cōgere, coēgī, coāctum *v.t.* drive together; gather together, assemble; urge, compel (+ acc. + infv. *or* + **ut** or **nē** + subjv.)

cohaereō, -haerēre, -haesī, -haesum *v.t.* cling together; be united, be connected with

cohibeō, -hibēre, -hibuī, -hibitum *v.t.* hold together, contain; repress, check

cohors, cohortis *nf.* enclosure; crowd, throng; cohort (*the tenth part of a legion*); the general's staff; bodyguard

cohortātiō, -ōnis *nf.* exhorting, encouragement

cohortor, cohortārī, cohortātus sum *v.d.t.* encourage, admonish; address

coitus *or* **coetus, -ūs** *nm.* coming together, assembly, joining together; sexual intercourse

collābor (conl-), collabī, collapsus sum *v.d.i.* fall together; fall in ruins; faint, swoon

collāre, -is *nnt.* collar for a dog or prisoner; neck-chain

collātiō (conl-), -ōnis *nf.* bringing together; hostile meeting; collision; contribution

collēga (conl-), -ae *nm.* colleague, associate in office

collēgium (conl-), -ī *nf.* colleagueship, association, guild, corporation, college

colligō (conl-), -ligere, -lēgī, -lectum *v.t.* gather, collect, acquire; deduce, infer

collis, -is *nm.* hill; height

collocō (conl-), -locāre, -locāvī, -locātum *v.t.* set, place, set up, locate, station (+ **in** + abl.); arrange

collocūtiō (conl-), -ōnis *nf.* conversation, chat, talk; conference

colloquium (conl-), -ī *nnt.* conversation; conference

colloquor (conl-), colloquī, collocūtus sum *v.d.i.t.* speak, talk, converse; negotiate with

collum, -ī *nnt.* neck

colluviō (conl-), -ōnis *nf.* dirt, dregs, impurities, pollution

colō, -āre, -āvī, -ātum *v.t.* strain, filter; purify

colō, colere, coluī, cultum *v.t.* cultivate; abide, inhabit; care for, love; adore, worship; seek; practice, adhere to

cōlon, -ī *nnt.* colon; colic

colōnia, -ae *nf.* settlement, colony

colōnus, -ī *nm.* farmer; settler, colonist

color, -ōris *nm.* color, hue; complexion; appearance

colōrō, -āre, -āvī, -ātum *v.i.* tan (*become darkened by the sun*)

cōlum, -ī *nnt.* filter, strainer

columba, -ae *nf.* female pigeon, dove

columbus, -ī *nm.* male pigeon, dove

columen, -inis *nnt.* top, summit, ridge, highest part, acme; pillar, support; gable, roof

columna, -ae *nf.* column, pillar, post; support

combibō, -bibere, -bibī, --- *v.t.* drink with a companion; drink up completely, absorb

comes, comitis *nm/f.* companion, associate; attendant

cōmicus, -a, -um *adj.* comic, pertaining to comedy

cōmis, -is, -e *adj.* mellow, gentle, affable, polite

cōmitās, -ātis *nf.* courtesy, kindness, politeness

comitātus, -ūs *nm.* escort, retinue; company, band

comitia, -ōrum *nnt./pl.* comitia, meeting of citizens

comitium, -ī *nnt.* meeting place; the Comitium (*the place of assembly of the people in the Forum*)

comitor, comitārī, comitātus sum *v.d.i.t.* attend; accompany, escort

commemorātiō, -ōnis *nf.* reminding, remembrance

commemorō, -memorāre, -memorāvī, -memorātum *v.t.* remember, recall, recount

commendātiō, -ōnis *nf.* recommendation, commending

commendō, -mendāre, -mendāvī, -mendātum *v.t.* leave for safe keeping, entrust; commend, recommend

commentārium, -ī *nnt.* notebook, memorandum, notes, commentary

commentum, -ī *nnt.* invention; falsehood; embellishment

commercium, -ī *nnt.* commerce, trade; fellowship; communication

commercor, commercārī, commercātus sum *v.d.t.* trade, buy up

commereō, -merēre, -meruī, -meritum *v.t.* deserve, merit; commit an offence, be guilty

comminuō, -minuere, -minuī, -minūtum *v.t.* break into pieces, crumble; lessen; impair

comminus *adv.* hand-to-hand, at close quarters

committō, -mittere, -mīsī, -missum *v.t.* bring together, combine; fight, carry on; entrust (+ acc. + dat.); expose; be guilty of; practice

commoditās, -ātis *nf.* convenience, fitness; suitable occasion; advantage; courtesy, forbearance

commodō, -modāre, -modāvī, -modātum *v.t.* lend; supply

commodum, -ī *nnt.* convenience; advantage, gain

commodus, -a, -um (w. comp. + sup.) *adj.* complete; suitable, comfortable; useful; pleasant, polite; **commodē** (w. comp. + sup.) *adv.* properly; skillfully; suitably

commoror, commorārī, commorātus sum *v.d.i.t.* tarry, linger, stay for a while

commōtiō, -ōnis *nf.* motion; excitement, agitation, commotion

commoveō, -movēre, -mōvī, -mōtum *v.t.* stir, shake; affect, move emotionally; influence

commūnicātiō, -ōnis *nf.* communication, imparting

commūnicō, -mūnicāre, -mūnicāvī, -mūnicātum *v.t.* share (+ acc. + **cum** + abl.); join, unite; confer with, communicate (+ **dē** + abl.); participate in (+ acc.)

commūnis, -is, -e *adj.* common, general, public (+ gen. *or* + dat. *or* + **inter** + acc.); courteous, sociable

commūnitās, -ātis *nf.* sharing in common, fellowship; affability

commūtō, -mūtāre, -mūtāvī, -mūtātum *v.t.* change, convert, exchange, substitute

cōmō, -ere, cōmpsī, cōmptum *v.t.* bring together, construct; dress hair, style hair, braid

cōmoedia, -ae *nf.* comedy

compāgēs, -is *nf.* joining together; frame, structure

comparātiō, -ōnis *nf.* comparison; trial of skill

comparō, -parāre, -parāvī, -parātum *v.t.* make ready; provide; collect; levy; couple together, pair up, match; count as equal

compellō, -pellere, -pulī, -pulsum *v.t.* drive together; force; incite; constrain

compēnsō, -pēnsāre, -pēnsāvī, -pēnsātum *v.t.* balance; compensate, make up

comperio, -perīre, -perī, -pertum *v.t.* find out, learn (+ acc. *or* + acc. + infv. in indirect discourse)

compēs, -pedis *nf.* shackle, fetter, chain

competītor, -ōris *nm.* rival, opponent

compitum, -ī *nnt.* crossroad

complector, complectī, complexus sum *v.d.t..* clasp, embrace, encircle, seize; understand; explain, describe

compleō, -plēre, -plēvī, -plētum *v.t.* fill up (+ abl.); complete, finish; live through; pass

complexus, -ūs *nm.* embrace, embracing

complicō, -plicāre, -plicāvī, -plicātum *v.t.* fold up, fold together, roll up

complūrēs, complūrēs, complūria *adj.* many, several

compluvium, -ī *nnt.* the compluvium (*pool in the atrium that collected rainwater from the roof*)

compōnō, -pōnere, -posuī, -positum *v.t.* put, place, lay; mix, bring together, join; collect; bring together in hostility; contrast, compare; construct; compose, write; put away, store up; lay at rest, pacify, reconcile, compromise, settle, set in order, adjust; dispose; arrange, devise; contrive, feign

compositē *adv.* in an orderly way (*in a composed manner*)

comprehendō, -prehendere, -prehendī, -prehēnsum *v.t.* seize, grasp; lay hold of; capture, arrest; comprehend; recount

comprehēnsiō, -ōnis *nf.* seizure, arrest; comprehension, perception; ability to comprehend

comprimō, -primere, -pressī, -pressum *v.t.* press together; check, restrain; suppress, silence

comptus, -a, -um (w. comp.) *adj.* embellished, adorned
computātiō, -ōnis *nf.* calculation, reckoning
computō, -putāre, -putāvī, -putātum *v.t.* add up, reckon, calculate
cōnātus, -ūs *nm.* attempt, effort, undertaking
concēdō, cēdere, -cessī, -cessum *v.i.* withdraw, depart; yield, submit, concede, allow; acknowledge, admit
concentus, -ūs *nm.* harmony, blended sounds; concord, agreement
concerpō, -cerpere, -cerpsī, -cerptum *v.t.* tear in pieces; gather; pluck
concertō, -certāre, -certāvī, -certātum *v.i.* contend with, debate with, argue with (+ dat. *or* + **cum** + abl.)
concessiō, -ōnis *nf.* granting, concession, yielding
concha, -ae *nf.* shellfish, mollusk; shell
concidō, -cidere, -cidī, --- *v.i.* fall down; fall dead; fail; be destroyed;
   concīdō, -cīdere, -cīdī, -cīsum *v.t.* cut, cut up; ruin, destroy, kill; defeat soundly
conciliō, -ciliāre, -ciliāvī, -ciliātum *v.t.* procure, gain; win over, conciliate
concilium, -ī *nnt.* meeting, assembly; council
conciō *or* **concieō -cīre** *or* **-ciēre, -cīvī, -cītum** *v.t.* bring together, collect; shake; attract; excite, provoke
concipiō, -cipere, -cēpī, -ceptum *v.t.* receive; imagine, conceive of, plan; understand; harbor
concitō, -citāre, -citāvī, -citātum *v.t.* stir up, excite, urge, instigate
conclāmō, -clāmāre, -clāmāvī, -clāmātum *v.t.* shout together; cry for help; exclaim
conclāve, -is *nnt.* room; dining-hall; cage, stall
conclūdō, -clūdere, -clūsī, -clūsum *v.t.* shut up, enclose, restrain; conclude; argue; demonstrate
concolor (concolōr-) *adj.* of same color (+ dat.)
concoquo, -coquere, -cōxī, -coctum *v.t.* boil together; digest; prepare; ripen; endure, put up with; think upon, ponder
concordia, -ae *nf.* union, concord, unanimity
concors (concord-) (w. comp. + sup.) *adj.* unanimous, agreeing, harmonious
concrēscō, -crēscere, -crēvī, -crētum *v.i.* grow together; harden, congeal, thicken; increase
concupīscō, -cupīscere, -cupīvī, -cupītum *v.t.* long for, covet
concurrō, -currere, -currī *or* **-cucurrī, -cursum** *v.i.* run together; assemble, meet; come together in combat; make haste; coincide, meet; happen
concursus, -ūs *nm.* running together; assembly; assault; collision (+ gen.)

concutiō, -cutere, -cussī, -cussum *v.t.* shake, strike together, agitate

condemnō, -demnāre, -demnāvī, -demnātum *v.t.* find guilty, convict, condemn (+ gen. of charge)

condiciō, -ōnis *nm.* agreement, compact, proposal, terms; position, circumstances

condimentum, -ī *nnt.* spice, seasoning

condiō, -īre, -īvī, -ītum *v.t.* preserve, conserve; pickle, season

conditor, -ōris *nm.* founder, maker, builder

condītus, -a, -um (w. comp.) *adj.* spicy, well-seasoned

condō, -dere, -didī, -ditum *v.t.* found; build; write; store up; preserve; bury, hide

condōnō, -dōnāre, -dōnāvī, -dōnātum *v.t.* present, deliver up, surrender, sacrifice, remit; pardon

condūcō, -dūcere, -dūxī, -ductum *v.t.* draw together, assemble, unite; hire, rent, employ; be of use

conductiō, -ōnis *nf.* bringing together; hiring

cōnectō, -nectere, -nexuī, -nexum *v.t.* tie together, connect, link

cōnfectiō, -ōnis *nf.* preparing, finishing, ending, completion

cōnfectus, -a, -um *adj.* tired out, weakened, consumed

cōnferō, -ferre, -tulī, collātum *or* **conlātum** *v.t.* bring together, collect, join; match against; compare; consult; carry; employ; lend, grant; refer; assign; postpone; blame; transfer

cōnfertus, -a, -um (w. comp. + sup.) *adj.* crowded, crammed; dense; stuffed, full (+ abl.)

cōnfessiō, -ōnis *nf.* acknowledgment, admission

cōnficiō, -ficere, -fēcī, -fectum *v.t.* accomplish, complete, do, bring about; provide, prepare; draw up; wear out, subdue; kill

cōnfīdō, -fīdere, -fīsus sum *v.i.* rely, trust, believe (+ dat.); be confident

cōnfirmātiō, -ōnis *nf.* securing, establishing; encouragement; confirmation, verification

cōnfirmō, -firmāre, -firmāvī, -firmātum *v.t.* strengthen, reinforce; encourage; establish; assert, prove

cōnfiteor, cōnfitērī, cōnfessus sum *v.d.i.t.* confess, admit, acknowledge

cōnflagrō, -flagrāre, -flagrāvī, -flagrātum *v.t., v.i.* burn up

cōnflīgō, -flīgere, -flīxī, -flīctum *v.t., v.i.* collide, dash together, fight, contend

cōnflō, -flāre, -flāvī, -flātum *v.t.* kindle, inflame; bring together; cause, bring about

cōnfluō, -fluere, -flūxī, --- *v.i.* flow together; crowd; assemble

cōnfodiō, -fodere, -fōdī, -fossum *v.t.* dig up; stab, pierce through; kill, assassinate

cōnformātiō, -ōnis *nf.* shaping, form, fashion, training; culture

cōnfugiō, -fugere, -fūgī, --- *v.i.* take refuge, flee to refuge

cōnfundō, -fundere, -fūdī, -fūsum *v.t.* pour; mingle; unite; spread over; confuse, jumble

cōnfūsiō, -ōnis *nf.* mingling, mixing; confusion, disorder

confūsus, -a, -um (w. comp.) *adj.* chaotic; perplexed (+ abl.)

congerlēs, -ēi *nf.* heap, pile

congerō, -gerere, -gessī, -gestum *v.t.* bring together, heap up, accumulate, build

congius, -ī *nm.* measure of about three quarts

congredior, congredī, congressus sum *v.d.i.* gather, come together; contend, fight

congregō, -gregāre, -gregāvī, -gregātum *v.t.* make flock together, assemble, gather together, unite

congressus, -ūs *nm.* meeting together; interview; fight, battle

congruō, -ere, -uī, --- *v.i.* agree; harmonize (+ dat. *or* + **cum** + abl. *or* + **inter** + acc.); correspond

coniciō (conj-), -icere, -iēcī, -iectum *v.t.* cast together, unite; hurl; aim; urge, force; place, put; guess; foretell

coniectūra, -ae *nf.* guess; inference

coniugium, -ī *nnt.* connection; union; marriage

coniūnctiō, -ōnis *nf.* union, agreement; close friendship

coniūnctus, -a, -um *adj.* united, allied (+ dat.); connected; intimate (+ **cum** + abl. *or* + abl. alone)

coniungō, -iungere, -iūnxī, -iūnctum *v.t.* combine, unite; associate, act in common

coniūnx *or* **coniux, coniugis** *nm/f.* spouse, husband, wife

coniūrātiō, -ōnis *nf.* plot, conspiracy

coniūrō, -iūrāre, -iūrāvī, -iūrātum *v.t.* swear together; unite; conspire, plot

cōnīveō, -nivēre, -nīvī *or* **-nīxī, ---** *v.i.* close one's eyes; overlook; wink at; connive

cōnor, cōnārī, cōnātus sum *v.d.i.t.* attempt, try, undertake (+ infv.); seek

conqueror, conquerī, conquestus sum *v.d.i.t.* complain, bewail

conquiēscō, -quiēscere, -quiēvī, -quiētum *v.i.* rest; cease; be at rest, enjoy peace

conquīrō, -quirere, -quīsīvī, -quīsītum *v.t.* seek for; bring together, gather

cōnsalūtō, -salūtāre, -salūtāvī, -salūtātum *v.t.* greet, greet together

cōnsanguineus, -a, -um *adj.* related by blood

cōnscelerātus, -a, -um *adj.* stained with guilt, wicked, criminal

cōnscientia, -ae *nf.* common knowledge; feeling, consciousness; conscience

cōnscīscō, -scīscere, -scīvī, -scītum *v.t.* vote together, approve of, resolve; adjudge; bring on oneself

cōnscius, -a, -um *adj.* conscious with, knowing in common (+ gen. of person *or* + dat. of what is known *or* + **in** *or* **dē** + abl.); *nm., nf.* participant; accomplice

cōnscrībō, -scrībere, -scrīpsī, -scrīptum *v.t.* write together; raise, collect, enlist; compose, write

cōnscrīptus, -a, -um *nm.* one enrolled (*used particularly in addressing the Senate*)

cōnsecrātiō, -ōnis *nf.* consecration, religious dedication

cōnsecrō, -secrāre, -secrāvī, -secrātum *v.t.* offer as sacred, consecrate; deify

cōnsenēscō, -senēscere, -senuī, --- *v.i.* grow old together, become old

cōnsēnsiō, -ōnis *nf.* agreement, unanimity

cōnsēnsus, -ūs *nm.* agreement, unanimity

cōnsentiō, -sentīre, -sēnsī, -sēnsum *v.t.* agree (+ dat. *or* + **cum** + abl.); resolve together; conspire

cōnsequor, cōnsequī, cōnsecūtus sum *v.d.i.t.* follow after, pursue; overtake, catch up with; arrive at, attain, achieve; imitate, adopt; result

cōnserō, -serēre, -seruī, -sertum *v.t.* connect together, entwine, tie, join

cōnservātiō, -ōnis *nf.* saving, preservation

cōnservātor, -ōris *nm.* savior, defender, keeper

cōnservō, -servāre, -servāvī, -servātum *v.t.* preserve, keep safe, maintain, guard

cōnsessus, -ūs *nm.* assembly

cōnsīderātus, -a, -um (w. comp. + sup.) *adj.* deliberate, cautious

cōnsīderō, -sīderāre, -sīderāvī, -sīderātum *v.t.* examine, look closely at, consider, contemplate

cōnsīdō, -sīdere, -sēdī, -sessum *v.i.* settle, settle down, sink down

cōnsilium, -ī *nnt.* council; deliberation; plan, measure, purpose, resolution; advice; understanding; judgment, decision

cōnsistō, -sistere, -stitī, -stitum *v.i.* stand still; stand fast, halt; find a foothold; stand forth; consist of, depend upon

cōnsōbrīna, -ae *nf.* maternal cousin

cōnsōbrīnus, -ī *nm.* maternal cousin

cōnsociō, -sociāre, -sociāvī, -sociātum *v.t.* associate, ally oneself, join, agree with

cōnsōlātiō, -ōnis *nf.* comfort, consolation

cōnsōlō, -sōlāre, -sōlāvī, -sōlātum *v.t.* console, comfort, cheer

cōnsōlor, cōnsōlārī, cōnsōlātus sum *v.d.t.* comfort, console, cheer

cōnspectus, -ūs *nm.* sight, view; presence

cōnspiciō, -spicere, -spexī, -spectum *v.t.* observe, gaze upon, perceive, face towards

cōnspicuus, -a, -um *adj.* visible, apparent; distinguished; conspicuous

cōnspīrō, -spīrāre, -spīrāvī, -spīrātum *v.t.* blow in unison; harmonize, agree; plot

cōnstāns (constant-) (w. comp. + sup.) *adj.* unchanging, constant; trustworthy, steadfast, faithful; **cōnstanter** *adv.* firmly, resolutely; evenly, consistently

cōnstantia, -ae *nf.* firmness, steadiness; perseverance, determination; uniformity

cōnsternō, -sternere, -strāvī, -strātum *v.t.* strew over, cover by strewing; thatch; pave; cover

cōnstituō, -stituere, -stituī, -stitūtum *v.t.* put, place, set up, station, establish, prepare, found, build; appoint; regulate, administer; decide, agree upon; halt

cōnstitūtum, -ī *nnt.* ordinance; appointment; agreement, compact

cōnstō, -stāre, -stitī, -stātum *v.i.* agree, be correct, be certain, be clear; be established, stand firm; cost; **cōnstat, -stāre, -stitit, ---** *v.i.* (imp.) it is agreed (+ acc. + infv.)

cōnstringō, -stringere, -strinxī, -strictum *v.t.* bind together, fetter; curb, hold firmly

cōnsuēscō, -suēscere, -suēvī, -suētum *v.t., v.i.* habituate, form a habit

cōnsuētūdō, -inis *nf.* custom, habitual practice; companionship, close friendship

cōnsul, -sulis *nm.* consul (*one of two chief magistrates of the Roman republic*)

cōnsulāris, -is, -e *adj.* of a consul; of consular rank

cōnsulātus, -ūs *nm.* consulship, consulate

cōnsulō, -sulere, -suluī, -sultum *v.i.* ask advice, deliberate (+ dat.); *v.t.* decide; look out for the interests of

cōnsultātiō, -ōnis *adj.* consultation, request for advice

cōnsultō *adv.* on purpose; **cōnsultō, -sultāre, -sultāvī, -sultātum** *v.t., v.i.* consult; reflect; provide for

cōnsultum, -ī *nnt.* decree; deliberation

cōnsūmō, -sūmere, -sūmpsī, -sūmptum *v.t.* use up, consume; waste, weaken, wear away; *v.i.* spend time

cōnsūmptor, -ōris *nm.* consumer; destroyer

cōnsurgō, -surgere, -surrēxī, -surrēctum *v.i.* stand up, rise together in a body; arise, originate

contactus, -ūs *nm.* touching, contact; contagion, infection

contāgiō, -ōnis *nf.* touching, contact; infection, contagion; pollution; bad companionship

contāminō, -tāmināre, -tāminavī, -tāminātum *v.t.* blend, mingle; contaminate, pollute

contegō, -tegere, -tēxī, -tēctum *v.t.* cover up, conceal, bury

contemnō, -temnere, -tempsī, -temptum *v.t.* scorn, despise; disparage; defy; slight, neglect

contemplor, contemplārī, contemplātus sum *v.d.t.* gaze at, observe; consider

contemptiō, -ōnis *nf.* scorn, disdain

contemptus *or* **contemtus, -a, -um** (w. comp. + sup.) *adj.* despised, vile

contendō, -tendere, -tendī, -tentum *v.t., v.i.* stretch tight, strain; aim; hasten; struggle, contest, dispute, protest; contrast; maintain, affirm

contentiō, -ōnis *nf.* struggle, effort, strife, dispute; comparison

contentus, -a, -um (w. sup.) *adj.* content, satisfied, happy

conterō, -terere, -trīvī, -trītum *v.t.* grind, pound; wear; rub on; wear away, wear out; destroy

conterreō, -terrēre, -terruī, -territum *v.t.* terrify, alarm

conticēscō, -ticēscere, -ticuī, --- *v.i.* become silent, cease to speak, be hushed; stop

contignātiō, -ōnis *nf.* floor, flooring; story (*in a building*)

contiguus, -a, -um *adj.* adjacent, bordering upon, touching (+ dat.)

continēns (continent-) (w. comp. + sup.) *adj.* bordering; connected, consecutive; self-restrained, temperate

continentia, -ae *nf.* self-restraint, self-control, temperance

contineō, -tinēre, -tinuī, -tentum *v.t.* hold together, contain; repress, check; include, involve

contingō, -tingere, -tigī, -tāctum *v.t., v.i.* touch, grasp; extend to; affect; reach, arrive at; happen, occur

continuō, -tinuāre, -tinuāvī, -tinuātum *v.t.* join together, make continuous, unite; continue without interruption, do one thing after another

continuō *adv.* immediately, directly; necessarily

continuus, -a, -um *adj.* continuous, adjoining; incessant, uninterrupted

cōntiō, -ōnis *nf.* gathering, assembly; address

cōntiōnātor, -ōris *nm.* one who harangues, demagogue

contorqueō, -torquēre, -torsī, -tortum *or* **-torsum** *v.t.* twist, hurl, throw

contrā *adv.* opposite, face to face; in opposition; on the contrary; in reply; *prep.* (+ acc.) against, facing, contrary to; in reply to; in hostility to; in spite of

contrāctiō, -ōnis *nf.* contraction; abbreviation, abridging; shortness

contractus, -a, -um (w. comp.) *adj.* drawn together; short, narrow; shrunken, pinched

contrahō, -trahere, -trāxī, -trāctum *v.t.* draw together, collect; contract, shorten, shrink, diminish; bring about, accomplish

contrārius, -a, -um *adj.* opposite; lying over against (+ gen. *or* +dat.); contrary, opposed, conflicting; uncongenial

contrīstō, -trīstāre, -trīstāvī, -trīstātum *v.t.* sadden, make sorry; darken, cloud, dim

contrōversia, -ae *nf.* debate, dispute, quarrel

contubernium, -ī *nnt.* the dwelling together of people in the same tent; relationship of a general and his personal followers; company

contumēlia, -ae *nf.* insult, reproach

contumēliōsus, -a, -um (w. comp. + sup.) *adj.* abusive, insolent

contundō, -tundere, -tutudī, -tūsum *or* **-tūnsum** *v.t.* beat, bruise, pound, mash

cōnūbium, -ī *nnt.* the right to marry; marriage

cōnus, -ī *nm.* cone; apex of a helmet

convalēscō, -valēscere, -valuī, --- *v.i.* grow strong; get well, recuperate, regain health, regain strength

cōnvenae, -ārum *nm/f./pl.* people who assemble together, multitude

conveniēns (convenient-) (w. sup.) *adj.* compatible, appropriate, agreeing, unanimous (+ dat.)

convenientia, -ae *nf.* harmony, agreement

conveniō, -venīre, -vēnī, -ventum *v.i.* come together, assemble; be agreed upon; be appropriate to

conventus, -ūs *nm.* meeting, convention, assembly; throng; court; corporation

conversiō, -ōnis *nf.* revolution, revolving; inversion; alteration, change; repetition

convertō, -vertere, -vertī, -versum *v.i.* turn; reverse, throw back; direct; change, alter; be changed

convīcium, -ī *nnt.* outcry; noise; altercation; insult
convincō, -vincere, -vīcī, -victum *v.t.* overcome, refute; prove clearly
convīva, -ae *nm/f.* guest, dinner guest
convīvium, -ī *nnt.* dinner party, banquet
convocō, -vocāre, -vocāvī, -vocātum *v.t.* call together, summon, convene
cooperiō, -operīre, -operuī, -opertum *v.t.* overwhelm, envelop; bury
coorior, coorīrī, coortus sum *v.d.i.* appear; break forth, break out; rise in
    opposition; begin
cōpia, -ae *nf.* plenty, abundance, copiousness; quantity; multitude; ability,
    power; **cōpiae, -ārum** *nf./pl.* wealth, resources, prosperity; troops
cōpiōsus, -a, -um (w. comp. + sup.) *adj.* well-supplied, abounding in (+
    abl. *or* + **ab** + abl.); fluent; eloquent
cōpula, -ae *nf.* band, rope, leash, bond, tie
coquō, -ere, coxī, coctum *v.t.* cook, bake; heat, parch; ripen; plan; vex,
    disturb
coquus *or* **cocus, -ī** *nm.* cook
cor, cordis *nnt.* heart; person; soul; feeling
corālium *or* **corallum** *or* **cūrālium, -ī** *nnt.* coral
cōram *adv.* publicly, openly; in person; *prep.* (+ abl.; sometimes postpos.).
    in the presence of, before
corbis, -is *nm/f.* basket
corium, -ī *nnt.* or **corius, -ī** *nm.* leather, skin, hide, bark, rind
cornīx, -nīcis *nf.* crow
cornū, -ūs *nnt.* horn of an animal; horn (*musical instrument*); wing of an
    army
corōna, -ae *nf.* crown, chaplet, wreath; cluster, crowd of people
corpulentus, -a, -um (w. comp.) *adj.* stout, corpulent
corpus, corporis *nnt.* body; living body; corpse; bulk, mass; matter
    (*physics*)
corrēctiō, -ōnis *nf.* amendment, correction; improvement
corrigia, -ae *nf.* shoelace
corrigō, -rigere, -rēxī, -rēctum *v.t.* align, straighten out, correct, amend,
    improve
corrōborō, -rōborāre, -rōborāvī, -rōborātum *v.t.* strengthen, fortify;
    encourage
corrumpō, -rumpere, -rūpī, -ruptum *v.t.* spoil, waste, mar, ruin; corrupt;
    bribe; falsify, tamper with
corruō, -ruere, -ruī, --- *v.t.*, throw down, overthrow; *v.i.* fall down, fall life-
    less, collapse

corruptēla, -ae *nf.* corruption, seduction
corruptiō, -ōnis *nf.* corruption, seduction
corruptus, -a, -um (w. comp. + sup.) *adj.* corrupt, bad
cortex, -ticis *nm/f.* bark, rind, shell; cork
costa, -ae *nf.* rib
cotīdiānus *or* **quotīdiānus, -a, -um** *adj.* daily
cotīdiē *or* **quotīdiē** *adv.* daily
coturnīx, -īcis *nf.* quail
coxa, -ae *nf.* hip
crās *adv.* tomorrow
crassitūdō, -inis *nf.* thickness, density
crassus, -a, -um (w. comp. + sup.) *adj.* thick, dense, fat; heavy
crātēra, -ae *nf.* mixing bowl, bowl, jar
crāticulus, -a, -um *adj.* wicker
crēber, crēbra, crēbrum (comp. **crēbrior**; sup. **crēberrimus)** *adj.* thick, close, numerous, crowded, abundant, frequent; **crēbrō** *adv.* frequently, repeatedly
crēbrēscō, -ere, crēbruī, --- *v.i.* become frequent, increase; gather strength
crēbritās, -ātis *nf.* frequency; thickness; closeness
crēdibilis, -is, -e (w. comp.) *adj.* believable, likely, credible; **crēdibile est**, it is credible that (+ acc. + infv.)
crēditor, -ōris *nm.* creditor
crēdō, -ere, -didī, -ditum *v.t.* think, suppose (+ acc. + infv.); lend; *v.i.* believe in, trust (+ dat.)
crēdulus, -a, -um *adj.* credulous, unsuspecting; simple
cremō, -āre, -āvī, -ātum *v.t.* burn, burn up
creō, -āre, -āvī, -ātum *v.t.* create; cause; appoint, choose, elect (+ double acc.)
crepīdō, -inis *nf.* foundation, basis; brim, border, edge; pedestal; dam; pier
crepundia, -ōrum *nnt./pl.* child's rattle
crepusculum, -ī *nnt.* dusk, twilight
crēscō, -ere, crēvī, crētum *v.i.* grow, spring up; increase, enlarge; wax; grow strong
crēta, -ae *nf.* chalk; white clay
crībrō, -āre, -āvī, -ātum *v.t.* sift, sieve
crībrum, -ī *nnt.* sieve
crīmen, -inis *nnt.* accusation, reproach; crime, offense
crīminātiō, -ōnis *nf.* accusation, charge, complaint

crīminor, crīminārī, crīminātus sum *v.d.t.* accuse of a crime, denounce, charge (+ acc. *or* + acc. + infv.)

crīnis, -is *nm.* hair (*usu. of the head*)

crispō, -āre, -āvī, -ātum *v.t.* curl; make rough, make uneven; make tremble, make wave

crispus, -a, -um (w. comp. + sup.) *adj.* curly, curled; uneven, wrinkled

crista, -ae *nf.* crest (*of a bird or a helmet*)

crocus, -ī *nm.or* **crocum, - ī** *nnt.* saffron

cruciātus, -ūs *nm.* torment, torture; pain

cruciō, -āre, -āvī, -ātum *v.t.* crucify; torment, torture

crūdēlis, -is, -e (w. comp.) *adj.* cruel, merciless, harsh, bitter

crūdēlitās, -ātis *nf.* harshness, cruelty

crūditās, -ātis *nf.* indigestion, excessive stuffing of the stomach

crūdus, -a, -um (w. comp.) *adj.* crude; bloody; raw, unripe; stuffed with food, undigested; vigorous, fresh; cruel, merciless

crūs, crūris *nnt.* leg

crusta, -ae *nf.* rind, bark, crust; scab

crustulum, -ī *nnt.* small pastry

crustum, -ī *nnt.* pastry, anything baked

crux, crucis *nf.* cross, frame for execution; torture, misery

crystallum, -ī *nnt. or* **crystallus, - ī** *nf.* crystal

cubiculum, -ī *nnt.* bedroom

cūbīle, -is *nnt.* place to rest, bed, nest, lair, kennel

cubitum, -ī *nnt.* elbow; bending; cubit

cubō, -ere, -uī, -itum *v.i.* lie down, recline; sleep; lie sick; slope

cūcullus, -ī *nm.* cap; hooded cloak

cucurbita, -ae *nf.* squash, gourd (*bot.*)

cūiusmodī *adj.* (indecl.) of whatever kind

culcita, -ae *nf.* mattress, cushion, pillow

culex, -icis *nm.* mosquito, gnat

culīna, -ae *nf.* kitchen

culmen, -inis *nnt.* top, summit, acme; ridge; pillar, support; roof

culpa, -ae *nf.* fault, blame, reproach; crime

culter, -trī *nm.* plowshare; knife

cultiō, -ōnis *nf.* cultivation; preparation

cultūra, -ae *nf.* cultivation, care; training, education; culture; style; worship

cultus, -ūs *nm.* labor, cultivation; culture, training, education; way of life, civilization; reverence; clothing, way of dressing

cum *or* **quom** *conj.* when, at the time when; while, as long as; as often as, whenever; since, because; although; **cum … tum** *conj.* both … and; **cum praesertim** *conj.* especially since; **cum** (*not* **quom**) *prep.* (+ abl.) with; along with, together with; compared with

cumulātē (w. comp. + sup.) *adv.* copiously, abundantly, with much interest

cumulō, -āre, -āvī, -ātum *v.t.* pile, heap up; increase; overload, overwhelm

cumulus, -ī *nm.* heap, pile; addition, surplus, increase

cūnābula, -ōrum *nnt./pl.* cradle

cūnae, -ārum *nf./pl.* cradle

cunctātiō, -ōnis *nf.* delay, hesitation; doubt

cunctor, cunctārī, cunctātus sum *v.d.i.* delay, cause to delay, hesitate; doubt

cunctus, -a, -um *adj.* all, all together, entire, whole

cuneus, -ī *nm.* wedge, plug; wedge formation

cunīculus, -ī *nm.* rabbit, hare; tunnel, hole, canal

cūpa, -ae *nf.* barrel, cask

cupiditās, -ātis *nf.* desire, craving, passion, ambition; love, lust

cupīdō, -inis *nf. or* **cūpēdō (cuppēdō), -inis** *nm.* desire, craving, passion, love, lust; **Cupīdō, -inis** *nm.* Cupid (*the god of love*)

cupidus, -a, -um (w. comp. + sup.) *adj.* ambitious, eager, desirous; loving, lustful; greedy (+ gen.)

cupiō, cupere, cupīvī, cupītum *v.t.* desire, wish for; favor; be devoted to

cūr *or* **quor** *adv.* why, wherefore

cūra, -ae *nf.* care, attention; anxiety; concern; sorrow; healing; administration

cūratē (w. comp.) *adv.* carefully, diligently

cūrātiō, -ōnis *nf.* management, oversight, administration

cūrātor, -ōris *nm.* inspector, manager; guardian, curator

cūria, -ae *nf.* curia, association; one of the thirty divisions of the patricians; the senate house

cūriōsus, -a, -um (w. comp. + sup.) *adj.* attentive, full of care, devoted; inquiring, curious, inquisitive; meddling, prying

cūrō, -āre, -āvī, -ātum *v.t.* attend to, take care of, preside over, manage, command (+ **ut** + subjv.)

curriculum, -ī *nnt.* running; race; career; small chariot

currō, -ere, cucurrī, cursum *v.i.* run; sail; fly; flow, spread

currus, -ī *nm.* chariot, wagon, triumphal chariot

cursō, -āvī ---, --- *v.i.* run here and there

cursor, -ōris *nm.* runner; courier

cursus, -ūs *nm.* running; course, way; voyage, journey; progress, direction; speed, race; **cursus pūblicus, cursūs pūblicī** *nm.* the post, government system for transporting communications; **cursus honōrum, cursūs honōrum** *nm.* career in public office

curvō, -āre, -āvī, -ātum *v.t.* bend, curve; move

curvus, -a, -um *adj.* bent, curved, crooked; winding; wrong; perverse

custōdia, -ae *nf.* guarding, guard, protection; confinement

custōdiō, -īre, -īvī, -ītum *v.t.* protect, guard; restrain, hold captive

custōdītē *adv.* cautiously, carefully

custos, -ōdis *nm/f.* guard, protector, overseer

cutis, -is *nf.* skin, hide, leather, rind, surface; external appearance

cȳgnus *or* **cȳcnus, -ī** *nm.* swan

cylindrus, cylindrī *nm.* cylinder

D

damnātiō, -ōnis *nf.* conviction, condemnation

damnō, -āre, -āvī, -ātum *v.t.* inflict injury on; condemn, find guilty (+ acc. of person + gen. of offence)

damnum, -ī *nnt.* damage, loss, harm; penalty

dē *prep.* (+ abl.) from, down from, away from, out of; after; during, in the course of; of, from among; made of; in regard to, concerning, about

dea, -ae (dat. + abl. pl. **deābus**) *nf.* goddess

dealbō, -āre, ---, -ātum *v.t.* whiten

dēbeō, -ēre, debuī, dēbitum *v.i.* keep back, withhold; owe, be in debt to; ought, should, must

dēbilis, -is, -e (+ comp.) *adj.* weak, frail, helpless; disabled

dēbilitās, -ātis *nf.* weakness

dēbilitō, -āre, -āvī, -ātum *v.t.* weaken, disable; dishearten, discourage

dēbitus, -a, -um *adj.* fitting, appropriate; doomed

dēcēdō, -cēdere, -cessī, -cessum *v.i.* go away, depart, retire, leave; go astray

decem *num.* (indecl.) ten

December, -bris *nm.* December (*usu. w.* **mēnsis**); **December, Decembris, Decembre** *adj.* of or pertaining to December

dēcernō, -cernere, -crēvī, -crētum *v.i.* decide, vote, decree (+ acc. + infv. *or* + **ut** *or* **nē** + subjv.); *v.t.* fight, contend

dēcertō, -certāre, -certāvī, -certātum *v.i.* fight out a contest, contend, vie (+ **cum** + abl.)

decet, decēre, decuit, --- *v.i.* (imp.) be fitting, be proper (+ acc. *or* + acc. + infv.)

dēcidō, -cidere, -cidī, --- *v.i.* fall down; perish

deciēs (deciēns) *adv.* ten times

decimus, -a, -um *adj.* tenth

dēcipiō, -cipere, -cēpī, -ceptum *v.t.* catch; deceive, cheat; beguile

dēclārō, -clārāre, -clārāvī, -clārātum *v.t.* declare, make known, proclaim, announce; prove

dēclīnātiō, -ōnis *nf.* bending to one side; deviation; avoidance

dēclīnō, -clīnāre, -clīnāvī, -clīnātum *v.t., v.i.* swerve, bend aside, turn aside, digress, avoid; let sink

decorō, -āre, -āvī, -ātum *v.t.* adorn, embellish; honor

decōrus, -a, -um *adj.* proper, seemly, right; adorned, beautiful (+ dat. *or* + abl. *or* + **ad** + acc. *or* + **prō** + abl.)

dēcrēscō, -crēscere, -crēvī, -crētum *v.i.* decrease, grow less, become fewer, wane, shrink

dēcrētum, -ī *nnt.* decision, decree, vote

dēcurrō, -currere, -currī (-cucurrī), -cursum *v.i.* run down, hasten down, run through, traverse, march, maneuver; come away

decus, -oris *nnt.* glory, honor, adornment; moral dignity, propriety

dēdecus, -oris *nnt.* shame, disgrace; cause of shame

dēdicātiō, -ōnis *nf.* dedication, consecration

dēdicō, -dicāre, -dicāvī, -dicātum *v.t.* dedicate, consecrate

dēditiō, -ōnis *nf.* giving up, surrender; betrayal

dēditus, -a, -um (w. comp. + sup.) *adj.* devoted to, addicted to (+ dat.)

dēdō, -dere, -didī, -ditum *v.t.* surrender, give up, betray; devote; submit

dēdūcō, -dūcere, -dūxī, -ductum *v.t.* lead down, bring down, draw off, remove, bring out, lead away

dēductiō, -ōnis *nf.* leading down or away; colonizing, settling

dēfatīgātiō, -ōnis *nf.* weariness, exhaustion

dēfatīgō *or* **dēfetīgō, -fatīgāre, -fatīgāvī, -fatīgātum** *v.t.* tire out, weary

dēfectiō, -ōnis *nf.* failure; disappearance; revolt, desertion

dēfectus, -ūs *nm.* failure, ceasing; **dēfectus sōlis, dēfectūs sōlis** *nm.* solar eclipse; **dēfectus lūnae, dēfectūs lūnae** *nm.* lunar eclipse

dēfendō, -fendere, -fendī, -fēnsum *v.t.* repel, ward off; protect, defend

dēfēnsiō, -ōnis *nf.* apology; defense

dēferō, -ferre, -tulī, -lātum *v.t.* bring down; bear off; grant, give, deliver; take; report, announce; bring before, refer to; denounce, accuse

dēfessus, -a, -um *adj.* faint, weary, exhausted

dēficiō, -ficere, -fēcī, -fectum *v.i.* revolt, withdraw; fail, cease; become exhausted; abandon

dēfīgō, -fīgere, -fīxī, -fīxum *v.t.* fasten, affix; thrust; set up, direct; plunge

dēfīniō, -fīnīre, -fīnīvī, -fīnītum *v.t.* limit; determine, establish, define

dēfīnītiō, -ōnis *nf.* limiting; definition

dēfīnītīvus, -a, -um *adj.* explanatory; definitive

dēfīnītus, -a, -um *adj.* definite, distinct

dēflagrō, -flagrāre, -flagrāvī, -flagrātum *v.t., v.i.* burn down, destroy by fire

dēflectō, -flectere, -flexī, -flexum *v.t.* bend aside; lead astray; digress

dēfleō, -flēre, -flēvī, -flētum *v.t.* weep over; deplore

dēflōrēscō, -flōrēscere, -flōruī, --- *v.i.* fade, wither

dēfōrmis, -is, -e *or* **dēfōrmus, -a, -um** (w. comp. + sup.) *adj.* ugly, deformed

dēfōrmō, -fōrmāre, -fōrmāvī, -fōrmātum *v.t.* disfigure, ruin; deteriorate; dishonor

dēfringō, -fringere, -frēgī, -frāctum *v.t.* detach, break off

dēfungor, dēfungī, dēfunctus sum *v.d.i.* perform, fulfill (+ abl.)

dēgō, dēgere, dēgī, --- *v.t., v.i.* spend; pass

dēiciō (dēj-), -icere, -iēcī, -iectum *v.t.* throw, hurl, throw away; kill

dein(de) *adv.* thereafter, since; afterwards, next; besides

deinceps *adv.* one after another, in order, next in order

dēlābor, dēlābī, dēlāpsus sum *v.d.i.* glide down, descend, sink, drop, fall

dēlectātiō, -ōnis *nf.* enjoyment, pleasure, amusement, entertainment

dēlectō, -āre, -āvī, -ātum *v.t.* delight, please, amuse, entertain

dēlectus, -a, -um *adj.* choice, chosen, elect; **dēlectus, -ūs** *nm.* selection, choice

dēleō, -ēre, -ēvī, -ētum *v.t.* erase, delete, obliterate, overthrow

dēlīberātiō, -ōnis *nf.* consideration, thought

dēlīberō, -līberāre, -līberāvī, -līberātum *v.t.* consider, deliberate; consult; resolve, determine

dēlīcātus, -a, -um (w. comp. + sup.) *adj.* charming, delightful; voluptuous; fastidious

dēlīciae, -ārum *nf./pl.* pleasure, delight, luxury; frivolity; pet; darling

dēlīctum, -ī *nnt.* misdeed, fault, crime, wrong

dēlīgō, -ligere, -lēgī, -lectum *v.t.* choose, select, designate

dēlīrātiō, -ōnis *nf.* folly, silliness

delphīnus, -ī *nm.* dolphin

dēlūbrum, -ī *nnt.* place of expiation; shrine, temple

dēmēns (dēment-) (w. comp. + sup.) *adj.* out of one's mind, distracted, insane; foolish, rash, infatuated; **dēmenter** *adv.* recklessly, rashly, foolishly

dēmergō, -mergere, -mersī, -mersum *v.t.* sink, submerge, bury; overwhelm

dēmetō, -metere, -messuī, -messum *v.t.* mow, reap, harvest, gather

dēmigrō, -migrāre, -migrāvī, -migrātum *v.i.* migrate, go off, depart

dēminuō, -minuere, -minuī, -minūtum *v.t.* decrease, make smaller, reduce; impair

dēminūtiō, -ōnis *nf.* reduction, diminution, lessening, loss

dēmissus, -a, -um (w. comp.) *adj.* lowered, sunken; downcast, dejected; humble, shy, timid, unassuming

dēmittō, -mittere, -mīsī, -missum *v.t.* lower, send down, put down, drop, let fall; lead down, march down; sink, bury

dēmō, -ere, dēmpsī, dēmptum *v.t.* take away, withdraw; dispel, count out

dēmōnstrātiō, -ōnis *nf.* pointing out; explanation

dēmōnstrō, -mōnstrāre, -mōnstrāvī, -mōnstrātum *v.t.* show, demonstrate, point out; prove

dēmum *adv.* at last, finally; certainly, in fact

dēnārius, -ī *nm.* denarius (*a silver coin*)

dēnegō, -negāre, -negāvī, -negātum *v.t.* say no, reject, deny, refuse

dēnique *adv.* at last, finally; in brief

dēnotō, -notāre, -notāvī, -notātum *v.t.* specify, mark out, designate

dēns, dentis *nm.* tooth

dēnsitās, -ātis *nf.* density, thickness

dēnsō, -āre, -āvī, -ātum *v.t.* thicken, condense; press together, crowd together

dēnsus, -a, -um (w. comp. + sup.) *adj.* dense, crowded, full, thick

dēnūntiātiō, -ōnis *nf.* notification, announcement, declaration

dēnūntiō, -nūntiāre, -nūntiāvī, -nūntiātum *v.t.* notify, announce, warn; denounce; order

dēpellō, -pellere, -pulī, -pulsum *v.t.* drive out, expel, ward off, thwart, force; dissuade

dēpendeō, -pendēre, -pendī, -pēnsum *v.i.* depend; hang down; pay

dēpingō, -pingere, -pinxī, -pīctum *v.t.* depict, portray, paint

dēplōrō, -plōrāre, -plōrāvī, -plōrātum *v.t., v.i.* lament, weep over; deplore; abandon

dēpōnō, -pōnere, -posuī, -positum *v.t.* unload, set down, place, put off, lay aside; entrust; give up, resign

dēportō, -portāre, -portāvī, -portātum *v.t.* carry down, take away, bring away; bring home

dēposcō, -poscere, -poposcī, --- *v.t.* demand, call for, request

dēpositum, -ī *nnt.* thing deposited; trust, deposit

dēprāvō, -prāvāre, -prāvāvī, -prāvātum *v.t.* pervert, distort, corrupt, deprave

dēprecātor, -ōris *nm.* averter, advocate, one who intercedes; **dēprecātor, dēprecārī, dēprecātus sum** *v.d.i.t.* plead against, pray to avert; intercede for

dēprehendō (dēprend-), -prehendere, -prehendī, -prehēnsum *v.t.* take away, seize, capture; surprise; detect; understand

dēprehēnsiō, -ōnis *nf.* detection; catching, seizing

dēprimō, -primere, -pressī, -pressum *v.t.* press down, sink, overwhelm

dēprōmō, -prōmere, -prōmpsī, -prōmptum *v.t.* draw out, bring out; obtain

dērēctō *adv.* straightway, directly

dērelinquō, -linquere, -līquī, -līctum *v.t.* abandon, forsake

dēscendō, -scendere, -scendī, -scēnsum *v.i.* descend, go down, climb down; sink; fall; penetrate; yield, agree to

dēscēnsus, -ūs *nm.* descent, slope; going down

dēscrībō, -scrībere, -scrīpsī, -scrīptum *v.t.* copy, transcribe, draw; describe, define; arrange

dēscrīptiō, -ōnis *nf.* copy, representation, sketch; description

dēserō, -serere, -seruī, -sertum *v.i.* desert, abandon, leave; forfeit

dēsertus, -a, -um *adj.* deserted; lonely

dēsīderātiō, -ōnis *nf.* longing; regret

dēsīderium, -ī *nnt.* longing, wish; regret, grief

dēsīderō, -āre, -āvī, -ātum *v.t.* miss, feel the want of, long for, wish for; demand, call for

dēsīdō, -sīdere, -sēdī, --- *v.i.* sink, fall, settle; deteriorate, worsen; waste time

dēsignātiō *or* **dissignātiō, -ōnis** *nf.* marking out, specifying; appointment to office

dēsignō *or* **dissgnō, -signāre, -signāvī, -signātum** *v.t.* mark out, trace, point out, designate, appoint, choose, nominate, elect

dēsinō, -sinere, dēsiī, dēsitum *v.t., v.i.* cease, leave off, quit (+ infv.), come to an end

dēsipiēns (desipient-) *adj.* silly, foolish

dēsistō, -sistere, -stitī, -stitum *v.i.* quit, cease

dēsōlō, -sōlāre, -sōlāvī, -sōlātum *v.t.* forsake, abandon

dēsperātiō, -ōnis *nf.* despair

dēspērō, -spērāre, -spērāvī, -spērātum *v.i.* despair, be hopeless, give up hope

dēspiciō, -spicere, -spexī, -spectum *v.t., v.i.* look down on, disdain

dēspūmō, -spūmāre, -spūmāvī, -spūmātum *v.t.* skim, remove scum

dēstinō, -āre, -āvī, -ātum *v.t.* bind, make firm; resolve, determine; assign, appoint

dēstituō, -stituere, -stituī, -stitūtum *v.t.* put away, leave, abandon, betray

dēstringō, -stringere, -strinxī, -strictum *v.t.* strip off; draw a weapon

dēsuētūdō, -inis *nf.* disuse

dēsum, -esse, -fuī, -futūrus *v.i.* be absent, be missing, fail, be inadequate, be at fault, neglect

dētergeō, -tergere, -tersī, -tersum *v.t.* wipe off, dust, sweep

dēterreō, -terrēre, -terruī, -territum *v.t.* frighten; discourage, hinder, repress

dētestābilis, -is, -e (w. comp.) *adj.* detestable, abominable

dētestor, dētestārī, dētestātus sum *v.d.t.* call down against, curse; avert

dētorqueō, -torquēre, -torsī, -tortum *v.t.* turn away; twist out of shape, distort

dētrahō, -trahere, -trāxī, -trāctum *v.t.* draw off, pull down, take away, remove, withdraw, rob; belittle

dētrīmentum, -ī *nm.* loss, hurt, harm

dēturbō, -turbāre, -turbāvī, -turbātum *v.t.* strike down; expel; deprive of

deus, -ī *nm.* (nom. pl. **deī** *or* **dī**; dat + abl. pl. **deīs** *or* **dīs**) god

dēversor, dēversārī, dēversātus sum *v.d.i.* lodge, stay as a guest

dēversōrium *or* **dēvorsōrium, -ī** *nnt.* lodging, place to stay

dēvincō, -vincere, -vīcī, -victum *v.t.* conquer, subdue, overpower

dēvocō, -vocāre, -vocāvī, -vocātum *v.t.* call away, call off, recall

dēvoveō, -vovēre, -vōvī, -vōtum *v.t.* vow, consecrate

dexter, dextera, dexterum *or* **dexter, dextra, dextrum** (comp. **dexterior**; sup. **dextimus**) *adj.* right, right-handed

dextera (dextra), -ae *nf.* the right hand

diabolus, -ī *nm.* devil

diadēma, -atis *nnt.* royal headband

diagōnālis, -is, -e *adj.* diagonal

dialecticus, -a, -um *adj.* pertaining to discussion; logical

dialectus (dialectos), -ī *nm.* dialect

diametros, -ī *nf.* diameter

diārium, -ī *nnt.* daily allowance of food; diary; **diāria, -ōrum** *nnt./pl.* daily pay

dīciō, -ōnis *nf.* domination, rule, jurisdiction

dīcō, -ere, dīxī, dictum *v.t.* say, speak, state, affirm, maintain (+ acc. *or* + acc. + infv.); name, appoint; settle

dictātor, -ōris *nm.* dictator (*a Roman magistrate, appointed in great emergencies for six months, with unlimited power*)

dictātūra, -āe *nf.* office of dictator

dictiō, -ōnis *nf.* act of saying, delivery, oratory, diction style; pleading;

dictitō, -āre, -āvī, -ātum *v.t.* keep saying; declare, assert, allege

dictō, -āre, -āvī, -ātum *v.t.* speak on behalf of another; suggest; dictate to a secretary

dictum, -ī *nnt.* remark, word, saying, speech

didūcō, -dūcere, -dūxī, -ductum *v.t.* draw apart, separate; distribute

diēs, diēī *nm./f.* day, daylight; appointed time; time interval, period; **in diēs** *adv.* day by day

differō, -ferre, distulī, dīlātum *v.i.* bear apart, disperse; defer, postpone; differ, be unlike

difficilis, -is, -e (comp. **difficilior**; sup. **difficillimus**) *adj.* hard, difficult; perilous; hard to manage, ill-tempered, obstinate

difficultās, -ātis *nf.* trouble, difficulty, distress

diffidentia, -ae *nf.* distrust, want of confidence; despair

diffīdō, -fīdere, -fīsus sum *v.i.* distrust, lack confidence in (+ dat.)

diffluō, -fluere, -flūxī, --- *v.i.* flow in different directions; be dissolved; melt away

diffugiō, -fugere, -fūgī, --- *v.i.* scatter, fly in different directions

diffundō, -fundere, fūdī, -fūsum *v.t.* pour forth, spread, diffuse; make relax, make happy

dīgerō, -gerere, -gessī, -gestum *v.t.* separate, spread, divide, sort

digitus, -ī *nm.* finger, toe

dignitās, -ātis *nf.* importance, worth, distinction, eminence, reputation

dignus, -a, -um (w. comp. + sup.) *adj.* worthy, deserving, suitable, becoming, fit, proper (+ abl.)

dīgressus, -ūs *nm.* departure, separation

dīiūdicō (dīj-), -iūdicāre, -iūdicāvī, -iūdicātum *v.t.* discern, decide, settle

dīlābor, dīlābī, dīlapsus sum *v.d.i.* fall to pieces, fall to ruin; scatter; perish

dīlātiō, -ōnis *nf.* postponement, delay

dīlātō, -lātāre, -lātāvī, -lātātum *v.t.* expand, spread out

dīlectus, -ūs *nm.* choosing, selection; levy, recruiting

dīligēns (diligent-) (w. comp. + sup.) *adj.* careful, conscientious, attentive, scrupulous, faithful

dīligentia, -ae *nf.* carefulness, attentiveness, diligence

dīligō, -ligere, -lēxī, -lēctum *v.t.* single out; value, esteem, appreciate; love

dīlūcēscō, -lūcēscere, -lūxī, --- *v.i.* grow light, lighten, dawn

dīlūtum, -ī *nnt.* solution (*liquid in which a thing has been dissolved*)

dīlūvium, -ī *nnt.* flood, inundation

dīmētior, dīmētīrī, dīmēnsus sum *v.d.t.* measure out, lay out

dīmicātiō, -ōnis *nf.* fight, combat, contest

dīmicō, -micāre, -micāvī, -micātum *v.i.* contend, fight; be in danger

dīmidius, -a, -um *adj.* halved, divided in half; **dīmidium, -ī** *nnt.* half

dīmittō, -mittere, -mīsī, -missum *v.t.* send out in different directions, send away, dismiss, discharge; forsake, leave

dīnumerō, -numerāre, -numerāvī, -numerātum *v.t.* count, number, reckon

dīrēctus *or* **dērēctus, -a, -um** (w. comp.) *adj.* straight (*in any direction*), level; upright, steep

dīreptiō, -ōnis *nf.* plundering

dīrimō, -imere, -ēmī, -ēmptum *v.t.* divide, cut off, interrupt, separate; destroy

dīripiō, -ripere, -ripuī, -reptum *v.t.* tear apart; lay waste, ransack, rob

dīritās, -ātis *nf.* calamity, misfortune; cruelty

dīrumpō, -rumpere, -rūpī, -ruptum *v.t.* break to pieces, shatter, sever

dīrus, -a, -um (w. comp.) *adj.* awful, dreadful, ill-omened; producing fear; cruel, fierce

discēdō, -cēdere, -cessī, -cessum *v.i.* leave, go away, withdraw (+ **ab, dē,** or **ex** + abl.); be left, remain

discernō, -cernere, -crēvī, -crētum *v.t.* separate, divide; distinguish, discern

discerpō, -cerpere, -cerpsī, -cerptum *v.t.* tear into pieces, mutilate

discessiō, -ōnis *nf.* separation, division; voting

discessus, -ūs *nm.* departure, separation

discidium, -ī *nf.* dissension, discord

disciplīna *or* **discipulīna, -ae** *nf.* training, instruction, education, study; discipline; culture

discipula, -ae *nf.* female student, pupil

discipulus, -ī *nm.* male student, pupil

discō, -ere, didicī, --- *v.t.* learn, become acquainted with, learn how

discordia, -ae *nf.* disagreement, quarrel; civil strife

discrepō, -crepāre, -crepuī, --- *v.i.* differ, disagree, be unlike

discrībō, -scrībere, -scrīpsī, -scrīptum *v.t.* classify, define; allot, appoint

discrīmen, -inis *nnt.* interval, separation, distinction; crisis, peril

discrīminō, -āre, -āvī, -ātum *v.t.* divide, separate

discursus, -ūs *nm.* running about, bustling; discourse, discussion

dīsertus, -a, -um (w. comp. + sup.) *adj.* skillful, clever; eloquent

disiciō (disj-), -icere, -iēcī, -iectum *v.t.* scatter, tear to pieces, disperse; destroy, overthrow; frustrate

disiungō (disj-), -iungere, -iūnxī, -iūnctum *v.t.* detach, loosen, separate

dispār (dispar-) *adj.* unlike, unequal (+ dat. *or* + gen.)

dispēnsātor, -ōris *nm.* treasurer, steward

dispēnsō, -pēnsāre, -pēnsāvī, -pēnsātum *v.t.* pay out, distribute; manage

dispergō, -spergere, -spersī, -spersum *v.t.* scatter, bestrew

dispersus, -a, -um *adj.* scattered

displiciō, -plicere, -plicuī, -itum *v.i.* displease (+ dat.)

dispōnō, -pōnere, -posuī, -positum *v.t.* arrange; distribute, post, assign

disputātiō, -ōnis *nf.* reckoning, considering; debate, argument

disputō, -putāre, -putāvī, -putātum *v.t., v.i.* investigate; argue, debate

dissēminō, -sēmināre, -sēmināvī, -sēminātum *v.t.* scatter, spread abroad, disseminate

dissēnsiō, -ōnis *nf.* conflict of opinion, disagreement, discord

dissentiō, -sentīre, -sēnsī, -sēnsum *v.i.* disagree, dissent (+ **ab** or **cum** + abl. of person *or* + **dē** + abl. of disagreement)

disserō, -serere, -seruī, -sertum *v.t.* argue about, discuss, explain

dissimilis, -is, -e (comp. **dissimilior**; sup. **disimillimus**) *adj.* different, unlike (+ dat.)

dissimilitūdō, -inis *nf.* difference, dissimilarity

dissimulō, -simulāre, -simulāvī, -simulātum *v.t., v.i.* keep secret, dissemble

dissipō *or* **dissupō, -āre, -āvī, -ātum** *v.t.* scatter, disperse, spread abroad

dissociō, -sociāre, -sociāvī, -sociātum *v.t.* disunite, separate, divide, estrange

dissolūtiō, -ōnis *nf.* destroying, destruction; looseness

dissolūtus, -a, -um *adj.* loose; remiss; dissolute

dissolvō, -solvere, -solvī, -solūtum *v.t.* unloose, separate; destroy; dissolve; free from debt

dissuādeō, -suādēre, -suāsī, -suāsum *v.t.* advise against, oppose by argument (+ **dē** + abl. *or* + acc. + infv. *or* + acc. + infv.)

distantia, -ae *nf.* remoteness; divergence, difference

distineō, -tinēre, -tinuī, -tentum *v.t.* hold apart; keep back, detain

distō, stare, ---, --- *v.i.* stand apart, be distant, be separate

distrahō, -trahere, -trāxī, -trāctum *v.t.* pull apart, pull to pieces, break up; distract

distribuō, -tribuere, -tribuī, -tribūtum *v.t.* distribute, apportion

distribūtiō, -ōnis *nf.* distribution, division

diū (comp. **diūtius**; sup. **diūtissimē**) *adv.* for a long time, too long

diurnus, -a, -um *adj.* of or belonging to the day, daily

diūturnus, -a, -um (w. comp. + sup.) *adj.* long-lasting, prolonged

dīvellō, -vellere, -vellī, -vulsum *v.t.* tear apart, separate; destroy

dīversōrium *or* **dīvorsōrium, -ī** *nnt.* inn

dīversus, -a, -um (w. comp. + sup.) *adj.* opposite, contrary, conflicting, different; separate, remote; **dīversē** (w. sup.) *adv.* in different directions

dīves (dīvit-) *or* **dīs (dīt-)** (comp. **dīvitior** *or* **dītior**; sup. **dīvitissimus** *or* **dītissimus**) *adj.* wealthy, rich (+ gen.); costly

dīvidō, -videre, -vīsī, -vīsum *v.t.* divide, separate; distribute, scatter; extend

dīvīnitus *adv.* by inspiration, divinely; admirably

dīvīnus, -a, -um (w. comp. + sup.) *adj.* of god, divine, godlike, sacred; inspired, prophetic

dīvīsiō, -ōnis *nf.* division, distribution

dīvitiae, -ārum *nf./pl.* wealth, riches, treasure

dīvortium, -ī *nnt.* divergence, parting of ways, divorce

dīvulgō, -vulgāre, -vulgāvī, -vulgātum *v.t.* spread, publish, divulge

dīvus *or* **dīus, -a, -um** *adj.* divine, deified; **dīvus, -ī** *nm.* god; **dīva, -ae** *nf.* goddess; **dīvum, -ī** *nnt.* sky, open air

dō, dare, dedī, datum *v.t.* give, offer; yield, permit; afford; supply; cause, bring about; exhibit

doceō, -ēre, docuī, doctum *v.t.* instruct, teach, explain, tell

doctrīna, -ae *nf.* teaching; scholarship, learning

doctus, -a, -um (w. comp. + sup.) *adj.* trained, learned, skilled; profound, cultured

doleō, -ēre, doluī, -itum *v.t., v.i.* feel pain, feel hurt, hurt, suffer; grieve; be sorry

dolor, -ōris *nm.* pain, suffering, grief, trouble, woe

dolus, -ī *nm.* trick, craft, cunning, deception

domesticus, -a, -um *adj.* pertaining to the house; private, personal

domī *adv.* at home

domicilium, -ī *nnt.* home, dwelling, habitation

domina, -ae *nf.* mistress of the household, wife; lady; empress

dominātiō, -ōnis *nf.* mastery, rule, domination

dominor, dominārī, dominātus sum *v.d.i.* have power, rule, govern, reign

dominus, -ī *nm.* master of a household; owner, proprietor; ruler, lord, emperor

domō *or* **domū** *adv.* from home; **domō, -āre, -āvī, -ātum** *v.t.* tame, train; master, conquer

domum *adv.* home, homewards

domus, -ūs *or* **- ī** (dat. sg. **domuī** *or* **domō**; abl sg. **domō** *or* **domū**; gen. pl. **domōrum** *or* **domuum**; dat. + abl. pl. **domibus**; acc. pl. **domūs** *or* **domōs**) *nf.* home, house, residence; household, family

dōnec *conj.* (w. indv.) until; (w. indv.or subjv.) so long as

dōnō, -āre, -āvī, -ātum *v.t.* present, give; cancel a debt

dōnum, -ī *nnt.* present, gift; religious offering

dormiō, -īre, -īvī, -ītum *v.i.* sleep, take rest, be at ease

dōs, dōtis *nf.* dowry

dracō, -ōnis *nm.* dragon, a kind of snake

dubitātiō, -ōnis *nf.* hesitation, uncertainty

dubitō, -āre, -āvī, -ātum *v.t., v.i.* doubt, hesitate, waver; consider, deliberate

dubius, -a, -um *adj.* doubtful, wavering, hesitant, uncertain; precarious

ducentī, -ae, -a *num.* two hundred

dūcō, -ere, dūxī, ductum *v.t.* conduct, lead; draw along; calculate, consider

dūdum *adv.* a little while ago, before; **iam dūdum** (+ a past tense) for a long time now

dulcēdō, -inis *nf.* sweetness, pleasantness, charm

dulcis, -is, -e (w. comp. + sup.) *adj.* sweet, pleasant

dum *conj.* (+ present indv.) as, while; (+ subjv. *or* + perfect indv.) until; (+ subjv.) provided that; **dummodō** *conj.* (+ subjv.) provided that, if only

dumtaxat *adv.* to this extent, so far, at least, at most

duo, duae, duo *num.* two

duodecim *num.* (indecl.) twelve

duodecimus, -a, -um *adj.* twelfth

duodēvīcēsimus, -a, -um *adj.* eighteenth

duodēvīgintī *num.* (indecl.) eighteen
dūplex (dūplic-) *adj.* double, two-fold; twice as much
dūplicō, -plicāre, -plicāvī, -plicātum *v.t.* double, increase by doubling, bend double
dūplus, -a, -um *adj.* double, twice as much
dūrēscō, -ere, dūruī, --- *v.i.* harden, grow hard; freeze
dūritia, -ae *nf.* hardness; austerity, harshness; insensibility
dūrō, -āre, -āvī, -ātum *v.t.* make hard, stiffen; make hardy, harden; *v.i.* endure, last
dūrus, -a, -um (w. comp. + sup.) *adj.* hard, tough; rude, unfeeling; cruel; hard to bear; enduring
dux, ducis *nm/f.* guide; leader, master, commander, ruler, chief
dyspnoea, -ae *nf.* difficulty in breathing

E

ē *See* **ex**.
ēbrius, -a, -um *adj.* full; drunk
ebur, -oris *nnt.* ivory
eburneus, -a, -um *adj.* ivory (*made from ivory*)
ecclēsia, -ae *nf.* assembly of the Greek people; assembly of Christians, church
ecquī, ecquae (equa), equod *adj.* is there any?; whether any
ecquid *adv.* at all, if at all, whether
edāx (edāc-) *adj.* greedy, gluttonous
ēdīcō, -dīcere, -dīxī, -dictum *v.t.* proclaim, announce, decree, ordain by proclamation
ēdictum, -ī *nnt.* edict, proclamation
ēdiscō, -discere, -didicī, --- *v.t.* memorize, learn thoroughly, study
ēditiō, -ōnis *nf.* putting forth, statement, publication (*of a book*)
ēdō, -dere, -didī, -ditum *v.t.* give out; bring forth, produce, bear; tell, publish, disclose
edō, -edere *or* **esse, ēdī, ēsum** *v.t.* eat, devour
ēdūcātiō, -ōnis *nf.* education; rearing of children
ēdūcō, -dūcāre, -dūcāvī, -dūcātum *v.t.* educate; rear, bring up; **ēdūcō, -dūcere, -dūxī, -ductum** *v.t.* lead out, draw out; bring up
effectus, -ūs *nm.* performance; result, effect
efferō, -ferāre, -ferāvī, -ferātum *v.t.* make wild, barbarize; brutalize; **efferō (ecferō), efferre, extulī, ēlātum** *v.t.* carry forth, bring out, produce, bear; raise, lift up; proclaim

efficāx (efficāc-) (w. comp. + sup.) *adj.* efficient, effective

efficiēns (efficient-) *adj.* effective

efficiō, -ficere, -fēcī, -fectum *v.t.* bring about, accomplish; produce, yield; show; prove

effigiēs, -ēī *nf.* image, likeness, copy

effingō, -fingere, -finxī, -fictum *v.t.* stroke; wipe clean; form, mold; represent

efflōrēscō, -flōrēscere, -flōruī, --- *v.i.* bloom, flourish

effodiō, -fodere, -fōdī, -fossum *v.t.* dig, mine, excavate

effrēnātus, -a, -um (w. comp.) *adj.* unbridled, uncontrolled

effugiō, -fugere, -fūgī, --- *v.t., v.i.* flee away, avoid, escape

effugium, -ī *nnt.* escape, flight

effundō, -fundere, -fūdī, -fūsum *v.t.* pour, pour out; drive out; throw down; produce abundantly; waste, empty; abandon, resign

effūsiō, -ōnis *nf.* spill, pouring forth; violent movement; extravagance

egēns (egent-) (w. comp. + sup.) *adj.* lacking, destitute, needy

egeō, egēre, eguī, --- *v.i.* be in want of, need; be without (+ gen. *or* + abl.)

egestās, -ātis *nf.* want, need, necessity; poverty

egō *pron.* I

ēgredior, ēgredī, ēgressus sum *v.d.i.t.* go out, depart, come forth, disembark; ascend

ēgregius, -a, -um *adj.* excellent, remarkable

ēgressus, -ūs *nm.* going out, departure, disembarking

ēiciō (ēji-), -icere, -iēcī, -iectum *v.t.* throw out, hurl forth, drive away, banish; wreck

ēiusmodī (ēji-) *adj. (indecl.)* of this kind, such

ēlābor, ēlābī, ēlāpsus sum *v.d.i.* slip away, escape; drop

ēlabōrātus, -a, -um *adj.* finished; highly decorated

ēlabōrō, -labōrāre, -labōrāvī, -labōrātum *v.t., v.i.* struggle, take pains, make an effort

ēlectiō, -ōnis *nf.* selection, choice

ēlegāns (ēlegant-) (w. comp. + sup.) *adj.* fastidious; delicate, select, elegant

ēlegantia, -ae *nf.* taste (*good style*)

elementum, -ī *nnt.* element, first principle; letter of the alphabet

elephās, -antis (elephantus, -ī) *nm.* elephant

ēlevō, -levāre, -levāvī, -levātum *v.t.* lift up; alleviate, diminish; disparage

ēlīdō, -līdere, -līsī, -līsum *v.t.* strike, knock; crash, shatter

ēligō, -ligere, lēgī, -lēctum *v.t.* pick out, choose

ēloquentia, -ae *nf.* eloquence

ēlūceō, -lūcēre, -lūxī, --- *v.i.* gleam; be conspicuous; appear

ēlūdō, -lūdere, -lūsī, -lūsum *v.t., v.i.* avoid, evade; deceive; mock

ēmendātiō, -ōnis *nf.* correction, improvement

ēmendātus, -a, -um (w. comp. + sup.) *adj.* faultless, correct, free from mistakes

ēmendō, -mendāre, -mendāvī, -mendātum *v.t.* correct, amend, revise; compensate for

ēmentior, ēmentīrī, ēmentītus sum *v.d.t.* lie, falsify; pretend

ēmergō, -mergere, -mersī, -mersum *v.t., v.i.* bring to life; come forth, emerge, escape

ēmigrō, -migrāre, -migrāvī, -migrātum *v.i.* migrate, move from place to place

ēmittō, -mittere, -mīsī, -missum *v.t.* send forth, expel, hurl; publish; set free; express, say

emō, -ere, ēmī, ēmptum *v.t.* buy, purchase

emorior, -morīrī, -mortuus sum *v.d.i.* die, die off

ēmoveō, -movēre, -mōvī, -mōtum *v.t.* move away; expel

ēmptiō, -ōnis *nf.* purchase

ēmptor, -ōris *nm.* customer, buyer

ēnarrō, -narrāre, -narrāvī, -narrātum *v.t.* tell in detail, describe

enim *conj.* (postpos.) for; because; in fact, indeed, certainly

ēnitēscō, -nitēscere, -nituī, --- *v.i.* begin to shine forth; be eminent; be displayed

ēnotō, -notāre, -notāvī, -notātum *v.t.* write down, note down

ēnūntiō, -nūntiāre, -nūntiāvī, -nūntiātum *v.t.* divulge, disclose, speak out

eō *adv.* there; for that reason; to that place; so far; **eō, īre, īvī (iī), itum** *v.i.* (*irreg.*) go, depart; come, enter; march, advance

eōdem *adv.* in the same place; to the same place; for the same purpose; besides

ephippium, -ī *nnt.* saddle blanket

epistula *or* **epistola, -ae** *nf.* letter, epistle

epitomē, -ēs *nf.* summary, abridgment

epulae, -ārum *nf./pl.* dishes; banquet, feast

equa, -ae (dat. + abl. pl. **equābus**) *nf.* mare

eques, -itis *nm.* horseman, rider; cavalryman, knight, member of the equestrian order

equidem *adv.* indeed, certainly, by all means; at least

equitātus, -ūs *nm.* cavalry; equestrian order
equitō, -āre, -āvī, -ātum *v.t.* ride on a horse
equus *or* **ecus, -ī** *nm.* horse
ērēctus, -a, -um (w. comp. + sup.) *adj.* upright; high, lofty; noble, haughty; intent
ergā *prep.* (+ acc.) towards
ergō *adv.* therefore, accordingly
ērigō, -rigere, -rēxī, -rēctum *v.t.* raise up, erect, elevate; stir up, arouse
ēripiō, -ripere, -ripuī, -reptum *v.t.* rescue; snatch from
ērogō, -rogāre, -rogāvī, -rogātum *v.t.* take out; pay, expend
errō, -āre, -āvī, -ātum *v.i.* lose one's way, wander; be in error, mistake
error, -ōris *nm.* wandering, straying; error, mistake; uncertainty
ērubēscō, ērubēscere, ērubuī, --- *v.i.* blush, grow red
ērudiō, -rudīre, -rudīvī, -ērudītum *v.t.* teach, educate; polish, refine
ērudītus, -a, -um (w. comp. + sup.) *adj.* learned, educated; polished, refined
ērumpō, -rumpere, -rūpī, -ruptum *v.t., v.i.* break forth; make break forth; hurl forth
ēruncō, -āre, ---, --- *v.t.* weed
ēruptiō, -ōnis *nf.* bursting forth; attack
esculentus, -a, -um *adj.* edible
ēsuriō, -īre, ---, -ītum *v.i.* be hungry
et *adv.* also, too, besides; *conj.* and; **et ... et** *conj.* both ... and
etenim *conj.* for; truly; because; since
etiam *adv.* too, and also, likewise; certainly; **etiam nunc** *conj.* even now, yet still
etiamsī *conj.* even if, although
etsī *conj.* although, even if; and yet
eucharistia, -ae *nf.* thanksgiving; communion (*ecclesiastical*)
ēvādō, -vādere, -vāsī, -vāsum *v.t., v.i.* go forth; escape; prove to be, result in
ēvānēscō, -vānēscere, -vānuī, --- *v.t.* pass away; disappear
ēvangelium, -ī *nnt.* good news; gospel
ēvehō, -vehere, -vexī, -vectum *v.t.* carry out, lead forth; spread abroad; raise, promote in rank
ēvellō, -vellere, -vellī, -volsum *v.t.* tear out, eradicate, pull off
ēveniō, -venīre, -vēnī, -ventum *v.i.* come forth, come out; turn out; result in
ēventus, -ūs *nm.* outcome, result, consequence; event

ēversiō, -ōnis *nf.* overthrow; ruin

ēvertō, -vertere, -vertī, -versum *v.t.* pull down, overturn, throw down; destroy

ēvidēns (evident-) (w. comp. + sup.) *adj.* looking out; obvious, unconcealed

ēvītō, -vītāre, -vītāvī, -vītātum *v.t.* shun, avoid

ēvolvō, -volvere, -volvī, -volūtum *v.t.* roll out, unwrap, unroll, disclose, unravel, explain

ōvomō, -vomere, -vomuī, -vomitum *v.t.* vomit forth; expel

ex (*before vowels and consonants*); **ē** (*before consonants*) *prep.* (+ abl.) out of, out from; from since, after; made of; from among; by reason of; according to

exaequō, -aequāre, -aequāvī, -aequātum *v.t.* make equal; attain equality with

exaggerō, -aggerāre, -aggerāvī, -aggerātum *v.t.* heap up; accumulate; magnify

exagitō, -agitāre, -agitāvī, -agitātum *v.t.* drive out; rouse; harass, disturb; incite, irritate

exāmen, exāminis *nnt.* bee swarm; crowd; testing; consideration

exanimis, -is, -e *adj.* lifeless, dead, breathless; frightened

exārdēscō, -ārdēscere, -ārsī, -ārsum *v.i.* blaze up, take fire, become inflamed

exaudiō, -audīre, -audīvī, -audītum *v.t.* hear clearly; perceive; obey

excēdō, -cēdere, -cessī, -cessum *v.t., v.i.* leave; exceed, pass

excellō, -cellere, -celluī, -celsum *v.t., v.i.* be eminent; excel, surpass

excelsus, -a, -um (w. comp. + sup.) *adj.* high, elevated

exceptiō, -ōnis *nf.* exception, restriction; objection

excerpō, -cerpere, -cerpsī, -cerptum *v.t* select, choose; omit

excidō, -cidere, -cidī, --- *v.i.* fall away; escape; perish

excipiō, -cipere, -cēpī, -ceptum *v.t.* withdraw; exclude; welcome, receive; take, capture

excitō, -citāre, -citāvī, -citātum *v.t.* stir up, rouse, incite; build; inspire, awaken

exclūdō, -clūdere, -clūsī, -clūsum *v.t.* exclude, shut out; prevent, hinder

excolō, -colere, -coluī, -cultum *v.t.* cultivate; improve

excruciō, -cruciāre, -cruciāvī, -cruciātum *v.t.* torture, torment

excūdō, -cūdere, -cūdī, -cūsum *v.t.* strike out, hammer, forge; mold; compose; hatch eggs

excurrō, -currere, -cucurrī (-currī), -cursum *v.i.* run forwards, hasten; attack; spread

excūsātiō, -ōnis *nf.* apology, excuse, defense

excūsō, -cūsāre, -cūsāvī, -cūsātum *v.t.* excuse; make an excuse; plead

excutiō, -cutere, -cussī, -cussum *v.t.* shake out, drive out, discard, throw; investigate; extort

exedō, -edere *or* **-esse, -ēdī, -ēsum** *v.t.* consume; destroy

exemplar, -āris *nnt.* copy; type, model

exemplum, -ī *nnt.* sample; pattern; warning, example, lesson; way, manner

exeō, -īre, -īvī (-iī), -itum *v.i.* go out; depart; result; run out, expire

exerceō, -ercēre, -ercuī, -ercitum *v.t.* keep occupied; practice, exercise, train; disturb, annoy

exercitātiō, -ōnis *nf.* training, practice

exercitus, -ūs *nm.* army

exhālō, -hālāre, -hālāvī, -hālātum *v.i.* exhale, breathe out

exhauriō, -haurīre, -hausī, -haustum *v.t.* draw off, take out, remove, pump out, empty

exigō, -igere, -ēgī, -āctum *v.t.* drive out; thrust; demand; collect

exiguus, -a, -um *adj.* meager, insufficient

exīlis, -is, -e *adj.* narrow, meager, inadequate; comfortless; worthless

eximius, -a, -um *adj.* fine, excellent; extraordinary

eximō, -imere, -ēmī, -ēmptum *v.t.* take away; release; consume; waste

existimō, -istimāre, -istimāvī, -istimātum *v.i.* think, believe, suppose, consider; esteem

exitiōsus, -a, -um (w. comp. + sup.) *adj.* deadly, harmful

exitium, -ī *nnt.* ruin, death, destruction

exitus, -ūs *nm.* exit, departure, way out, ending, result, conclusion; passage; death

exonerō, -onerāre, -onerāvī, -onerātum *v.t.* unload, unburden, free, relieve

exoptō, -optāre, -optāvī, -optātum *v.t.* desire earnestly, wish for greatly

exordium, -ī *nnt.* opening, preface, beginning

exorior, -orīrī, -ortus sum *v.d.i.* appear; rise; begin

exornō, -ornāre, -ornāvī, -ornātum *v.t.* equip, provide; decorate, embellish

expedītus, -a, -um *adj.* free, unencumbered; prompt; easy; convenient

expellō, -pellere, -pulī. -pulsum *v.t.* drive forward, drive out, expel

expergīscor, expergīscī, experrēctus sum *v.d.i.* awake; be alert

experientia, -ae *nf.* test, trial; proof

experīmentum, -ī *nnt.* test, trial; proof

experior, experīrī, expertus sum *v.d.t.* try, test, undertake, undergo; prove

expers (expert-) *adj.* having no part in; devoid of (+ gen. *or* + abl.)

expetō, -petere, -petīvī, -petītum *v.t.* seek after, aim for; demand; wish

expleō, -plēre, -plēvī, -plētum *v.t.* satisfy, fill up, appease; finish

explicātiō, -ōnis *nf.* unfolding, uncoiling; interpretation, explanation

explicō, -plicāre, -plicāvī, -plicātum *v.t.* unfold, spread out; release; develop; explain

explōrātor, -ōris *nm.* scout, spy, explorer

explōrō, -āre, -āvī, -ātum *v.t.* explore, investigate; reconnoiter

expōnō, -pōnere, -posuī, -positum *v.t.* put forth, exhibit, disembark, explain

exportō, -portāre, -portāvī, -portātum *v.t.* carry out, export

exposcō, -poscere, -poposcī, --- *v.t..* beg earnestly for; demand; claim

exprimō, -primere, -pressī, -pressum *v.t.* squeeze out, extort; represent, portray

exprobō, -probāre, -probāvī, -probātum *v.t., v.i.* blame for, reproach

exprōmō, -prōmere, -prōmpsī, -prōmptum *v.t.* exhibit, show forth; utter, state

expūgnātiō, -ōnis *nf.* reduction, subjugation

expūgnō, -pūgnāre, -pūgnāvī, -pūgnātum *v.t.* capture, take by storm, overcome; extort; accomplish

exscrībō, -scrībere, -scrīpsī, -scrīptum *v.t.* write out; copy; resemble

exsecrātiō, -ōnis *nf.* curse, execration

exsecror, exsecrārī, exsecrātus sum *v.d.t.* curse

exsequor, exsequī, exsecūtus sum *v.d.t.* follow after; accompany; pursue; enforce; execute, fulfill; investigate; punish

exsiliō, -silīre, -siluī, --- *v.i.* leap up, leap out

exsilium (exilium), -ī *nnt.* exile, banishment

exsistō, -sistere, -stitī, -stitum *v.i.* come forth, appear

exsolvō, -solvere, -solvī, -solūtum *v.t.* loosen, untie; release; explain; pay off, discharge

exspectātiō, -ōnis *nf.* anticipation, expectation, longing for

exspectō, -spectāre, -spectāvī, -spectātum *v.t.* wait for, anticipate, expect; dread

exspīrō, -spīrāre, -spīrāvī, -spīrātum *v.t., v.i.* breathe out; perish

exspoliō, -spoliāre, -spoliāvī, -spoliātum *v.t.* pillage, rob

exstīnguō, -stinguere, -stīnxī, -stīnctum *v.t.* put out, extinguish; kill, destroy

exstruō, -struere, -strūxī, -strūctum *v.t.* heap up, heap full; raise, erect, build

exsul *or* **exul, -sulis** *nm/f.* outcast, exile

exsultō, -sultāre, -sultāvī, -sultātum *v.i.* leap up; exult in

exta, -ōrum *nnt./pl.* internal organs, entrails

extemplō *adv.* immediately, directly

extendō, -tendere, -tendī, -tēnsum (tentum) *v.t.* spread, stretch out, prolong; strain

extenuō, -tenuāre, -tenuāvī, -tenuātum *v.t.* make thin; lessen

exter (exterus), extera, exterum (comp. **exterior**; sup. **extrēmus** *or* **extimus**) *adj.* outward; foreign, strange

exterminō, -termināre, -termināvī, -terminātum *v.t.* exile, drive out

externus, -a, -um *adj.* outward; foreign (*of another country*)

exterreō, -terrēre, -terruī, -territum *v.t.* frighten, terrify

extollō, -tollere, ---, --- *v.t.* lift up, raise; praise highly

extorqueō, -torquēre, -torsī, -tortum *v.t.* wrench away; extort

extrā *adv.* on the outside; *prep.* (+ acc.) outside of, beyond, aside from, except

extrahō, -trahere, -trāxī, -trāctum *v.t.* drag forth, remove, extricate; prolong

extrēmus, -a, -um *adj.* extreme, farthest, utmost

exūrō, -ūrere, -ussī, -ūstum *v.t.* burn up, consume

F

faba, -ae *nf.* bean

faber, fabrī *nm.* worker (*especially in metals and other hard materials*)

fabrica, -ae *nf.* workshop; architecture

fabricātor, -ōris *nm.* maker

fabricō, fabricāre, fabricāvī, fabricātum *v.t.* form, forge, make

fābula, -ae *nf.* account; fable, myth; matter; play, plot

facētiae, -ārum *nf./pl.* wit, humor

facētus, -a, -um (w. sup.) *adj.* elegant; witty

faciēs, -ēī *nf.* kind, class; appearance, face, form

facilis, -is, -e (comp. **facilior**; sup. **facillimus**) *adj.* easy; approachable, kindly; **facile** (comp. **facilius**; sup. **facillimē**) *adv.* easily; promptly

facilitās, -ātis *nf.* facility; readiness; courtesy

facinus, -oris *nnt.* deed, act; offense, crime

faciō, -ere, fēcī, factum *v.t.* make, construct; do, perform; cause; choose, appoint

factiō, -ōnis *nf.* preparing; partisanship, association, party

factiōsus, -a, -um *adj.* heading a party; partisan, seditious, intriguing, treasonable

factum, -ī *nnt.* deed, achievement, event; result

facultās, -ātis *nf.* facility, capability, power, means; natural talent, natural capability; possibility

faeneror, faenerārī, faenerātus sum *v.d.i.t.* loan at interest

faenīlia, -um *nnt. /pl.* loft, hay loft

faenum, -ī *nnt.* hay

faenus, -oris *nnt.* interest, profit, gain

fallācia, -ae *nf.* deceit, fraud

fallō, -ere, fefellī, falsum *v.t., v.i.* deceive, cheat; disappoint; escape notice; break a promise

falsus, -a, -um (w. comp. + sup.) *adj.* deceptive, false, untrue, misleading

falx, falcis *nf.* scythe, sickle, pruning hook

fāma, -ae *nf.* report, rumor; renown, fame

famēs, -is *nf.* hunger, starvation; want

familia, -ae *or* **-ās** *nf.* household; family; estate

familiāris, -is, -e (w. comp. + sup.) *adj.* belonging to a household; private, intimate, familiar; **familiāris, -is** *nm/f.* acquaintance

familiāritās, -ātis *nf.* intimacy, close acquaintance

famula, -ae *nf.* female servant

famulus, -ī *nm.* male servant

fānum, -ī *nnt.* shrine, sanctuary

farcīmen, -minis *nnt.* sausage

farciō, -īre, farsī, fartum *v.t.* stuff

fās *nnt. (indecl.)* right according to divine law; divine law, divine justice; **fās est** *v.i.* it is allowed, it is lawful (+ infv. *or* + acc. + infv.)

fascia, -ae *nf.* band, bandage

fasciculus, -ī *nm.* small parcel, small bundle

fascinātiō, -ōnis *nf.* fascination, bewitchment

fascinō, -āre, -āvī, -atum *v.t.* fascinate, bewitch

fascinum (fascinus), -ī *nnt.* charm, amulet; bewitching

fascis, -is *nm.* bundle; **fascēs, -um** *nf./pl.* fasces (*the bundle of rods carried before magistrates as a sign of authority*)

fastīdiōsus, -a, -um (w. comp. + sup.) *adj.* nice; fussy, selective; causing disgust

fāstus, -a, -um *adj.* day open for law courts, court-day; **fastī, -ōrum** *nm./pl.* calendar (*list of magistrates*)

fātālis, -is, -e *adj.* destined; fatal, dangerous

fateor, fatērī, fassus sum *v.d.t.* acknowledge, admit; show

fātīgātiō, -ōnis *nf.* tiredness

fatīgō, -āre, -āvī, -ātum *v.t.* weary, tire out; vex, harass, beseige

fātum, -ī *nnt.* prophecy, oracle; fate, destiny, ill fate; ruin; death

fatuus, -a, -um *adj.* idiotic, silly, foolish

faucēs, -ium *nf./pl.* throat; jaws; entrance, pass

fautor, -ōris *nm.* sponsor, promoter, patron

faveō, -ēre, fāvī, fautum *v.i.* be well disposed toward, favor, befriend (+ dat.); protect

favor, -ōris *nm.* favor, goodwill; partiality; approval, encouragement, support

fax, facis *nf.* torch; meteor, comet; fire

febris, -is *nf.* fever

Februārius, -a, -um *adj.* February (*usu. w.* **mēnsis**); **Februārius, -ī** *nm.* February

fel, fellis *nnt.* gall

fēlēs (fēlis), -is *nf.* cat

fēlicitās, -ātis *nf.* good luck; success; happiness

fēlix (fēlic-) (w. comp. + sup.) *adj.* fruitful; of good omen, fortunate, lucky

fēmina, -ae *nf.* female, woman

fēmineus, -a, -um *adj.* female

femur, -oris (-inis) *nnt.* thigh

fenestra, -ae *nf.* window

fera, -ae *nf.* wild beast, animal

ferculum, -ī *nnt.* tray; litter, bier

ferē *adv.* (postpos.) almost, nearly, usually, for the most part

fēriae, -ārum *nf./pl.* festival

feriō, -īre, ---, --- *v.t.* strike, hit; kill; impress

fermē *adv.* nearly, almost; hardly

fermentō, -āre, -āvī, -ātum *v.t.* ferment

fermentum, -ī *nnt.* yeast, leaven

ferō, ferre, tulī, lātum *v.t.* bear, carry; lead, drive; produce, yield; endure, tolerate; report; allow

ferōcia, -ae *nf.* wildness, fierceness, ferocity; bravery

ferōx (ferōc-) (w. comp. + sup.) *adj.* wild, bold, impetuous, high-spirited; courageous; fierce, savage, cruel

ferrāmentum, -ī *nnt.* iron tool, hatchet

ferreus, -a, -um *adj.* made of iron, hard-hearted, cruel

ferrum, -ī *nnt.* iron; iron tool

fertilis, -is, -e (w. comp. + sup.) *adj.* fertile, fruitful, productive

ferula, -ae *nf.* fennel; stick

ferus, -a, -um *adj.* savage, wild, fierce

fervefaciō, -facere, -fēcī, -factum *v.t.* boil, heat, melt

fervidus, -a, -um (w. comp.) *adj.* boiling; passionate, ardent

fervor, -ōris *nm.* boiling; glowing heat; heat of passion

fessus, -a, -um *adj.* exhausted, worn out; weak, infirm

festīnātiō, -ōnis *nf.* hurry, haste; eagerness

festīnō, -āre, -āvī, -ātum *v.t.* accelerate, hasten; *v.i.* hurry

festīvus, -a, -um *adj.* pleasing; witty, entertaining; elegant

festus, -a, -um *adj.* gay, festive, happy

fētus *or* **foetus, -ūs** *nm.* bearing of young, hatching; litter, brood

fibra, -ae *nf.* fiber, filament

fibula, -ae *nf.* garment pin; clamp

fictilia, -um *nnt./pl.* pottery, earthenware vessels

fictum, -ī *nnt.* falsehood, fiction

ficus, -ī *nf.* fig tree; fig

fidēlis, -is, -e (w. comp. + sup.) *adj.* sure, faithful, trustworthy, trusted

fidēlitās, -ātis *nf.* loyalty, fidelity, trustworthiness

fidēs, -eī *nf.* trust, confidence; trustworthiness, honor, credibility; promise;
    fidēs, -ium *nf./pl.* lyre, stringed instrument

fidicen, -inis *nm.* lyre-player

fidō, -ere, fīsus sum *v.i.* rely upon, confide in (+ dat. *or* + abl.)

fidūcia, -ae *nf.* trust; assurance, self-confidence; pledge

fidus, -a, -um (w. comp. + sup.) *adj.* trustworthy, credible, faithful

figō, -ere, fīxī, fixum *v.t.* set up, place; fasten, affix

figūra, -ae *nf.* figure, mold, form; style, manner

filia, -ae (dat. + abl. pl. **fīliābus**) *nf.* daughter

filius, -ī *nm.* son

filix, -icis *nf.* fern

filum, -ī *nnt.* yarn, thread, cord

fingō, -ere, finxī, fictum *v.t.* shape, fashion, make; represent; imagine;
    feign

finiō, -īre, -īvī, -ītum *v.t.* confine, restrain; appoint; finish, come to an end

finis, -is *nm.* period, termination; **finēs, -ium** *nm./pl.* borders; territory,
    country

finitimus, -a, -um *adj.* adjacent, bordering on (+ dat.)

fīō, fierī, factus sum *v.i.* (irreg.) become, be made; happen, take place

firmāmentum, -ī *nnt.* means of strengthening; support, prop

firmō, -āre, -āvī, -ātum *v.t.* make firm, fortify; encourage; establish

firmus, -a, -um (w. sup.) *adj.* steadfast, strong, sound, valid

fistula, -ae *nf.* tube; pipe (*musical instrument*)

flābellum, -ī *nnt.* small fan

flāgitiōsus, -a, -um *adj.* shameful, disgraceful, dissolute

flāgitium, -ī *nnt.* shameful act, disgrace

flāgitō, -āre, -āvī, -ātum *v.t.* demand earnestly, request, demand to know, summon

flagrō, -āre, -āvī, -ātum *v.t.* burn, glow; be on fire

flāmen, flāminis *nm.* flamen (*a priest of a particular deity*)

flāminica, -ae *nf.* wife of the flamen

flamma, -ae *nf.* flame; passion; rage

flammeum, -ī *nnt.* bridal veil

flātus, -us *nm.* blast; a blowing of air or wind; arrogance

flāvus, -a, -um *adj.* yellow, gold-colored

flēbilis, -is, -e *adj.* pathetic, lamentable

flectō, flectere, flexī, flectum *v.t.* bend, turn aside; change; persuade, appease

fleō, -ēre, flēvī, flētum *v.t.* weep; drip, trickle; *v.i.* weep for, lament

flētus, -ūs *nm.* crying, weeping

flexus, -ūs *nm.* turn, the act of bending or curving

flō, flāre, flāvī, flātum *v.t.* blow

flōreō, -ēre, flōruī, --- *v.i.* bloom; succeed, prosper

flōridus, -a, -um *adj.* gay, brightly colored

flōs, flōris *nm.* flower

fluctuō, -āre, -āvī, -ātum *v.i.* waver, move up and down

fluctus, -ūs *nm.* flowing; flood, tide, billow; commotion

fluidus, -a, -um *adj.* fluid

fluitō, -āre, -āvī, -ātum *v.i.* flow hither and thither, flutter, waver

flūmen, flūminis *nnt.* stream, river; flow, fluency

fluō, -ere, flūxī, flūxum *v.i.* flow, run, overflow, pour; vanish; sink; proceed; issue

fōcāle, -is *nnt.* scarf

focus, -ī *nm.* hearth, fireplace; home

fodiō, -ere, fōdī, fossum *v.t.* dig, prod

foederātus, -a, -um *adj.* allied, confederate

foedus, -a, -um (w. comp. + sup.) *adj.* nasty, shameful, vile; **foedus, -eris** *nnt.* treaty, union, alliance, agreement

folium, -ī *nnt.* leaf (*bot.*)

fōns, fontis *nm.* spring; fountain; source

forāmen, -inis *nnt.* pore, hole, opening

forās *adv.* out(side), outdoors; forth

forceps, -cipis *nm/f.* pincers, tongs

forfex, -ficis *nf.* pair of scissors

foris *adv.* out(side), outdoors

forma, -ae *nf.* shape, form; appearance, image; plan

formica, -ae *nf.* ant

formīcō, -āre, -āvī, -ātum *v.i.* creep like an ant; feel like ants crawling, tingle

formīdō, -āre, -āvī, -ātum *v.t.* dread, fear; *v.i.* be frightened; **formīdō, -inis** *nf.* dread, terror

formō, -āre, -āvī, -ātum *v.t.* form, shape, influence; train

formōsus, -a, -um (w. comp. + sup.) *adj.* beautiful, lovely

formula, -ae *nf.* physical beauty; rule, formula, method

fornāx, -ācis *nf.* furnace, oven, kiln

fornix, -icis *nm.* vault, arch; cellar

fors, fortis *nf.* luck, chance, accident

forsitan *adv.* perhaps

fortasse *adv.* perhaps, possibly

forte *adv.* by chance, accidentally; perhaps

fortis, -is, -e (w. comp. + sup.) *adj.* strong; brave, valiant; impetuous

fortitūdō, -inis *nf.* strength; courage, fortitude

fortuītus, -a, -um *adj.* random, accidental, casual

fortūna, -ae *nf.* fortune, chance, luck; lot, circumstances; prosperity; adversity

fortūnātus, -a, -um *adj.* prosperous, lucky, happy

forum, -ī *nnt.* open space; marketplace; principal site for affairs of state and public business

fossa, -ae *nf.* ditch, trench

foveō, -ēre, fōvī, fōtum *v.t.* keep warm; cherish; encourage

fraga, -ōrum *nnt./pl.* strawberries

fragilis, -is, -e *adj.* fragile, brittle, weak

frāgmentum, -ī *nnt.* fragment

fragor, -ōris *nm.* breaking; crack, loud noise

frangō, -ere, frēgī, frāctum *v.t.* break, shatter; wreck, break down; subdue

frāter, frātris *nm.* brother

fraudātor, -ōris *nm.* swindler

fraudō, -āre, -āvī, -ātum *v.t.* swindle, cheat, steal
fraus, fraudis *nf.* fraud, cheating; offense; error; harm
fraxinus, -ī *nf.* ash tree
fremitus, -ūs *nm.* roaring, growling
fremō, -ere, -uī, --- *v.i.* roar, growl, grumble
frēnō, - āre, -āvī, -ātum *v.t.* curb a horse
frēnum, -ī *nnt.* horse's bit, bridle
frequēns (frequent-) (w. comp. + sup.) *adj.* numerous, crowded; regular;
　repeated
frequentia, -ae *nf.* large assembly, crowd, multitude
frequentō, -āre, -āvī, -ātum *v.t.* visit often; throng, gather in great
　numbers
frētus, -a, -um *adj.* depending on, trusting (+ abl. *or* + acc. + infv.)
fricō, -āre, fricuī, frictum *v.t.* rub
frīgeō, -ēre, ---, --- *v.i.* be cold; be inactive; be slighted
frīgidus, -a, -um (w. comp. + sup.) *adj.* cold, cool; indifferent; without
　force; dull, trivial
frīgō, -ere, frīxī, frictum *v.t.* roast, parch
frīgus, -oris *nnt.* cold
friō, -āre, -āvī, -ātum *v.t.* crumble
frōns, frontis *nf.* forehead; face; front; appearance
frūctuōsus, -a, -um *adj.* abounding in fruit; profitable
frūctus, -ūs *nm.* fruit, produce; delight; yield, profit, reward
frūgālis, -is, -e *adj.* thrifty, economical
frūgālitās, -ātis *nf.* thrift, frugality, temperance
frūmentum, -ī *nnt.* grain
fruor, fruī, fructus sum *v.d.i.* enjoy, receive pleasure from (+ abl.)
frūstrā *adv.* in a deceitful way; in vain; without reason
frūstrātiō, -ōnis *nf.* deception; disappointment, frustration
frūstror, frustrārī, frustrātus sum *v.d.t.* frustrate, bring to naught,
　disappoint
frustum, -ī *nnt.* scrap, morsel
frūx, frūgis *nf.* fruit, produce; result, success
fūcōsus, -a, -um *adj.* dyed; spurious, counterfeit
fūcus, -ī *nm.* rouge, red or purple dye
fuga, -ae *nf.* flight, escape; exile
fugiō, -ere, fūgī, fūgitum *v.i.* flee, run away, escape, go into exile, vanish;
　shun
fugitīvus, -a, -um *adj.* fugitive, runaway

fulcīmentum

fulcīmentum, -ī *nnt.* support, prop
fulgeō, -ēre, fulsī, --- *v.i.* flash, gleam, shine
fulgor, -ōris *nm.* lightning flash; destructive power
fullōnica, -ae *nf.* laundry
fulmen, -inis *nnt.* stroke of lightning; destructive power
fūmō, -āre, ---, --- *v.i.* smoke, steam
fūmōsus, -a, -um *adj.* smoky; smoked
fūmus, -ī *nm.* smoke, steam, vapor
functiō, -ōnis *nf.* performance, performing
funda, -ae *nf.* sling (*weapon for hurling stones*); sling-stone
fundāmentum, -ī *nnt.* foundation, basis; anus
fundō, -āre, -āvī, -ātum *v.t.* found, establish; **fundō, -ere, fūdī, fūsum**
    v.t. shower, pour; scatter; bring forth; overthrow
fundus, -ī *nm.* base, bottom; estate, farm
funestus, -a, -um (w. comp.) *adj.* deadly, destructive; mournful
fungor, fungī, fūnctus sum *v.d.i.t.* be engaged in, perform, do, fulfill
    (+ abl.)
fungus, -ī *nnt.* fungus, mushroom
fūnis, -is *nm.* rope, cord
fūnus, -eris *nnt.* corpse; funeral rites; death, murder; ruin
fūr, fūris *nm.* thief
furca, -ae *nf.* fork, pitchfork
furia, -ae *nf.* madness; fury; curse; **furiae, -ārum** *nf./pl.* violent passion
furiōsus, -a, -um (w. comp. + sup.) *adj.* full of rage
furnus, -ī *nm.* oven
furō, -ere, furuī, --- *v.i.* be made; rage
fūror, fūrārī, fūrātus sum *v.d.t.* steal
furor, -ōris *nm.* rage, frenzy, prophetic frenzy
fūrtim *adv.* stealthily
fūrtum, -ī *nnt.* theft, robbery; item stolen; deceit
fuscus, -a, -um *adj.* sunburnt
fustis, -is *nm.* club, cudgel
fūsus, -ī *nm.* spool; spindle
fūtūrum, -ī *nnt.* future

G

galea, -ae *nf.* helmet
gallīna, -ae *nf.* fowl, chicken, hen
gallus, -ī *nm.* rooster, cock
gargarizō, -āre, -āvī, -ātum *v.i.* gargle
garriō, -īre, -īvī (-iī), -ītum *v.i.* chatter; gossip
gaudeō, -ēre, gāvīsus sum *v.i.* be glad, rejoice, delight in (+ abl.)
gaudium, -ī *nnt.* joy, delight, pleasure
gavia, -ae *nf.* seagull
gaza, -ae *nf.* wealth, riches, treasure
gelidus, -a, -um *adj.* very cold, icy
gelō, -āre, -āvī, -ātum *v.t.* make freeze, congeal; *v.i.* freeze, stiffen
gelum, -ī *or* **gelū, -ūs** *nnt. or* **gelus, -ī** *nm.* frost, icy coldness
gemellus, -a, -um *adj.* twin, double
geminus, -a, -um *adj.* born together, twin, paired, double; similar, corresponding
gemitus, -ūs *nm.* groan, moan, lamentation; pain, sorrow; roar
gemma, -ae *nf.* gemstone, jewel; bud; eye
gemō, -ere, -uī, -itum *v.i.* groan, wail, sigh, lament
gena, -ae *nf.* cheek
gener, generī *nm.* son-in-law; suitor
generālis, -is, -e *adj.* belonging to a kind; general (*not specific*)
generātim *adv.* according to kind or class; generally, universally, in general
generō, -āre, -āvī, -ātum *v.t.* beget, produce, generate
generōsus, -a, -um (w. comp. + sup.) *adj.* of noble birth; noble
genitālis, -is, -e *adj.* belonging to birth; fruitful
genius, -ī *nm.* guardian deity of a place or person
gēns, gentis *nf.* offspring; clan, nation, tribe; people, race; species, breed; **gentēs, -ium** *nf./pl.* world; nations
genū, genūs *nnt.* knee
genus, -eris *nnt.* birth, descent; family, race, stock; sort, kind, class, order; gender
geōgraphia, -ae *nf.* geography
germānus, -a, -um *adj.* akin, of the same stock; **germānus, -ī** *nm.* full brother; **germāna, -ae** *nf.* full sister
germen, -inis *nnt.* germ, plant embryo
germinō, -āre, ---, --- *v.i.* sprout

gerō, -ere, gessī, gessum *v.t.* bear, carry, have; entertain; perform, do, accomplish; manage, transact; wear clothes

gestus, -ūs *nm.* posture; gesture

gibber, -eris *nm.* hump

gignō, -ere, genuī, genitum *v.t.* give birth to, bring forth, bear children; give rise to

gingīva, -ae *nf.* gum (*of the mouth*)

glaciēs, -ōī *nf.* ice, frost, cold

gladiātor, -ōris *nm.* gladiator, swordsman

gladius, -ī *nm.* sword

glāns, glandis *nf.* acorn, chestnut; bullet

globus, -ī *nm.* globe, sphere, ball; band, crowd

glōria, -ae *nf.* glory, fame; ambition; pride

glōrior, glōriārī, glōriātus sum *v.d.i.* glory, boast

glōriōsus, -a, -um (w. sup.) *adj.* full of glory, renowned; vain, conceited, bragging

glōs, glōris *nf.* sister-in-law, husband's sister

glōssārium, -ī *nnt.* dictionary, glossary

glūten, -inis *nnt.* glue

glūtinō, -āre, -āvī, -ātum *v.t.* glue

gnārus (nārus), -a, -um *adj.* acquainted with, knowing; practiced, expert (+ gen. *or* + acc. + infv.); known

gossypion *or* **gossipion, gossypiī** *nnt.* cotton; cotton-tree

gracilis, -is, -e (comp. **gracilior**; sup. **gracillimus**) *adj.* slender, slim

gradātiō, -ōnis *nf.* climax in a speech

gradior, gradī, gressus sum *v.d.i.* walk, go, proceed

gradus, -ūs *nm.* pace, gait, walk; position, base; stairs; approach; degree, rank

grāmen, -inis *nnt.* grass; grassy plain

grammaticus, -a, -um *adj.* concerned with reading and writing, literary, grammatical

grandaevus, -a, -um *adj.* aged, old

grandis, -is, -e (w. comp.) *adj.* full-grown, large; grown-up, tall; aged, old; great, strong; weighty

grandō, grandinis *nf.* hail

grānum, -ī *nnt.* grain, seed, kernel

grātia, -ae *nf.* grace; favor, esteem; kindness, courtesy; thanks; influence; **grātiā** *prep.* (+ gen.) for the sake of; **Grātiae, -ārum** *nf./pl.* the Graces (*goddesses of music, poetry, and the arts*)

grātuītus, -a, -um *adj.* free, without cost; unbribed

grātulātiō, -ōnis *nf.* rejoicing, congratulation; public thanksgiving

grātulor, grātulārī, grātulātus sum *v.d.i.* show joy, rejoice; congratulate

grātus, -a, -um (w. comp. + sup.) *adj.* agreeable, pleasing; thankful, grateful; beloved

gravātiō, -ōnis *nf.* oppression, heaviness

gravidus, -a, -um *adj.* heavy; laden; teeming; pregnant

gravis, -is, -e (w. comp. + sup.) *adj.* heavy, burdensome, laden; oppressive, severe, difficult; weighty, important; eminent, revered, having influence

gravitās, -ātis *nf.* weight; severity; importance; dignity

gremium, -ī *nnt.* lap, bosom, breast; embrace

gressus, -ūs *nm.* step, pace, gait; way

grex, gregis *nm.* flock, herd, band, group, crew

grillus (gryllus), -ī *nm.* grasshopper; cricket

grūs, gruis *nm/f.* crane (*zool.*)

gubernāculum, -ī *nnt.* helm, rudder; control; government

gubernātor, -ōris *nm.* pilot, helmsman; governor, ruler

gubernō, -āre, -āvī, -ātum *v.t.* steer, direct, control, guide

gula, -ae *nf.* gullet, throat; appetite

gummis, -is *nf.* (**gummi** *nnt. indecl.*) gum, sticky substance

gurges, -itis *nm.* whirlpool; gulf, abyss; wave, tide; sea, ocean; flood

gustātus, -ūs *nm.* sense of taste; appetite for; flavor

gustō, -āre, -āvī, -ātum *v.t.* taste, lunch, eat; enjoy

gustus, -ūs *nm.* taste, nibble; hors d'oeuvre

gutta, -ae *nf.* drop

guttur, gutturis *nnt.* throat; mouth

gymnasium, -ī *nnt.* gymnasium, public school of gymnastics; place for philosophical discussion

gypsum, -ī *nnt.* plaster

H

habeō, -ēre, habuī, habitum *v.t.* have, hold, possess; wear; detain; inhabit; rule; treat; use; intend; believe, think (+ acc. + infv.); practice; accept

habilis, -is, -e (comp. **habilior**) *adj.* easily handled; proper; swift; expert

habilitās, -ātis *nf.* aptitude

habitātiō, -ōnis *nf.* dwelling, habitation, house, lodging

habitō, -āre, -āvī, -ātum *v.t.* live, dwell, inhabit

habitus, -ūs *nm.* bearing, attitude; condition; style of dress; quality
habēna, -ae *nf.* strap; bridle, rein
haedus, -ī *nm.* kid, young goat
haereō, -ēre, haesī, haesum *v.i.* stick to, adhere to (+ abl. *or* + **in** + abl.); hesitate, be perplexed
haesitātiō, -ōnis *nf.* stammer, hesitation, irresolution
haesitō, -āre, -āvī, -ātum *v.i.* be stuck, stick fast; hesitate, doubt
hama *or* **ama, -ae** *nf.* bucket
hāmus, -ī *nm.* hook
harēna *or* **arēna, -ae** *nf.* sand; desert; sea shore
harundō, -inis *nf.* reed, shaft; pen
haruspex, -spicis *nm.* soothsayer, deviner from entrails of sacrificed animals
hasta, -ae *nf.* pole; spear
hastīle, -is *nnt.* shaft of a spear; spear
haud *or* **haut** *adv.* not at all, by no means
haudquāquam *adv.* by no means, not at all
hauriō, -īre, hausī, haustum *v.t.* draw off, empty; penetrate; imbibe; receive
haustus, -ūs *nm.* drawing of water; draft, drink
hebes (hebet-) (w. comp.) *adj.* dumb, dull-witted, sluggish, weak
hebēscō, -ere, ---, --- *v.i.* become blunt, grow dull
hedera, -ae *nf.* ivy
herba, -ae *nf.* blade of grass; plant
hērēditās, -ātis *nf.* inheritance
hērēs, -ēdis *nm/f.* heir
herī *adv.* yesterday
hernia, -ae *nf.* hernia, rupture
hesternus, -a, -um *adj.* of yesterday
hiātus, -ūs *nm.* opening, aperture; a gaping
hībernō, -āre, -āvī, -ātum *v.i.* spend the winter, be in winter quarters
hībernus, -a, -um *adj.* of winter
hīc *adv.* here, in this place, on this point, now
hic, haec, hoc *adj.* this, this one here; *pron.* he, she, it; the latter
hiems *or* **hiemps, hiemis** *nf.* winter; wintry weather
hilaris, -is, -e *or* **hilarus, -a, -um** (w. comp. + sup.) *adj.* merry, joyful
hinc *adv.* from this side, hence
hirsūtus, -a, -um (w. comp.) *adj.* shaggy, covered with hair
hirundō, -dinis *nf.* swallow (*zool.*)
historia, -ae *nf.* history, narrative of past events; report

histriō, -ōnis *nm.* player, actor

hodiē *adv.* today, at this time

hodiernus, -a, -um *adj.* of today, today's

holitor *or* **olitor, -ōris** *nm.* gardener

holus *or* **olus, holeris** *or* **oleris** *nnt.* vegetable, pot-herb

homō, hominis *nm./f.* human being; man; **hominēs, hominum** *nm./pl.* mankind, human race

honestās, -ātis *nf.* honor, integrity; reputation

honestō, -āre, -āvī, -ātum *v.t.* bestow honor upon, adorn

honestus, -a, -um (w. comp. + sup.) *adj.* respected; noble, of high character

honōrificus, -a, -um (comp. **honōrificentior**; sup. **honōrificentissimus**) *adj.* bringing honor, honorable

honōs (honor), -ōris *nm.* honor, esteem, respect; glory; election to public office

hōra, -ae *nf.* hour

hordeum, -ī *nnt.* barley

hōrologium, -ī *nnt.* clock, sundial, water-clock

horreō, -ēre, horruī, --- *v.i.* stand on end, bristle; tremble, shiver; be afraid of

horreum, -ī *nnt.* magazine, warehouse; barn

horribilis, -is, -e (w. comp.) *adj.* fearful, terrible, horrible

horridus, -a, -um (w. comp.) *adj.* rough; shaggy; bristling; uncouth

horror, -ōris *nm.* shuddering, trembling; horror, fear; veneration

hortor, hortārī, hortātus sum *v.d.t.* encourage, incite, exhort (+ **ut** or **nē** + subjv.)

hortus, -ī *nm.* garden, park

hospes, -itis *nm.* guest, lodger; host; stranger, foreigner

hospita, -ae *nf.* guest, lodger; hostess; stranger, foreigner

hospitālis, -is, -e (w. sup.) *adj.* pertaining to guest or host; friendly, hospitable

hospitium, -ī *nnt.* reception of guests, entertainment of guests; friendship; inn

hostia, -ae *nf.* sacrifice; sacrificial victim

hostīlis, -is, -e *adj.* pertaining to an enemy; aggressive, hostile

hostis, -is *nm./f.* enemy, public enemy; stranger

hūc *adv.* hither, to this point, to this place

hūiusmodī *adj. (indecl.)* of this a kind, of such a kind, such

hūmānitās, -ātis *nf.* humanity, human nature; politeness, culture

hūmānus, -a, -um (w. sup.) *adj.* human; courteous, cultured

humilis, -is, -e (comp. **humilior**; sup. **humillimus**) *adj.* low; slight; mean, of low social rank

hūmor, -ōris *nm.* fluid, moisture
humus, -ī *nf.* ground, soil; country; **humī** *adv.* on the ground

I

iaceō,-ēre, iacuī, --- *v.i.* lie, rest, recline; lie dead; be level; be dejected; be despised
iaciō (jac), -ere, iēcī, iactum *v.t.* throw; build; throw out, mention
iactō (jact-), -āre, -āvī, -ātum *v.t.* toss, hurl; shake; utter
iactūra (jac-), -ae *nf.* throwing away; loss; expense
iactus (jac-), -ūs *nm.* throwing; range of a missile
iam (jam) *adv.* by now, now already; immediately; indeed; moreover; **iam prīdem** *adv.* long since, long ago; **nec iam** *adv.* and now no longer
iānitor (jān-), -ōris *nm.* porter, door-keeper
iānua (jān-), -ae *nf.* door; house-gate
Iānuārius, -a, -um *adj.* January (*usu. w.* **mēnsis**); **Iānuārius, -ī** *nm.* January
ibī *adv.* there, in that place, thereupon; on that occasion
ictus, -ūs *nm.* stroke, blow, hit
idcircō *adv.* therefore, on that account
īdem, eadem, idem *adj., pron.* the same
identidem *adv.* again and again, continually; now and then
ideō *adv.* for that reason, therefore
idōneus, -a, um *adj.* adequate, suitable (+ dat. *or* + **ad** or **in** + acc.)
Īdūs, Īduum *nf./pl.* the Ides (*One of the three days by which dates were calculated. In March, May, July and October, the Ides fell on the thirteenth, in the remaining months on the fifteenth.*)
iecur (jec-), iecoris *or* **iocineris** *nnt.* liver
iēiūnium (jēj-), -ī *nnt.* fast; hunger
iēiūnus (jēj-), -a, -um *adj.* fasting, hungry; barren; insignificant, lowly
ientāculum (jent-), -ī *nnt.* breakfast
igitur *adv.* (usu. postpos.) now, accordingly, therefore
ignārus, -a, -um *adj.* unfamiliar with, unacquainted with; unskilled in (+ gen.)
ignāvus, -a, -um (w. comp. + sup.) *adj.* slothful, lazy, listless; cowardly
ignis, -is *nm.* fire
ignōminia, -ae *nf.* disgrace, infamy
ignōrantia, -ae *nf.* ignorance, want of knowledge
ignōrō, -āre, -āvī, -ātum *v.t., v.i.* be ignorant, not know, be unacquainted with

ignōscō, -nōscere, -nōvī, -nōtum *v.i.* overlook, excuse, pardon (+ dat.)

ignōtus, -a, -um (w. comp. + sup.) *adj.* unfamiliar, unknown; obscure

illacrimō (inl-), -lacrimāre, -lacrimāvī, -lacrimātum *v.i.* weep, shed tears

illaesus (inl-), -a, -um *adj.* unharmed, unhurt

ille, illa, illud *adj.* that; well-known; *pron.* he, she, it; the former, the other

illecebra (inl-), -ae *nf.* attraction, charm

illīberālis (inl-), -is, -e *adj.* mean, ungenerous

illīc *adv.* yonder, in that place; in that matter

illicitus (inl-), -a, -um *adj.* unauthorized, not allowed

illinc *adv.* on that side; from that place

illō *adv.* to that place, thither

illūc *adv.* to that place; to that end; to such a degree

illūdō (inl-), -lūdere, -lūsī, -lūsum *v.t.* play at; mock, jeer at

illūminō (inl-), -lūmināre, -lūmināvī, -lūminātum *v.t.* light, illuminate

illūstris (inl-), -is, -e (w. comp.) *adj.* light, full of light; clear, plain; famous; noble

illūstrō (inl-), -āre, -āvī, -ātum *v.t.* make light; make clear, explain; make famous

imāgō, -inis *nf.* copy; statue, image, portrait; ghost; thought

imbēcillitās, -ātis *nf.* weakness, helplessness

imbēcillus, -a, -um (w. comp.) *adj.* weak, delicate, feeble

imber, -bris *nm.* rain, storm, shower

imbuō, -buere, -buī, -būtum *v.t.* fill; moisten; infect; stain, tint

imitātiō, -ōnis *nf.* imitation, copy

imitor, imitārī, imitātus sum *v.d.t.* imitate, copy

immānis, -is, -e *adj.* enormous, huge; terrible, savage, monstrous

immānitās, -ātis *nf.* hugeness; savageness; monstrosity

immātūrus, -a, -um *adj.* unripe, premature

immemor (-oris) *adj.* not thinking, unmindful, heedless (+ gen.)

immēnsus, -a, -um *adj.* immense, vast

immeritō *adv.* undeservedly, unjustly

immineō, -minēre, ---, --- *v.i.* overhang; be near at hand, impend, threaten (+ dat.)

imminuō, -minuere, -minuī, -minūtum *v.t.* decrease, lessen; infringe upon

imminūtiō, -ōnis *nf.* diminishing, weakening

immittō, -mittere, -mīsī, -missum *v.t.* send in, admit; send against

immō *adv.* on the contrary, no indeed

immōbilis, -is, -e *adj.* stationary, unmovable

immoderātus, -a, -um *adj.* immeasurable; excessive

immodicus, -a, -um *adj.* enormous; excessive

immolō, -molāre, -molāvī, -molātum *v.t.* sacrifice

immortālis, -is, -e *adj.* immortal, deathless, imperishable

immortālitās, -ātis *nf.* immortality, undying fame

immūnis *or* **immoenis, -is, -e** *adj.* exempt from a public office; unburdened, free from (+ gen.)

immūnitās *or* **immoenitās, -ātis** *nf.* exemption from public offices or duties

impār (impar-) *adj.* odd in number, uneven, unequal (+ dat.)

impatiēns (impatient-) *adj.* impatient, unable to endure

impedīmentum, -ī *nnt.* hindrance, impediment; **impedīmenta, -ōrum** *nnt./pl.* baggage, baggage-train; check, hindrance

impediō, -pedīre, -pedīvī, -pedītum *v.t.* compromise, entangle; impede, prevent

impellō, -pellere, -pulī, -pulsum *v.t.* strike against; push, thrust away; incite, persuade

impendeō, -pendēre, ---, --- *v.i.* hang over, be near at hand, impend, threaten (+ dat.)

impendium, -ī *nnt.* expense, cost; interest

impendō, -pendere, -pendī, -pēnsum *v.t.* measure out according to weight; expend

impēnsa, -ae *nf.* expense

imperātor, -ōris *nm.* chief commander, leader, emperor

imperfectus, -a, -um *adj.* incomplete, unfinished; imperfect

imperītus, -a, -um (w. comp. + sup.) *adj.* unskilled, inexperienced (+ dat.)

imperium, -ī *nnt.* order, command; authority, jurisdiction; right of commanding; empire; rule, government

imperō, -āre, -āvī, -ātum *v.t.* dictate, command (+ **ut** or **nē** + subjv.); control, rule, govern

impetrō, -petrāre, -petrāvī, -petrātum *v.t.* get, obtain; accomplish, effect; get by asking

impetus, -ūs *nm.* attack, assault; rush; violence, fury

impiētās, -ātis *nf.* undutifulness; impiety

impius, -a, -um *adj.* undutiful, irreverent; wicked

impleō, -plēre, -plēvī, -plētum *v.t.* fill up; finish; fulfill, satisfy (+ abl. *or* + gen.)

implicō, -plicāre, -plicāvī, -plicātum *v.t.* tangle, encircle; unite

implōrō, -plōrāre, -plōrāvī, -plōrātum *v.t., v.i.* beg, implore

impluvium, -ī *nnt.* the skylight opening in the atrium of a house

impōnō, -pōnere, -posuī, -positum *v.t.* place upon; establish, set up, set over; assign; deceive

importō, -portāre, -portāvī, -portātum *v.t.* import, bring in

importūnus, -a, -um *adj.* unsuitable; rude; cruel

imprimō, -primere, -pressī, -pressum *v.t.* impress; press upon, press into

improbitās, -ātis *nf.* wickedness

improbō, -probāre, -probāvī, -probātum *v.t.* censure, blame

improbus, -a, -um (w. comp. + sup.) *adj.* wicked; shameless

imprōvīsus, -a, -um *adj.* unforeseen, unexpected

imprūdēns (imprūdent-) *adj.* not expecting, unsuspecting, heedless (+ gen.)

impūbēs (impūber-) *or* **impūbēs, -is** *adj.* under age, young

impudēns (impudent-) (w. comp. + sup.) *adj.* without sense of shame, indecent

impudentia, -ae *nf.* shamelessness

impudīcus, -a, -um *adj.* shameless, unchaste

impulsus, -ūs *nm.* pushing; impulse

impūnē *adv.* without punishment; unharmed

impūnitās, -ātis *nf.* exemption from punishment, impunity, pardon

impūrus, -a, -um (w. comp. + sup.) *adj.* unclean, defiled

in *prep.* (*of motion*, + acc.) into, towards, against; *prep.* (*of rest*, + abl.) in, within, on, upon, among

inanimus, -a, -um *adj.* lifeless

inānis, -is -e (w. comp. + sup.) *adj.* void, empty; without effect

inaugurō, -augurāre, -augurāvī, -augurātum *v.t.* act as an augur, consult omens from birds; divine; consecrate; inaugurate

inaurēs, -ium *nf./pl.* earring

inaurō, -aurāre, -aurāvī, -aurātum *v.t.* gild, cover with gold

incēdō, -cēdere, -cessī, -cessum *v.i.* advance, proceed; attack

incendium, -ī *nnt.* fire, conflagration; vehemence, passion

incendō, -cendere, -cēnsī, -cēnsum *v.t.* set alight, burn; inflame, incite

inceptum, -ī *nnt.* beginning; attempt; enterprise

incertus, -a, -um (w. comp. + sup.) *adj.* undetermined, uncertain, doubtful, wavering

incessus, -ūs *nm.* walk, gait; manner of walking

incidō, -cidere, -cidī, -cāsum *v.t.* fall in; light upon; occur, happen

incipiō, -cipere, -cēpī, -ceptum *v.t.* take hold of; commence

incīsiō, -ōnis *nf.* cut, incision

incitāmentum, -ī *nnt.* motivation, inducement

incitō, -citāre, -citāvī, -citātum *v.t.* hasten; urge on, rouse

inclīnātiō, -ōnis *nf.* inclination, propensity

inclīnō, -clīnāre, -clīnāvī, -clīnātum *v.t., v.i.* bend; incline; be inclined to, be favorable towards

inclūdō, -clūdere, -clūsī, -clūsum *v.t.* enclose; put inside; obstruct; include

incognitus, -a, -um *adj.* unknown, not examined

incohō, -āre, -āvī, -ātum *v.t., v.i.* begin, commence; take in hand, propose

incola, -ae *nm/f.* inhabitant; immigrant

incolō, -colere, -coluī, -cultum *v.t.* inhabit, dwell in

incolumis, -is, -e *adj.* safe, unharmed, out of danger (+ **ab** + abl.)

incommodus, -a, -um (w. sup.) *adj.* troublesome, inconvenient

incōnstantia, -ae *nf.* inconstancy, fickleness

incrēbrēscō, -crēbrēscere, -crebuī, --- *v.i.* become strong; increase, spread

incrēdibilis, -is, -e *adj.* incredible, extraordinary

incrēmentum, -ī *nnt.* increase, growth

increpitō, -crepitāre, -crepitāvī, -crepitātum *v.t.* cry out; blame, scold

increpō, -crepāre, -crepāvī, -crepātum *v.t., v.i.* make a noise; occur; scold

incruentus, -a, -um *adj.* without bloodshed

incultus, -a, -um (w. comp.) *adj.* untilled; rough, savage; uneducated

incumbō, -cumbere, -cubuī, -cubitum *v.i.* lie upon, recline; oppress; make an effort

incurrō, -currere, -cucurrī (-currī), -cursum *v.t.* run into, meet; attack; offend; happen

incursiō, -ōnis *nf.* running against; clash, raid, attack

incursō, -cursāre, -cursāvī, -cursātum *v.t.* run against; raid, attack

inde *adv.* from that place; from that time; therefore

indecōrus, -a, -um *adj.* improper, unbecoming, disgraceful

index, -dicis *nm/f.* witness, informer; sign; label; forefinger

indicium, -ī *nnt.* proof, evidence, testimony; mark, token, sign

indicō, -dicāre, -dicāvī, -dicātum *v.t.* indicate, point out, reveal, accuse

indifferēns (indifferent-) *adj.* indifferent

indigena, -ae *adj.* native

indigentia, -ae *nf.* need, want

indignātiō, -ōnis *nf.* indignation

indignus, -a, -um (w. comp. + sup.) *adj.* unworthy; unbecoming; shameful (+ abl. *or* + gen.)

indoctus, -a, -um (w. comp. + sup.) *adj.* ignorant, unlearned, unskilled

indolēs, -is *nf.* natural quality; nature, disposition

indūcō, -dūcere, -dūxī, -ductum *v.t.* lead in, bring forward; spread over; persuade

indulgēns (indulgent-) (w. comp.) *adj.* kind, indulgent

induō, -duere, -duī, -dūtum *v.t.* assume, put on clothes; cover; entangle

indūsium, -ī *nnt.* shift, undergarment

industria, -ae *nf.* industry, activity

industrius, -a, -um *adj.* industrious, active

indūtiae, -ārum *nf./pl.* truce, armistice

ineō, -īre, -īvī (-iī), -ītum *v.t., v.i.* go into, enter; enter upon, begin, undertake

ineptia, -ae *nf.* folly, foolishness

inermis, -is, -e *or* **inermus, -a, -um** *adj.* unarmed, defenseless

iners (inert-) (w. comp. + sup.) *adj.* awkward; unskillful; passive, inactive, idle

inertia, -ae *nf.* unskillfulness; idleness

inēvītābilis, -is, -e *adj.* unavoidable

inexplicābilis, -is, -e *adj.* intricate, difficult; unaccountable

īnfāmis, -is, -e *adj.* infamous, disreputable

īnfāns (īnfant-) *adj.* infant; **īnfāns, īnfantis** *nm/f.* baby, infant

īnfantia, -ae *nf.* inability to speak; childhood

īnfaustus, -a, -um *adj.* unfortunate, unlucky

īnfēlīx (īnfēlīc-) (w. comp. + sup.) *adj.* unfruitful, barren; ill-fated, unlucky, unsuccessful; unhappy

īnfēnsus, -a, -um *adj.* hostile, enraged

īnferior, īnferior, īnferius (īnferiōr-) *adj.* lower, further down

īnferō, -ferre, -tulī, -lātum *v.t.* carry in, bring in; wage; bring forward; excite; inflict

īnferus, -a, -um *adj.* lower, underneath, underground; of the underworld; **īnferī, -ōrum** *nm./pl.* spirits of the underworld, the dead

īnfēstus, -a, -um *adj.* unsafe, hostile (+ dat. *or* + **in** + acc.), dangerous

īnfidus, -a, -um *adj.* untrustworthy; treacherous

īnfimus, -a, -um *adj.* lowest; last, most base

īnfinītus, -a, -um *adj.* without limit, endless

īnfirmitās, -ātis *nf.* weakness, infirmity, illness

īnfirmō, -firmāre, -firmāvī, -firmātum *v.t.* weaken; disprove; impair

īnfirmus, -a, -um (w. comp. + sup.) *adj.* weak, feeble, unhealthy; inconstant; invalid, inconclusive

īnfitior, īnfitiārī, īnfitiātus sum *v.d.t.* deny, disown

īnflammātiō, -ōnis *nf.* inflammation

īnflammō, -flammāre, -flammāvī, -flammātum *v.t.* set on fire; inflame, arouse

īnflātiō, -ōnis *nf.* inflation; flatulence

īnflexibilis, -is, -e *adj.* unbendable, unchangeable, inflexible

īnflō, -flāre, -flāvī, -flātum *v.t.* blow into, breathe upon; inspire; elate

īnfluō, -fluere, -flūxī, -flūxum *v.i.* flow into, pour in; invade

īnformō, -formāre, -formāvī, -formātum *v.t.* shape, mold; educate; describe

īnfrā *adv.* below, beneath, under; *prep.* (+ acc.) below, underneath

īnfundō, -fundere, -fūdī, -fūsum *v.t.* pour in, inject; administer; crowd into; mix

īnfūsiō, -ōnis *nf.* pouring into, watering

ingeniōsus, -a, -um (w. comp. + sup.) *adj.* talented, clever by nature

ingenium, -ī *nnt.* innate quality, character, temper; ability, genius, power of the mind

ingēns (ingent-) *adj.* big beyond natural size, great

ingenuus, -a, -um *adj.* native; free-born, noble

ingrātus, -a, -um (w. comp. + sup.) *adj.* unacceptable; thankless (+ dat.)

ingravēscō, -gravēscere, ---, --- *v.i.* grow worse, become burdensome; increase

ingredior, ingredī, ingressus sum *v.d.i.t.* go forward, go into, undertake

ingressiō, -ōnis *nf.* entry; act of entering; beginning

inguen, inguinis *nnt.* groin

inhabilis, -is, -e *adj.* unmanageable, awkward, clumsy, unfit

inhabitō, -habitāre, -habitāvī, -habitātum *v.t.* inhabit, dwell in

inhaereō, -haerēre, -haesī, -haesum *v.i.* adhere, stick fast, cling to (+ dat.)

inhiō, -hiāre, -hiāvī, -hiātum *v.t., v.i.* gape; be amazed

inhonestus, -a, -um *adj.* dishonorable

inhospitus, -a, -um *adj.* bleak, unwelcoming, inhospitable

inhūmānus, -a, -um (w. comp. + sup.) *adj.* brutal, inhuman, uncouth, coarse, unkind

inhumātus, -a, -um *adj.* unburied

inibī *adv.* in that place, there

iniciō (inj-), -icere, -iēcī, -iectum *v.t.* cast into; heap up, build; take possession of

inimīcitia, -ae *nf.* hostility, personal enimity

inimīcus, -a, -um (w. comp. + sup.) *adj.* unfriendly, hostile (+ dat.)

inīquitās, -ātis *nf.* unevenness, inequity; difficulty

inīquus, -a, -um (w. comp. + sup.) *adj.* uneven, unequal; unfavorable; wrong, unjust; hostile (+ dat.); steep

initium, -ī *nnt.* entrance; start, beginning

iniūcundus (inj-), -a, -um (w. comp.) *adj.* unpleasant, disagreeable

iniungō (inj-), -iungere, -iūnxī, -iūnctum *v.t.* join; impose

iniūria (inj-), -ae *nf.* grievance, wrong, injustice, insult

iniūstus (inj-), -a, -um (w. comp.) *adj.* wrong, unjust; oppressive

innāscor, innāscī, innātus sum *v.d.i.* be born, grow, arise in

innītor, innītī, innīxus sum *v.d.i.* lean upon, support oneself (+ abl.)

innocēns (innocent-) (w. sup.) *adj.* harmless; innocent, upright

innocentia, -ae *nf.* blamelessness, uprightness

innocuus, -a, -um *adj.* innocent, harmless

innoxius, -a, -um *adj.* harmless; blameless; unhurt

innumerābilis, -is, -e *adj.* countless

innuō, -nuere, -nuī, -nūtum *v.i.* nod, hint (+ dat.)

innupta, -ae *nf.* unmarried woman, virgin

inoffēnsus, -a, -um *adj.* unhindered; without injury

inopia, -ae *nf.* want, lack, need, scarcity; poverty

inquam, inquit, inquiunt *v.i.* (*def.*) say (*used parenthetically*)

inquiēs, -ētis *nf.* unrest

inquiētus, -a, -um (w. comp. + sup.) *adj.* restless

inquilīnus, -a, -um *adj.* inhabiting a place that one does not own; *nm/f.* tenant, immigrant; resident

inrītō (irr-) -rītāre, -rītāvī, -rītātum *v.t.* stir up, incite; anger

īnsalūbris, -is, -e (w. comp. + sup.) *adj.* unhealthy

īnsānus, -a, -um (w. comp. + sup.) *adj.* unsound in mind

īnscientia, -ae *nf.* ignorance, want of knowledge

īnscius, -a, -um *adj.* ignorant, not knowing (+ gen.)

īnscrībō, -scrībere, -scrīpsī, -scrīptum *v.t.* inscribe; assign

īnscrīptiō, -ōnis *nf.* writing on, writing in

īnsectum, -ī *nnt.* insect

īnsequōr, īnsequī, īnsecūtus sum *v.d.i.t.* follow, pursue; succeed; censure

īnserō, -serere, -seruī, -sertum *v.t.* insert; join, associate, mix with

īnsidiae, -ārum *nf./pl.* ambush, plot, trap

īnsidior, īnsidiārī, īnsidiātus sum *v.d.i.* ambush, lie in wait for, plot against

īnsigne, -is *nnt.* mark, sign; proof; badge, decoration

īnsignis, -is, -e (w. sup.) *adj.* remarkable, striking, extraordinary

īnsimulō, -simulāre, -simulāvī, -simulātum *v.t.* charge, accuse (*usu. falsely;* + gen. of charge)

īnsistō, -sistere, -stitī, --- *v.t., v.i.* go towards; tread on; halt; pursue; persist

īnsolēns (īnsolent-) (w. comp. + sup.) *adj.* unusual, strange; arrogant

īnsolentia, -ae *nf.* strangeness; arrogance

īnsolitus, -a, -um *adj.* strange, unusual (+ **ad** + acc. *or* + gen.)

īnsomnia, -ae *nf.* insomnia

īnsōns (īnsont-) *adj.* innocent, not guilty (+ gen.; rarely + abl., *of the offence*)

īnspectiō, -ōnis *nf.* inspection, scrutiny

īnspectō, -spectāre, -spectāvī, -spectātum *v.t., v.i.* look at, observe

īnspērātus, -a, -um (+ sup.) *adj.* beyond hope; not expecting

īnspiciō, -spicere, -spēxī, -spectum *v.t.* look into, examine, inspect

īnstabilis, -is, -e *adj.* rickety, tottering, unstable

īnstaurō, -staurāre, -staurāvī, -staurātum *v.t.* renew, repeat, refresh

īnstituō, -stituere, -stituī, -stitūtum *v.t.* put in place, found, arrange, build; provide; begin; decide; educate, train in a branch of knowledge

īnstitūtum, -ī *nnt.* purpose, plan; precedent; rule

īnstō, -stāre, -stitī, -stātum *v.t.* stand near; approach; urge, press on, harass; menace

īnstrūmentum, -ī *nnt.* equipment, instrument, tool

īnstruō, -struere, -strūxī, -strūctum *v.t.* build in; prepare; draw up, arrange; inform

īnsula, -ae *nf.* island; apartment house

īnsuper *adv.* upon, above; over and above

integer, integra, integrum (comp. **integrior**; sup. **integerrimus**) *adj.* untouched, whole, unhurt; fresh, not tired out; undecided; blameless

integritās, -ātis *nf.* completeness; integrity

intellegō, -legere, -lēxī, -lēctum *v.t.* see into, perceive, realize, understand (+ acc. *or* + acc. + infv.)

intemperantia, -ae *nf.* excess, over-indulgence

intempestus, -a, -um *adj.* unseasonable, unpropitious; unhealthy

intendō, -tendere, -tendī, -tēnsum *v.t.* stretch out, strain; aim; intend

intentiō, -ōnis *nf.* straining, stretching, effort; intention; attention

intentus, -a, -um (w. comp.) *adj.* earnest, eager; vigilant (+ dat. *or* + abl.)

inter *prep.* (+ acc.) amid, among; between; during

intercēdō, -cēdere, -cessī, -cessum *v.t.* come between, intervene; come to pass

interdīcō, -dīcere, -dīxī, -dictum *v.t.* forbid, prohibit; command

interdictum, -ī *nnt.* prohibition

interdiū *adv.* during the day, by day

interdum *adv.* sometimes, now and then

intereā *adv.* meanwhile

intereō, -īre, -īvī (-iī), -itum *v.i.* be lost among, perish, go to ruin, decay

interest, interesse, interfuī, --- *v.i.* (imp. v.) it makes a difference, it is of importance, it concerns (*the person or thing concerned is expressed by the gen. or the abl. f. of the personal adjs.; the degree of importance by a nt. acc., an adv., or a gen. of value; the cause of concern by the infv. or the acc. + infv. or by* **ut** *or* **nē** + *the subjv. or by an indirect question*)

interfector, -ōris *nm.* murderer, killer

interficiō, -ficere, -fēcī, -fectum *v.t.* kill, murder; destroy

interim *adv.* meanwhile; nevertheless

interimō, -imere, -ēmī, -ēmptum *v.t.* destroy; kill

interior, interior, interius (interiōr-) *adj.* inner; nearer; deepest

interitus, -ūs *nm.* ruin, destruction; death

intermissiō, -ōnis *nf.* pause

intermittō, -mittere, -mīsī, -missum *v.t.* suspend, interrupt; pause, cease

internecetiō, -ōnis *nf.* slaughter, mass destruction

internus, -a, -um *adj.* internal; domestic; civil

interpellātiō, -ōnis *nf.* interruption

interpellō, -pellāre, -pellāvī, -pellātum *v.t.* interrupt; obstruct

interpōnō, -pōnere, -posuī, -positum *v.t.* place between, insert

interpres, -pretis *nm/f.* negotiator; messenger; explainer, translator, interpreter

interpretātiō, -ōnis *nf.* explanation, interpretation, translation

interpretor, interpretārī, interpretātus sum *v.d.t.* interpret, explain; understand; decide

interpūnctiō, -ōnis *nm.* punctuation

interpungō, -pungere, -pūnxī (-pupugī), -pūnctum *v.t.* punctuate

interrēgnum, -ī *nnt.* interval between two reigns; the time between the death or departure of the consuls and the election of new consuls

interrogātiō, -ōnis *nf.* examination, interrogation; argument

interrogō, -rogāre, -rogāvī, -rogātum *v.t.* examine, inquire, interrogate

interrumpō, -rumpere, -rūpī, -ruptum *v.t.* break apart, break up

intersum, -esse, -fuī, -futūrum *v.i.* lie in between, intervene (+ **inter** + acc.); differ (+ **ab** + abl.); take part in, participate in (+ dat. *or* + **in** + abl.)

intervallum, -ī *nnt.* break, gap, pause; distance

interveniō, -venīre, -vēnī, -ventum *v.t.* come between, interrupt; occur; hinder

interventus, -ūs *nm.* coming between, intervention

intestīnus, -a, -um *adj.* internal; **intestīnum, -ī** *nnt. or* **intestīna, -ōrum** *nnt./pl.* the gut, bowels, intestines

intimus, -a, -um *adj.* inmost, deepest; intimate

intorqueō, -torquēre, -torsī, -torsum *v.t.* twist, turn; hurl

intrā *prep.* (+ acc.) within, inside of; in the course of

intrō *adv.* within, inward; **intrō, -āre, -āvī, -ātum** *v.t.* come in; penetrate, reach

intrōdūcō, -dūcere, -dūxī, -ductum *v.t.* lead in, present

intrōductiō, -ōnis *nf.* introduction, bringing in

introitus, -ūs *nm.* entrance, approach, door; beginning

intueor, intuērī, intuitus sum *v.d.t.* regard, consider, look upon

intus *adv.* within, inside

inultus, -a, -um *adj.* unavenged; unpunished

inurbānus, -a, -um *adj.* impolite, boorish

inūrō, -ūrere, -ussī, -ustum *v.t.* burn into, brand

inūtilis, -is, -e (w. comp. + sup.) *adj.* worthless, useless, unprofitable (+ **ad** + acc. *or* + dat.)

invādō, -vādere, -vāsī, -vasum *v.t., v.i.* enter; charge, attack; seize; begin

invalidus, -a, -um (w. comp. + sup.) *adj.* not strong, powerless, inadequate

invehō, -vehere, -vexī, -vectum *v.t.* bring into, carry against; ride on, be carried by; attack

inveniō, -venīre, -vēnī, -ventum *v.t.* come across, find, discover, find out, learn; invent

inventārium, -ī *nnt.* list, inventory

inventiō, -ōnis *nf.* invention; faculty of invention

inventum, -ī *nnt.* invention, device

invenustus, -a, -um *adj.* unattractive, awkward, inelegant

invertō, -vertere, -vertī, -versum *v.t., v.i.* tip, turn over; alter

investīgātiō, -ōnis *nf.* examination, investigation

investīgō, -vestīgāre, -vestīgāvī, -vestīgātum *v.t.* track, search into, examine, inquire

inveterāsco, -veterāscere, -veterāvī, --- *v.i.* become old, become established, become rooted

invicem *adv.* in turn, alternately; mutually, for each other

invictus, -a, -um (w. comp. + sup.) *adj.* unconquered; unconquerable

invideō, -vidēre, -vīdī, -vīsum *v.i.* envy, begrudge (+ dat.)

invidia, -ae *nf.* envy; dislike, hatred, ill will

invidus, -a, -um *adj.* envious, jealous (+ gen.)

inviolātus, -a, -um *adj.* unharmed, inviolable

invīsus, -a, -um (w. comp. + sup.) *adj.* disliked, hated

invītātiō, -ōnis *nf.* invitation, inducement

invītō, -āre, -āvī, -ātum *v.t.* invite, ask, allure; entertain

invītus, -a, -um (w. sup.) *adj.* unwilling, against one's will

involūcrum, -ī *nnt.* wrap, cover

involūtus, -a, -um (w. sup.) *adj.* rolled up; complicated

involvō, -volvere, -volvī, -volūtum *v.t.* envelop, roll in, cover, roll upon

iō *interj.* hurray!

iocor (joc-), iocārī, iocātus sum *v.d.i.* joke, say jestingly

ipse, ipsa, ipsum *dem. pron.* self; myself, yourself, *etc.*

īra, -ae *nf.* passion, violent anger, wrath

īrācundia, -ae *nf.* inclination to anger; anger, violence

īrācundus, -a, -um (w. comp. + sup.) *adj.* irascible, prone to anger, passionate, hot-headed

īrāscor, īrāscī, īrātus sum *v.d.i.* be angry, become angry, be furious (+ dat.)

īrātus, -a, -um (w. comp. + sup.) *adj.* furious, angry

īrōnīa, -ae *nf.* irony

irrēpō (inr-), -rēpere, -rēpsī, -rēptum *v.i.* creep stealthily into

irrīdeō (inr-), -rīdēre, -rīsī, -rīsum *v.t., v.i.* laugh at, mock

irrigātiō (inr-), -ōnis *nf.* irrigation

irrigō (inr-), -rigāre, -rigāvī, -rigātum *v.t.* water, conduct water

irritus (inr-), -a, -um *adj.* null, invalid, ineffectual

irrumpō (inr-), -rumpere, -rūpī, -ruptum *v.t.* burst in, break into, invade

irruptiō (inr-), -ōnis *nf.* bursting into; descent; attack

is, ea, id *dem. pron.* this, that; he, she, it

iste, ista, istud *dem. pron.* that, this; that of yours

istīc *adv.* over there, in that place; on this occasion

istinc *adv.* from over there, from there

istūc *adv.* to that place

ita *adv.* thus, so, as follows; to such a degree

itaque *conj.* and so, accordingly, therefore

item *adv.* likewise, moreover

iter, itineris *nnt.* trip, journey; road, route, path, passage; march

iterātiō, -ōnis *nf.* repetition

iterō, -āre, -āvī, -ātum *v.t.* repeat, do again

iterum *adv.* again, a second time; **iterum atque iterum**, again and again

iubeō (jub-), -ēre, iussī, iussum *v.t.* order, command (+ acc. + infv.; rarely + **ut** or **nē** + subjv.)

iūcundus (jūc-), -a, -um *or* **iocundus (joc-), -a, -um** (w. comp. + sup.) *adj.* pleasant, agreeable

iūdex (jūd-), -icis *nm/f.* judge, decider; juror

iūdicium (jūd-), -ī *nnt.* trial; sentence, judicial decision; opinion

iūdicō (jūd-), -dicāre, -dicāvī, -dicātum *v.t.* criticize, judge; proclaim

iugālis (jug-), -is, -e *adj.* yoked together

iūglāns (jūg-), -glandis *nf.* walnut; walnut tree

iugum (jug-), -ī *nnt.* yoke; team; mountain ridge

Iūlius, -a, -um *adj.* July (*usu. w.* **mēnsis**); **Iūlius, - ī** *nm.* July

iungō (jung-), -ere, iūnxī, iūnctum *v.t.* join, unite, ally; yoke

iurgium (jurg-), -ī *nnt.* quarrel, dispute

Iūnius, -a, -um *adj.* June (*usu. w.* **mēnsis**); **Iūnius, -ī** *nm.* June

iurgō (jurg-), -āre, -āvī, -ātum *v.i.* quarrel

iūriscōnsultus (jūr-), -ī *nm.* lawyer, one learned in law

iūrō (jūr-), -āre, -āvī, -ātum *v.i.* swear, take an oath

iūs (jūs), iūris *nnt.* broth, soup; law, right, duty, justice; authority, power; **iūs iūrandum, iūris iūrandī** *nnt.* oath

iussū (jus-) *nnt. (indecl.)* by order, by command

iussum (jus-), -ī *nnt.* command, order

iūstitia (jūs-), -ae *nf.* justice; clemency

iūstus (jūs-), -a, -um (w. comp. + sup.) *adj.* just, fair, proper, right

iuvenīlis (juv-), -is, -e *or* **iuvenalis (juv-), -is, -e** (w. comp.) *adj.* youthful

iuvenis (juv-), -is, -e (comp. **iūnior** *or* **iuvenior**) *adj.* young; **iuvenis (juv-), -is** *nm/f.* youth

iuventus (juv-), -ūs *nf.* youth, the youth, young men

iuvō (juv-), -āre, iūvī, iūtum *v.t.* help, support; please

iūxtā (jūx-) *adv.* close, near to; in like manner; *prep.* (+ acc.) beside, next to; near; almost the same as

K

Kalendae *or* **Calendae, -ārum** *nf./pl.* the Kalends (*the first day of the month*)

L

labefaciō, -facere, -fēcī, -factum *v.t.* cause to totter, shake, loosen; impair

labefactō, -factāre, -factāvī, -factātum *v.t.* cause to totter, shake; impair, weaken; disturb; overthrow, destroy

labēs, -is *nf.* fall, giving way; taint, stain, impurity

lābor, lābī, lāpsus sum *v.d.i.* glide, slide, slip, sink, fall; perish; err, go astray

labor *or* **labōs, -ōris** *nm.* labor, toil, exertion; hardship

labōriōsus, -a, -um (w. comp. + sup.) *adj.* laborious, tiresome; troubled

labōrō, -āre, -āvī, -ātum *v.t., v.i.* toil, labor; be in trouble, suffer; totter

labrum, -ī *nnt.* lip, margin, rim

labyrinthus, -ī *nm.* labyrinth

lac, lactis *nnt.* milk

lacer, lacera, lacerum *adj.* torn, mangled, bruised, disfigured

lacerō, -āre, -āvī, -ātum *v.t.* tear, mangle, rend

lacerta, -ae *nf.* lizard

lacertōsus, -a, -um *adj.* muscular, brawny

lacertus, -ī *nm.* upper arm; muscle

lacessō, -ere, lacessīvī, lacessītum *v.t.* excite, provoke, irritate, harass; defy

lacinia, -ae *nf.* flap, piece of hanging cloth; corner of cloth

lacrima *or* **lacruma, -ae** *nf.* tear, teardrop

lacrimō *or* **lacrumō, -āre, -āvī, -ātum** *v.i.* weep, mourn

lactūca, -ae *nf.* lettuce

lacūnar, -āris *nnt.* paneled ceiling, ceiling

lacus, -ūs *nm.* lake, pond, pool; river, stream; reservoir, tank, cistern

laedō, -ere, laesī, laesum *v.t.* hurt, damage, wound, injure, offend, pain, vex, betray, violate

laena, -ae *nf.* cloak, mantle

laetitia, -ae *nf.* happiness, joy, delight, gladness, pleasure

laetor, laetārī, laetātus sum *v.d.i.* rejoice, be glad (+ abl.)

laetus, -a, -um (w. comp. + sup.) *adj.* happy, pleased, delighted, glad, joyful

laevus, -a, -um *adj.* left, on the left hand; foolish; ominous, boding

lāmentābilis, -is, -e *adj.* lamentable, pitiable

lāmentum, -ī *nnt.* shriek, groan, lamentation, cry

lāmina, -ae *nf.* thin metal plate, metal leaf; blade of knife or sword

lampas, -adis *nf.* light, torch

lāna, -ae *nf.* wool; wool-working; soft hair, soft feathers

lancea, -ae *nf.* lance, spear

lāneus, -a, -um *adj.* woolen; covered with wool

langueō, -ēre, ---, --- *v.i.* be faint, be weary, be languid, be listless; hesitate; sink; be heavy

languēscō, -ere, languī, --- *v.i.* become faint, become weak, become listless, become feeble

languidus, -a, -um (w. comp.) *adj.* weak, sluggish, inactive, apathetic, listless

lāniger, lānigera, lānigerum *adj.* wool-bearing, fleecy, tufted with wool

laniō, -āre, -āvī, -ātum *v.t.* mangle, rend, mutilate

lanista, -ae *nm.* trainer of gladiators; inciter, instigator

lanterna, -ae *nf.* lantern, torch, lamp

lānūgō, -inis *nf.* down, fine hair

lapicīdīnae, -ārum *nf./pl.* quarry, excavation

lapidōsus, -a, -um (w. comp.) *adj.* stony, hard as stone

lapillus, -ī *nm.* pebble, little stone; precious stone, jewel

lapis, lapidis *nm.* stone; landmark; statue

lāpsō, -āre, -āvī, -ātum *v.i.* slip

lāpsus, -ūs *nm.* falling, lapse, gliding, slip; any gliding motion

laqueus, -ī *nm.* loop, noose; snare, trap

lārdum (lāridum), -ī *nnt.* lard, bacon fat

largior, largīrī, largītus sum *v.d.t.* lavish, dispense, bestow; bribe

largus, -a, -um (w. comp. + sup.) *adj.* wide, spacious, copious, abundant; free

lascīvia, -ae *nf.* sportiveness, playfulness; wantonness, licentiousness

lassus, -a, -um *adj.* tired, weary

latebra, -ae *nf.* hiding place, retreat; pretense, excuse

lateō, -ēre, latuī, --- *v.i.* lie hidden, lurk, be concealed, escape notice

latex, laticis *nm.* fluid, liquid

lātitūdō, -inis *nf.* width, breadth, extent; size; compass

lātrātus, -ūs *nm.* bark, barking

lātrīna, -ae *nf.* toilet, latrine; bath

latrō, -ōnis *nm.* mercenary soldier; outlaw, highwayman, bandit; hunter

latrōcinium, -ī *nnt.* highway robbery; band of robbers

latrōcinor, latrōcinārī, latrōcinātus sum *v.d.i.* serve as mercenary soldier; plunder, rob, practice highway robbery

lātus, -a, -um (w. comp. + sup.) *adj.* wide, broad, extensive (*in breadth*), extending; **lātē** (w. sup) *adv.* broadly, widely, far and wide

latus, -eris *nnt.* side, flank

laudābilis, -is, -e *adj.* praiseworthy, commendable

laudō, -āre, -āvī, -ātum *v.t.* praise, commend; eulogize, deliver funeral oration

laurea, -ae or **laurus, -ī** *nf.* bay tree, laurel tree; laurel garland, crown of laurel

laus, laudis *nf.* praise, commendation, glory, renown, credit, merit

lavō, -āre, lāvī, lautum (lōtum) *v.t.* wash, bathe; moisten

laxō, -āre, -āvī, -ātum *v.t.* extend, make wide, enlarge; loosen, release, lighten, relieve, lessen; moderate

laxus, -a, -um (w. comp. + sup.) *adj.* wide, open, loose; indulgent

lea (leaena), -ae *nf.* lioness

lectīca, -ae *nf.* litter, portable couch

lectiō, -ōnis *nm.* gathering, selecting; reading, that which is read

lector, -ōris *nm.* reader

lectulus, -ī *nm.* cot, little couch

lectus, -ī *nm.* bed, couch

lēgātiō, -ōnis *nf.* embassy, legation; ambassador, legate

lēgātum, -ī *nnt.* bequest, legacy

lēgātus, -ī *nm.* ambassador, envoy, legate; lieutenant

lēgifer, lēgifera, lēgiferum *adj.* lawgiving

legiō, -ōnis *nf.* legion, troop

legionārius, -a, -um *adj.* pertaining to legion, legionary

lēgitimus, -a, -um *adj.* fixed or appointed by law, legal, lawful, legitimate

legō, -ere, lēgī, lēctum *v.t.* collect; select, choose, elect, appoint; read

lēniō, -īre, -īvī, -ītum *v.t.* soften, mollify, calm, appease

lēnis, -is, -e (w. comp. + sup.) *adj.* soft, mild, gentle, calm, smooth, kind, moderate

lēns, lentis *nf.* lentil

lentus, -a, -um (w. comp. + sup.) *adj.* pliant, yielding, slow, idle, backward, easy, unconcerned; tough; **lentē** *adv.* slowly

leō, leōnis *nm.* lion

lepidus, -a, -um (w. comp. + sup.) *adj.* pleasant, agreeable, fine, nice, pretty

lepōs *or* **lepor, lepōris** *nm.* pleasantness, charm, politeness; humor, wit

lepus, leporis *nm.* hare

lētālis *or* **lēthālis, -is, -e** *adj.* mortal, fatal, deadly

lētifer (lēth-), lētifera, lētiferum *adj.* mortal, fatal, deadly

lētō (lēth-), -āre, -āvī, -ātum *v.t.* kill, slay

lētum (lēth-), -ī *nnt.* death; ruin, destruction

levāmen, -inis *nnt.* consolation, solace

levātiō, -ōnis *nf.* lifting up, elevation, relief, alleviation

levis, -is, -e (w. comp. + sup.) *adj.* light (*not heavy*), slight, trifling; swift; easy; moderate; capricious; untrustworthy

levō, -āre, -āvī, -ātum *v.t.* raise; lighten, relieve, lessen, release; remove; console

lēx, lēgis *nf.* written law, statute, rule, regulation; manner; agreement, condition, terms

lībāmen, -inis *nnt.* libation; offering

libellus, -ī *nm.* little book, pamphlet, notice, information; complaint, indictment, accusation,

libenter *or* **lubenter** (w. comp. + sup.) *adv.* willingly, cheerfully, gladly

līber, lībera, līberum (comp. **līberior**; sup. **līberrimus**) *adj.* free, unrestricted, unimpeded

liber, librī *nm.* book; bark (*bot.*)

līberālis, -is, -e (w. comp. + sup.) *adj.* pertaining to freedom; worthy of a free man, noble, dignified, honorable; kind, gracious; generous, liberal

līberātiō, -ōnis *nf.* delivery, release; rescue

līberī, -ōrum *nm./pl.* free persons; children

līberō, -āre, -āvī, -ātum *v.t.* set free, liberate, rescue, deliver, release, save, acquit, absolve

lībertās, -ātis *nf.* freedom, liberty, independence

libet (lub-), libēre, libuit (libitum est) *v.i.* (*imp.*) it pleases, it is agreeable, it seems good to (+ dat. *or* + infv. *or* + acc. + infv.)

libīdinōsus (lub-), -a, -um (w. comp. + sup.) *adj.* lustful, sensual, self-willed; arbitrary; eager

libīdō (lub-), -inis *nf.* desire, inclination, passion, inordinate desire, sensuality, lust; pleasure

lībō, -āre, -āvī, -ātum *v.t.* make libation, pour an offering; taste, drink, sip

lībra, -ae *nf.* Roman pound (*twelve ounces*); balance, pair of scales; plummet-level, level; counterpoise

librārius, -ī *nm.* copyist, transcriber; scribe; library slave

lībrō, -āre, -āvī, -ātum *v.t.* balance, poise; swing, hurl

licentia, -ae *nf.* license, unrestrained freedom, wantonness, lawlessness; boldness, presumption, insolence

licet, licēre, licuit (licitum est) *v.i.* (*imp.*) it is allowed, it is lawful, it is permitted (+ infv. *or* + acc. of permitted + infv. *or* + dat. of person permitted + infv. *or* + subjv.); **licet** *conj.* (+ subjv.) although, though

lictor, -ōris *nm.* lictor (*an official attendant or magistrate*)

lignum, -ī *nnt.* wood; fuel, firewood

ligō, -āre, -āvī, -ātum *v.t.* tie

līlium, -ī *nnt.* lily

līma, -ae *nf.* file

līmāx, -ācis *nf.* slug, snail

limbus, -ī *nm.* fringe, border

līmen, -inis *nnt.* threshold, door, entrance; house, palace, temple; starting post of race; the beginning

līmes, līmitis *nm.* by-way, path, track; boundary line, fortified boundary line

līmō, -āre, -āvī, -ātum *v.t.* file, file off; diminish; polish, finish; investigate thoroughly

līmōsus, -a, -um *adj.* muddy, swampy

līmum, -ī *nnt.* mud, slime, clay, soil

līnea, -ae *nf.* linen thread, string; net; plumb-line; stroke, mark, line; boundary-line, limit, goal; feature, lineament; line of descent, lineage; outline, sketch

līneāmentum, -ī *nnt.* line, stroke, mark; feature, lineament

līneus, -a, -um *adj.* of flax, linen

lingua, -ae *nf.* tongue (*anat.*); language, dialect; boastful speech; voice

linter, lintris *nf.* boat, ferry-boat

linteum, -ī *nnt.* linen cloth, napkin; scarf; sail-cloth

līnum, -ī *nnt.* flax; flaxen thread, cord, rope; linen cloth; net

liquefaciō, -facere, -fēcī, -factum *v.t.* make melt, dissolve, make liquid

liqueō, -ēre, licuī, --- *v.i.* flow; be limpid, be clear

liquēscō, -ere, ---, --- *v.i.* begin to melt

liquidus, -a, -um *adj.* liquid, flowing; clear, pure; serene

liquor, -ōris *nm.* fluidity, liquid

līs, lītis *nf.* quarrel, dispute; lawsuit, litigation

litō, -āre, -āvī, -ātum *v.t., v.i.* sacrifice, appease god; offer successfully, perform acceptably

littera *or* **lītera, -ae** *nf.* letter of the alphabet, written character; **litterae** *or* **līterae, -arum** *nf./ pl.* correspondence, letter, epistle

lītus, lītoris *nnt.* seashore, seaside; strand; beach; riverbank

lituus, -ī *nm.* the curved staff used in augury; trumpet, horn

līveō, -ēre, ---, --- *v.i.* be livid; be dusky

līvidus, -a, -um *adj.* black and blue, bruised, dark blue, dusky

līvor, -ōris *nm.* blue (*color*); black and blue spot; envy, spite

lixīvium, -ī *nnt.* lye

locō, -āre, -āvī, -ātum *v.t.* put, place (+ **in** + abl.); arrange; rank; let, lease, hire

locuplēs (locuplēt-) (w. comp. + sup.) *adj.* rich, wealthy; well supplied; trustworthy

locus, -ī *nm.* place, spot; post, station; topic; passage; opportunity; room; **loca, -ōrum** *nnt./pl.* region, country

locusta, -ae *nf.* lobster; locust

locūtiō, -ōnis *nf.* speaking, speech, discourse; way of speaking, pronunciation; utterance, phrase

lōdīx, -icis *nf.* sheet, covering for bed; blanket

longaevus, -a, -um *adj.* aged, of great age; in old age

longinquitās, -ātis *nf.* distance, remoteness; length, duration (*of time*)

longīnquus, -a, -um (w. comp.) *adj.* long, extensive; remote, far off; longlasting

longitūdō, -inis *nf.* length; long duration

longurius, -ī *nm.* long pole

longus, -a, -um (w. comp. + sup.) *adj.* long, extended, far-reaching; of long duration; tedious; distant, remote; **longē** (w. comp. + sup.) *adv.* far away, at distance; for a long time; long; greatly, by far; **longē lātēque** *adv.* far and wide

loquāx (loquāc-) (w. comp.) *adj.* talkative, full of words

loquēla, -ae *nf.* speech, discourse; **loquēlae, -ārum** *nf./pl.* words

loquor, loquī, locūtus sum *v.d.i.t.* speak, say, talk, tell, mention, declare; show; testify

lōrīca, -ae *nf.* mail, armor, cuirass

lōrum, -ī *nnt.* thong, strap; lace; rein, bridle

lūbricus, -a, -um *adj.* slippery, slimy

lūceō, -ēre, lūxī, --- *v.i.* be bright, shine, gleam, be splendid, be resplendent; show itself, appear

lūcerna, -ae *nf.* lamp

lūcēscō, -ere, lūxī, --- *v.i.* begin to shine, grow light, dawn

lūcidus, -a, -um (w. comp. + sup.) *adj.* bright, shining, radiant

lūcifer, lūcifera, lūciferum *adj.* light-bringing

lūcrum, -ī *nnt.* profit, advantage; avarice

luctātor, -ōris *nm.* wrestler; foe

luctor, luctārī, luctātus sum *v.d.i.* wrestle, struggle, strive

lūctus, -ūs *nm.* mourning, grief, distress

lūculentus, -a, -um (w. sup.) *adj.* full of light, bright, splendid; distinguished

lūcus, -ī *nm.* wood or grove dedicated to some deity, sacred grove or park of temple

lūdibrium, -ī *nnt.* mockery, ,jest, dishonoring; laughing-stock; wantonness

lūdō, -ere, lūsī, lūsum *v.t.* play (+ acc. *or* + abl. of game), sport, frolic; participate in public game; ridicule

lūdus, -ī *nm.* pastime, play, sport; joke; place for exercising the mind or body, school; **ludī, -ōrum** *nm./pl.* public games, spectacles

luēs, -is *nf.* plague, pestilence, blight

lūgeō, -ēre, lūxī, lūctum *v.t.* mourn, lament

lūgubris *or* **lūgŭbris, -is, -e** *adj.* mournful, grieving

lūmen, -inis *nnt.* light; source of light, lamp; light of the eye, eye; brightness

lūna, -ae *nf.* moon

lūnāris, -is, -e *adj.* lunar, of the moon

lūnātus, -a, -um *adj.* crescent, half-moon shaped

luō, -ere, luī, --- *v.t.* loose; pay, atone for, expiate; undergo

lupa, -ae *nf.* she-wolf

lupus, -ī *nm.* wolf

lūsor, -ōris *nm.* player, gambler

lūstrātiō, -ōnis *nm.* lustration (*the religious rite of purification*), purification; sacrifice

lūstrō, -āre, -āvī, -ātum *v.t.* purify with religious ceremony, lustrate; make light, light up; wander over, pass over, sail over; reconnoiter; track, trace; observe, survey

lūstrum, -ī *nnt.* purification

lustrum, -ī *nnt.* den, lair

lūsus, -ūs *nm.* sport, play

lūteum, -ī *nnt.* yolk of an egg; yellow (*color*)

lūteus, -a, -um *adj.* (*colors*) yellow, saffron yellow; orange

lutulentus, -a, -um *adj.* sloppy, muddy, filthy

lutum, -ī *nnt.* mire, mud, clay

lūx, lūcis *nf.* light, brightness, daylight; light of life; eyesight

lūxuria, -ae *nf.* extravagance, excess, luxury; sensuality

lūxuriō, -āre, -āvī, -ātum *v.i.* be rank, be luxuriant, abound excessively; swell, enlarge; be self-indulgent, be dissolute

lūxuriōsus, -a, -um (w. comp. + sup.) *adj.* luxurious, exuberant, immoderate, wanton, profuse

lūxus, -ūs *nm.* luxury; wantonness; splendor, pomp

lychnus, -ī *nm.* lamp

lympha, -ae *nf.* water

lynx, lyncis *nm/f.* lynx

lyra, -ae *nf.* lyre, harp

M

macellum, -ī *nnt.* market for food

macer, macra, macrum (comp. **macrior**; sup. **macerrimus**) *adj.* meager, poor, barren; thin

māchina, -ae *nf.* machine; device for performing some sort of work; strategem

māchinātiō, -ōnis *nf.* machinery, contrivance; cunning device; plot

māchinor, māchinārī, māchinātus sum *v.d.t.* hatch a plan, contrive, plot

maciēs, -ēī *nf.* thinness, leanness; poverty

mactō, -āre, -āvī, -ātum *v.t.* glorify; sacrifice; put to death

macula, -ae *nf.* spot, stain, mark; disgrace

maculō, -āre, -āvī, -ātum *v.t.* spot, stain; pollute

madefaciō, -facere, -fēcī, -factum *v.t.* soak, moisten; dye deeply

madeō, -ēre, maduī, --- *v.i.* be wet, be moist; soak, steep

madidus, -a, -um (w. comp.) *adj.* soaking, wet

maeror, -ōris *nm.* sadness, mourning

maestus, -a, -um (w. sup.) *adj.* sorrowful, sad, melancholy

magicus, -a, -um *adj.* magical, pertaining to magic

magis *adv.* more, far more; rather

magister, magistrī *nm.* teacher, leader, guide, guardian

magistra, -ae *nf.* teacher; director

magistrātus, -ūs *nm.* magistrate; office of a magistrate

magnēs, magnētis *nm.* magnet

magnēticus, -a, -um *adj.* magnetic

magnificentia, -ae *nf.* grandeur, splendor; boastfulness

māgnificus, -a, -um (comp. **māgnificentior**; sup. **māgnificentissimus**) *adj.* magnificent; elevated, noble, distinguished; splendid; costly

māgnitūdō, -inis *nf.* greatness, volume, size, magnitude; abundance

māgnopere *adv.* particularly, very much, exceedingly

māgnus, -a, -um (comp. **māior**; sup. **māximus**) *adj.* great, wide, tall, large, abundant, grand, stately, eminent; **māgnā vōce** *adv.* loudly

magus, -ī *nm.* learned scholar among the Persians; magician

māiestās (māj-), -ātis *nf.* grandeur, dignity, majesty; treason

māior, māior, māius (māiōr-) *adj.* greater, larger, higher; **māiōrēs, māiōrum** *nm./pl.* ancestors

Māius, -a, -um *adj.* May (*usu. w.* **mēnsis**); **Māius, -ī** *nm.* May

malē (comp. **pēius**; sup. **pessimē**) *adv.* badly, awkwardly; evilly; unfortunately; unsuccessfully

maledīcō, -dīcere, -dīxī, -dictum *v.t.* curse, slander, abuse

maledictum, -ī *nnt.* curse, reproach

maleficium, -ī *nnt.* evil deed, wickedness, wrong

malignus, -a, -um (w. comp. + sup.) *adj.* malicious, malignant, evil

malleus, -ī *nm.* hammer

mālō, mālle, māluī, --- *v.t.* (*irreg.*) prefer

mālum, -ī *nnt.* apple; any apple-like fruit

malum, -ī *nnt.* evil; misfortune; hurt; punishment; crime

malus, -a, -um (comp. **pēior**; sup. **pessimus**) *adj.* bad, evil; malformed; adverse, hostile, destructive

mālus, -ī *nf.* apple tree; *nm.* mast, upright pole, beam, staff

mandātum, -ī *nnt.* commission, task; command

mandō, -dāre, -dāvī, -dātum *v.t.* charge with, entrust; order (+ **ut** or **nē** + subjv.)

māne *adv.* early in the morning, in the morning

māneō, -ēre, mānsī, mānsum *v.i.* remain, stay, last; await, expect

Mānēs, -ium *nm./pl.* shades of the dead, spirits of the dead

manica, -ae *nf.* sleeve

manifestus, -a, -um (w. comp. + sup.) *adj.* plain, apparent; caught in the act

manipulus, -ī *nm.* small bundle, handful; company of soldiers, military unit

mānō, -āre, -āvī, -ātum *v.t., v.i.* trickle, flow; spread abroad

mānsiō, -ōnis *nf.* sojourn, stay; station, inn

mānsuēfaciō, -facere, -fēcī, -factum *v.t.* tame, soften, civilize

mānsuētūdō, -inis *nf.* gentleness, mildness; clemency

mānsuētus, -a, -um (w. comp. + sup.) *adj.* tame, soft, gentle, quiet

mantēle, -is *nnt.* napkin; towel

manūbiae, -ārum *nf./pl.* booty taken in war, spoils, prize money

manūmittō, -mittere, -mīsī, -missum *v.t.* release, free, manumit

manus, -ūs *nf.* hand; legal power of male relative or husband over a
    woman; body or group of people

mappa, -ae *nf.* napkin

mare, -is *nnt.* sea

margarīta, -ae *nf.* pearl

margō, -inis *nm/f.* border, edge, boundary, limit

marīnus, -a, -um *adj.* marine, of the sea

maritimus, -a, -um *adj.* of the sea, maritime

marītus, -ī *nm.* husband, married man

marmor, -oris *nnt.* marble, block of marble; statue

marsūpium, -ī *nnt.* purse, pouch

Mārtius, -a, -um *adj.* March (*usu. w.* **mēnsis**); **Mārtius, -ī** *nm.* March

mās, māris *nm.* male, manly; vigorous

māsculīnus, -a, -um *adj.* masculine, male

massa, -ae *nf.* lump, mass

māter, mātris *nf.* mother, dam (*female parent of an animal*); origin; **māter
    familiās, mātris familiās** *nf.* mistress of a house

māteria, -ae *nf.* matter, stuff; that which

māteriēs, -ēī *nf.* matter, stuff; that which

mātertera, -ae *nf.* maternal aunt

mathēmaticus, -a, -um *adj.* pertaining to mathematics

mātrimōnium, -ī *nnt.* marriage

mātrōna, -ae *nf.* married woman, matron, noble woman

mātūritās, -ātis *nf.* ripeness, maturity

mātūrō, -āre, -āvī, -ātum *v.t., v.i.* ripen, bring to maturity; hasten

mātūrus, -a, -um (comp. **mātūrior**; sup. **mātūrissimus** or **mātūrrimus**)
    adj. ripe; **mātūrē** (sup. **mātūrissimē** or **mātūrrimē**) *adv.* proper;
    early

mātūtīnus, -a, -um *adj.* early in the morning, early

māximus, -a, -um *adj.* largest, greatest, tallest, maximum; **maximē** *adv.*
    in the highest degree; especially, particularly; very

meātus, -ūs *nm.* passing, motion; path, passage

medeor, medērī, ---, --- *v.d.i.t..* cure, heal, relieve, restore

medicāmentum, -ī *nnt.* drug, medicine; **medicāmina faciēī,
    medicāminum faciēī** *nnt./pl.* make-up

medicīna, -ae *nf.* medicine, remedy; art of medicine

medicus, -ī *nm.* physician, doctor

mediocris, mediocris, mediocre *adj.* moderate, ordinary; inferior

mediocritās, -ātis *nf.* moderation, medium, middle state

meditor, meditārī, meditātus sum *v.d.i.t.* consider, think over, devise, plan

medius, -a, -um *adj.* in the middle (of), middle, between, among; **medium, -ī** *nm.* the middle; public eye, the midst of the community

medulla, -ae *nf.* core, medulla, pith

mel, mellis *nnt.* honey, sweetness

melior, melior, melius (meliōr-) *adj.* superior, better; **melius** *adv.* better

membrāna, -ae *nf.* skin, membrane; parchment

membrum, -ī *nnt.* member, limb, part, portion

meminī, meminisse, --- *v.t., v.i.* (*def. v.*) remember, bear in mind (+ gen.)

memor (memor-) *adj.* mindful, remembering (+ gen.)

memoria, -ae *nf.* memory, recollection

memorō, -āre, -āvī, -ātum *v.t.* mention, recount, tell

mendācium, -ī *nnt.* lie, fiction

mendāx (mendāc-) (w. sup.) *adj.* lying, false, deceitful

mendīcō, -āre, -āvī, -ātum *v.i.* beg for money

mendīcus, -ī *nm.* beggar

mendōsus, -a, -um (w. comp.) *adj.* wrong, incorrect, inaccurate

mēns, mentis *nf.* mind, intellect; feeling, spirit; plan; courage

mēnsa, -ae *nf.* counter, table; dinner course

mēnsis, -is *nm.* month

mēnsūra, -ae *nf.* measuring, measure, amount, quantity, degree

menta, -ae *nf.* mint (*bot.*)

mentiō, -ōnis *nf.* mention

mentior, mentīrī, mentītus sum *v.d.i.t.* lie, deceive, mislead

mentum, -ī *nnt.* chin

mercātor, -ōris *nm.* dealer, trader, merchant

mercātūra, -ae *nf.* trade, commerce; traffic

mercēs, -ēdis *nf.* price, fee; wages; reward

mercor, mercārī, mercātus sum *v.d.t.* trade, carry on trade, buy

mereō, -ēre, meruī, meritum *v.t., v.i.* deserve, earn, gain; buy; serve for pay

meretrīx, -trīcis *nf.* prostitute

mergō, -ere, mersī, mersum *v.i.* dip, plunge, dive; sink

merīdiānus, -a, -um *adj.* of midday, meridian; southern

merīdiēs, -ēī *nm.* midday, noon; south; **merīdiē** *adv.* at noon; **ad merīdiem** *adv.* at midday

meritus, -a, -um (w. sup.) *adj.* deserving; deserved; **meritō** *adv.* deservedly, rightly; **meritum, -ī** *nnt.* merit, service, favor

merus, -a, -um *adj.* pure, unmixed, undiluted; naked; mere; genuine

merx, mercis *nf.* merchandise, goods
messis, -is *nf.* harvest, crop
-met *enclitic suffixed to pronouns to add emphasis*
mēta, -ae *nf.* cone; goal, goal post; end, boundary
metallum, -ī *nnt.* metal; **metalla, -ōrum** *nnt./pl.* mine, quarry; income
mētiōr, mētīrī, mēnsus sum *v.d.t.* measure; distribute; traverse; estimate, value
metō, -ere, messuī, messum *v.t.* reap, harvest, mow down
metuō, -ere, -uī, -ūtum *v.t.* fear, dread; be apprehensive (+ **ut** or **nē** + subjv.)
metus, -ūs *nm.* fear, dread, apprehension
meus, -a, -um *adj.* my, mine, my own
mīca, -ae *nf.* crumb, grain, bit
micō, -āre, -uī, --- *v.i.* move quickly; tremble; twinkle, glitter, shine brightly
migrō, -āre, -āvī, -ātum *v.t., v.i.* move from one place to another, migrate
mīles, -itis *nm/f.* soldier, foot soldier; **mīlitēs, -um** *m./pl.* infantry, army
mīlitāris, -is, -e *adj.* pertaining to soldiery or war
mīlitia, -ae *nf.* military service, soldiery; warfare
mīlitō, -āre, -āvī, -ātum *v.t.* serve in the army
mīlle *num.* (*indecl.*) thousand; **mīlia (mīllia), -ium** *nnt./pl.* thousand; **mīlle passūs** *nnt.* (*indecl.*) mile; **mīlia passuum, mīlium passuum** *nnt./pl.* miles
mīllēsimus, -a, -um *adj.* thousandth
mīlliārium, -ī *nnt.* milestone; mile
milvus, -ī *nm.* kite (*a bird of prey*)
minae, -ārum *nf./pl.* threats, menaces
minimus, -a, -um *adj.* smallest; least; **minimē** *adv.* by no means, at least; **minimum, -ī** *nnt.* minimum
minister, ministrī *nm.* servant, attendant, helper
ministerium, -ī *nnt.* service, assistance, attendance; employment
ministra, -ae *nf.* female attendant, maid servant
ministrō, -āre, -āvī, -ātum *v.t.* serve, attend to, take care of
minor, minārī, minātus sum *v.d.i.t.* threaten, menace (+ dat.); **minor, minor, minus (minōr-)** *adj.* smaller, less; **minus** *adv.* less
minuō, -ere, -uī, -ūtum *v.t.* reduce, make small; weaken
minūtus, -a, -um *adj.* little, minute, insignificant
mīrābilis, -is, -e *adj.* admirable, wonderful, extraordinary
mīrāculum, -ī *nnt.* strangeness; marvelous thing, miracle

mīrandus, -a, -um *adj.* wonderful, marvelous

mīrātiō, -ōnis *nf.* surprise, wonder

mīrificus, -a, -um (w. sup. **mīrificissmis** *or* **mīrificentissimus**) *adj.* causing wonder, extraordinary

mīror, mīrārī, mīrātus sum *v.d.i.t.* wonder at, be amazed; admire, esteem

mīrus, -a, -um (w. comp.) *adj.* miraculous, wonderful, astonishing

misceō, -ēre, miscuī, mīxtum *v.t.* mix, blend; unite, join; stir up, disturb

miser, misera, miserum (comp. **miserior**; sup. **miserrimus**) *adj.* unhappy, pitiable, sad; worthless

miserābilis, -is, -e *adj.* pitiable, wretched

misereō, -ēre, miseruī, miseritum *v.t., v.i.* feel pity, have compassion for; **miseret, miserēre, miseruit, ---** *v.i.* causes pity, one feels pity for

miseria, -ae *nf.* distress, suffering

misericordia, -ae *nf.* sympathy, compassion, mercy

misericors (misericord-) (w. comp. + sup.) *adj.* sympathetic, compassionate, merciful

miseror, miserārī, miserātus sum *v.d.i.t.* deplore; feel compassion for, sympathize

mistūra, -ae *nf.* mixing, mingling; sexual intercourse

mītigō, -āre, -āvī, -ātum *v.t.* make mild, tame, pacify, appease; ripen

mītis, -is, -e (w. comp. + sup.) *adj.* mild, soft, gentle

mittō, -ere, mīsī, missum *v.t.* send; report; cease, dismiss; release, shoot, throw; omit

mīxtus, -a, -um *adj.* mixed, confused

moderātiō, -ōnis *nf.* regulation, self-control, moderation

moderātor, -ōris *nm.* controller, governor, manager

moderātus, -a, -um (w. comp. + sup.) *adj.* restrained, moderate

moderor, moderārī, moderātus sum *v.d.i.t.* limit, regulate, control, restrain

modestia, -ae *nf.* moderation, self-control; sense of honor or shame

modestus, -a, -um (w. comp. + sup.) *adj.* gentle, forbearing, discreet

modicus, -a, -um *adj.* moderate, limited, not excessive, not deep, not extravagant, temperate, ordinary

modō *adv.* only, merely; just now, recently; ~...~ *adv.* now...now; *conj.* (+ subjv.) if only, on condition that; **nē** ~ *conj.* (+ subjv.) on condition that not

modus, -ī *nm.* measure, extent; rhythm; way, manner; limit

moenia, -ium *nnt./pl.* city walls, fortifications; fortified city

mola, -ae *nf.* millstone, hand mill; grits

mōlēs, -is *nf.* mass, bulk; dam, mole, barrier; weight, strength; difficulty
molestia, -ae *nf.* annoyance, trouble
molestus, -a, -um (w. comp. + sup.) *adj.* troublesome, annoying
mōlior, mōlīrī, mōlītus sum *v.d.t.* endeavor, toil, labor upon, undertake, build
molitor, -ōris *nm.* miller
mollis, -is, -e (w. comp. + sup.) *adj.* pliant, soft, gentle, delicate, weak
molo, -ere, -uī, -itum *v.t.* grind in a mill
mōmentum, -ī *nnt.* impulse; movement; influence; importance
monacha, -ae *nf.* nun
monachus, -ī *nm.* monk
monastērium, -ī *nnt.* monastery
moneō, -ēre, monuī, monitum *v.t.* warn, remind; teach; announce
monēta, -ae *nf.* currency, money; mint
monīle, -is *nnt.* collar, necklace
monitiō, -ōnis *nf.* warning, advice
monopōlium, -ī *nnt.* monopoly
mōns, montis *nm.* mountain; mountain range; mass, heap
mōnstrō, -āre, -āvī, -ātum *v.t.* show, point out; inform
mōnstrum, -ī *nnt.* sign, portent; monstrosity
monumentum *or* **monimentum, -ī** *nnt.* means of reminding; record; monument
mora, -ae *nf.* stay, delay; obstacle
mōrālis, -is, -e *adj.* ethical, moral
morbus, -ī *nm.* illness, disease
mordāx (mordāc-) (w. comp. + sup.) *adj.* sharp, biting, pungent; corroding
mordeō, -ēre, momordī, morsum *v.t.* bite, nip, sting; annoy; cut into
mōrigeror, mōrigerārī, mōrigerātus sum *v.d.i.* accommodate, comply with
morior, morī (morīrī), mortuus sum *v.d.i.* die; wither, decay
moror, morārī, morātus sum *v.d.i.t..* delay, stay, retard, hinder
mōrōsus, -a, -um *adj.* surly, hard to please, ill-tempered, capricious
mors, mortis *nf.* death; dead body
morsus, -ūs *nm.* bite; devouring
mortālis, -is, -e *adj.* mortal; human; transitory
mortifer, -fera, -ferum *adj.* malignant, deadly
mortuus, -a, -um *adj.* lifeless, dead
mōs, mōris *nm.* custom, habitual practice; fashion; **mōrēs, mōrum** *nm./pl.* manners; character

mōtus, -ūs *nm.* motion, movement, disturbance; emotion; rebellion

moveō, -ēre, mōvī, mōtum *v.t., v.i.* move, disturb, affect, stir up; promote; change

mox *adv.* presently, soon; thereupon, then

mūcidus *or* **muccidus, -a, -um** *adj.* stale, moldy, musty

mūcor, -ōris *nm.* mold, moldiness

mūcrō, -ōnis *nm.* point, edge; sharpness

mulier, mulieris *nf.* woman; wife

multa, -ae *nf.* fine

multiplex (multiplic-) *adj.* with many folds or windings; manifold; changeable; deceitful, intricate

multiplicātiō, -ōnis *nf.* multiplying

multiplicō, -plicāre, -plicāvī, -plicātum *v.t.* multiply, increase by many times

multitūdō, -inis *nf.* host, large number, crowd

multō, -āre, -āvī, -ātum *v.t.* punish; fine

multus, -a, -um (comp. **plūs**; sup. **plūrimus**) *adj.* much; **multī, -ae, -a** *adj./pl.* many, in large numbers; **multō** *adv.* by much, much; far, by far, greatly; **multum** *adv.* much, often; greatly

mundus, -a, -um (w. comp. + sup.) *adj.* clean, neat; elegant; **mundus, -ī** *nm.* decoration; dress of women; universe, world

mūniceps, mūnicipis *nm/f.* citizen of a free town; fellow citizen

mūnicipium, -ī *nnt.* free city, municipality

mūnificentia, -ae *nf.* benevolence, generosity

mūnimentum, -ī *nnt.* fortification, bulwark, protection, defense

mūniō *or* **moeniō, -īre, -īvī, -ītum** *v.t.* fortify, strengthen; defend, guard

mūnītiō, -ōnis *nf.* defenses, fortification; engineering work

mūnus, -eris *nnt.* service, employment, function, duty; charge, tax; gift; public show (*especially gladiator games*)

muria, -ae *nf.* pickle, brine

murmur, murmuris *nnt.* rumble, murmur; crashing

mūrus, -ī *nm.* wall; city wall

mūs, mūris *nm/f.* rat, mouse

musca, -ae *nf.* fly

mūsculus, -ī *nm.* little mouse; muscle

mūsica, -ae *nf.* music

mūsicus, -ī *nm.* musician

mūtābilis, -is, -e (w. comp. + sup.) *adj.* changeable, variable

mūtātiō, -ōnis *nf.* alteration, change

mūtō, -āre, -āvī, -ātum *v.t.* shift, change, alter; remove; exchange
mūtus, -a, -um *adj.* mute (*without speech or voice*), silent
mūtuus, -a, -um *adj.* borrowed; loaned; mutual, reciprocal; **mutuum, -ī**
   nnt. loan
mystērium, -ī *nnt.* secret rite, secret worship; mystery, secret

N

nam *conj.* for
namque *conj.* for, in fact, inasmuchas
nancīscor, nancīscī, nactus (nanctus) sum *v.d.t.* obtain, secure; meet
   with; light upon; incur
nāris, -is *nf.* nostril
nārrātiō, -ōnis *nf.* relation, narrative
nārrātor, -ōris *nm.* narrator
nārrō, -āre, -āvī, -ātum *v.t.* narrate, tell
nāscēns (nascent-) *adj.* young, rising
nāscor, nāscī, nātus sum *v.d.i.* be born
nāsus, -ī *nm.* nose; nozzle
nāta *or* **gnāta, -ae** *nf.* daughter; offspring
nātālis, -is, -e *adj.* of or belonging to one's birth, natal
natātiō, -ōnis *nf.* swimming
natātor, -ōris *nm.* swimmer
nātiō, -ōnis *nf.* birth; breed, kind; nation, people
nātīvitās, nātīvitātis *nf.* birth, nativity; generation
natō, -āre, -āvī, -ātum *v.i.* swim, float; be flooded
nātū *nm.* (*indecl.*) by birth
nātūra, -ae *nf.* birth; nature, the world; quality; character
nātūrālis, -is, -e *adj.* natural, by birth; not artificial
nātus *or* **gnātus, -ī** *nm.* son; offspring
naufragium, -ī *nnt.* shipwreck
nausea, -ae *nf.* nausea, seasickness
nauseabundus, -a, -um *adj.* inclined to vomit
nauseō, -āre, ---, --- *v.i.* vomit, be seasick
nauta, -ae *nm.* sailor, boatman
nāvālis, -is, -e *adj.* naval, of ships; **nāvālia, -ium** *nnt./pl.* dockyard
nāvigātiō, -ōnis *nf.* navigation, voyage
nāvigium, -ī *nnt.* boat, ship
nāvigō, -igāre, -igāvī, -igātum *v.i.* sail, embark; sail upon, navigate

nāvis, -is *nf.* vessel, ship

-ne *enclitic particle that marks a question*

nē *adv.* not, no; **nē ... quidem** *adv.* not even

nebula, -ae *nf.* haze, mist, fog

nebulōsus, -a, -um *adj.* misty, foggy

nec (neque) *adv., conj.* nor, and not, nor yet; **nec (neque) ... nec (neque)** *conj.* neither ... nor

necessārius, -a, -um *adj.* inevitable, necessary, unavoidable; **necessāriō** *adv.* necessarily

necesse *adj./nt. (indecl.)* unavoidable, necessary, inevitable; **necesse est, esse, fuit** *v.i. (imp. v.)* it is necessary (+ infv. *or* + dat. + infv.)

necessitās, -ātis *nf.* exigency, necessity, need; relationship

necessitūdō, -inis *nf.* necessity; intimate relationship; distress

necne *conj.* or not

necō, -āre, -āvī, -ātum *v.t.* execute, kill

nectō, -ere, nexuī (nexī), nexum *v.t.* lace, tie together, bind, attach

nefandus, -a, -um *adj.* unutterable; impious, heinous

nefārius, -a, -um *adj.* impious, heinous, wicked

nefās *nnt. (indecl.)* that which is against divine command; impious deed, sin, crime; **nefās est** *v.i.* it is forbidden, it is wrong (+ infv.)

nefāstus, -a, -um *adj.* not right; contrary to religion,; impious; unpropitious

negātiō, -ōnis *nf.* denying

neglegēns (negligent-) (w. comp. + sup.) *adj.* careless, neglectful, inattentive; improvident

neglegentia, -ae *nf.* carelessness, neglect

neglegō, -legere, -lēxī, -lectum *v.t.* ignore, pay no attention to; despise

negō, -āre, -āvī, -ātum *v.t.* say no, refuse, deny, decline

negōtior, negōtiārī, negōtiātus sum *v.d.i.* deal in, trade in

negōtium, -ī *nnt.* business, occupation; matter; difficulty

nēmō, -inis *pron. m/f.* no one, nobody

neō, nēre, nēvī, nētum *v.i.* spin, twist fibers

nepōs, -ōtis *nm.* grandson; nephew; prodigal

neptis, -is *nf.* granddaughter

nēquāquam *adv.* by no means, not at all

neque (nec) *adv., conj.* nor, and not, nor yet; **neque (nec) ... neque (nec)** *conj.* neither ... nor

nequeō, -quīre, -quīvī (-iī), -itum *v.i.* be unable (+ infv.)

nēquīquam *adv.* needlessly, in vain

nēquitia, -ae *nf.* worthlessness; wickedness

nervus, -ī *nm.* sinew, muscle, tendon; bow-string; string

nesciō, -scīre, -scīvī, -scītum *v.t.* not know, be ignorant; **nesciō quid** *nnt.* something; **nesciō quō modō** *adv.* somehow

neu *or* **nēve** *conj.* (+ subjv.) and not, or not, nor

neuter, neutra, neutrum *adj.* neither the one nor the other; neuter in gender

nēve *conj.* (+ subjv.) and not, nor; and in order that not

nex, necis *nf.* death by slaughter, murder

nī *adv.* not; **quid ~** *adv.* why not?; *conj.* not, that not; if not, unless

nictātiō, -ōnis *nf.* wink

nictō, -āre, -āvī, -ātum *v.i.* blink, wink; strive

nīdus, -ī *nm.* nest; nestlings

niger, nigra, nigrum (comp. **nigrior**; sup. **nigerrimus**) *adj.* glossy black; gloomy, ill-omened; wicked

nihil *nnt.* (*indecl.*) none, nothing

nihilōminus *adv.* nevertheless, still

nihilum, -ī *nnt.* nothing, not a bit

nīl *nnt.* (*indecl.*) nothing

nimbus, -ī *nm.* storm; rain cloud; heavy rain; throng

nimīrum *adv.* doubtless, certainly, to be sure

nimis *adv.* too much, excessively

nimius, -a, -um *adj.* too much, excessive, too great; **nimium** *adv.* too much, too; greatly, very; **nimium** *nnt.* (*indecl.*) a great deal

ningit (ninguit), -ere, ninxit, --- *v.i.* (*imp.*) it is snowing

nisi *conj.* if not, unless, except

niteō, -ēre, ---, --- *v.i.* glitter, be bright; flourish

nitidus, -a, -um (w. comp. + sup.) *adj.* shining, bright; sleek, spruce; handsome

nītor, nītī, nīxus (nīsus) sum *v.d.i.* rest, lean upon, depend upon (+ abl.); strive, make an effort (+ infv.); **nītor, -ōris** *nm.* brilliance, sheen, splendor

nitrum, -ī *nnt.* soda, natron

niveus, -a, -um *adj.* snowy

nīx, nivis *nf.* snow

nōbilis, -is, -e (w. comp. + sup.) *adj.* famous, well-known; noble, of high rank

nōbilitās, -ātis *nf.* fame; high birth, aristocracy, nobility

nōbilitō, -āre, -āvī, -ātum *v.t.* make known

noceō, -ēre, nocuī, nocitum *v.t.* harm, hurt, injure (+ dat.)

noctū *adv.* at night, by night

nocturnus, -a, -um *adj.* by night, nocturnal

nōdō, -āre, -āvī, -ātum *v.t.* knot, tie in a knot

nōdus, -ī *nm.* knot; band

nōlō, nōlle, nōluī, --- *v.i.* not wish, refuse, be unwilling (+ infv.)

nōmen, -inis *nnt.* name, title, designation; gentile name; fame, repute

nōminātim *adv.* by name; specially, in particular

nōminātiō, -ōnis *nf.* nomination

nōminō, -āre, -āvī, -ātum *v.t.* call by name, name; make famous; nominate; mention

nōn *adv.* no, not at all, by no means; **nōn modo (sōlum)** ... **sed (etiam)** *conj.* not only ... but also; **nōn nihil** *nnt.* (*indecl.*) a dash, small amount

Nōnae, -ārum *nf./pl.* the Nones (*one of the days of the month by which the dates were calculated; the Nones fell on the seventh day of March, May, July, and October, but on the fifth day of the other months*)

nōnāgintā *num.* (*indecl.*) ninety

nōndum *adv.* not yet

nōnne *adv. introduces a question and indicates that a positive answer is expected*

nōnnūllus, -a, -um *adj.* some; **nōnnūllī, -ae, -a** *adj./pl.* several

nōnnumquam *adv.* sometimes

nōnus, -a, -um *adj.* ninth

norma, -ae *nf.* carpenter's square; rule, standard

nōs *pron.* we

nōscō, -scere, nōvī, nōtum *v.t.* know, become acquainted with, learn

noster, nostra, nostrum *adj.* our, ours, our own, of us

nota, -ae *nf.* mark; stamp; letter, note; token; disgrace

notātiō, -ōnis *nf.* marking; taking notice of

nōtiō, -ōnis *nf.* making oneself acquainted with; notion, concept

notō, -āre, -āvī, -ātum *v.t.* note, designate with a mark; write down; censure

nōtus, -a, -um (w. comp. + sup.) *adj.* known, familiar, well-known, famous, notorious; of ill-repute

novācula, -ae *nf.* razor, sharp knife

novem *num.* (*indecl.*) nine

Novembris (November), Novembris, Novembre *adj.* November (*usu. w.* **mēnsis**); **November, -bris** *nm.* November

noverca, -ae *nf.* stepmother

novissimus, -a, um *adj.* the latest, the last; the rear (*of an army*); extreme

novitās, -ātis *nf.* newness, novelty

novō, -āre, -āvī, -ātum *v.t.* make new, renew; invent; change, alter

novus, -a, -um (w. sup.) *adj.* new, young, fresh; strange; latest, last

nox, noctis *nf.* night; darkness; **nocte** *adv.* by night, at night; **mediā nocte** *adv.* at midnight

noxius, -a, -um *adj.* bad, harmful; guilty (+ gen.)

nūbēs, -is *nf.* cloud, mist; swarm

nūbilus, -a, -um *adj.* dull, cloudy, overcast

nucleus, -ī *nm.* pit, kernel

nūditās, -ātis *nf.* nudity, nakedness

nūdō, -āre, -āvī, -ātum *v.t.* expose, lay bare, strip

nūdus, -a, -um (w. sup.) *adj.* bare, naked; lightly clad; vacant

nūgae, -ārum *nf./pl.* nonsense, trifles

nūllus, -a, -um *adj.* no, none, not any

num *adv.* introduces a direct question and indicates that a negative answer is expected; *adv.* whether (*in indirect questions*)

nūmen, -inis *nnt.* nod; command; divine will of the gods; divinity; divine favor

numerō, -āre, -āvī, -ātum *v.t.* count, number; pay

numerus, -ī *nm.* number; quantity; rank; measure of music, rhythm

nummus, -ī *nm.* coin, money

numquam *adv.* never, by no means

nunc *adv.* now, at the present time; under these circumstances

nundinae, -ārum *nf./pl.* fair, market day

nūntiō, -āre, -āvī, -ātum *v.t.* announce, declare, report

nūntius, -ī *nm.* information, news; messenger

nūper (comp. **nūperius**; sup. **nūperrimē**) *adv.* lately, recently

nūptiae, -ārum *nf./pl.* marriage, wedding

nurus, -ūs *nf.* daughter-in-law

nūsquam *adv.* nowhere; on no occasion; to no purpose

nūtriō, -īre, -īvī, -ītum *v.t.* nurse, suckle; rear, foster; support

nūtrīx, -īcis *nf.* nurse, wet-nurse

nūx, nucis *nf.* nut; nut tree

nympha, -ae (nymphē, -ēs) *nf.* bride; nymph

O

ob *prep.* (+ acc.) to, towards; for, on account of

obeō, -īre, -īvī (-iī), -itum *v.t., v.i.* go to meet; reach; traverse; enter upon; perform, accomplish

ōbex, -icis *nm/f.* latch, bar, bolt; barricade

obiciō (obj-), -icere, -iēcī, -iectum *v.t.* throw before; offer; reproach

obiūrgō (obj-), -iūrgāre, -iūrgāvī, -iūrgātum *v.t.* scold, reprove; urge

oblectāmentum, -ī *nnt.* delight, amusement, enjoyment

oblectō, -lectāre, -lectāvī, -lectātum *v.t.* delight, divert

obligātiō, -ōnis *nf.* bond, tie

obligō, -ligāre, -ligāvī, -ligātum *v.t.* fasten to, tie up, bind; oblige, make liable

oblīquus, -a, -um *adj.* slanting, sideways; indirect; covert

oblīviō, -ōnis *nf.* forgetfulness

oblīviōsus, -a, -um (w. sup.) *adj.* forgetful

oblīvīscor, oblīvīscī, oblītus sum *v.d.i.t.* forget; ignore, disregard (+ gen.)

oblongus, -a, -um (w. comp.) *adj.* oblong

obmūtēscō, -mūtēscere, -mūtuī, --- *v.i.* become silent; cease

obnoxius, -a, -um (w. comp.) *adj.* addicted to; guilty; submissive, timid; be a slave to (+ dat.)

oboedientia, -ae *nf.* obedience, compliance

oboediō, -oedīre, -oedīvī, -oedītum *v.i.* listen to, obey (+ dat.)

obruō, -ruere, -ruī, -rutum *v.t.* overwhelm, bury; destroy

obscēnus *or* **obscaenus, -a, -um** (w. comp. + sup.) *adj.* filthy, offensive; ill-omened

obscūritās, -ātis *nf.* darkness; obscurity

obscūrō, -āre, -āvī, -ātum *v.t.* darken, obscure, hide, suppress

obscūrus, -a, -um (w. comp. + sup.) *adj.* dark, obscure; unfamiliar; hard to understand; humble, low

obsecrō, -secrāre, -secrāvī, -secrātum *v.t.* appeal, entreat, beg

obsequium, -ī *nnt.* deference; compliance, obedience; flattery

obsequor, obsequī, obsecūtus sum *v.d.i.* comply with, yield to, obey; indulge (+ dat.)

obserō, -serāre, -serāvī, -serātum *v.t.* latch, bolt, bar

observātiō, -ōnis *nf.* observation, noticing, watching

observō, -servāre, -servāvī, -servātum *v.t.* observe, notice; attend to; guard

obses, -sidis *nm/f.* hostage; surety, pledge
obsideō, -sidēre, -sēdī, -sessum *v.t., v.i.* stay; besiege; lie in wait for
obsidiō, -ōnis *nf.* siege; blockade
obsignō, -signāre, -signāvī, -signātum *v.t.* seal, stamp with a seal; seal up
obsistō, -sistere, -stitī, -stitum *v.t.* cross, oppose (+ dat.)
obsolētus, -a, -um (w. comp.) *adj.* worn out, decayed; poor; ordinary
obstetrīx, -trīcis *nf.* midwife
obstinātiō, -ōnis *nf.* firmness; stubbornness
obstō, -stāre, -stitī, -stātum *v.t.* stand before; hinder, obstruct; oppose (+ dat.)
obstruō, -struere, -strūxī, -strūctum *v.t.* build against; block, impede
obstupefaciō, -facere- fēcī, -factum *v.t.* amaze, astound
obsum, -esse, -fuī, -futūrum *v.i.* be against; hurt (+ dat.)
obtegō, -tegere, -tēxī, -tēctum *v.t.* cover over, protect, keep secret
obtemperō, -temperāre, -temperāvī, -temperātum *v.t.* comply, obey
obterō, -terere, -trīvī, -trītum *v.t.* crush, trample; destroy
obtestor, obtestārī, obtestātus sum *v.d.t.* protest; call as witness; implore in the name of the gods
obtineō, -tinēre, -tinuī, -tentum *v.t., v.i.* hold fast, maintain, assert
obtingō, -tingere, -tigī, --- *v.t., v.i.* befall, happen
obtrectō, -trectāre, -trectāvī, -trectātum *v.t., v.i.* disparage; be opposed to
obtūrō, -āre, ---, -ātum *v.t.* plug, stop up
obveniō, -venīre, -vēnī, -ventum *v.i.* meet on the way; go to meet; befall
obviam *adv.* in the way, against, in face of; to meet
obvius, -a, -um *adj.* in the way, across the path; to meet; against; open, exposed
occāsiō, -ōnis *nf.* occasion, opportunity; excuse, pretext
occāsus, -ūs *nm.* setting of a heavenly body; the west; fall, destruction; death
occidēns, -entis *nm.* west; evening
occidentālis, -is, -e *adj.* west, western
occīdiō, -ōnis *nf.* slaughter, utter extermination
occīdō, -cīdere, -cīdī, -cīsum *v.t.* strike down; kill
occidō, -cidere, -cidī, -cāsum *v.i.* fall, perish; set (*of heavenly bodies*)
occlūdō, -clūdere, -clūsī, -clūsum *v.t.* stop up, close, obstruct, prevent
occultō, -āre, -āvī, -ātum *v.t.* conceal, hide
occultus, -a, -um (w. comp. + sup.) *adj.* concealed, hidden, secret
occupātiō, -ōnis *nf.* seizure; business
occupātus, -a, -um *adj.* busy, engaged (+ **in** + abl.)

occupō, -āre, -āvī, -ātum *v.t.* seize; attack; surprise; anticipate; take up

occurrō, -currere, -currī, -cursum *v.i.* meet, encounter; attack; oppose; occur

ōceanus, -ī *nm.* ocean, the outer sea

octāvus, -a, -um *adj.* eighth

octō *num.* (*indecl.*) eight

Octōber, Octōbris, Octōbre *adj.* October (*usu. w.* **mēnsis**); **Octōber, -bris** *nm.* October

octōgintā *num.* (*indecl.*) eighty

oculus, -ī *nm.* eye

ōdī, ōdisse, ōsūrum *v.t.* (*def.*) hate, dislike, be displeased with

odiōsus, -a, -um (w. comp.) *adj.* offensive, hateful, unpleasant

odium, -ī *nnt.* hatred, enmity; offense; disgust

odor, odōris *nm.* aroma, scent, perfume, odor, stench

odōrātus, -ūs *nm.* smell; sense of smell

offendō, -fendere, -fendī, -fēnsum *v.i.* stumble, blunder; find; offend, displease

offēnsiō, -ōnis *nf.* stumbling; aversion; misfortune

offēnsus, -a, -um *adj.* vexed; offensive

offerō, -ferre, obtulī, oblātum *v.t.* present, bring before, offer; inflict

officīna, -ae *nf.* workshop, manufactory

officiō, -ficere, -fēcī, -fectum *v.i.* hinder, oppose; hurt

officium, -ī *nnt.* service, favor, duty; office; function

offirmō, -firmāre, -firmāvī, -firmātum *v.t., v.i.* make firm; persevere, be obstinate

olea, -ae *nf.* olive; olive tree

oleō, -ēre, oluī, --- *v.i.* smell (*emit an odor*)

oleōsus, -a, -um *adj.* oily, full of oil

oleum, -ī *nnt.* oil

ōlim *adv.* formerly, once, long since; ever; some time, some day

olfaciō, -facere, -fēcī, -factum *v.t.* smell (*track by smell*)

olla, -ae *nf.* pot, jar

ōmen, -inis *nnt.* omen, sign

ōminor, ōminārī, ōminātus sum *v.d.t.* predict, augur

omittō, -mittere, -mīsī, -missum *v.t.* let go, let loose; give up; throw away; omit

omnīnō *adv.* quite, completely; certainly, no doubt

omnis, -is, -e *adj.* every, all, entire; **omnēs, -ium** *nm/f./pl.* everybody, all; **omnia, -ium** *nnt./pl.* everything, all things

onerō, -āre, -āvī, -ātum *v.t.* load, burden; oppress, make worse

onus, oneris *nnt.* freight, load, burden
opera, -ae *nf.* work, effort, labor
operārius, -ī *nm.* workman, laborer
operculum, -ī *nnt.* lid, cover
operiō, -perīre, operuī, opertum *v.t.* conceal, close; burden
operōsus, -a, -um (w. comp. + sup.) *adj.* painstaking; industrious; troublesome, difficult
opifex, -ficis *nm/f.* maker, workman, artisan
opiniō, -ōnis *nf.* opinion, belief; conjecture
opinor, opīnārī, opīnātus sum *v.d.i.t.* suppose, imagine, think; judge
oportet, oportēre, oportuit, --- *v.i.* (*imp.*) it is necessary, one must (+ subjv. *or* + acc. + infv.)
oppidum, -ī *nnt.* town; city
oppōnō, -pōnere, -posuī, -positum *v.t.* oppose, place opposite; bring forward, present
opportūnitās, -ātis *nf.* suitableness, advantage
opportūnus, -a, -um *adj.* suitable, convenient; useful, advantageous
opprimō, -primere, -pressī, -pressum *v.t.* press against; oppress, treat cruelly; put down, crush, sink; surprise
opprobrium, -ī *nnt.* scandal, disgrace, reproach
oppūgnātiō, -ōnis *nf.* assault, attack
oppūgnō, -pūgnāre, -pūgnāvī, -pūgnātum *v.t.* attack, assault
ops, opis *nf.* aid, help; power; **opēs, opum** *nf./pl.* substance, wealth
optābilis, -is, -e *adj.* desirable
optātiō, -ōnis *nf.* wish
optātum, -ī *nnt.* wish, desire
optātus, -a, -um *adj.* wished for, desired; pleasing
optimus, -a, -um *adj.* best, excellent; aristocratic; **optimē** *adv.* best
optiō, -ōnis *nf.* option, choice
optō, -āre, -āvī, -ātum *v.t.* wish, choose, prefer; long for
opus, -eris *nnt.* labor, work; building; work of art; deed, action; **opus est, esse, fuit** *v.i.* (*imp.*) there is need of, it is necessary (+ abl. of the thing needed *or* + acc. + infv.)
ōra, -ae *nf.* edge, border, boundary; territory, region; seacoast
ōrāculum, -ī *nnt.* oracle; divine response; prophecy
ōrātiō, -ōnis *nm.* speaking, speech; diction, style; set speech, oration; subject, theme; eloquence
ōrātor, -ōris *nm.* orator, speaker; legate, ambassador
orbis, -is *nm.* circle, ring; disk; wheel; region, territory; circuit

orbitās, -ātis *nf.* destitution; childlessness; orphanhood

orbō, -āre, -āvī, -ātum *v.t.* deprive; rob; make destitute; bereave

orbus, -a, -um *adj.* destitute; bereaved; orphaned; childless

ōrdinātiō, -ōnis *nf.* act of arrangement

ōrdinātus, -a, -um *adj.* orderly, arranged

ōrdinō, -āre, -āvī, -ātum *v.t.* adjust, set in order; govern

ordior, ordīrī, orsus sum *v.d.i.t.* begin, undertake

ōrdō, -inis *nm.* row, line; arrangement; rank; social class

oriēns, orientis *nm.* rising sun, morning sun; east

orientālis, -is, -e *adj.* east, eastern

orīgō, -inis *nf.* origin, source, start; lineage, descent

orior, orīrī, ortus sum *v.d.i.* arise, come into existence; descend; begin; be born, descend from

ōrnāmentum, -ī *nnt.* decoration, ornament; mark of honor

ōrnātiō, -ōnis *nf.* decoration, adornment

ōrnātrīx, -trīcis *nf.* hairdresser

ōrnō, -āre, -āvī, -ātum *v.t.* furnish, equip; adorn; honor

ōrō, -āre, -āvī, -ātum *v.i.* plead, beg, entreat; argue

ortus, -ūs *nm.* rise, origin, source; rising of a heavenly body; birth

ōs, ōris *nnt.* mouth; opening, aperture

os, ossis *nnt.* bone; marrow

oscillō, -āre, -āvī, -ātum *v.t., v.i.* swing

oscitātiō, -ōnis *nf.* yawn, gaping

oscitō, -āre, -āvī, -ātum *v.i.* yawn, gape

ōsculor, osculārī, osculātus sum *v.d.t.* kiss; **osculum, -ī** *nnt.* kiss

ostendō, -tendere, -tendī, -tentum *v.t.* stretch out; show, disclose, make known

ostentātiō, -ōnis *nf.* show, display; pomp, parade

ostentō, -āre, -āvī, -ātum *v.t.* show, exhibit; show off, boast

ostium, -ī *nnt.* door, entrance, mouth

ostrea, -ae *nf.* oyster, mussel

ōtiōsus, -a, -um (w. comp. + sup.) *adj.* idle, at leisure; neutral, indifferent; peaceful

ōtium, -ī *nnt.* relaxation, leisure, quiet, peace

ovātiō, -ōnis *nf.* ovation, a lesser triumph

ōvātus, -a, -um *adj.* oval

ovis, -is *nf.* sheep

ovō, -āre, -āvī, -ātum *v.i.* rejoice; receive an ovation

ōvum, -ī *nnt.* egg

P

pabulum, -ī *nnt.* fodder; nourishment
pacīscor, pacīscī, pactus sum *v.d.i.t.* agree upon, form a compact, stipulate
pācō, -āre, -āvī, -ātum *v.t.* subdue, pacify
pactiō, -ōnis *nf.* agreement, contract
pactum, -ī *nnt.* agreement, contract
paedagōgus, -ī *nm.* slave that attended children; tutor
paene *adv.* almost, nearly, practically
paenitentia, -ae *nf.* repentance
paeniteō, -ēre, paenituī, --- *v.t.* make sorry; be sorry, repent; **paenitet, paenitēre, paenituit, ---** *v.t.* (*imp.*) it repents, it is sorry, it grieves; it displeases, it offends (+ acc. of person + gen. of thing)
pāgānus, -a, -um *adj.* belonging to a village; rustic, rural
pāgina, -ae *nf.* page
pāla, -ae *nf.* spade
palam *adv.* openly, publicly
palla, -ae *nf.* palla (*woman's mantle*)
palleō, -ēre, palluī, --- *v.i.* be pale
pallidus, -a, -um *adj.* pale
pallium, -ī *nnt.* pallium (*man's mantle*)
palma, -ae *nf.* palm of the hand; palm branch, palm tree; oar blade
palpebra, -ae *nf.* eyelid; eyelash
palpitō, -āre, -āvī, -ātum *v.i.* throb, tremble
pālus, -ī *nm.* stake, post
palus, palūdis *nf.* swamp, marsh
pandō, -ere, pandī, passum *v.t.* spread, spread out, unfold; throw open; reveal, explain
pangō, -ere, pepigī (pēgī), pāctum *v.t.* fasten; agree upon, contract; betroth
pānis, -is *nm.* bread
pannōsus, -a, -um *adj.* ragged, tattered
pannus, -ī *nm.* piece of cloth, patch, rag
pāpiliō, -ōnis *nm.* butterfly
papilla, -ae *nf.* nipple; breast
papyrus, -ī *nf.* papyrus
pār (par-) *adj.* equal, alike, matching (+ dat.); suitable; **pāriter** *adv.* equally, in similar manner; at the same time; **pār, paris** *nnt.* couple, pair

parallēlus, -a, -um *adj.* parallel
paralysis, -is *nf.* paralysis
parasīticus, -a, -um *adj.* parasitic
parasītus, -ī *nm.* guest; toady, parasite
parātus, -a, -um (w. comp. + sup.) *adj.* ready, prepared (+ **ad** + acc.);
  provided; skilled
parcō, -ere, pepercī (parsī), parsum *v.t.* spare; treat forbearingly;
  abstain, cease
parcus, -a, -um (w. sup.) *adj.* economical, thrifty; stingy (+ gen.); moderate; spare, little; **parcē** (w. comp. + sup.) *adv.* sparingly, thriftily;
  stingily
parēns, parentis *nm/f.* parent; ancestor
pāreō, -ēre, pāruī, pāritum *v.i.* appear, be visible; obey, submit
pariēs, pariētis *nm.* wall, house wall
pariō, -ere, peperī, partum *v.t.* bring forth; give birth to; acquire, gain
pāriter *adv.* equally, alike; at the same time, together
parma, -ae *nf.* small round cavalry shield
parō, -āre, -āvī, -ātum *v.t.*, vi. prepare, make ready; design, intend; get,
  acquire
parricīda, -ae *nm.* one that commits parricide; murderer, assassin
parricīdium, -ī *nnt.* parricide; murder, assassination
pars, partis *nf.* part, portion; party, side; office; role; region; direction
parsimōnia, -ae *nf.* economy, frugality
particeps (particip-) *adj.* sharing, partaking in (+ gen.); **particeps, -cipis**
  nm. partner, colleague
particula, -ae *nf.* particle
partim *adv.* partly, in part
partiō, -īre, -īvī, -ītum *v.t.* share, divide; take a share in
partītiō, -ōnis *nf.* partition, division
parturiō, -īre, -īvī, --- *v.t.* be pregnant, have a baby
partus, -ūs *nm.* bearing; childbirth, delivery; motherhood; offspring
parum *adv.* too little, insufficiently
parvus, -a, -um (comp. **minor**; sup. **minimus**) *adj.* little, insignificant
pascō, -ere, pāvī, pastum *v.t.*, v.i. feed, support, nourish; graze
passim *adv.* here and there
passus, -a, -um *adj.* spread out, outstretched; spread out to dry; **passus, -ūs**
  nm. step, pace, footstep; track, trace
pāstor, -ōris *nm.* shepherd
pāstus, -ūs *nm.* feeding, pasture, fodder

patefaciō, -facere, -fēcī, -factum *v.t.* open up, reveal
patefactiō, -ōnis *nf.* revelation, disclosing
pateō, -ēre, patuī, --- *v.i.* lie open, be accessible, be evident
pater, patris *nm.* father; **patrēs, patrum** *nm./pl.* ancestors; senators;
    pater familiās, patris familiās *nm.* male head of the household
paternus, -a, -um *adj.* of a father, paternal; pertaining to one's native
    country
patēscō, -ēre, patuī, --- *v.i.* spread, open out, extend, lie open
patiēns (patient-) (w. comp. + sup.) *adj.* supporting; enduring; able to
    endure
patientia, -ae *nf.* endurance, suffering, patience, indulgence
patina, -ae *nf.* plate, dish
patior, patī, passus sum *v.d.t.* bear, endure; allow, permit
patria, -ae *nf.* country, native land; home
patricius, -a, -um *adj.* patrician, noble
patrimōnium, -ī *nnt.* patrimony
patrius, -a, -um *adj.* pertaining to a father, fatherly; hereditary, ancestral;
    native
patrōna, -ae *nf.* patroness, protector
patrōnus, -ī *nm.* patron, defender
patruēlis, -is *nm/f.* paternal cousin
patruus, -ī *nm.* paternal uncle
paucus, -a, -um *adj.* few; small, little; **paucī, -ōrum** *nm./pl.* a few;
    pauca, -ōrum *nnt./pl.* a few things, a few words
paulātim *adv.* little by little, gradually
paulisper *adv.* for a short time, for a little while
paulus *or* **paullus, -a, -um** *adj.* little, slight, small; **paulō** *adv.* by a little, a
    little; **paulō post** *adv.* soon after; **paulum** *adv.* a little, somewhat
pauper (pauper-) (comp. **pauperior**; sup. **pauperrimus**) *adj.* poor, not
    wealthy; scanty
paupertās, -ātis *nf.* poverty
paveō, -ēre, pāvī, --- *v.t., v.i.* be struck with terror, tremble, be terrified
pavīmentum, -ī *nnt.* pavement
pāvō, -ōnis *nm.* peacock
pavor, -ōris *nm.* trembling, fear, dread, panic
pāx, pācis *nf.* peace, harmony, tranquillity; pact of peace
peccātum, -ī *nnt.* sin, moral wrong
peccō, -āre, -āvī, -ātum *v.t., v.i.* offend, transgress, commit a fault
pecten, -inis *nm.* comb; rake

pectō, -ere, pexī, pectum (pectitum) *v.t.* comb

pectus, -oris *nnt.* chest, breast, upper body

pecūliāris, -is, -e *adj.* belonging to one's private property; special, particular

pecūnia, -ae *nf.* money, wealth

pecus, -oris *nnt.* herd (*especially of cattle*); **pecus, -udis** *nf.* herd of cattle, herd of sheep

pedes, -itis *nm.* one traveling on foot; foot soldier; **peditēs, -itum** *nm./pl.* infantry

pedester, pedestris, pedestre (pedestr-) *adj.* pedestrian, on foot; on land

pedica, -ae *nf.* trap, snare

pēgma, -atis *nnt.* bookcase

pēierō (pēiūrō), -ierāre, -ierāvī, -ierātum *v.t.* swear falsely, perjure

pēior (peji-), pēior, pēius (pēiōr-) *adj.* worse; **pēius** *adv.* worse, rather badly

pellis, -is *nf.* hide, skin; leather

pellō, -ere, pepulī, pulsum *v.t.* strike; push, force back; banish, remove

pelvis, -is *nf.* basin

pendeō, -ēre, pependī, --- *v.i.* hang, hang down, overhang; be dependent; hesitate

pendō, -ere, pependī, pēnsum *v.t.* weigh, consider, value, judge

penes *prep.* (+ acc.) in the power of, in the possession of

penetrō, -āre, -āvī, -ātum *v.i.* penetrate, enter; reach

pēnicillus, -ī *nm.* brush

pēnis, -is *nm.* tail; penis

penitus *adv.* inwardly, deeply; throughout

penna, -ae *nf.* feather; pen, quill

pēnsiō, -ōnis *nf.* payment

pēnsum, -ī *nnt.* allotment of wool; charge; weight, importance

pēnūria, -ae *nf.* want, lack

pepō, -onis *nm.* melon, pumpkin

per *prep.* (+ acc.) through, across, along; during, in the course of; by means of, for the sake of

pēra, -ae *nf.* wallet, bag, backpack

peragō, -agere, -ēgī, -āctum *v.t.* drive through, pierce; pass through; disturb; accomplish; describe

percellō, -ere, -culī, -culsum *v.t.* beat down; overthrow; dishearten

percipiō, -cipere, -cēpī, -ceptum *v.t.* seize; perceive; learn, understand; gather

percontor (percunctor), percontārī, percontātus sum *v.d.t.* inquire, investigate

percurrō, -currere, -cucurrī (currī), -cursum *v.t.* travel; hasten, pass over quickly

percutiō, -cutere, -cussī, -cussum *v.t.* pierce; kill, strike down

perditus, -a, -um (w. comp. + sup.) *adj.* miserable, desperate, wretched; ruined; corrupt, profligate

perdō, -dere, -didī, -ditum *v.t.* waste; ruin; lose completely

perdūcō, -dūcere, -dūxī, -ductum *v.t.* lead through; prolong; induce

peregrīnātiō, -ōnis *nf.* traveling abroad, wandering

peregrīnor, peregrīnārī, peregrīnātus sum *v.d.i.* travel abroad, wander

peregrīnus, -a, -um *adj.* foreign, strange; **peregrīnus, -ī** *nm.* alien, foreigner

perennis, -is, -e *adj.* lasting through the year; lasting

pereō, -īre, -īvī (-iī), -itum *v.i.* pass away, disappear; perish; fail

perfectus, -a, -um (w. comp. + sup.) *adj.* complete, finished; excellent, perfect

perferō, -ferre, -tulī, -lātum *v.t.* sustain, endure, put up with; bring; announce; accomplish

perficiō, -ficere, -fēcī, -fectum *v.t.* complete, carry out, perform; cause

perfidia, -ae *nf.* treachery, faithlessness

perfluō, -fluere, -flūxī, -flūxum *v.t., v.i.* leak, stream through

perforō, -forāre, -forāvī, -forātum *v.t.* pierce, bore through

perfringō, -fringere, -frēgī, -frāctum *v.t.* shatter, fracture; violate

perfruor, perfruī, perfrūctus sum *v.d.i.* be delighted (+ abl.)

perfugiō, -fugere, -fūgī, --- *v.i.* flee, escape; desert; take refuge

perfugium, -ī *nnt.* refuge, asylum

perfundō, -fundere, -fūdī, -fūsum *v.t.* pour over, drench; dye; scatter; inspire; fill

perfungor, perfungī, perfūnctus sum *v.d.i.* perform; undergo; pass through (+ abl.)

pergō, -ere, perrēxī, perrēctum *v.t., v.i.* proceed, march; hasten

perīclitor, perīclitārī, perīclitātus sum *v.d.i.t.* try, test; risk; be in danger

perīculōsus, -a, -um (w. comp. + sup.) *adj.* dangerous

perīculum, -ī *nnt.* trial, lawsuit; risk, danger

perimō, -imere, -ēmī, -emptum *v.t.* take away completely, annihilate; prevent; kill

perinde *adv.* just so, in the same manner

periodus, -ī *nf.* period; a complete sentence

peristylum, -ī *nnt.* peristyle (*an open court surrounded by a colonnade*)

perītus, -a, um (w. comp. + sup.) *adj.* competent, experienced (+ gen.)

periūrium (perj-), -ī *nnt.* false oath, perjury

permaneō, -manēre, -mānsī, -mānsum *v.i.* remain, abide, last, continue, persist

permittō, -mittere, -mīsī, -missum *v.t.* let go, surrender; put in charge of, entrust; allow, grant

permoveō, -movēre, -mōvī, -mōtum *v.t.* move deeply, impress, influence; arouse, agitate

permultus, -a, -um *adj.* very much; **permultī, -ae, -a** *adj./pl.* very many, in great numbers

permūtātio, -ōnis *nf.* change; exchange

permūtō, -mūtāre, -mūtāvī, -mūtātum *v.t.* change; exchange

perna, -ae *nf.* ham

perniciēs, -ēī *nf.* destruction, overthrow, disaster

perniciōsus, -a, -um (w. comp. + sup.) *adj.* destructive, pernicious

pernīx (pernīc-) *adj.* nimble, agile

pernoctō, -noctāre, -noctāvī, -noctātum *v.i.* spend the night, pass the night

perpellō, -pellere, -pulī, --- *v.t.* drive, compel; induce

perpetuitās, -ātis *nf.* continuous duration, perpetuity

perpetuus, -a, -um *adj.* continuous, uninterrupted

perscrībō, -scrībere, -scrīpsī, -scrīptum *v.t.* write out, detail, put on record, register

persequor, persequī, persecūtus sum *v.d.t.* follow, pursue; prosecute; avenge; accomplish; relate

persevērō, -sevērāre, -sevērāvī, -sevērātum *v.t., v.i.* persist, persevere

persolvō, -solvere, -solvī, -solūtum *v.t.* unravel, solve; explain; pay out; give, inflict

persōna, -ae *nf.* mask; part, character in a play; person

perspiciō, -spicere, -spexī, -spectum *v.t.* look into, examine, discern

perstō, -stare, -stitī, -stātum *v.i.* stand firm, persist, endure

perstringō, -stringere, -strīnxī, -strictum *v.t.* touch deeply, affect; wound; thrill

persuādeō, -suādēre, -suāsī, -suāsum *v.t.* persuade; prevail upon (+ dat. of person persuaded *or* + **ut** or **nē** + subjv.)

perterreō, -terrēre, -terruī, -territum *v.t.* terrify

pertinācia, -ae *nf.* stubbornness, persistence

pertināx (pertināc-) *adj.* tenacious, stubborn, persistent

pertineō, -tinēre, -tinuī, --- *v.i.* reach, extend to; belong; concern; conduce

perturbō, -turbāre, -turbāvī, -turbātum *v.t.* agitate, disturb greatly

pervagor, pervagārī, pervagātus sum *v.d.i.t.* wander about; spread through; be known

perveniō, -venīre, -vēnī, -ventum *v.i.* arrive, come to the end of a journey, reach (+ **ad** + acc.)

pervium, -ī *nnt.* passage

pervulgō, -vulgāre, -vulgāvī, -vulgātum *v.t.* publish; make available; frequent a place

pēs, pedis *nm.* foot

pessimus, -a, -um *adj.* worst, very evil, very bad; **pessimē** *adv.* very badly

pestilentia, -ae *nf.* pestilence, plague

pestis, -is *nf.* plague, pestilence; ruin, death

petasus, -ī *nm.* broad-brimmed hat

petītiō, -ōnis *nf.* thrust, blow, attack; canvassing for votes; application, request, claim

petītor, -ōris *nm.* suitor, plaintiff, petitioner; candidate

petō, -ere, -īvī, -ītum *v.t.* aim at, strive toward; attack; demand (+ **ut** or **nē** + subjv.); entreat office

petulantia, -ae *nf.* pertness, impudence

pharus, -ī *nm.* lighthouse

phasēlus, -ī *nm.* bean, kidney bean

phāsiānus, -ī *nm.* pheasant

philosophia, -ae *nf.* philosophy

philosophus, -ī *nm.* philosopher

phōca, -ae *nf.* seal (*zool.*)

physicus, -a, -um *adj.* belonging to natural philosophy

piāculum, -ī *nnt.* expiation of sin; placating of a deity; punishment for sacrilege

pictor, -ōris *nm.* painter

pictūra, -ae *nf.* drawing, painting

pietās, -ātis *nf.* dutifulness towards parents and country; gratitude; loyalty, patriotism

piger, pigra, pigrum (comp. **pigrior**; sup. **pigerrimus**) *adj.* inactive, lazy, sluggish

piget, pigēre, piguit (pigitum est), --- *v.t.* (*imp.*) it annoys; it disgusts; it makes sorry (+ acc. of person + gen. of thing)

pigmentum, -ī *nnt.* paint, pigment

pignerō, -āre, -āvī , -ātum *v.t.* take as a pledge, lay claim to

pignus, -oris (-eris) *nnt.* pawn; pledge; security; hostage; wager
pila, -ae *nf.* ball; ball game
pilula, -ae *nf.* small ball
pīlum, -ī *nnt.* pilum (*heavy javelin*)
pilus, -ī *nm.* a hair; trifle
pingō, -ere, pinxī, pictum *v.t.* paint, depict; stain; decorate
pinguis, -is, -e (w. comp. + sup.) *adj.* fertile; plump, chubby; stupid
pīnus, -ūs (-ī) *nf.* pine tree, fir tree
piper, piperis *nnt.* pepper
pīrāta, -ae *nm.* pirate
pirum, -ī *nnt.* pear
piscātor, -ōris *nm.* fisherman
piscātus, -ūs *nm.* fishing, catching of fish
piscis, -is *nm.* fish
piscor, piscārī, piscātus sum *v.d.i.* fish
pistor, -ōris *nm.* miller; baker
pistrīnum, -ī *nnt.* mill; bakery
pistrīx, -strīcis *nf.* shark
pīsum, -ī *nnt.* pea
pītuīta, -ae *nf.* phlegm
pius, -a, -um (w. sup.) *adj.* dutiful, conscientious, devout, devoted, faithful, loving
pix, picis *nf.* tar, pitch
placenta, -ae *nf.* cake
placeō, -ēre, placuī, placitum *v.t.* please; meet with approval; satisfy (+ dat.); **placet, placēre, placuit (placitum est)** *v.i.* (*imp.*) it pleases, it seems good to (+ **ut** + subjv. *or* + infv. *or* + acc. + infv.)
plācō, -āre, -āvī, -ātum *v.t.* quiet, calm, appease
plaga, -ae *nf.* mesh, net
planta, -ae *nf.* green twig, cutting, graft; sole of the foot
plānus, -a, -um (w. comp. + sup.) *adj.* level, flat; humble; clear, distinct; **plānē** (w. comp. + sup.) *adv.* plainly, clearly; wholly
plaudō, plaudere, plausī, plausum *v.t.* applaud, clap, praise
plaustrum *or* **plōstrum, -ī** *nnt.* cart, wagon
plausus, -ūs *nm.* applause
plēbēius, -ī *nm.* plebeian
plēbiscītum, -ī *nnt.* plebiscite, decree of the people
plēbs, plēbis (plēbēs, -ēī) *nf.* the common people, the plebs, plebeian order; mass, multitude

plēnus

plēnus, -a, -um (w. comp. + sup.) _adj._ full, filled with (+ gen. _or_ + abl.);
    complete
plērusque, plēraque, plērumque _adj._ most, majority; **plērumque** _adv._
    generally, for the most part; **plērique, plērōrumque** _nm./pl._ the
    majority, almost all
plōrātus, -ūs _nm._ cry of distress, lamenting
pluit, pluere, pluit, --- _v.i._ (_imp._) it is raining
plūma, -ae _nf._ down, fine feathers
plumbārius, -ī _nm._ plumber
plumbum, -ī _nnt._ lead
plūres, plūrēs, plūra (plūr-) _adj./pl._ more
plūrimus, -a, -um _adj._ most; **plūrimum** _adv._ very much; for the most part
plūs, plūris _nnt._ more
pluteus, -ī _nm._ shelter; shelf; bookcase
pluvia, -ae _nf._ rain, shower
pluvius, -a, -um _adj._ rainy, stormy
pōculum, -ī _nnt._ cup
poēma, -atis _nnt._ poem, poetry
poena, -ae _nf._ penalty, punishment, vengeance, recompense
poēta, -ae _nm._ poet
poliō, -īre, -īvī, -ītum _v.t._ refine, polish, embellish
pollex, -licis _nm._ thumb
polliceor, pollicērī, pollicitus sum _v.d.t._ promise (+ present infv. _or_ +
    acc. + future infv.); offer
polluō, -ere, polluī, pollūtum _v.t._ stain, pollute, desecrate, violate, disgrace
polus, -ī _nm._ axis; pole of the earth
pōmārium, -ī _nnt._ orchard
pompa, -ae _nf._ solemn procession; retinue
pōmum, -ī _nnt._ fruit, orchard fruit
pondus, -eris _nnt._ weight, mass, load; importance, authority
pōne _adv._ behind; _prep._ (+ acc.) behind
pōnō, -ere, posuī, positum _v.t._ lay, place, put (+ **in** + abl.); lay aside;
    allay; spend
pōns, pontis _nm._ bridge
pontifex, -ficis _nm._ high priest, pontifex
popīna, -ae _nf._ place that served food and drink, shop
populāris, -is, -e _adj._ popular, of the people; democratic; political;
    populārēs, -ium _nm./pl._ the popular party
populātiō, -ōnis _nf._ devastation, ravaging

populor, populārī, populātus sum *v.d.t.* pillage, devastate

populus, -ī *nm.* nation, people; multitude

porcus, -ī *nm.* pig, hog

porrigō, -rigere, -rēxī, -rēctum *v.t.* hold forth, hold out; reach; offer

porrō *adv.* forward, onward; at a distance; formerly; in the future; again, next; moreover

porta, -ae *nf.* gate, city-gate, gate of a camp

portentum, -ī *nnt.* portent, omen; monster

porticus, -ūs *nf.* covered walkway, colonnade

portō, -āre, -āvī, -ātum *v.t.* carry, bear, take

portōrium, -ī *nnt.* tariff, customs

portus, -ūs *nm.* harbor, port; refuge

poscō, -ere, poposcī, --- *v.t.* require, demand, need

possessiō, -ōnis *nf.* occupation, seizure

possideō, -sidēre, -sēdī, -sessum *v.t.* own, hold, occupy

possum, posse, potuī, --- *v.i.* be able, can (+ infv.); have power, have influence

post *adv.* behind, backwards; afterwards, later; next; *prep.* (+ acc.) after; behind; inferior to

posteā *adv.* after that, later, afterwards; **posteāquam** (+ indv.) *conj.* afterwards, thereafter

posterior, posterior, posterius (posteriōr-) *adj.* latter; later; **posterius** *adv.* later, at a later date

posteritās, -ātis *nf.* the future; future generations

posterus, -a, -um *adj.* subsequent, following, future; **posterī, -ōrum** *nm./pl.* posterity

posthāc *adv.* after this, in the future

postis, -is *nm.* doorpost; door

postmerīdiānus (pōmerīdiānus), -a, -um *adj.* afternoon

postmodum *adv.* after a while, afterwards

postquam (w. indv. in direct discourse; w. subjv. in indirect discourse) *conj.* after; when; as soon as; because

postrēmus, -a, -um *adj.* last, hindmost; **postrēmō** *adv.* at last, finally

postrīdiē *adv.* next day

postulātiō, -ōnis *nf.* demand, claim; complaint

postulō, -āre, -āvī, -ātum *v.t.* ask; demand (+ **ut** or **nē** + subjv.)

pote (potis) *adj.* (*indecl.*) capable, able

potēns (potent-) (w. comp. + sup.) *adj.* strong, able, powerful, having influence (+ gen. *or* + abl.)

potentia, -ae *nf.* power, might; authority; influence

potestās, -ātis *nf.* power, control; legal power or authority

pōtiō, -ōnis *nf.* beverage, drink; drinking

potior, potior, potius (potiōr-) *adj.* better, preferable; more important;
    potius *adv.* rather, more;

potior, potīrī, potītus sum *v.d.i.t.* take possession of, become master of;
    possess (+ abl. *or* + gen. *or* + acc.)

potis (pote) *adj.* (*indecl.*) capable, able

potissimus, -a, -um *adj.* most important, chief

prae *prep.* (+ abl.) in front of; compared with; because of

praeacūtus, -a, -um *adj.* pointed, sharpened

praebeō, -bēre, -buī, -bitum *v.t.* hold forth, offer, present, supply, grant

praecaveō, -cavēre, -cāvī, -cautum *v.i.* safeguard, take precautions (+
    dat.)

praeceps (praecipit-) *adj.* headlong; in haste, hasty; steep

praeceptum, -ī *nnt.* maxim, teaching; order

praecīdō, -cīdere, -cīdī, -cīsum *v.t.* cut short, abbreviate; mutilate

praecipiō, -cipere, -cēpī, -ceptum *v.t.* anticipate; instruct, command (+
    dat. of person + **ut** or **nē** + subjv.)

praecipuus, -a, -um *adj.* particular, special, outstanding; **praecipuē** *adv.*
    especially

praeclārus, -a, -um (w. comp. + sup.) *adj.* outstanding, remarkable,
    excellent; **praeclārē** (w. sup.) *adv.* very plainly; excellently

praeda, -ae *nf.* plunder, booty; prey; gain

praedīcō, -dīcere, -dīxī, -dictum *v.t., v.i.* prophesy, predict; advise, warn

praeditus, -a, -um *adj.* gifted, endowed, provided (+ abl.)

praedō, -ōnis *nm.* robber, plunderer

praedor, praedārī, praedātus sum *v.d.i.t.* plunder, rob

praeeō, -īre, -īvī (-iī), -itum *v.t.* precede (+ dat. *or* + acc.); prescribe (+ acc.)

praefectus, -ī *nm.* overseer, superintendant; civil or military officer; prefect;
    praefectus classis, praefectī classis *nm.* officer of a fleet, admiral

praeferō, -ferre, -tulī, -lātum *v.t.* carry in front of; set before; prefer;
    reveal

praeficiō, -ficere, -fēcī, -fectum *v.t.* put in charge of, appoint

praemium, -ī *nnt.* recompense, reward

praenōmen, -inis *nnt.* praenomen (*first name of a Roman male*)

praepōnō, -pōnere, -posuī, -positum *v.t.* place before, place in command;
    set before, prefer

praepositiō, -ōnis *nf.* placing before; preposition; preference

praescrībō, -scrībere, -scrīpsī, -scrīptum *v.t.* write before; determine beforehand, prescribe

praesēns (praesent-) (w. comp. + sup.) *adj.* at hand, imminent; instant, prompt; powerful; propitious

praesentia, -ae *nf.* presence; present time

praesertim *adv.* especially, particularly

praesidium, -ī *nnt.* protection, defense; post, garrison, camp

praestāns (praestant-) (w. comp. + sup.) *adj.* excellent, superior

praestō *adv.* at hand, present

praestō sum, ~ esse, ~ fuī, ~ futūrum *v.i.* be at hand, be of help, be of service (+ dat.); **praestō, -stāre, -stitī, -stitum** *v.t.* stand out, excel; be responsible for; perform; maintain; **praesum, -esse, -fuī, -futūrum** *v.i.* be in command, head, preside over (+ dat.)

praesūmō, -sūmere, -sūmpsī, -sūmptum *v.t.* anticipate, take in advance; take for granted

praetendō, -tendere, -tendī, -tentum *v.t.* extend; offer as a pretext

praeter *prep.* (+ acc.) past; by; before; against; except

praetereā *adv.* besides, moreover

praetereō, -īre, -īvī (-iī), -itum *v.t.* go by, go past; pass by without noticing; omit

praeteritus, -a, -um *adj.* past, gone by; **praeteritia, -ōrum** *nnt./pl.* the past

praetermissiō, -ōnis *nf.* omission

praetermittō, -mittere, -mīsī, -missum *v.t.* let pass; omit, overlook

praetexta, -ae *nf.* purple border on clothing; purple bordered toga worn by the higher Roman magistrates and Roman children

praetor, -ōris *nm.* commander; praetor (*magistrate in charge of administering justice*)

praetūra, -ae *nf.* office of praetor

praevertō, -vertere, -vertī, -versum *v.t.* put first; anticipate, forestall; surprise

prandeō, -ēre, prandī, prānsum *v.i.* have lunch

prandium, -ī *nnt.* lunch

prātum, -ī *nnt.* meadow

prāvus, -a, -um (w. comp. + sup.) *adj.* crooked, wrong, immoral

precor, -ārī, precātus sum *v.d.t.* beg, entreat (+ **ut** or **nē** + subjv.); invoke

prehendō (prēnd-), -hendere, -hendī, -hēnsum *v.t.* clutch, seize; detect; arrest; reach

prēlum, -ī *nnt.* clothes press, wine or olive press

premō, -ere, pressī, pressum *v.t.* press, press hard; pursue; cover; burden, sink, crush; urge

pressūra, -ae *nf.* pressure

pressus, -a, -um *adj.* depressed, pressed down

pretiōsus, -a, -um (w. comp. + sup.) *adj.* valuable, costly

pretium, -ī *nnt.* value, price; recompense

prex, precis *nf.* (*irreg.*) plea, prayer; curse

prīdom *adv.* a long time ago

prīdiē *adv.* on the previous day

prīmus, -a, -um *adj.* first, foremost; eminent; **prīmō** *adv.* at first; **prīmum** *adv.* originally

prīnceps (prīncip-) *adj.* chief, first; **prīnceps, -cipis** *nm.* chief, leader; originator

prīncipālis, -is, -e *adj.* original, first

prīncipium, -ī *nnt.* origin, beginning; **prīncipia, -ōrum** *nnt./pl.* military headquarters

prior, prior, prius (priōr-) *adj.* former, earlier; first; **prius** *adv.* sooner; previously

prīscus, -a, -um *adj.* ancient; old-fashioned

prīstinus -a, -um *adj.* former, original

priusquam (+ subjv. to denote anticipation or prevention, otherwise + indv.) *conj.* before

prīvātus, -a, -um *adj.* personal, private

prīvigna, -ae *nf.* stepdaughter; **prīvignus, -ī** *nm.* stepson

prīvō, -āre, -āvī, -ātum *v.t.* rob, deprive; free, release

prō *prep.* (+ abl.) for; in place of; on behalf of; in comparison with; on account of

proavia, -ae *nf.* great-grandmother

proavus, -ī *nm.* great-grandfather; ancestor

probitās, -ātis *nf.* honesty, goodness

probō, -āre, -āvī, -ātum *v.t.* approve, recommend; show, prove, convince

proboscis, -scidis *nf.* trunk, snout

prōbrōsus, -a,-um *adj.* scandalous, shameful

probrum, -ī *nnt.* shameful deed, crime; unchastity, immodesty; dishonor; insult

probus, -a, -um *adj.* good, excellent; honest; **probē** *adv.* rightly, correctly; thoroughly

prōcēdō, -cēdere, -cessī, -cessum *v.i.* advance, proceed, arise, make progress, prosper

procella, -ae *nf.* storm, violent wind; commotion
procellōsus, -a, -um *adj.* rough, stormy
prōcērus, -a, -um (w. comp. + sup.) *adj.* tall
prōcōnsul, prōcōnsulis *nm.* proconsul (*governor of a province*)
prōcreātiō, -ōnis *nf.* generation, begetting, procreation
prōcreō, -creāre, -creāvī, -creātum *v.t.* bring forth, procreate, cause
procul *adv.* far off, far away; from afar
prōcūrātiō, -ōnis *nf.* administration, management
prōcūrātor, -ōris *nm.* agent, steward, manager
prōcūrō, -cūrāre, -cūrāvī, -cūrātum *v.t.* look after, administer, supervise
procus, -ī *nm.* suitor, wooer; canvasser
prōdeō, -īre, -īvī (-iī), -itum *v.i.* go out; stand out; proceed
prōdigium, -ī *nnt.* omen, portent; monster
prōdigus, -a, -um *adj.* lavish, wasteful (+ gen. *or* + **in** + abl.)
prōditor, -ōris *nm.* traitor, betrayer
prōdō, -ere, -didī, -ditum *v.t.* put forth, make known, report; betray
prōdūcō, -dūcere, -dūxī, -ductum *v.t.* bring forward, lead forward;
    extend, lengthen, prolong; postpone
proelior, proeliārī, proeliātus sum *v.d.i.* battle
proelium, -ī *nnt.* battle, fight
profānus, -a, -um *adj.* not sacred, secular, impious
profectiō, -ōnis *nf.* start of a journey, setting out
profectō *adv.* really, indeed, in fact
prōferō, -ferre, -tulī, -lātum *v.t.* produce, bring forward, publish, reveal;
    enlarge, extend
professiō, -ōnis *nf.* declaration, acknowledgment
professor, -ōris *nm.* authority; teacher, professor
prōficiō, -ficere, -fēcī, -fectum *v.t., v.i.* advance; succeed, accomplish;
    gain; help
prōficīscor, prōficīscī, prōfectus sum *v.d.i.* start, set out on a journey
prōfiteor, prōfitērī, professus sum *v.d.t.* declare publicly; acknowledge;
    promise
prōfugiō, -fugere, -fūgī, --- *v.t., v.i.* flee, escape; take refuge
profugus, -a, -um *adj.* fugitive; **profugus, -ī** *nm.* refugee
prōfundō, -fundere, -fūdī, -fūsum *v.t.* pour out; spend lavishly, squander
prōfūsus, -a, -um *adj.* hanging down; lavish, generous, immoderate,
    wasteful (+ gen.)
prōgeniēs, -ēī *nf.* descent, family; descendants; offspring
prōgredior, prōgredī, prōgressus sum *v.d.i.* advance, go forward

prōgressus, -ūs *nm.* advance; progress, improvement

prohibeō, -hibēre, -hibuī, -itum *v.t.* hold before; prevent, restrain; forbid; protect

prōiciō (prōj-), -icere, -iēcī, -iectum *v.t.* throw out, expel; extend; resign, throw away

proinde *adv.* accordingly; just so, equally

prōlātō, -lātāre, -lātāvī, -lātātum *v.t.* extend, enlarge; postpone, delay

prōlēs, -is *nf.* growth; children, descendants; child, offspring

prōlixus, -a, -um (w. comp.) *adj.* widespread, broad, long; willing; favorable

promiscuus, -a, -um *adj.* mixed; common, ordinary

prōmissum, -ī *nnt.* promise

prōmittō, -mittere, -mīsī, -missum *v.t.* put forth; promise; foretell, give hope of

prōmoveō, -movēre, -mōvī, -mōtum *v.t.* push onwards, advance, carry forward; bring to light; increase

prōmptus, -a, -um (w. comp. + sup.) *adj.* set forth; disclosed; ready for (+ **ad** + acc. *or* + abl. *or* + **in** + abl. *or* + dat.)

prōnōmen, -inis *nnt.* pronoun

prōnūntiātiō, -ōnis *nf.* public announcement; judicial decision

prōnūntiō, -nūntiāre, -nūntiāvī, -nūntiātum *v.t.* pronounce, state publicly, recite

prōnus, -a, -um *adj.* inclined forward, stooping forward (+ **ad** + acc.); inclined to, favorable (+ **in** + acc.)

prōpāgātiō, -ōnis *nf.* propagating; extension; perpetuation

prope *adv.* near; nearly, almost; *prep.* (+ acc.) near, near to, in the vicinity of

prōpellō, -pellere, -pulī, -pulsum *v.t.* drive forth, drive away; impel

properō, -āre, -āvī, -ātum *v.t., v.i.* hurry, hasten, accelerate

propinquitās, -ātis *nf.* nearness, relationship

propinquus, -a, -um *adj.* close, close to, near (+ dat.); related, kin; **propinquus, -ī** *nm.* male relation, relative; **propinqua, -ae** *nf.* female relation, relative

propior, propior, propius (propiōr-) *adj.* nearer, closer; later; of greater concern

prōpōnō, -pōnere, -posuī, -positum *v.t.* put forth, put up a notice, display; intend; point out

prōpositum, -ī *nnt.* aim, purpose, intention; theme

prōpraetor, -ōris *nm.* propraetor (*governor of a Roman province*)

proprius, -a, -um *adj.* particular, individual, private, one's own; exact, appropriate; enduring

propter *adv.* near, at hand, near by; *prep.* (+ acc.) near, close to; on account of, because of

proptereā *adv.* therefore

prōpūgnātor, -ōris *nm.* champion, defender

prōripiō, -ripere, -ripuī, -reptum *v.t.* drag out; impel

prōrsus *adv.* forward; certainly; in short, in fact

proscēnium *or* **proscaenium, -ī** *nnt.* stage of the theater

prōscrībō, -scrībere, -scrīpsī, -scrīptum *v.t.* advertise, publish a notice; confiscate property; outlaw, proscribe

prōscrīptiō, -ōnis *nf.* notice, advertisement; confiscation; proscription

prōsequor, prōsequī, prōsecūtus sum *v.d.t.* follow, escort; pursue; honor

prōsper *or* **prōsperus, -a, -um** *adj.* as desired, favorable, prosperous

prōspiciō, -spicere, -spexī, -spectum *v.t.* look out, behold; provide for

prōsum, prōdesse, prōfuī, prōfutūrum *v.t.* be of use, help (+ dat. *or* + **ad** + acc.)

prōtegō, -tegere, -tēxī, -tēctum *v.t.* cover, protect

prōtinus *or* **prōtenus** *adv.* onward; directly, without interruption, immediately

prout *adv.* accordingly, proportionately, as

prōverbium, -ī *nnt.* proverb, adage

prōvidentia, -ae *nf.* foresight, precaution

prōvideō, -vidēre, -vīdī, -vīsum *v.t., v.i.* foresee; discern; look after, be careful

prōvidus, -a, -um *adj.* foreseeing (+ gen.); prudent

prōvincia, -ae *nf.* duty; public office; command; province

prōvocō, -vocāre, -vocāvī, -vocātum *v.t.* call forth, summon; challenge

proximus, -a, -um *adj.* next, closest (+ dat.); **proximē** *adv.* next; lately; most closely

prūdēns (prūdent-) (w. comp. + sup.) *adj.* foreseeing; experienced; discreet, prudent

prūdentia, -ae *nf.* foresight; knowledge; discretion

prūnum, -ī *nnt.* plum

prūriō, -īre, -īvī, -ītum *v.i.* itch

prūrītus, -ūs *nm.* itch

psittacus, -ī *nm.* parrot

pūbertās, -ātis *nf.* puberty; age of maturity

pūbēs, -īs *nf.* young men able to bear arms; youth; throng

pūblicus, -a, -um *adj.* of the people, public; common, general, usual, ordinary

pudeō, -ēre, puduī, puditum *v.t., v.i.* feel shame, make ashamed; **pudet,
  pudēre, puduit (puditum est)** *v.i.* (*imp.*) be ashamed (+ acc. of person shamed + gen. of thing shaming)

pudor, -ōris *nm.* reserve, shame, sense of modesty or propriety; cause for
  shame, disgrace

puella, -ae *nf.* girl, maiden, young woman

puer, puerī *nm.* boy, youth; slave; **ā puerō** *adv.* from boyhood, from childhood

puerīlis, -is, -e *adj.* childish, youthful; trivial

pueritia, -ae *nf.* childhood, youth

pugillārēs, -ium *nm./pl.* notebook, writing tablets

pūgna, -ae *nf.* fist; fight, battle

pūgnō, -āre, -āvī, -ātum *v.t.* battle, fight, dispute, struggle

pulcher (pulc-), pulchra, pulchrum (comp. **pulchrior**; sup. **pulcherrimus**)
  adj. beautiful, fair, handsome; excellent; noble; glorious

pulchritūdō (pulc-), -inis *nf.* beauty; excellence

pūlex, -icis *nm.* flea

pullātus, -a, -um *adj.* dressed in mourning, dressed in dark garments

pullus, -ī *nm.* young animal; chick

pulmō, -ōnis *nm.* lung

pulsātiō, -ōnis *nf.* knocking, beating

pulsō -āre, -āvī, -ātum *v.t.* knock, beat, strike

pulsus, -ūs *nm.* beating, striking, blow; pulse of the veins; impulse; influence

pulverulentus, -a, -um *adj.* dusty

pulvīnus, -ī *nm.* cushion, pillow

pulvis, pulveris *nm.* dust, powder

pūnctum, -ī *nnt.* prick, small hole, puncture; small point of time, moment;
  small measure

pungō, -ere, pupugī, pūnctum *v.t.* puncture, stab, prick, penetrate;
  sting; vex

pūniō *or* **poeniō, -īre, -īvī, -ītum** *v.t.* punish, correct

pūpa, -ae *nf.* doll

puppis, -is *nf.* stern of a ship; ship

pūpula, -ae *nf.* eyeball

pūrgāmentum, -ī *nnt.* refuse, sweepings

purgātiō, -ōnis *nf.* purification, cleansing

purgō, -āre, -āvī, -ātum *v.t.* purify, purge, cleanse; justify

purpureus, -a, -um *adj.* purple

pūrus, -a, -um (w. comp. + sup.) *adj.* pure, clean, innocent, free from
  pollution, chaste; naked, unadorned; flawless

pūs, pūris *nnt.* pus; corrupt matter
pustula, -ae *nf.* pimple
putāmen, -inis *nnt.* nutshell
pūtēscō, -ere, pūtuī, --- *v.i.* rot, decay
puteus, -ī *nm.* pit, well
putō, -āre, -āvī, -ātum *v.t.* think, suppose, value, regard (+ acc. + infv.)
pūtridus, -a, -um *adj.* rotten, decayed
pȳramis, -idis *nf.* pyramid

Q

quā *adv.* on which side, at what place, by which way, where
quadrāgēsimus, -a, -um *adj.* fortieth
quadrāgintā *num.* (*indecl.*) forty
quadrātus, -a, -um *adj.* square, squared; **quadrātum, -ī** *nnt.* square
quadrīduum, -ī *nnt.* period of four days
quadrīgae, -ārum *nf./pl.* four-horse chariot
quadringentī, -ae, -a *num.* four hundred
quadrirēmis, -is *nf.* quadrireme (*a ship with four banks of oars*)
quadrupēs (quadruped-) *adj.* having four feet, going on four feet, on all fours
quaerō, -ere, quaesīvī, quaesītum *v.t.* seek, look for, strive to obtain (+
    ab, dē, or **ex** + abl. of person *or* + indirect question); save, acquire;
    miss, lack; demand; investigate; plan, aim at
quaesītor, -ōris *nm.* investigator, prosecuting officer
quaesō, -ere, ---, --- *v.t., v.i.* beg, beseech
quaestiō, -ōnis *nf.* inquiry, investigation; trial, court; subject of investiga-
    tion; question
quaestor, -ōris *nm.* quaestor (*a Roman magistrate charged with various
    duties, including public monies and military stores*)
quaestus, -ūs *nm.* acquisition, gain, profit, advantage; business, employment
quālis, -is, -e *adj.* of what sort?, what kind of?; of such a kind, such
quāliscumque, quāliscumque, quālecumque *adj.* of what quality
    whatsoever, of whatever kind, of any kind whatever
quālus, -ī *nm.* hamper, basket
quam *adv.* in what manner?, how?; how much?; as, just as, even as; *conj.*
    than (after comps.); ~ (+ sup adv. *or* + adj.) as . . . as possible;
    ~ **prīmum** *conj.* as soon as possible
quamlibet *or* **quamlubet** *adv.* at pleasure; however much, to any extent
quamobrem *adv.* why?, wherefore?, for which reason?; therefore

quamquam (*usu.* + indv.) *conj.* although, though, notwithstanding that, however, and yet

quamvīs *adv.* as you will; however much; *conj.* (+ subjv. *or* + indv.) however much, although, no matter how much

quandō *adv.* when?, at what time?; *conj.* when, at the time that; since; because

quandōque *adv.* whenever, at some time or other; as often as; since

quandōquidem *conj.* since indeed, seeing that

quantulus, -a, -um *adj.* how little, how small

quantum *adv.* so much as, so far as, as far as; how much?, how great?

quantus, -a, -um *adj.* how much?, how great?; **tantus, -a, -um** ... **quantus, -a, -um** *adj.* as great as, as much as; **quantō** *adv.* how much more; the more

quāpropter *adv.* by what means?, how?, on what account?, why?; *adv.* wherefore, therefore, so that

quārē *adv.* why?; wherefore?, by what means?, how?

quārtus, -a, -um *adj.* fourth

quārtus decimus, quārta decima, quārtum decimum *adj.* fourteenth

quasi *adv.*, *conj.* (+ subjv.) as if, as though, as it were

quassō, -āre, -āvī, -ātum *v.t.* shake; brandish; shatter

quātenus *adv.* how far; as far as; till when, how long; in so far as

quater *adv.* four times

quatiō, -ere, ---, quassum *v.t.* shake, cause to tremble; strike, crush; move, affect; vex, weary

quattuor *num.* (*indecl.*) four

quattuordecim *num.* (*indecl.*) fourteen

-que *enclitic conj.* and, and so

quemadmodum *adv.* in what way?, how?; *adv.* in what way, how; just as

queō, -īre, quīvī (quiī), quitum *v.i.* be able, can (+ infv.)

quercus, -ūs *nf.* oak; oak leaves

querella, -ae *nf.* grievance, complaint, lament

queror, querī, questus sum *v.d.i.t.* complain, lament, bewail

querulus, -a, um *adj.* complaining; uttering a plaintive sound

questus, -ūs *nm.* complaint

quī *adv.* how? by what means?; whereby, wherewith; **quī, quae, quod** *adj.* which? what? what sort of a?; any (*after* **sī, nisi, nē, num**); *pron.* who, which, what; that; these who, those who

quia *conj.* (+ indv when the writer gives his own reason; + subjv. when he gives another's reason) because, since

quīcumque, quaecumque, quodcumque *pron.* whoever, whichever; whatsoever, any whatever, every

quīdam, quaedam, quoddam *adj.* certain, particular; **quīdam, quaedam, quiddam** *pron.*, somebody, something

quidem *adv.* (postpos.) in fact, indeed; at least

quies, -ētis *nf.* rest, repose, quiet

quiēscō, -ere, quiēvī, quiētum *v.i.* keep quiet, be silent; rest, sleep

quiētus, -a, -um (w. comp. + sup.) *adj.* at rest, undisturbed, at peace

quīn *adv., conj.* why not?; but indeed, in fact; so that not, but; without (*in dependent clauses*); that (*after words of doubting*); from (*after words of hindering*)

quīndecim *num.* (*indecl.*) fifteen

quīnquāgēsimus, -a, -um *adj.* fiftieth

quīnquāgintā *num.* (*indecl.*) fifty

quīnque *num.* (*indecl.*) five

quīntus, -a, -um *adj.* fifth

quīntus decimus, quīnta decima, quīntum decimum *adj.* fifteenth

quippe *adv.* of course, naturally, certainly; *conj.* since, seeing that; for

quis, qua, quid *pron.* anyone, any, anything (*after sī, nisi, nē, num*); **quis, quae, quid** *pron.* who?, which?, what?

quisnam, quaenam, quidnam *pron.* who then?, what then?, who?, what?

quispiam, quaepiam, quidpiam *adj.* any; *pron.* anyone, anything

quisquam, quaequam, quicquam (quidquam) *pron.* any, anyone, anything (*usu. in negative sentences*)

quisque, quaeque, quidque *pron.* each, every, everyone, everything

quisquiliae, -ārum *nf./pl.* waste, trash, garbage

quisquis, quaeque, quicquid (quidquid) *pron.* whoever, whatever, everyone who, everything which

quīvīs, quaevīs, quidvīs *pron.* whom you please, what you please; anyone, anything

quō *adv.* whither?, to what end?, why?; *conj.* (+ subjv.) that, in order that

quoad *adv.* how long?, how far?; as long as, as far as; so far as, as much as; with respect to, as to; *conj.* (+ subjv.; sometimes + indv.) until

quōcircā *conj.* for which reason, and therefore

quōcumque *adv.* to whatever place

quod *conj.* that, the fact that; because, since (+ indv. when the writer gives his own reason; + subjv. when the writer gives another's reason); as regards the fact that; so far as, to the extent that

quōdammodō *adv.* in a certain way, in a certain manner

quōminus *adv.* by which the less; *conj.* (+ subjv.) so that not
quōmodō *adv.* how, in what way, in what manner
quondam *adv.* formerly; at times
quoniam *conj.* seeing that; now that
quoque *adv.* (postpos.) also, too, even
quot *adj.* (*indecl.*) how many?
quotannīs *adv.* yearly
quotīdiānus *or* **cotīdiānus, -a, -um** *adj.* daily
quotīdiē *or* **cotīdiē** *adv.* daily
quotiēns *adv.* how often
quōusque (quō usque) *adv.* till what time?, how long?

R

rabiēs, -ēī *nf.* madness, rage
racēmus, -ī *nm.* cluster of grapes
radiāns (radiant-) *adj.* radiant
radius, -ī *nm.* spoke of a wheel; shuttle; ray of light
rādīx, -dīcis *nf.* root; radish
rādō, -ere, rāsī, rāsum *v.t.* scrape smooth, shave; graze; erase; hurt
rāmus, -ī *nm.* branch
rāna, -ae *nf.* frog
rancidus, -a, -um (w. comp.) *adj.* rancid, stinking
rapāx (rapāc-) (w. comp. + sup.) *adj.* greedy, rapacious, prone to grab
rapidus, -a, -um *adj.* tearing; seizing; rapid, swift
rapīna, -ae *nf.* robbery, plundering, pillage
rapiō, -ere, rapuī, raptum *v.t.* snatch, seize, carry off; hurry along, impel;
     rob, plunder, lay waste; rape
raptus, -ūs *nm.* tearing off; abduction; plundering
rārus, -a, -um (w. comp. + sup.) *adj.* loose in texture, thin, scanty; scattered;
     infrequent, scarce, uncommon, rare; extraordinary; **rārō** *adv.* seldom
rastrum, -ī *nnt.* rake
ratiō, -ōnis *nf.* reckoning, calculation, account; transaction, business mat-
     ter; consideration; reason, motive; plan, scheme; theory; faculty of
     reasoning
ratiōcinor, ratiōcinārī, ratiōcinātus sum *v.d.i.t.* calculate, compute;
     reason, argue; consider, deliberate
ratis, -is *nf.* raft; ship, vessel
raucus, -a, -um *adj.* harsh, hoarse

rea, -ae *nf.* female prisoner; defendant in a legal action
rebelliō, -ōnis *nf.* renewal of war; rebellion
rebellis, -is, -e *adj.* rebellious, insurgent
rebellō, -bellāre, -bellāvī, -bellātum *v.i.* renew a war; revolt
recēdō, -cēdere, -cessī, -cessum *v.i.* go back, go away, withdraw; vanish, disappear
recēns (recent-) (w. comp. + sup.) *adj.* recent, new, fresh, young; vigorous
recēnseō, -cēnsēre, -cēnsuī, -cēnsum *v.t.* count, number; revise, go over, examine, review; enroll; recount
receptor, -ōris *nm.* receiver, harborer
recessus, -ūs *nm.* withdrawal, retreat, departure
recipiō, -cipere, -cēpī, -ceptum *v.t.* take back, regain, recover; admit, welcome, receive; gain, acquire; promise
recitō, -citāre, -citāvī, -citātum *v.t.* recite, read aloud, rehearse
reclāmō, -clāmāre, -clāmāvī, -clāmātum *v.t., v.i.* cry out against, protest
recognitiō, -ōnis *nf.* review, inspection
recognōscō, -gnōscere, -gnōvī, -gnitum *v.t.* recall to mind, recollect; review, look over
recolō, -colere, -coluī, -cultum *v.t.* cultivate again, resume, renew
reconciliātiō, -ōnis *nf.* renewal, restoration
reconciliō, -conciliāre, -conciliāvī, -conciliātum *v.t.* make good again, repair; restore good feelings, reconcile
reconditus, -a, -um (w. comp.) *adj.* put away, concealed; profound; reserved, reticent
recondō, -condere, -condidī, -conditum *v.t.* put back; put away, hide, conceal
recoquō, -coquere, -coxī, -coctum *v.t.* boil again; burn, melt, forge again
recordatiō, -ōnis *nf.* recollection, remembrance
recordor, recordārī, recordātus sum *v.d.t.* recall to mind, remember (+ gen. *or* + acc. *or* + acc. + infv.)
recreō, -creāre, -creāvī, -creātum *v.t.* re-create, refresh, renew, reinvigorate
rēctor, -ōris *nm.* ruler, governor, guide
rēctus, -a, -um (w. comp. + sup.) *adj.* straight, upright; correct, proper; virtuous, just; **rēctā** *adv.* directly, straightway; **rēctē** (w. comp. + sup.) *adv.* in a straight line; right, correctly, suitably, well, appropriately
recubō, -cubāre, ---, --- *v.i.* lie upon the back, lie down, recline
recuperō (reciperō), -cuperāre, -cuperāvī, -cuperātum *v.t.* get back, regain, recover
recurrō, -currere, -currī, --- *v.i.* run back, hasten back, return, recur

recūsātiō, -ōnis *nf.* refusal, protest, declining

recūsō, -āre, -āvī, -ātum *v.t.* refuse, reject, decline, protest

reddo, reddere, reddidī, redditum *v.t.* give back, return, pay back; grant; surrender; report

redēmptiō, -ōnis *nf.* buying up; bribery, ransoming

redeō, -īre, -īvī (-iī), -itum *v.i.* return, go back; be brought back, be restored

redigō, redigere, redēgī, redāctum *v.t.* drive back, bring back; reduce; compel, subdue

redimō, redimere, redēmī, redēmptum *v.t.* ransom, buy back; buy up, take by contract; gain, secure

reditus, -ūs *nm.* return, journey back; income

redūcō, -dūcere, -dūxī, -ductum *v.t.* lead back, bring back, accompany; cause to retreat; restore

redundō, -undāre, -undāvī, -undātum *v.i.* run over, overflow, be in excess; swim; reek; remain

referō, -ferre, rettulī (retulī), relātum *v.t.* bring back, carry back; give back, restore; reply; repeat; report; consider, refer; recall; reproduce

rēfert, rēferre, rētulit, --- *v.i.* (*imp.*) it is of advantage; it is important; it concerns (the person concerned is denoted by the abl. f. sg. of a poss. adj., *or* by the gen.; the matter concerned is denoted by **ad** + acc., *or* an infv. *or* acc. + infv., *or* an indirect question, a conditional clause, *or* rarely by the nom.; the degree of concern is expressed by an adv. *or* by the gen.)

refertus, -a, -um (w. comp. + sup.) *adj.* crowded, full, replete (+ abl. *or* + gen. *or* + **dē** + abl.)

reficiō, -ficere, -fēcī, -fectum *v.i.* make over, reconstruct, restore, reestablish, renew, reinvigorate

reformīdō, -formīdāre, -formīdāvī, -formīdātum *v.t.* shrink from, fear greatly, be afraid of

refrīgerō, -frīgerāre, -frīgerāvī, -frīgerātum *v.t.* cool, chill

refrīgēscō, -frīgēscere, -frīxī, --- *v.i.* grow cold, become chilled; become remiss, abate, fail

refugiō, -fugere, -fūgī, --- *v.i.* flee back, take refuge; shrink from, avoid

refugium, -ī *nnt.* asylum, place of refuge

refūtō, -fūtāre, -fūtāvī, -fūtātum *v.t.* repel, oppose, withstand; refute, discredit

rēgālis, -is, -e *adj.* royal, kingly

regenerō, -generāre, -generāvī, -generātum *v.t.* reproduce, bring forth again; bring forth something similar

rēgia, -ae *nf.* palace

rēgīna, -ae *nf.* princess, queen, ruler, woman of rank

rēgiō, -ōnis *nf.* direction; boundary line; region, district; quarter, tract

rēgius, -a, -um *adj.* royal, kingly

rēgnō, -āre, -āvī, -ātum *v.t., v.i.* rule, reign; prevail

rēgnum, -ī *nnt.* kingship; dominion, kingdom; government, power

regō, -ere, rēxī, rēctum *v.t.* keep straight; direct, guide, control, govern, rule

rēgula, -ae *nf.* ruler, a straight length of wood

rēgulus, -ī *nm.* prince; petty monarch

reiciō (rej-), -icere, -iēcī, -iectum *v.t.* throw back, force back, repel; refuse

reiectiō (rej-), -ōnis *nf.* throwing back; rejection; challenge

relābor, relābī, relapsus sum *v.d.i.* slip back, glide back; fall back

relanguēscō, -languēscere, -languī, --- *v.i.* become faint

relaxō, -laxāre, -laxāvī, -laxātum *v.t.* make wide, loosen; open; relieve, lighten

relevō, -levāre, -levāvī, -levātum *v.t.* lift up, lighten, relieve, free; soothe, console

religiō, -ōnis *nf.* sense of right, conscientiousness; devoutness, piety, holiness, religious scruple; fear of the gods; worship of the gods, religion

religiōsus, -a, -um (w. comp. + sup.) *adj.* conscientious, devout; scrupulous; sacred, holy

relinquō, -linquere, -līquī, -līctum *v.t.* leave behind, abandon, desert; relinquish, bequeath

reliquiae, -ārum *nf./pl.* that which is left, residue, relics, remains, remnant, fragments, ashes

reliquus *or* **relicus, -a, -um** *adj.* left, remaining; future, subsequent; other, the rest; **reliquum** *or* **relicum, -ī** *nnt.* the rest, remainder; the future

relūceō, -lūcēre, -lūxī, --- *v.i.* shine back, blaze, glow

remaneō, -manēre, -mānsī, --- *v.i.* stay behind, remain, be left; continue, endure

remedium, -ī *nnt.* remedy, cure, antidote, medicine

rēmex, -micis *nm.* rower

rēmigō, -āre, -āvī, -ātum *v.t., v.i.* row a boat

remissiō, -ōnis *nf.* sending back; relaxation, abatement, easing

remissus, -a, -um (w. comp.) *adj.* slack, remiss; relaxed, mild, indulgent

remittō, -mittere, -mīsī, -missum *v.t., v.i.* send back, make return, give back, restore; loosen, relax; give up, grant, pardon

remoror, remorārī, remorātus sum *v.d.i.t.* hold back, delay, hinder

remōtus, -a, -um (w. comp. + sup.) *adj.* remote, distant (+ **ab** + abl.); retired, secluded

removeō, -movēre, -mōvī, -mōtum *v.t.* move back; remove, take away; withdraw; abolish

remūnerātiō, -ōnis *nf.* recompense, reward

remūneror, -mūnerārī, -mūnerātus sum *v.d.t.* reward, recompense

rēmus, -ī *nm.* oar

rēnēs, rēnum *nm./pl.* kidneys

renovātiō, -ōnis *nf.* renewal, renovation

renovō, -novāre, -novāvī, -novatum *v.t.* renew, restore, revive

renūntiātiō, -ōnis *nf.* formal report, public announcement

renūntiō, -nūntiāre, -nūntiāvī, -nūntiātum *v.t.* report, announce, proclaim (+ acc. + infv.); declare elected

reor, rērī, ratus sum *v.d.i.* reckon, judge, think, believe (+ acc. + infv *or* + double acc.)

reparō, -parāre, -parāvī, -parātum *v.t.* recover; restore; purchase, obtain; refresh; take in exchange

repellō, -pellere, reppulī, -pulsum *v.t.* drive back, repel; keep back, repulse; banish

rependō, -pendere, -pendī, -pēnsum *v.t.* weigh again; repay, reimburse

repente *adv.* suddenly

repentīnus, -a, -um *adj.* sudden, unexpected, hasty

reperiō, -īre, repperī, repertum *v.t.* find again; find out, learn; invent

repetō, -petere, -petīvī, -petītum *v.t.* seek again; attack again; demand anew; repeat, undertake again; recall; revive

repleō, -plēre, -plēvī, -plētum *v.t.* refill, fill up, satisfy, fill (+ abl.)

rēpō, -ere, rēpsī, rēptum *v.i.* crawl, creep

repōnō, -pōnere, -posuī, -positum *v.t.* lay back, bend back; put aside, deposit; replace, put back; substitute

reportō, -portāre, -portāvī, -portātum *v.t.* carry back; obtain, gain

repraesentātiō, -ōnis *nf.* representation

repraesentō, -praesentāre, -praesentāvī, -praesentātum *v.t.* make present again; exhibit, manifest, represent; pay down; perform immediately; hasten

reprehendō (reprēnd-), -hendere, -hendī, -hēnsum *v.t.* hold back, seize, restrain; criticize, find fault

reprimō, -primere, -pressī, -pressum *v.t.* press back; restrain, confine

repudiō, -pudiāre, -pudiāvī, -pudiātum *v.t.* cast off, reject, refuse, scorn

repuerāscō, -puerāscere, ---, --- *v.i.* become a child again; play like a child

repūgnō, -pūgnāre, -pūgnāvī, -pūgnātum *v.t.* oppose, resist, contend against

repulsa, -ae *nf.* rejection, repulse, refusal

reputō, -putāre, -putāvī, -putātum *v.t.* count over, compute; think over, meditate, reflect on

requiēs, -ētis *nf.* rest, pause, recreation, relaxation; relief

requīrō, -quīrere, -quīsīvī, -quīsītum *v.t.* seek again, search for; ask; require, need

rēs, reī *nf.* thing, object, matter; affair; event, circumstance; fact; property, possessions; profit, advantage; cause, reason; business; battle; state, government; **rēs adversae, rērum adversārum** *nf./pl.* misfortune; **rēs familiāris, reī familiāris** *nf.* private property; **rēs gestae, rērum gestārum** *nf./pl.* act, deed, achievement; **rēs novae, rērum novārum** *nf./pl.* revolution; **rēs pūblica, reī pūblicae** *nf.* politics, state, the Roman state; **rēs secundae, rērum secundārum** *nf./pl.* success, prosperity

rescrībō, -scrībere, -scrīpsī, -scrīptum *v.t.* answer, reply, respond in writing

reservō, -servāre, -servāvī, -servātum *v.t.* keep back, save up, retain

resideō, -sidēre, -sēdī, --- *v.t., v.i.* remain sitting; stay, reside; remain behind

resīdō, -sīdere, -sēdī, --- *v.i.* sit down, sink; subside, abate

resignō, -signāre, -signāvī, -signātum *v.t.* unseal, open; annul, destroy

rēsīna, -ae *nf.* resin

resistō, -sistere, -stitī, --- *v.t.* stand back; remain behind, stay; resist (+ dat.)

resolvō, -solvere, -solvī, -solūtum *v.t.* untie again, unfasten, open; relax; make void

resonō, -sonāre, -sonāvī, -sonātum *v.t., v.i.* echo, resound

respectō, -spectāre, -spectāvī, -spectātum *v.t., v.i.* look back upon; gaze at; await; regard, care for

respectus, -ūs *nm.* looking back; care, consideration, regard

respergō, -spergere, -spersī, -spersum *v.t.* sprinkle; defile

respiciō, -spicere, -spexī, -spectum *v.t., v.i.* look back; gaze upon; look out for, consider

respondeō, -spondēre, -spondī, -spōnsum *v.t.* answer, reply (+ acc. of answer + dat. of person answered); be a match for; agree

respōnsum, -ī *nnt.* answer, reply

restinguō

restinguō, -stinguere, -stīnxī, -stīnctum *v.t.* quench, extinguish; annihilate

restituō, -stituere, -stituī, -stitūtum *v.t.* restore, reinstate, replace, revive

restitūtiō, -ōnis *nf.* return, restoring

restō, -stāre, -stitī, --- *v.i.* withstand, resist; remain, be left over

resūmō, -sūmere, -sūmpsī, -sūmptum *v.t.* take up again, resume

retardō, -tardāre, -tardāvī, -tardātum *v.t., v.i.* keep back, impede, delay

rēte, -is *nnt.* net, snare

retegō, -tegere, -tēxī, -tēctum *v.t.* uncover, open, disclose, reveal

reticentia, -ae *nf.* silence

reticeō, -ticēre, -ticuī, --- *v.t., v.i.* be silent; keep secret

retineō, -tinēre, -tinuī, -tentum *v.t.* hold back; detain, repress; keep, maintain

retrāctātiō, -ōnis *nf.* drawing back, shrinking; refusal; retraction

retrāctō, -tractāre, -tractāvī, -tractātum *v.t.* handle again, undertake again; draw back, refuse, be reluctant, retract

retrahō, -trahere, -trāxī, -trāctum *v.t.* draw back, bring back; remove

retrō *adv.* backward, to the rear; behind, in the rear; in past times, formerly; on the contrary

retrōrsum *adv.* backward(s), behind

retundō, -tundere, rettudī, retūsum *v.t.* beat back; blunt, dull; restrain

reus, -ī *nm.* male prisoner, defendant in a legal action

revellō, -vellere, -vellī, -volsum (-vulsum) *v.t.* pluck, pull away, tear off; abolish

revereor, reverērī, reveritus sum *v.d.t.* revere, feel awe for; fear

revertor, revertī, reversus sum *v.d.i.* return, go back

revincō, -vincere, -vīcī, -victum *v.t.* conquer; refute

revīvīscō, -vīvīscere, -vīxī, --- *v.i.* come back to life, be revived, recover

revocō, -vocāre, -vocāvī, -vocātum *v.t.* call back, bring back, recover, restore; withdraw, divert

revolvō, -volvere, -volvī, -volūtum *v.t.* roll backwards; go over again

rēx, rēgis *nm.* king, chief, monarch, ruler

rīdeō, -ēre, rīsī, rīsum *v.t., v.i.* laugh; laugh at, deride

rīdiculus, -a, -um *adj.* comic, ridiculous; contemptible

rigēscō, -ere, riguī, --- *v.i.* stiffen, freeze

rigidus, -a, -um *adj.* stiff, hard; unbending, stern

rigō, -āre, -āvī, -ātum *v.t.* conduct water; moisten

rīma, -ae *nf.* crack, fissure

ringor, ringārī, rictus sum *v.d.i.* snarl, be angry

rīpa, -ae *nf.* bank of a lake or river

rīsus, -ūs *nm.* laughter; ridicule; object of ridicule

rītē *adv.* with due ceremony, properly

rīvālis, -is, -e *adj.* pertaining to a rivulet, sharing a brook; neighbor; suitor

rīvus, -ī *nm.* stream

rōbīgō, -inis *nf.* rust, metallic oxide; blight, smut

rōbur, -oris *nnt.* hard wood; oak tree; strength, vigor, force

rōbustus, -a, -um (w. comp.) *adj.* oaken; strong, hardy, robust

rogātiō, -ōnis *nf.* question, entreaty; proposed law, resolution

rogitō, -āre, ---, --- *v.t.* ask eagerly, keep asking

rogō, -āre, -āvī, -ātum *v.t.* ask, entreat, beg for; bring forward, introduce, propose

rogus, -ī *nm.* funeral pyre; death, destruction

rōs, rōris *nm.* dew

rosa, -ae *nf.* rose, rosebush

roseus, -a, -um *adj.* made of roses; rose-colored

rōstrum, -ī *nnt.* beak, mouth, bill; beak of a ship; orator's platform

rota, -ae *nf.* wheel; chariot

rotundus, -a, -um (w. comp.) *adj.* round, circular; perfect, complete

rubor, -ōris *nm.* redness; bashfulness, modesty; shame

rubus, -ī *nm.* blackberry; bramble-bush

rudis, -is, -e *adj.* rough, wild, coarse, rude, uncultivated, unpolished, unskilled, ignorant

rūfus, -a, -um *adj.* red

rūga, -ae *nf.* wrinkle

rūgōsus, -a, -um *adj.* wrinkled

ruīna, -ae *nf.* tumbling down; downfall, ruin; wreck, calamity; **ruīnae, -ārum** *nf./pl.* ruins of a building

rūmor, -ōris *nm.* report, rumor; general opinion, common talk; reputation

rumpō, -ere, -rūpī, ruptum *v.t.* break, burst open; force open, cause to break forth; break off, interrupt

ruō, -ere, ruī, rutum *v.t., v.i.* tumble down in ruins, collapse; go to ruin; hasten, hurry; fall in torrents

rūrsum (rūrsus) *adv.* backward, back; again, a second time; on the contrary

rūs, rūris *nnt.* country; farm, estate; **rūrī** *adv.* in the country

rūsticātiō, -ōnis *nf.* stay in the country; life in the country

rūsticor, rūsticārī, rūsticātus sum *v.d.i.* stay in the countryside

rūsticus, -a, -um *adj.* rural, rustic, coarse, simple; **rusticus, -ī** *nm.* peasant; countryman

S

s.d. *abb.* (**salūtem dīcit**) sends greetings
s.v.b.e.v. *abb.* (**sī valēs, bene est; valeō**) if you are well, it is well; I am
    well
sacculus, -ī *nm.* pouch, small bag
saccus, -ī *nm.* bag, sack
sacellum, -ī *nnt.* shrine
sacer, sacra, sacrum (sup. **sacerrimus**) *adj.* dedicated, consecrated,
    sacred; accursed, infamous
sacerdōs, -ōtis *nm/f.* priest(ess)
sacerdōtium, -ī *nnt.* priesthood, priestly office
sacrāmentum, -ī *nnt.* oath; military oath of allegiance
sacrārium, -ī *nnt.* shrine, sanctuary
sacrificium, -ī *nnt.* sacrifice
sacrificō, -ficāre, -ficāvī, -ficātum *v.i.* sacrifice
sacrōsānctus, -a, -um *adj.* revered as holy, inviolable
sacrum, -ī *nnt.* sacred thing, sacred place; sacred rite, sacrifice, worship
saeculum *or* **saeclum, -ī** *nnt.* generation; period of time, lifetime, century
saepe *adv.* often, frequently
saepēs, -is *nf.* fence, hedge
saepīmentum (sēp-), -ī *nnt.* railing, hedge, enclosure
saepiō, -īre, saepsī, -saeptum *v.t.* enclose, fence in, surround; protect,
    fortify
saeptum, -ī *nnt.* pen, enclosure, barrier, wall
saevus, -a, -um (w. comp. + sup.) *adj.* fierce, violent, savage
sagātus, -a, -um *adj.* wearing the sagum (*the military cloak*)
sagāx (sagāc-) (w. comp. + sup.) *adj.* keen-scented; quick, shrewd
sagitta, -ae *nf.* arrow
sagum, -ī *nnt.* coarse cloak, military cloak
sāl, salis *nnt.* salt; saltwater
salārium, -ī *nnt.* allowance, pay
salīnae, -ārum *nf./pl.* salt works
saliō, -īre, ---, salītum (salsum) *v.t.* salt
saliō, -īre, saluī, saltum *v.i.* leap, skip, bound
salīx, -icis *nf.* willow
salmō, -ōnis *nm.* salmon
salsus, -a, -um *adj.* salty; witty, biting, satirical**

saltātiō, -ōnis *nf.* dance
saltem *adv.* at least, at all events, anyhow
saltō, -āre, -āvī, -ātum *v.i.* dance
saltus, -ūs *nm.* leap, bound
salūbris *or* **salūber, salūbris, salūbre** (w. comp. + sup.) *adj.* healthy, healthful; useful, serviceable; vigorous
salūs, -ūtis *nf.* health; welfare, safety, deliverance; greeting
salūtāris, -is, -e *adj.* beneficial, healthful, salutary, useful, serviceable
salūtātiō, -ōnis *nf.* greeting, calling upon; ceremonial visit
salūtātor, -ōris *nm.* visitor, caller
salūtō, -āre, -āvī, -ātum *v.t.* greet, salute; wish good health to; visit, pay a call on
salveō, -ēre, ---, --- *v.i.* be healthy, be well
salvus, -a, -um *adj.* well, safe, unharmed, in good heath
sānātiō, -ōnis *nf.* cure, act of curing
sanciō, -īre, sānxī, sānctum *v.t.* make sacred, consecrate; ratify, approve; decree, enact
sānctiō, -ōnis *nf.* decree, ordinance; sanction
sānctus, -a, -um (w. comp. + sup.) *adj.* consecrated, holy, sacred, divine, pure; just, upright; inviolable
sānē *adv.* discreetly, sensibly; indeed, truly
sānēscō, -ere, sānuī, --- *v.i.* heal, get well
sanguis, sanguinis *nm. or* **sanguen, sanguinis** *nnt.* blood; bloodshed, slaughter; family, stock
sānitās, -ātis *nf.* good health, soundness; reasonableness, good sense, sanity
sānō, -āre, -āvī, -ātum *v.t.* heal, make sound, cure, restore, repair
sānus, -a, -um (w. comp. + sup.) *adj.* sound, healthy
sapiēns (sapient-) (w. comp. + sup.) *adj.* wise, sensible, discreet
sapientia, -ae *nf.* good sense, discretion, prudence, wisdom
sapiō, -ere, -īvī, --- *v.i.* taste; have taste, have discernment; be discreet; be wise
sāpō, -ōnis *nm.* soap
sapor, -ōris *nm.* taste, flavor
sapphīrus, -ī *nf.* sapphire
sarcina, -ae *nf.* package, load, bundle; **sarcinae, -ārum** *nf./pl.* luggage
sarciō, -īre, sarsī, sartum *v.t.* darn, mend, patch
sarcophagus, -ī *nm.* stone coffin
sarculum, -ī *nnt.* hoe

sarda, -ae *nf.* pickled fish
sartāgō, -inis *nf.* frying pan
satelles, -itis *nm/f.* guard, attendant; companion
satis *adj.* (*indecl.*) adequate, sufficient; *adv.* enough, sufficiently, amply;
    nnt. (*indecl.*) enough
satisfaciō, -facere, -fēcī, -factum *v.t.* content, satisfy; make amends
satur, satura, saturum *adj.* full, satiated; copious (+ *abl. or* + *gen.*)
saucius, -a, -um *adj.* wounded, hurt, injured, weakened
saxum, -ī *nnt.* rock
scabellum, -ī *nnt.* stool, footstool
scabiēs, -ēī *nf.* scabies, mange
scaena, -ae *nf.* scene, stage
scālae, -ārum *nf./pl.* flight of stairs; ladder
scalpō, -ere, scalpsī, scalptum *v.t.* carve, chisel
scalprum, -ī *nnt.* chisel
scalptūra, -ae *nf.* cutting, engraving
scandō, -ere, ---, --- *v.t.* rise, climb, ascend
scapha, -ae *nf.* skiff, boat
scarabaeus, -ī *nm.* beetle
scelerātus, -a, -um (w. comp. + sup.) *adj.* defiled, profaned; wicked,
    impious, sacrilegious
scelestus, -a, -um (w comp. + sup.) *adj.* wicked, impious; criminal
scelus, -eris *nnt.* crime, sin, wickedness
scēnographia, -ae *nf.* perspective (*in painting*)
schola, -ae *nf.* leisure time for learning; debate; school
scholasticus, -a, -um *adj.* academic; rhetorical
sciēns (scient-) (w. comp. + sup.) *adj.* intelligent, skilled, expert (+ *gen. or*
    + infv.)
scientia, -ae *nf.* knowledge, acquaintance; skill, art, science
scīlicet *adv.* certainly, of course, no doubt
scindō, -ere, scidī, scissum *v.t.* tear, cut, rip apart, divide, separate
scintilla, -ae *nf.* spark; trace
scintillō, -āre, ---, --- *v.i.* sparkle, glitter
sciō, -īre, -īvī, -ītum *v.t.* know, understand (+ acc. + infv.), have knowl-
    edge of
scirpus, -ī *nm.* rush (*bot.*)
scissūra, -ae *nf.* tear, rip, split
scītus, -a, -um *adj.* knowing (+ gen.); sensible, proper; clever, witty,
    shrewd

sciūrus, -ī *nm.* squirrel
scobis, -is *nf.* sawdust, chips, shavings
scopula, -ae *nf.* broom-twig
scopulōsus, -a, -um *adj.* rocky, craggy
scopulus, -ī *nm.* cliff, rock, crag
scopus, -ī *nm.* target, goal
scorpiō, -ōnis *nm.* scorpion
scortum, -ī *nnt.* prostitute, whore
scrība, -ae *nm.* clerk, scribe, secretary
scrībō, -ere, scrīpsī, scrīptum *v.t.* draw; write
scrīnium, -ī *nnt.* box for papers and books and documents
scrīptiō, -ōnis *nf.* writing, composition
scrīptor, -ōris *nm.* writer, scribe, author; narrator
scrīptum, -ī *nnt.* composition, writing
scrīptūra, -ae *nf.* composition, writing
scrūpulus, -ī *nm.* small stone; worry, anxiety; scruple
scrūtātiō, -ōnis *nf.* searching, investigation
scrūtor, scrūtārī, scrūtātus sum *v.d.t.* investigate, scrutinize, examine carefully
sculpō, -ere, sculpsī, sculptum *v.t.* carve, sculpt, engrave
sculptor, -ōris *nm.* sculptor
sculptūra, -ae *nf.* carving, sculpture
scurra, -ae *nm.* clown, jester; man-about-town
scutula, -ae *nf.* little square dish; diamond shape
scūtum, -ī *nnt.* oblong infantry shield; protection, shelter, defense
sē *pron. See* suī.
secāle, -is *nnt.* grain; rye, spelt
sēcēdō, -cēdere, -cessī, -cessum *v.i.* depart, separate, withdraw
sēcernō, -cernere, -crēvī, -crētum *v.t.* separate, divide, set apart
sēcessus, -ūs *nm.* going away, separation; retirement; hiding place, retreat
sēclūdō, -clūdere, -clūsī, -clūsum *v.t.* shut off, seclude, confine alone
secō, -āre, -uī, sectum *v.t.* slice, cut; wound; divide
sēcrētus, -a, -um (w. comp.) *adj.* separated, apart (+ abl.); remote, secret, lonely, private, secluded
secūndum *prep.* (+ acc.) after, next to, following; according to
secūndus, -a, -um *adj.* following, next; second; secondary, inferior; prosperous; favorable
secūris, -is *nf.* axe, battle axe
sēcūritās, -ātis *nf.* freedom from anxiety or alarm or danger; security

sēcūrus, -a, -um (w. comp.) *adj.* careless, free from care, carefree, tranquil, safe

secus *adv.* otherwise, not so; **~ atque (ac), ~ quam** *adv.* otherwise than, differently from; **nōn ~, haud ~** *adv.* just so

sed *conj.* but, on the contrary, however

sēdātus, -a, -um (w. comp.) *adj.* sedate, calm

sēdecim *num.* (*indecl.*) sixteen

sedeō, -ēre, sēdī, sessum *v.i.* sit, be idle, be settled

sēdēs, -is *nf.* chair; dwelling place; place, site

sēditiō, -ōnis *nf.* dissension, mutiny, uprising

sēdō, -āre, -āvī, -ātum *v.t.* calm, settle, check, allay, quiet

sēdūcō, -dūcere, -dūxī, -ductum *v.t.* lead apart, separate; rescue

sēdulitās, -ātis *nf.* persistency, zeal

sēiungō (sēj-), -iungere, -iūnxī, -iūnctum *v.t.* separate, sever, disconnect

sēlēctus, -a, -um *adj.* chosen, selected

sella, -ae *nf.* chair; magistrate's chair

semel *adv.* once, a single time, but once

sēmen, -inis *nnt.* seed; race; source; principle

sēmisomnus, -a, -um *adj.* sleepy

sēmita, -ae *nf.* path, lane

semper *adv.* always, ever, forever

sempiternus, -a, -um *adj.* everlasting, perpetual, eternal

senātor, -ōris *nm.* senator, member of the senate

senātus, -ūs *nm.* senate

senectūs, -ūtis *nf.* old age

senēscō, -ere, senuī, --- *v.i.* grow old; decay, become weak, decline

senex (sen-) (comp. **senior**) *adj.* elderly, old; **senex, senis** *nm.* old man

senīlis, -is, -e *adj.* of old age, old

sēnsim *adv.* gradually, little by little, slowly

sēnsus, -ūs *nm.* sense, consciousness; sensation, emotion, feeling, attitude; judgment, perception

sententia, -ae *nf.* opinion, judgment, view; proposal, motion; decision, resolution; determination; sentence

sentiō, -īre, sēnsī, sēnsum *v.t.* perceive, feel, hear, see, discern, think, judge (+ acc. + infv.)

seorsum *adv.* apart, separately

sēparātiō, -ōnis *nf.* separation

sēparātus, -a, -um *adj.* separate, apart, distinct

sēparō, -parāre, -parāvī, -parātum *v.t.* part, sever, separate

sepeliō, -pelīre, -pelīvī (-peliī), -pultum *v.t.* bury; overwhelm, wipe out

septem *num.* (*indecl.*) seven

September, -bris *nm.* September (*usu. w.* **mēnsis**); **September, -bris, -bre** *adj.* September

septemdecim *num.* (*indecl.*) seventeen

septentriō (septemtriō), -ōnis *nm.* north; **septentriōnālis, -is, -e** *adj.* north, northern

septimus, -a, -um *adj.* seventh

septuāgintā *num.* (*indecl.*) seventy

sepulcrum (sepulchr-), -ī *nnt.* tomb, grave

sepultūra, -ae *nf.* burial, funeral rites

sequāx (sequāc-) *adj.* following; pursuing

sequor, sequī, secūtus sum *v.d.t.* follow, attend; come next, result; seek, pursue, strive at

serēnus, -a, -um *adj.* fair, bright, clear; tranquil; joyful

sēricum, -ī *nnt.* silk

seriēs, -ēī *nf.* line, row; lineage

sērius, -a, -um *adj.* solemn, serious

sermō, -ōnis *nm.* conversation, talk, report, gossip

serō, -ere, sēvī, satum *v.t.* sow, plant; beget

serpō, -ere, serpsī, serptum *v.i.* crawl, creep, glide, come stealthily

serra, -ae *nf.* saw

sērus, -a, -um (w. comp.) *adj.* late; **sērō** *adv.* late; at a late hour

serva, -ae *nf.* female slave

servīlis, -is, -e *adj.* pertaining to a slave, servile

serviō, -īre, -īvī (-iī), -ītum *v.i.* be a slave, serve, labor for; gratify (+ dat.)

servitium, -ī *nnt.* slavery; group of slaves

servitūs, -ūs *nf.* slavery

servō, -āre, -āvī, -ātum *v.t.* save, preserve from danger; store away; observe

servus, -ī *nm.* male slave

sestertius, -ī *nm.* sestertius (*a small silver coin*)

seu *conj. See* **sīve.**

sevēritās, -ātis *nf.* gravity, solemnity, sternness

sevērus, -a, -um (w. comp. + sup.) *adj.* grave, solemn, stern, strict

sex *num.* (*indecl.*) six

sexāgintā *num.* (*indecl.*) sixty

sextārius, -ī *nm.* sixth part of a congius (*about a pint measure*)

Sextīlis, -is *nm.* August (*usu. w.* **mēnsis**) (*later renamed* **Augustus, -ī**, *nm., in honor of the emperor*); **Sextīlis, -is, -e** *adj.* of the sixth month, August

sextus, -a, -um *adj.* sixth
sexus, -ūs *nm.* sex, gender
sī *conj.* if; inasmuch as; even if; although
sibi *pron. See* **suī.**
sībilō, -āre, -āvī, -ātum *v.i.* whistle, hiss
sībulus, -ī *nm.* whistling, hissing
sīc *adv.* so, thus, in this way; in the same way
sīca *nf.* dagger
siccō, -āre, -āvī, -ātum *v.t.* dry, make dry; drain
siccus, -a, -um *adj.* dry; thirsty
sīcut(ī) *adv.* as, just as, as it were
sīdō, -ere, ---, --- *v.i.* settle, sink down; alight
sīdus, -eris *nnt.* group of stars, constellation; star; heaven
signifer, signiferī *nm.* military standard bearer
significātiō, -ōnis *nf.* indication, sign, token; approbation
significō, -ficāre, -ficāvī, -ficātum *v.t.* show, point out, indicate, portend
signō, -āre, -āvī, -ātum *v.t.* stamp, mark, imprint, seal; adorn; point out, note
signum, -ī *nnt.* token, mark, sign; standard, banner; signal; image, statue; omen
silentium, -ī *nnt.* silence, quiet
sileō, -ēre, siluī, --- *v.t., v.i.* be silent, keep still; suppress
siliqua, -ae *nf.* pod, husk
silva, -ae *nf.* forest, woods
silvestris, -is, -e *adj.* of a forest; wooded
simia, -ae *nf.* monkey, ape
similis, -is, -e (comp. **similior**; sup. **simillimus**) *adj.* alike, similar, resembling; **similiter** *adv.* similarly, likewise
similitūdō, -inis *nf.* resemblance, likeness, similarity
simplex (simplic-) (w. comp.) *adj.* simple, unmixed, single, not complicated; **simpliciter** (w. comp. + sup.) *adv.* simply, plainly; frankly
simul *adv.* at once, at the same time; **~ ac (atque)** *conj.* as soon as
simulācrum, -ī *nnt.* image, likeness, form, figure, appearance; semblance of a deity; vision, apparition
simulātiō, -ōnis *nf.* feigning, simulation, pretense
simulō, -āre, -āvī, -ātum *v.t.* make like, imitate, copy; feign, pretend
sin *conj.* but if, if however
sināpi, -is *nnt.* mustard
sincēritās, -ātis *nf.* purity; soundness; integrity, sincerity
sincērus, -a, -um *adj.* clean, pure; whole, entire; genuine, candid

sine *prep.* (+ abl.) without

singulāris, -is, -e *adj.* alone, single, individual; singular, extraordinary, unique

singulī, -ae, -a *adj./pl.* single, one at a time, individual, separate

singultiō, -īre, -īvī, --- *v.i.* hiccup, gasp; **singultō, -āre, ---, -ātum** *v.t., v.i.* hiccup, gasp, sob; **singultus, -ūs** *nm.* sobbing; rattling in the throat

sinister, sinistra, sinistrum *adj.* on the left hand, left; favorable, fortunate; unfavorable, inauspicious, adverse

sinō, -ere, sīvī, situm *v.t.* place, put down; let, allow, permit (+ infv. *or* + **ut** + subjv.)

sinus, -ūs *nm.* curve; bay, inlet, cove; fold of a garment or of land

sīquidem *conj.* if only, if indeed; since

sistō, -ere, stitī, statum *v.i.* set up, stand; lead, bring; establish; stop, halt

sitiō, -īre, -īvī, --- *v.t., v.i.* be thirsty, thirst for; **sitis, -is** *nf.* thirst; eagerness

situla, -ae *nf.* bucket

situs, -a, -um *adj.* placed, situated; buried; **situs, -ūs** *nm.* site, situation, position, location

sīve *or* **seu** *conj.* or if, or; **~ ... ~** *conj.* whether ... or, either or

socer, -erī *nm.* father-in-law

sociētās, -ātis *nf.* association, union, society, alliance

socius, -a, -um *adj.* sharing, associated, allied; **socius, -ī** *nm.* partner, associate, ally; **sociī, -ōrum** *nm./pl.* the military units of allies

socrus, -ūs *nf.* mother-in-law

sodālis, -is, -e *adj.* companionable, friendly; **sodālis, -is** *nm/f.* associate, companion, friend

sodālitās, -ātis *nf.* companionship, fellowship; club, association; secret society

sōl, sōlis *nm.* sun; sunshine

sōlācium, -ī *nnt.* consolation, comfort

sōlāris, -is, -e *adj.* solar, of the sun

sōlārium, -ī *nnt.* sun-dial; balcony exposed to the sun

solea, -ae *nf.* soul of the foot; sandal

sōleō, -ēre, solitus sum *v.i.* be in the habit, be accustomed, be wont to (+ infv.)

solidus *or* **soldus, -a, -um** (w. sup.) *adj.* entire, undivided; massive, solid; sound, trustworthy

sōlitārius, -a, -um *adj.* alone, lonely, isolated

sōlitūdō, -inis *nf.* being alone, loneliness, solitude; desert, waste place; deprivation, want

solitus, -a, -um *adj.* customary, usual

solium, -ī *nnt.* throne, chair of state; bathtub; sarcophagus

sollemnis, -is, -e (w. comp. + sup.) *adj.* celebrated every year; religiously established, sacred, solemn; festive; regular, usual

sollers (sollert-) (w. comp. + sup.) *adj.* bright, clever; skillful (+ gen.)

sollertia, -ae *nf.* skill, cleverness

sollicitātiō, -ōnis *nf.* an annoying, vexation; an inciting; solicitation

sollicitō, -āre, -āvī, -ātum *v.t.* agitate, disturb, urge, incite, tempt, instigate; worry

sollicitūdō, -inis *nf.* concern, worry, apprehension

sollicitus, -a, -um *adj.* uneasy, worried (+ **nē** + subjv. of thing worried about), agitated, alarmed; alarming, distressing

sōlor, sōlārī, sōlātus sum *v.d.t.* comfort, console; lessen, soothe, relieve

solum, -ī *nnt.* bottom, base; soil, ground; floor; country, region; sole of the foot

sōlus, -a, -um *adj.* alone, single, lonely, deserted, solitary; **sōlum** *adv.* only, merely; **nōn sōlum . . . sed etiam** *conj.* not only . . . but also

solūtiō, -ōnis *nf.* loosening; payment

solūtus, -a, -um (w. comp. + sup.) *adj.* unbound, loosened, freed (+ **ab** + abl. *or* + abl. alone *or* + gen.); lax, careless

solvō, -ere, solvī, solūtum *v.t.* loose, unfasten, free; break up; overcome; annul; fulfill; pay off; discharge

somnifer, somnifera, somniferum *adj.* narcotic

somniō, -āre, -āvī, -ātum *v.t., v.i.* dream; **somnium, -ī** *nnt.* dream

somnus, -ī *nm.* sleep

sonō, -āre, -uī, -itum *v.t., v.i.* sound, resound; sing of; speak

sōns (sont-) *adj.* guilty

sonus, -ī *nm.* sound, noise

sordidus, -a, -um (w. comp. + sup.) *adj.* filthy, dirty; vulgar, base, low; mean; miserly

soror, -ōris *nf.* sister

sors, sortis *nf.* lot; casting or drawing of lots; fortune, fate; share, part

sortītus, -ūs *nm.* drawing of lots, sortition

sōspitō, -āre, ---, --- *v.t.* save, protect; prosper

spargō, -ere, sparsī, sparsum *v.t.* scatter, hurl, disperse, disseminate, besprinkle

spatiōsus, -a, -um (w. comp. + sup.) *adj.* roomy, spacious; prolonged

spatium, -ī *nnt.* distance, interval; room, space; period of time

speciēs, -ēī *nf.* look, appearance; vision; beauty, splendor

spectāculum, -ī *nnt.* sight, spectacle; spectator's seat

spectātor, -ōris *nm.* watcher, observer

spectō, -āre, -āvī, -ātum *v.t.* witness, see, observe, inspect, look towards

speculātor, -ōris *nm.* spy, scout

speculor, speculārī, speculātus sum *v.d.t.* scout, search, examine

speculum, -ī *nnt.* mirror

specus, -ūs *nm/nt.* hollow, cave, den

spēlunca, -ae *nf.* cave, grotto, den

spērō, -āre, -āvī, -ātum *v.t.* hope, hope for, expect; trust, believe

spēs, speī *nf.* hope, expectation; trust; anticipation

sphaera, -ae *nf.* sphere, globe

spīca, -ae *nf.* ear of grain

spīna, -ae *nf.* thorn; spine, backbone

spīra, -ae *nf.* coil, twist

spīrāculum, -ī *nnt.* vent

spīritus, -ūs *nm.* breath; breathing; breeze; breath of a god, inspiration; breath of life; courage; pride

spīrō, -āre, -āvī, -ātum *v.t., v.i.* draw breath, breathe, exhale; be alive; be inspired with (+ acc. of specification)

splendēscō, -ere, ---, --- *v.i.* begin to shine, become bright

splendidus, -a, -um (w. comp. + sup.) *adj.* brilliant, shining; magnificent, illustrious; **splendidē** (w. comp. + sup.) *adv.* rightly, magnificently, nobly

splendor, -ōris *nm.* brightness; splendor, eminence; distinction

spoliātiō, -ōnis *nf.* plundering, robbing

spoliō, -āre, -āvī, -ātum *v.t.* strip, spoil, despoil, plunder

spolium, -ī *nnt.* skin; arms stripped from the enemy, spoils (*usually in pl.*)

spondeō, -ēre, spopondī, spōnsum *v.t., v.i.* promise solemnly, vow, betroth; agree

spongia (spongea), -ae *nf.* sponge

spōnsālia, -ium *nnt./pl.* betrothal, wedding

spōnsiō, -ōnis *nf.* engagement, betrothal; solemn promise

sponte *adv.* of one's own free will, willingly; **sponte meā** of my own accord; **sponte tuā** of your own accord; **sponte suā** of his/her/its own accord

spūma, -ae *nf.* foam, froth; scum

spuō, -ere, spuī, spūtum *v.t.* spit

squālor, -ōris *nm.* filthiness; garments dirtied in mourning

squāma, -ae *nf.* scale of a fish; thin metallic plate or scale

stabiliō, -āre, -āvī, -ātum *v.t.* establish, make firm, secure

stabilis, -is, -e (w. comp.) *adj.* stable, firm, fixed, lasting, enduring

stabilitās, -ātis *nf.* steadfastness, stability, durability

stabulum, -ī *nnt.* habitation; stable; cottage; tavern; brothel

stadium, -ī *nnt.* racetrack; stadium

stāgnum, -ī *nnt.* standing water; pond, marsh

statim *adv.* at once, immediately; regularly

statiō, -ōnis *nf.* standing, position; station, post

statua, -ae *nf.* statue, image

statuō, -ere, statuī, statūtum *v.t.* put, set up, establish; settle, decide (+ acc. + infv. of the writer's settlement or decision *or* + **ut** or **nē** + subjv. of another's settlement or decision)

status, -ūs *nm.* standing, situation; attitude

stella, -ae *nf.* star; planet; constellation

stercus, -oris *nnt.* dung, manure

sterilis, -is, -e *adj.* barren, unfruitful; vain, fruitless (+ gen.)

sternō, -ere, strāvī, strātum *v.t.* spread out, extend, scatter; overthrow

sternuō, -ere, sternuī, --- *v.i.* sneeze

sternūtāmentum, -ī *nnt.* sneeze

stertō, -ere, -stertuī, --- *v.i.* snore

stillō, -āre, -āvī, -ātum *v.i.* drop, fall in drops, trickle

stilus *or* **stylus, -ī** *nm.* stake; stylus (*instrument for writing*)

stimulō, -āre, -āvī, -ātum *v.t.* stimulate, rouse, annoy, disturb

stimulus, -ī *nm.* goad, spur, incentive; pain

stīpendium, -ī *nnt.* tax, tribute; income, salary; soldier's pay; military service

stīpes, -itis *nm.* log, trunk, stump

stīpō, -āre, -āvī, -ātum *v.t.* cram full, stuff, pack; accompany

stirps, stirpis *nm/f.* stalk, stem; family; descendant; source, origin

stō, -āre, stetī, statum *v.i.* stand; stand up; endure; stand still, tarry

stola, -ae *nf.* stola (*the garment of the married Roman woman*)

stolidus, -a, -um (w. comp. + sup.) *adj.* dense, stupid

stomachus, -ī *nm.* stomach; windpipe; liking; distaste, anger, vexation

strabō, -ōnis *nm.* squinter

strāgēs, -is *nf.* throwing down; massacre; wreck

strāgulum, -ī *nnt.* quilt, heavy blanket; rug

strāmentum, -ī *nnt.* straw

strangulō, -āre, -āvī, -ātum *v.t.* strangle, choke

strātum, -i *nnt.* covering; blanket, coverlet; bed

strēnuus, -a, -um (w. comp. + sup.) *adj.* energetic, active, restless

strepitus, -ūs *nm.* noise, racket, crash; murmur

strictus, -a, -um (w. comp.) *adj.* drawn together; tight, close; brief; strict; rigid

stringō, -ere, strinxī, strictum *v.t.* tighten, draw tight; tie; strip off, trim; unsheathe; graze, touch lightly; touch upon; wear away

strūctūra, -ae *nf.* a constructing, an erecting; arrangement; structure, building

struō, -ere, strūxī, strūctum *v.t.* heap up; build; arrange, put in order; devise, contrive

studeō, -ēre, studuī, --- *v.i.* be eager; strive after; study (+ dat.); attend school

studiōsus, -a, -um (w. comp. + sup.) *adj.* zealous, eager; assiduous; partial, devoted (+ gen. *or* + dat.)

studium, -ī *nnt.* enthusiasm, zeal; study; interest; partiality

stultitia, -ae *nf.* foolishness, silliness

stultus, -a, -um (w. comp. + sup.) *adj.* foolish, silly; stupid

stupefaciō, -facere, -fēcī, -factum *v.t.* stun, make senseless

stupidus, -a, -um *adj.* stunned; stupid; senseless

stupor, -ōris *nm.* mental shock, senselessness; amazement

stuprum, -ī *nnt.* disgrace; lewdness

suādeō, -ēre, suāsī, suāsum *v.i.* recommend, advise; exhort; persuade (+ dat. of person advised + acc. *or* + acc. + infv. *or* + **ut** or **nē** + subjv. of course advised)

suāsor, -ōris *nm.* adviser, proposer

suāvis, -is, -e (w. comp. + sup.) *adj.* sweet, pleasant

suāvitās, -ātis *nf.* sweetness, pleasantness

sub *prep.* (*of motion*, + acc.) under, along under; near to, up to, towards; down into; immediately after; under the power of; *prep.* (*of rest*, + abl.) beneath, under; close under; at the bottom of; at; under the power of

subdūcō, -dūcere, -dūxī, -ductum *v.t.* draw up from under, pull up, raise; steal, remove

subeō, -īre, -īvī (-iī), -itum *v.t., v.i.* pass under, enter; advance, approach; come up from below; follow; come and help

subiaceō (subj-), -iacēre, -iacuī, --- *v.i.* lie under, lie near (+ dat.)

subiciō (subj-), -icere, -iēcī, -iectum *v.t.* throw under, place under (+ acc. of what is under + dat. of what is above); submit (+ dat.); present; raise, lift; substitute, counterfeit

subigō, -igere, -ēgī, -āctum *v.t.* bring under; drive up from below; conquer, subjugate, constrain; train

subitus, -a, -um *adj.* unexpected, sudden; **subitō** *adv.* suddenly, unexpectedly

sublevō, -levāre, -levāvī, -levātum *v.t.* lift up from beneath, support; alleviate; encourage, help

sublica, -ae *nf.* pile, stake

subligāculum, -ī *nnt.* underwear, loincloth

sublīmus, -a, -um *or* **sublīmis, -is, -e** *adj.* lifted on high, aloft; eminent

subolēs, -is *nf.* shoot, sprout; offspring; stock, race, lineage

subrēpō, -rēpere, -rēpsī, --- *v.i.* steal, go stealthily; creep under; steal upon (+ **sub** + acc. *or* + acc. alone *or* + dat.)

subrūfus, -a, -um *adj.* reddish

subscrīptiō, -ōnis *nf.* subscription; signing, signature; record

subsellium, -ī *nnt.* bench, seat; court

subsequor, subsequī, subsecūtus sum *v.d.t.* follow after; follow in opinion, conform to, adhere to; copy, imitate

subsidium, -ī *nnt.* reserve; support, help; **subsidia, -ōrum** *nnt./pl.* reserve troops

subsīdō, -sīdere, -sēdī, -sessum *v.i.* sit down, crouch down; settle down, subside; submit; stay; lie in ambush

subsistō, -sistere, -stitī, --- *v.i.* make stop; make a stand, resist, halt; stay; cease

substituō, -stituere, -stituī, -stitūtum *v.t.* put next; put under; substitute

substructiō, -ōnis *nf.* that which is built beneath, substructure, foundation, base

subsum, -esse, -fuī, -futūrum *v.i.* be under; be close at hand (+ dat.)

subter *adv.* below, beneath, underneath; *prep.* (+ acc. *or* + abl.) beneath, below, along the underside of

subterrāneus, -a, -um *adj.* underground

subtīlis, -is, -e (w. comp.) *adj.* fine in texture, finely woven; slender; discriminating; simple, plain; **subtīliter** *adv.* accurately; simply, plainly

subtrahō, -trahere, -trāxī, -trāctum *v.t.* draw from beneath; remove, take away secretly

subūcula, -ae *nf.* shirt

suburbānus, -a, -um *adj.* suburban, near the city

subveniō, -venīre, -vēnī, -ventum *v.i.* come to the aid of, help (+ dat.); cure, relieve

subvolō, -āre, ---, --- *v.i.* soar up, fly up

succēdō, -cēdere, -cessī, -cessum *v.i.* enter; approach; follow, succeed

successiō, -ōnis *nf.* following after, succeeding, succession

succurrō, -currere, -currī, -cursum *v.i.* run to, run to help, relieve, assist (+ dat.); come into the mind

sūcus, -ī *nm.* sap, juice; flavor

sūdārium, -ī *nnt.* handkerchief; towel

sūdō, -āre, -āvī, -ātum *v.t., v.i.* sweat; sweat out

sūdor, -ōris *nm.* perspiration, sweat

sufferō, -ferre, sustulī, sublātum *v.t., v.i.* lay the foundation for; support, hold up; endure, suffer

sufficiō, -ficere, -fēcī, -fectum *v.t., v.i.* put under; dye, steep; provide; substitute; be sufficient

suffōcō, -fōcāre, -fōcāvī, -fōcātum *v.t.* choke, suffocate

suffrāgātor, -ōris *nm.* voter; political supporter

suffrāgium, -ī *nnt.* vote; voting tablet; right to vote

suffrāgor, suffrāgārī, suffrāgātus sum *v.d.i.* vote in favor, approve

suggestus, -ūs *nm.* raised height, platform

sūgō, -ere, sūxī, suctum *v.t.* suck

suī, sibi, sē, sē *refl. pron.* himself, herself, itself; themselves

suillus, -a, -um *adj.* of pigs

sum, esse, fuī, futūrum *v.i.* be, exist, be living; happen

summa, -ae *nf.* rank, leadership; top, highest place; main thing, most important point; summary

summittō (subm-), -mittere, -mīsī, -missum *v.t.* let down, send under; submit; subject; moderate; send up from below, lift

summoveō (subm-), -movēre, -mōvī, -mōtum *v.t.* move up from below; drive off, remove, force away, clear away, banish, suspend, remove from office

summus, -a, -um *adj.* highest; greatest, best; extreme, exceeding the usual limits

sūmō, -sūmere, -sūmpsī, -sūmptum *v.t.* take; assume; choose, obtain, buy; begin

sūmptuōsus, -a, -um (w. comp.) *adj.* expensive, costly; extravagant

sūmptus, -ūs *nm.* cost, expense; expenditure

suō, -ere, suī, sūtum *v.t.* sew, stitch

supellex, supellectilis *nf.* furniture

super *adv.* over, above; in addition, moreover; *prep.* (+ acc. *or* + abl.) over, upon; concerning

superbia, -ae *nf.* arrogance, pride, vanity; rudeness

superbus, -a, -um (w. comp. + sup.) *adj.* arrogant, proud

supercilium, -ī *nnt.* eyebrow; nod; arrogance

superficiēs, -ēī *nf.* surface, top

superior, superior, superius (superiōr-) *adj.* superior, higher, better; previous, former, earlier; **superiōre nocte** *adv.* last night

superō, -āre, -āvī, -ātum *v.t.* rise above; exceed, surpass; conquer, overcome

superstes (superstit-) *adj.* present, witnessing; surviving (+ dat. *or* + gen.)

superstitiō, -ōnis *nf.* fear of the supernatural, superstition; unreasonable idea; credulity

superstitiōsus, -a, -um *adj.* superstitious; credulous; prophetic

supersum, -esse, -fuī, -futūrum *v.i.* be left over, remain, survive, outlive; be plentiful

superus, -a, -um *adj.* upper, above, higher; **superī, -ōrum** *nm./pl.* the gods above

supervacāneus, -a, -um *adj.* over and above, superfluous, unnecessary

superveniō, -venīre, -vēnī, -ventum *v.t.* come upon; rise above; arrive; overtake; exceed, surpass

suppeditō, -peditāre, -peditāvī, -peditātum *v.t., v.i.* provide, supply; be at hand; suffice

suppetō, -petere, -petīvī (-petiī), -ītum *v.i.* be at hand, be available; suffice (+ dat.)

suppleō, -plēre, -plēvī, -plētum *v.t.* fill up, complete

supplex (supplic-) *adj.* bending the knee, kneeling; begging; suppliant (+ dat.); **supplex, -plicis** *nm.* suppliant, petitioner (+ gen. of person or god petitioned)

supplicātiō, -ōnis *nf.* public supplication; public day of prayer, public day of thanksgiving

supplicium, -ī *nnt.* kneeling, supplication; punishment, torture

supplicō, -plicāre, -plicāvī, -plicātum *v.t.* kneel down; implore; pray to the gods, supplicate (+ dat.)

supplōdō, -plōdere, -plōsī, --- *v.t.* stamp with the foot; **supplōsiō, -ōnis** *nf.* stamp of the foot

supprimō, -primere, -pressī, -pressum *v.t.* press down, press under; sink; hold down, repress; conceal, suppress

suprā *adv.* above, on top, over; *prep.* (+ acc.) above, beyond, more than

suprēmus, -a, -um *adj.* highest, topmost; final, last; greatest, best, utmost

sūra, -ae *nf.* calf of the leg

surculus, -ī *nm.* slip, sprout, twig

surdus, -a, -um (w. comp.) *adj.* deaf; deaf to (+ **ad** + acc.); not heard, silent

surgō, surgere, surrēxī, surrēctum *v.t., v.i.* get up, rise, stand up

surripiō (subr-), -ripere, -ripuī, -reptum *v.t.* take secretly, steal; take by surprise

sursum *or* **sursus** *or* **susum** *adv.* up, upward

sūs, suis *nm/f.* pig, sow, swine

suscēnseō, -cēnsēre, -cēnsuī, --- *v.i.* be provoked; bear a grudge

suscipiō, -cipere, -cēpī, -ceptum *v.t.* take up, undertake; support, raise; accept, receive

suspectus, -a, -um (w. comp.) *adj.* suspected, mistrusted (+ dat. of person suspected *or* + **dē** + abl. *or* + gen. *or* + infv. to express "suspected of")

suspendō, -pendere, -pendī, -pēnsum *v.t.* suspend, hang up; dedicate; leave undecided; check, stop

suspēnsus, -a, -um *adj.* raised up; doubtful, hesitant; depending on (+ **ex** + abl.)

suspiciō, -ōnis *nf.* suspicion, mistrust

suspiciōsus, -a, -um (w. sup.) *adj.* suspicious, mistrustful (+ **in** + abl.); causing suspicion

suspicor, suspicārī, suspicātus sum *v.d.t.* suspect, mistrust; suppose

suspīrium, -ī *nnt.* sigh, deep breath

suspīrō, -āre, -āvī, -ātum *v.i.* exhale, sigh; long for

sustentō, -tentāre, -tentāvī, -tentātum *v.t.* hold up, sustain, support; strengthen; hinder

sustineō, -tinēre, -tinuī, -tentum *v.t.* support, hold up; control; endure; sustain with food

susurrō, -āre, ---, --- *v.i.* whisper, mutter

susurrus, -ī *nm.* whispering, muttering

sūtūra, -ae *nf.* seam

suus, -a, -um *refl. adj.* his, her, its, their own; *adj.* favoring, propitious; suitable, fitting; **sua, suōrum** *nnt./pl.* one's own property

syllaba, -ae *nf.* syllable

synagōga, -ae *nf.* synagogue

syntaxis, -is *nf.* syntax, connection of words

T

tabella, -ae *nf.* tablet; writing tablet; **tabellae, -ārum** *nf./pl.* letter, dispatch

tabellārius, -ī *nm.* messenger, mail carrier

taberna, -ae *nf.* stall, small shop; inn

tabernāculum, -ī *nnt.* tent

tabernārius, -ī *nm.* shopkeeper

tābēs, -is *nf.* wasting away, decay, melting

tābēscō, -ere, tābuī, — *v.i.* decay, waste away, melt

tablīnum (tabulīnum), -ī *nnt.* tablinum (*the room where Roman family records were kept*)

tabula, -ae *nf.* board; tablet; writing tablet; record, account; picture; **tabulae pūblicae, tabulārum pūblicārum** *nf./pl.* public reqister, public records

tabulārium, -ī *nnt.* archive

tabulātum, -ī *nnt.* story, floor of a building

taceō, -ēre, tacuī, tacitum *v.i.* be silent, leave unspoken

tacitus, -a, -um *adj.* noiseless, silent, quiet; secret; unmentioned

tāctus, -ūs *nm.* touch; sense of touch; influence

taeda, -ae *nf.* torch

taedet, taedēre, taeduit (taesum est) *v.i.* (*imp.*) it disgusts, it offends, it wearies (+ acc. of person + gen. of thing)

taedium, -ī *nnt.* boredom; disgust

talentum, -ī *nnt.* talent (*a weight and denomination of money*)

tāliō, -ōnis *nf.* reprisal, retaliation

tālis, -is, -e *adj.* such, of such a kind; such as this; **tālis, -is, -e ... quālis, -is, -e** *adj.* such ... as

tālus, -ī *nm.* ankle, ankle bone

tam *adv.* so, so much, so far, to such a degree

tamen *conj.* (*sometimes postpos.*) however, still; nevertheless

tametsī *conj.* (+ indv.) although, though; and yet

tamquam *adv.* just as; as it were

tandem *adv.* at last, finally; (*in questions, usu. postpos.*) pray tell, may I ask, after all?

tangō, -ere, tetigī, tāctum *v.t.* touch; adjoin; arrive; be involved in; affect, impress, move

tantum *adv.* so much, so greatly; only so much, merely; **~modō** *adv.* only, merely

tantus, -a, -um *adj.* of such size, so great, such; so very great, so important; only so much; **tantō** *adv.* by so much; **tantus, -a, -um ... quantus, -a, -um** *adj.* so much as, so great as

tardō, -āre, -āvī, -ātum *v.t., v.i.* make slow, delay, impede; tarry

tardus, -a, -um (w. comp. + sup.) *adj.* heavy; slow; late; dull

tata, -ae *nm.* dad, daddy

taurus, -ī *nm.* bull

tēctum, -ī *nnt.* shelter, house, roof

teges, -etis *nf.* mat, covering

tegō, -ere, texī, tēctum *v.t.* cover, spread over; hide, veil; protect

tēgula, -ae *nf.* roof tile

tēla, -ae *nf.* weaving; web; loom

tēlum, -ī *nnt.* missile, spear, arrow, weapon

temerārius, -a, -um *adj.* accidental; rash, thoughtless

temerē *adv.* randomly, by chance; rashly, thoughtlessly; **nōn temerē est quod** (+ indv.), it is not for nothing that

temeritās, -ātis *nf.* chance; accident; rashness, recklessness

temperantia, -ae *nf.* self-control, moderation

temperātus, -a, -um (w. comp. + sup.) *adj.* correctly mixed, ordered; temperate, moderate

temperō, -āre, -āvī, -ātum *v.t., v.i.* be moderate, forbear, be temperate; control, regulate, restrain

tempestās, -ātis *nf.* time, season; weather; bad weather, storm; misfortune

templum, -ī *nnt.* sacred enclosure, temple, shrine; tomb

temporārius, -a, -um *adj.* temporary; seasonable

temptātiō, -ōnis *nf.* test, trial; seizure, attack, onset of illness

temptō, -āre, -āvī, -ātum *v.t.* feel, handle; try, attempt (+ infv.); attack

tempus, -oris *nnt.* period of time, interval, season; right time, right occasion, opportunity; temple of the head

tenāx (tenāc-) (w. comp. + sup.) *adj.* holding fast, sticky; steady; resolute (+ gen.)

tendō, -ere, tetendī, tentum (tēnsum) *v.t.* extend, stretch, distend; proceed; endeavor, aim at

tenebrae, -ārum *nf./pl.* darkness, shadows, night

tenebricōsus, -a, -um (w. sup.) *adj.* gloomy, dark, shadowy

teneō, -ēre, tenuī, tentum *v.t.* hold, have; keep, control; restrain, check; guard, defend

tener, tenera, tenerum (comp. **tenerior**; sup. **tenerrimus**) *adj.* tender, soft, gentle, sensitive

tenuis, -is, -e (w. comp. + sup.) *adj.* thin, slender, slight; subtle; unimportant, lowly; weak

tenuitās, -ātis *nf.* thinness, fineness; delicacy, refinement

tenus *prep.* (postpos. + gen *or* + abl.) up to, down to, as far as

tepidus, -a, -um *adj.* tepid, lukewarm

ter *adv.* three times, thrice

terebra, -ae *nf.* drill, gimlet

terebrō, -āre, ---, -ātum *v.t.* drill, pierce

tergeō, -ēre, tersī, tersum *v.t.* scour, wipe, scrub

tergum, -ī *nnt.* back, rear, reverse; skin, hide, leather

terminō, -āre, -āvī, -ātum *v.t.* limit, bound; finish, terminate

terminus, -ī *nm.* boundary marker, limit, end

ternī, -ae, -a *adj./pl.* three at a time, three each

terō, -ere, trīvī, trītum *v.t.* rub, wear away, use up, wear out

terra, -ae *nf.* earth, land, region, country; **orbis terrae (terrārum), orbis terrae (terrārum)** *nm.* the whole world

terreō, -ēre, terruī, territum *v.t.* frighten, scare; deter

terrestris, -is, -e *adj.* terrestrial, of the earth; on land

terribilis, -is, -e *adj.* terrible, frightening to (+ dat. *or* + abl.)

terror, -ōris *nm.* alarm, fear; terror, dread

tertius, -a, -um *adj.* third

tessera, -ae *nf.* cube of wood or stone, etc.; mosaic cube; die, gaming piece; token; watchword

testāmentum, -ī *nnt.* will, testament

testimōnium, -ī *nnt.* evidence, testimony, proof

testis, -is *nm/f.* witness; spectator

testor, testārī, testātus sum *v.d.t.* testify, serve as a witness; appeal to; declare

tēstūdō, -inis *nf.* turtle, tortoise (*defensive formation during battle in which the soldiers' shields were locked together*)

texō, -ere, texuī, textum *v.t.* weave, plait, braid

textile, -is *nnt.* textile, cloth

textor, -ōris *nm.* weaver

textum, -ī *nnt.* fabric, woven cloth

theātrum, -ī *nnt.* theater; place for games; audience

thēca, -ae *nf.* case, envelope; hull; sheath

thermae, -ārum *nf./pl.* warm springs or baths; public bathing building

thēsaurus *or* **thēnsaurus, -ī** *nm.* treasure, hoard; store house, treasury

tholus, -ī *nm.* dome

thymbra, -ae *nf.* savory

thymum, -ī *nnt.* thyme

tībia, -ae *nf.* leg, shin

tībiāle, -is *nnt.* hose, legging

tībīcen, -inis *nm.* flautist, piper

tignum, -ī *nnt.* beam of wood, timber

tigris, -is (-idis) *nm/f.* tiger

timeō, -ēre, timuī, --- *v.t., v.i.* be afraid (+ infv. of something to do), be anxious, fear (+ **nē** or **nē nōn** + subjv. of what may happen *or* + **ut** + subjv. of what may not happen)

timidus, -a, -um (w. comp. + sup.) *adj.* afraid, timid (+ **ad** + acc. *or* + **in** + abl.), cowardly

timor, -ōris *nm.* fear, alarm, dread; awe

tingō (tinguō), -ere, tinxī, tinctum *v.t.* moisten; dye

tinniō, -īre, ---, --- *v.t.* ring, tinkle

tintinnābulum, -ī *nnt.* bell

tīrō, -ōnis *nm.* beginner; recruit

tītillō, -āre, -āvī, -ātum *v.t.* tickle

titulus, -ī *nm.* inscription; label, title; notice

toga, -ae *nf.* toga

togātus, -a, -um *adj.* clad in a toga

tolerābilis, -is, -e (w. comp. + sup.) *adj.* bearable, tolerable

tolerō, -āre, -āvī, -ātum *v.t.* endure, tolerate, suffer

tollēnō, -ōnis *nm.* crane, machine for lifting, hoist

tollō, -ere, sustulī, sublātum *v.t.* erect, lift, raise high; bring up, educate; remove, lay aside; destroy, put an end to

tondeō, -ēre, totondī, tōnsum *v.t.* shave, clip, shear

tonitrus, -ūs *nm.* thunder

tōnsillae, -ārum *nf./pl.* tonsils

tōnsor, -ōris *nm.* barber, haircutter

tōnstrīna, -ae *nf.* barbershop

tormentum, -ī *nnt.* machine that hurled stones; missile; rack (*instrument of torture*); torture, pain

tornus, -ī *nm.* lathe

torpeō, -ēre, ---, --- *v.i.* be numb; be stiff; be inactive, be paralyzed; be stupid

torqueō, -ēre, torsī, tortum *v.t.* twist, wind, turn, whirl; distort; torture, torment

torques (torquis), -is *nm/f.* torque (*a twisted neck-chain*); yoke for oxen

torrēns, torrentis *nm.* torrent

torreō, -ēre, torruī, tostum *v.t.* burn, roast, parch; dry

tortuōsus, -a, -um *adj.* winding, full of twists and turns; intricate; confused; wily

torvus, -a, um *adj.* fierce, savage; gloomy

tot *adj.* (*indecl.*) so many, as many
totidem *adv.* just so many, the same number of
totiēns *or* **totiēs** *adv.* so often, so many times
tōtus, -a, -um (gen. sg. **tōtīus**; dat. sg. **tōtī**) *adj.* entire, total, the whole, all
trāctātiō, -ōnis *nf.* treatment, management
trāctātus, -ūs *nm.* handling, management
trāctō, -āre, -āvī, -ātum *v.t.* pull, draw; touch, handle, manipulate; manage, control; treat, deal with
trāctus, -ūs *nm.* region, territory
trāditiō, -ōnis *nf.* giving up, surrender; betrayal; instruction
trādō, -dere, -didī, -ditum *v.t.* deliver, hand over; entrust, confide; betray; surrender; relate
trādūcō, -dūcere, -dūxī, -ductum *v.t.* carry over or across, bring over or across, transfer; pass time; display; slander
tragicus, -a, -um *adj.* tragic
tragoedia, -ae *nf.* tragedy
trahō, -ere, trāxī, trāctum *v.t.* drag, pull; carry off; trace; assume, take on; influence; attract; obtain; protract, drag out
trāiciō *or* **trānsiciō (trāj-, trānsj-), -icere, -iēcī, -iectum** *v.t.* throw across, shoot across; carry over, transport; cross; pass through, pierce
tranquillitās, -ātis *nf.* calm, stillness, tranquillity
tranquillus, -a, -um (w. comp. + sup.) *adj.* quiet, calm, still, peaceful, undisturbed
trāns *prep.* (+ acc.) across, over, beyond
trānscendō, -scendere, -scendī, -scēnsum *v.t., v.i.* climb over, pass over; disregard; go beyond, overstep
trānscrībō, -scrībere, -scrīpsī, -scrīptum *v.t.* copy in writing, transcribe; transfer; assign
trānseō, -īre, -īvī (-iī), -itum *v.t., v.i.* cross over, go across, go through; pass by, disregard; go beyond, transgress
trānsferō, -ferre, -tulī, -lātum *v.t.* bear across, transport, transfer
trānsfigō, -figere, -fīxī, -fīxum *v.t.* pierce through, wound; transfix
trānsigō, -igere, -ēgī, -āctum *v.t.* pierce through; bring to an end, accomplish; settle, agree
trānsiliō, -silīre, -siluī (-silīvī), --- *v.t.* leap across, jump over; pass by, neglect; go beyond
trānsitus, -ūs *nm.* passage over, transit; passage; infection
trānsmittō, -mittere, -mīsī, -missum *v.t.* send across, transmit; pass over, traverse; hand over, assign

trānsportō, -portāre, -portāvī, -portātum *v.t.* carry across

trānsversus *or* **trāsversus** *or* **trānsvorsus, -a, -um** *adj.* turned across, crosswise; at cross purposes

trēdecim *num.* (*indecl.*) thirteen

tremefaciō, -facere, -fēcī, -factum *v.t.* cause to shake or tremble

tremō, -ere, -uī, --- *v.i.* shake, tremble; tremble at, shudder at

tremor, -ōris *nm.* trembling, shaking; earthquake

trepidātiō, -ōnis *nf.* alarm, agitation, trepidation

trepidō, -āre, -āvī, -ātum *v.i.* hasten in alarm; be agitated, be afraid of; hesitate, waver

trepidus, -a, -um *adj.* nervous, agitated, anxious (+ gen. of cause of anxiety)

trēs, trēs, tria *num.* three

triangulum, -ī *nnt.* triangle

triangulus, -a, -um *adj.* triangular

tribūnal, -ālis *nnt.* raised platform where magistrates sat; judgment-seat, judicial court, tribunal

tribūnus, -ī *nm.* tribune (*representative of the Roman people*); officer of a Roman legion

tribuō, -ere, tribuī, tribūtum *v.t.* assign, grant; concede, allow

tribus, -ūs *nf.* tribe (*division of the Roman people*)

tribūtum, -ī *nnt.* tribute, tax

trīclīnium, -ī *nnt.* dining couch; dining-room

tridēns, -dentis *nm.* trident

trīgintā *num.* (*indecl.*) thirty

tripūs, -podis *nm.* tripod

trīstis, -is, -e (w. comp. + sup.) *adj.* gloomy, sad, sullen, ill-humored, stern; **trīste** (w. comp. + sup.) *adv.* sadly, sorrowfully; severely; with difficulty

trīstitia, -ae *nf.* sadness, sorrow, depression; sternness

trīticum, -ī *nnt.* wheat

trītus, -a, -um (w. comp.) *adj.* much frequented, much used; worn out, exhausted

triumphō, -āre, -āvī, -ātum *v.t., v.i.* celebrate a triumph, exult

triumphus, -ī *nm.* triumph, victory celebration

triumvir, triumvirī *nm.* one of a board of three officials

trochlea (troclea), -ae *nm.* pulley

tropaeum, -ī *nnt.* trophy, memorial of a victory

trucīdō, -cīdāre, -cīdāvī, -cīdātum *v.t.* massacre, butcher

truculentus, -a, -um (w. comp.) *adj.* fierce, savage; rustic, churlish

trūdō, -ere, trūsī, trūsum *v.t.* shove, push, thrust; urge

trulla,-ae *nf.* ladle
truncus, -ī *nm.* trunk, stem (*bot.*)
trutīna, -ae *nf.* balance of a scales; scales
tū *pron.* you (sg.)
tuba, -ae *nf.* trumpet, war trumpet
tūber, -eris *nnt.* swelling, protuberance
tubus, -ī *nm.* pipe, tube
tueor, tuērī, tūtus sum *v.d.t.* look at, consider; protect, care for
tugurium, -ī *nnt.* hut
tum *adv.* then, at that time; then again, besides; ~ ... **cum** *adv.* not only
    ... but also
tumeō, -ēre, ---, --- *v.i.* swell, be puffed up
tumor, -ōris *nm.* swelling, protuberance; excitement; pride
tumultus, -ūs *nm.* uproar, tumult; insurrection
tumulus, -ī *nm.* mound, hill; burial mound, grave
tunc *adv.* then, at that time
tundō, -ere, tutudī, tūnsum (tūsum) *v.t.* pound, beat, thump; importune;
    deafen
tunica, -ae *nf.* tunic (*the basic garment of the Romans*); husk, peel
turba, -ae *nf.* turmoil, row; mob, crowd; riot
turbidus, -a, -um (w. comp. + sup.) *adj.* disordered, confused; stormy,
    turbulent
turbo, -āre, -āvī, -ātum *v.t.* disturb, throw into confusion, upset
turbulentus, -a, -um (w. comp. + sup.) *adj.* disturbed, stormy, disordered
turma, -ae *nf.* troop of cavalry
turpis, -is, -e (w. comp. + sup.) *adj.* ugly, repulsive; low, disgraceful, dis-
    honorable, shameful
turpitūdō, -inis *nf.* repulsiveness, ugliness; shamefulness, dishonorableness
turris, -is (acc. **turrim**; abl. **turrī**) *nf.* tower
tūs, tūris *nnt.* incense
tussiō, -īre, ---, --- *v.i.* cough
tussis, -is *nf.* cough
tūtēla, -ae *nf.* watching, protection, guardianship, wardship; charge, trust
tūtor, tūtārī, tūtātus sum *v.d.t.* guard, watch, protect
tūtus, -a, -um (w. comp. + sup.) *adj.* safe, free from danger; watchful;
    tūtō *adv.* safely, securely
tuus, -a, -um *adj.* your, yours (2nd person sg.)
tympanum, -ī *nnt.* drum
tyrannus, -ī *nm.* ruler, king; tyrant, despot

U

über, -eris *nnt.* udder, breast

übertās, -ātis *nf.* richness, fertility, productiveness

ubi (ubī) *adv.* where?, when?; where, when, whenever, as soon as; by whom, with whom

ubicumque *adv.* wherever

ubinam *adv.* where?, where on earth?

ubīque *adv.* anywhere, in any place; everywhere, in every place

ūdō, -ōnis *nm.* sock

ulcīscor, ulcīscī, ultus sum *v.d.t.* punish; revenge; require

ulcus, ulceris *nnt.* lesion, sore, ulcer

ūllus, -a, -um (gen. **ūllīus**; dat. **ūllī**) *adj.* any

ulterior, ulterior, ulterius (ulteriōr-) *adj.* farther, beyond, more distant; ulterius; *adv.* beyond, farther on, more, longer

ultimus, -a, -um *adj.* remote, farthest, last; uttermost, extreme

ultiō, -ōnis *nf.* revenge, vengeance

ultrā *adv.* beyond, on the other side, farther, besides, in addition; *prep.* (+ acc.) on the farther side of, beyond, past; over, across; above, exceeding

ultrō citrōque *adv.* hither and thither, to and fro, backwards and forwards, up and down

ululātus, -ūs *nm.* howling, shrieking

ululō, -āre, -āvī, -ātum *v.i.* howl, shriek, yell, wail; re-echo

umbella, -ae *nf.* sun-shade, parasol

umbilīcus, -ī *nm.* navel; umbilical cord; middle

umbra, -ae *nf.* shade, shadow; shady place; faint appearance; shelter; shade (*ghost of a person*)

umbrōsus, -a, -um (w. comp.) *adj.* shady

ūmectō, -āre, -āvī, -ātum *v.t.* dampen, moisten, wet; weep

umerus *or* **humerus, -ī** *nm.* upper bone of the arm; shoulder

ūmidus *or* **hūmidus, -a, -um** *adj.* damp, dank, wet, moist

ūmor *or* **hūmor, -ōris** *nm.* moisture, dew

umquam *adv.* ever, at any time

ūnā *adv.* together, at once, at the same time; **ūnā cum** (*prep.* + abl.) together with

uncia, -ae *nf.* the twelfth part of anything

unda, -ae *nf.* wave, surge; water, fluid, liquid

unde *adv.* whence, from which place; from which, from whom

ūndecim *num. (indecl.)* eleven

ūndecimus, -a, -um *adj.* eleventh

ūndēvīcēsimus, -a, -um *adj.* nineteenth

ūndēvīgintī *num. (indecl.)* nineteen

undique *adv.* on all sides, from all sides, everywhere, all around

ungō (unguō), -ere, ūnxī, ūnctum *v.t.* oil, smear, annoint

unguentum, -ī *nnt.* ointment, perfume

unguis, -is *nm.* fingernail, toenail; claw, talon, hoof

ūnicus, -a, -um *adj.* only, sole, single, unique; **ūnicē** *adv.* singularly, above all others, uniquely

ūniversus, -a, -um *adj.* whole, entire, all together; universal, general; **in ūniversum** *adv.* generally, in general, as a general rule

ūnus, -a, -um (gen. **ūnīus**; dat. **ūnī**) *adj.* single, one only, alone, sole

urbānitās, -ātis *nf.* city manners, courtesy, elegance, urbanity; wit, humor

urbānus, -a, -um *adj.* urban, of the city; in the manner of the city, refined, courteous

urbs, urbis *nf.* city; the city of Rome

urceus, -ī *nm.* pitcher, jug

urgeō, -ēre, ūrsī, --- *v.t., v.i.* press on, push, urge (+ **ut** or + **nē** + subjv.); press hard, oppress, urge on, drive

ūrīna, -ae *nf.* urine

ūrīnālis, -is, -e *adj.* urinary, pertaining to urine

urna, -ae *nf.* urn, water-pot, vessel, jar

ūrō, -ere, ussī, ustum *v.t.* burn, singe; pain; pinch; rub sore, chafe; dry up; inflame, burn with passion; disturb, harass

ursa, -ae *nf.* she-bear, sow bear

ursus, -ī *nm.* male bear

ūsitātus, -a, -um (w. comp. + sup.) *adj.* usual, customary, regular, common, ordinary, familiar; **ūsitātum est** it is usual, it is customary (+ infv.)

uspiam *adv.* at any place, somewhere, anywhere

usquam *adv.* anywhere

usque ad (*prep.* + acc.) as far as, even to; all the way; as long as

ūsūra, -ae *nf.* use, enjoyment; interest on money, usury

ūsūrpō, -āre, -āvī, -ātum *v.t.* make use of, employ; practice; adopt; talk of; resort to

ūsus, -ūs *nm.* use, employment, enjoyment; practice, experience, skill; familiarity; benefit, profit, need; intimacy

ut(ī) *adv.* where; as, as soon as; how?, in what way?, in what manner?; as for instance, as if; *conj.* that, so that; in order that; though, although

ūtēnsilia, -ium *nnt./pl.* utensils, materials

uter, utra, utrum (gen. **utrīus**; dat. **utrī**) *adj.* which of two, either of two

uterque, utraque, utrumque *adj.* each, either, both

uterus, -ī *nm.* uterus, womb; cavity; fruit of the womb

ūtilis, -is, -e (comp. **ūtilior**; sup. **ūtillimus**) *adj.* useful; profitable, advantageous; fit, suitable

ūtilitās, -ātis *nf.* utility, usefulness; profit, advantage, expediency

utinam *adv.* oh that!, would that!, if only! (+ subjv.)

utique *adv.* in any case, by all means; (+ neg.) not at all; especially, at least

ūtor, ūtī, ūsus sum *v.d.i.t.* use, employ; exercise, perform; enjoy, indulge in; enjoy someone's friendship (+ abl.)

utrimque *adv.* on both sides, from both sides, on either hand

utrōque *adv.* in either direction, to both places

utrum … an *adv.* whether … or

ūva, -ae *nf.* grape, bunch of grapes; cluster of fruit

uxor, -ōris *nf.* wife

V

vacātiō, -ōnis *nf.* freedom, release from, exemption, immunity

vacca, -ae *nf.* cow, heifer

vaccillō, -āre, -āvī, -ātum *v.i.* sway to and fro, stagger; waver, hesitate

vacō, -āre, -āvī, -ātum *v.i.* be empty, be free from, be unoccupied (+ abl. or + **ab** + abl.), be at leisure (+ dat.)

vacuēfaciō, -facere, -fēcī, -fectum *v.t.* evacuate, make empty

vacuus, -a, -um *adj.* empty, void, unoccupied; clear, unobstructed; worthless, useless; single (*unmarried*); widowed; carefree, idle, unengaged, at leisure (+ abl. or + **ab** + abl.)

vadimōnium, -ī *nnt.* bail, bail-bond, security

vādō, -ere, ---, --- *v.i.* go, proceed

vadōsus, -a, -um *adj.* shallow, full of shallows

vadum, -ī *nnt.* shallow place, ford; body of water, sea

vāgina, -ae *nf.* sheath, scabbard

vāgiō, -īre, -iī, --- *v.i.* squeal, wail, squall

vāgitus, -ūs *nm.* cry, wail of an infant

vagor, vagārī, vagātus sum *v.d.i.* ramble, rove, wander; spread abroad

vagus, -a, -um *adj.* astray, wandering; inconstant

valdē *adv.* strongly, exceedingly; very much; certainly

valeō, -ēre, valuī, valitum *v.i.* be strong, be vigorous, be healthy; have power; be able

valētūdinārium, -ī *nnt.* hospital, sick-room

valētūdō, -inis *nf.* health, state of health; illness, ill health, feebleness

validus, -a, -um (w. comp. + sup.) *adj.* powerful, strong, vigorous

vallis (vallēs), -is *nf.* valley, hollow

vallō, -āre, -āvī, -ātum *v.t.* fortify with a rampart

vallum, -ī *nnt.* rampart

valva, -ae *nf.* door

vānēscō, -ere, ---, --- *v.i.* pass away, vanish; get thinner

vānitās, -ātis *nf.* emptiness, aimlessness; deceit, fickleness; vanity, vain-glory

vānus, -a, -um (w. comp.) *adj.* empty, idle; baseless, vain; fruitless; false, deceitful; for naught

vapidus, -a, -um *adj.* flat, insipid

vapor, -ōris *nm.* vapor, steam

variētās, -ātis *nf.* variety, diversity; difference, disagreement; change, vicissitude

variō, -āre, -āvī, -ātum *v.t.* vary, change; *v.i.* be different, vary

varius, -a, -um *adj.* diverse, different, various, varying, changeful; varie-gated; **variē** *adv.* variously, differently; with varying fortune

vas, vadis *nm.* surety, bail

vās, vāsis *nnt.* vessel, vase

vāstātiō, -ōnis *nf.* laying waste, devastation

vāstitās, -ātis *nf.* wasteland, desert; ruin, desolation, destruction

vāstō, -āre, -āvī, -ātum *v.t.* lay waste, devastate, destroy

vastus, -a, -um (w. comp. + sup.) *adj.* dreary, desolate, laid waste; huge, immense, vast, boundless; mighty, frightful; deafening

vātes, -is *nm/f.* prophet, diviner, seer; inspired bard, poet

-ve *enclitic conj.* or, or also

vectīgālis, -is, -e *adj.* tributary; payer of tribute; **vectīgal, -ālis** *nnt.* state toll, tax, duty; income

vectis, -is *nm.* bolt, bar; lever

vectō, -āre, -āvī, -ātum *v.t.* carry, transport

vector, -ōris *nm.* carrier, bearer; passenger

vectūra, -ae *nf.* conveying, carrying; fare, money for transport

vehemēns *or* **vēmēns (vehement-, vēment-)** (w. comp. + sup.) *adj.* eager, ardent, vehement; aggressive, forceful

vehiculum, -ī *nnt.* vehicle, conveyance

veho, -ere, vexī, vectum *v.t.* carry, bear, convey; bring in; draw, lead, conduct, drive

vel *conj.* or, or if you will, or even; ~ ... ~ *conj.* either ... or, whether ... or; ~ **potius** *conj.* or rather

vēlāmen, -inis *nnt.* veil, covering; garment

vellicō, -āre, -āvī, -ātum *v.t.* pinch, nip; pluck

vellō, -ere, vellī (vollī), vulsum (volsum) *v.t.* pull, pluck, pull out; tear up, tear away

vellus, -eris *nnt.* fleece, lock of wool

vēlō, -āre, -āvī, -ātum *v.t.* veil, cover; crown; clothe

vēlōcitās, -ātis *nf.* swiftness, fleetness

vēlōx (velōc-) (w. comp. + sup.) *adj.* swift, rapid

vēlum, -ī *nnt.* cloth, covering; sail; curtain

velut *adv.* just as, as when, as, as if

vēna, -ae *nf.* blood vessel, vein

vēnābulum, -ī *nnt.* hunting spear

vēnālis, -is, -e *adj.* on sale, to be sold

vēnātiō, -ōnis *nf.* the chase, hunting; combat of wild beasts; game

vēnātor, -ōris *nm.* hunter

vēnātrīx, -īcis *nf.* huntress

vēnātus, -ūs *v.t.* hunt, chase

vēnditātiō, -ōnis *nf.* offering for sale; boasting, vaunting

vēnditiō, -ōnis *nf.* sale, selling

vēnditō, -āre, -āvī, -ātum *v.t.* keep offering for sale, try to sell; deal in, sell; give for a bribe; recommend

vēnditor, -ōris *nm.* seller

vēndō, -dere, -didī, -ditum *v.t.* sell; betray; bribe

venēfica, -ae *nf.* witch, sorceress

venēficium, -ī *nnt.* sorcery, poisoning; preparation of drugs

venēficus, -ī *nm.* sorcerer; poisoner

venēnātus, -a, -um *adj.* poisonous, poisoned, drugged; enchanted

venēnō, -āre, -āvī, -ātum *v.t.* poison, drug

venēnum, -ī *nnt.* poison, venom

vēneō, -īre, vēniī, vēnitum *v.i.* go to sale, be sold

venerābilis, -is, -e *adj.* venerable, revered

venerābundus, -a, -um *adj.* venerating, reverential, full of awe

venereus, -a, -um *adj.* of Venus; venereal, of sexual love

venero, -āre, -āvī, -ātum *v.t.* worship, reverence; pray, supplicate

veneror, venerārī, venerātus sum *v.d.t.* worship, reverence; pray, supplicate

venia, -ae *nf.* pardon, favor
veniō, -īre, vēnī, ventum *v.i.* come; come into, enter; approach; be
  descended
vēnor, vēnārī, vēnātus sum *v.d.i.t.* chase, hunt
venter, ventris *nm.* belly
ventilātiō, -ōnis *nf.* ventilation, airing
ventōsus, -a, -um (w. comp. + sup.) *adj.* windy, stormy
ventriculus, -ī *nm.* belly, stomach
ventus, -ī *nm.* wind
venustās, -ātis *nf.* beauty, grace, elegance; artistic taste; art
venustus, -a, -um *adj.* attractive, charming, graceful
vēr, vēris *nnt.* spring, springtime
vērāx (vērāc-) (w. comp.) *adj.* truthful
verber, verberis *nnt.* lash, blow of a whip, scourging
verberō, -āre, -āvī, -ātum *v.t.* beat, strike, lash
verbum, -ī *nnt.* term, word, expression; verb
vērē *adv.* really, truly, in fact; properly, rightly
verēcundia, -ae *nf.* shyness, modesty, sense of shame; respect
verēcundus, -a, -um *adj.* modest, shy
vereor, verērī, veritus sum *v.d.i.t.* reverence, stand in awe of, respect;
  fear, dread
vērisimilis, -is, -e (comp. **vērisimilior**; sup. **vērisimillimus**) *adj.* probable,
  likely; **vērisimiliter** *adv.* probably
vēritās, -ātis *nf.* truth; truthfulness, sincerity; reality, fact
vermis, -is *nm.* worm
vērnus, -a, -um *adj.* of spring, spring
vērō *adv.* truly, certainly; *conj.* (*often postpos.*) but in fact, however, but
verrō, -ere, verrī, versum *v.t.* sweep, skim
verrūca, -ae *nf.* wart; small fault
versātilis, -is, -e *adj.* turning around, revolving; versatile
versō, -āre, -āvī, -ātum *v.t.* roll, wheel, turn; drive this way and that; turn
  over, ponder
versor, versārī, versātus sum *v.d.i.* move about; dwell, remain; be associated, be situated, be engaged in, be busy (+ abl.)
versum (versus) *adv.* turned towards, in that direction; *prep.* (+ acc.)
  turned in the direction of, facing towards
versus, -ūs *nm.* turn, turning; line, row, line of poetry
vertebra, -ae *nf.* joint of the back, vertebra
vertex, -icis *nm.* whirlpool, eddy; the crown of the head; top, summit, zenith

vertīgō, -inis *nf.* whirling around; dizziness

vertō, -ere, versī, versum *v.t.* turn, change direction; turn away, divert; destroy; change, alter; ponder

vērus, -a, -um (w. comp. + sup.) *adj.* true, real, genuine; fair, reasonable; **vērē** (w. comp. + sup.) *adv.* truly; **vērō** *adv.* truly, doubtless; *conj.* however, but; **vērum** *adv.* truly; *conj.* but, notwithstanding, however, still; **vērum, -ī** *nnt.* truth, fact, reality

vēscor, vēscī, --- *v.d.i.* feed on, eat; feast on (+ abl.)

vēsīca, -ae *nf.* bladder, urinary bladder

vespa, -ae *nf.* wasp

vesper, vesperī (-eris) *nm.* eve, evening; the evening star; **vesperī, vespere** *adv.* in the evening; **vespera, -ae** *nf.* evening

vespertīliō, -ōnis *nm.* bat (*zool.*)

Vestālis, -is *nf.* Vestal, vestal virgin

vester (vos-), vestra, vestrum *adj.* your, yours (2nd person pl.)

vestiārium, -ī *nnt.* wardrobe, clothes-chest

vestibulum, -ī *nnt.* porch, portico, entrance

vestīgium, -ī *n.* track, trace, footprint; mark, indication, sign; feet; course

vestīgō, -āre, -āvī, -ātum *v.t.* stalk, track, trace, search for

vestīmentum, -ī *nnt.* clothing, garment

vestiō, -īre, -īvī, -ītum *v.t.* cover with a garment, provide with clothing, array, adorn

vestis, -is *nf.* garment, robe, apparel; fabric, cloth, drapery

vestītus, -ūs *nm.* clothing, dress, attire

veterānus, -a, -um *adj.* veteran, old; **veterānus, -ī** *nm.* veteran soldier, veteran

veto, -āre, -uī, -itum *v.t.* forbid, oppose, prohibit

vetus (veter-) (sup. **veterrimus**) *adj.* old, ancient; of long standing; of a former time, former, earlier

vetustās, -ātis *nf.* old age, age; long duration; great age, ancient times

vetustus, -a, -um (w. comp. + sup.) *adj.* ancient

vexātiō, -ōnis *nf.* harassment; distress, hardship, trouble

vexillum, -ī *nnt.* banner, flag, standard

vexō, -āre, -āvī, -ātum *v.t.* shake, toss; attack; aggravate, annoy

via, -ae *nf.* road, path, way, street; passage, journey, voyage

viāticum, -ī *nnt.* traveling money, traveling expenses

viātor, -ōris *nm.* traveler, wayfarer; magistrate's attendant, court-officer

vibrō, -āre, -āvī, -ātum *v.i.* vibrate, quiver; throw, hurl; gleam, flash

vicārius, -ī *nm.* substitute; under-slave

vicem *adv.* to the extent of; **in vicem** *adv.* by turns

vīcēsimus, -a, -um *adj.* twentieth

vīcinia, -ae *nf.* environs, neighborhood

vīcinitās, -ātis *nf.* neighborhood, vicinity

vīcīnus, -a, -um *adj.* neighboring, near, close by

vicis (**vicem** acc.; **vice** abl.) *nf.* (*irreg.*) change, interchange; remuneration; lot, condition; post, office, duty; **vicēs** (**vicēs** acc.; **vicibus** dat./abl.) *nf./pl.* (*irreg.*) changes; fortune; perils

vicissim *adv.* alternately, in turn

vicissitūdō, -inis *nf.* turn, change from one thing to another; alternation

victima, -ae *nf.* victim, beast for sacrifice, sacrificial victim

victor, -ōris *nm.* victor, conqueror

victōria, -ae *nf.* victory, triumph

victrīx, victrīcis *nf.* conqueror

victus, -ūs *nm.* food, sustenance, diet, provisions; way of life, mode of living

vīcus, -ī *nm.* abode; quarter of a city; street; village; country-seat

vidēlicet *adv.* clearly, plainly; of course, to be sure

videō, -ēre, vīdī, vīsum *v.t.* see, behold, witness; comprehend, understand; see to, care for; **videor, vidērī, vīsus sum** *v.* pass, look, appear, seem, be regarded

vidua, -ae *nf.* widow; unmarried woman

viduus, -a, um *adj.* deprived of wife or husband; widowed; unmarried

vigeō, -ēre, viguī, --- *v.i.* thrive, flourish; be powerful, gain strength

vigil (vigil-) *adj.* awake, watchful, unsleeping; **vigil, vigilis** *nm.* watchman, sentinel, guard; **vigilēs, -ium** *nm./pl.* the urban watchmen

vigilia, -ae *nf.* watching, wakefulness, vigilance; watch, guard

vigilō, -āre, -āvī, -ātum *v.t., v.i.* keep watch, be awake, wake up

vīgintī *num.* (*indecl.*) twenty

vigor, -ōris *nm.* activity, vigor; strength, force

vīlicus, -ī *nm.* steward (*caretaker of an estate*)

vīlis, -is, -e (w. comp. + sup.) *adj.* worthless, cheap

vīlitās, -ātis *nf.* cheapness

villa, -ae *nf.* villa, country-set, farm-dwelling

villōsus, -a, -um *adj.* shaggy

villus, -ī *nm.* coarse hair; pile, nap

vīmen, -inis *nnt.* twig, shoot (*bot.*)

vīnārius, -a, -um *adj.* of wine, for wine

vinciō, -īre, vīnxī, vīnctum *v.t.* tie up, bind, twine, encircle

vincō, -ere, vīcī, victum *v.t.* defeat, conquer, surpass, overcome, overpower, prevail

vinculum (vinclum), -ī *nnt.* link, bond, fetter, tie; band, strap, rope, cord,
cable

vindēmia, -ae *nf.* vintage

vindex, vindicis *nm/f.* defender, protector, champion; avenger, punisher

vindicō, -dicāre, -dicāvī, -dicātum *v.t.* lay claim to, assume; protect,
defend; release, free, set free; avenge, punish

vīnea, -ae *nf.* vineyard; shed for sheltering beseigers

vīnētum, -ī *nnt.* vineyard

vīnulentia, -ae *nf.* wine bibbing; intoxication from wine; tendency to drink
too much

vīnum, -ī *nnt.* wine

viola, -ae *nf.* violet (*bot.*); the color violet

violāceus, -a, -um *adj.* violet in color

violātiō, -ōnis *nf.* violation, profanation; injury

violentia, -ae *nf.* violence, fury

violentus, -a, -um (w. comp. + sup.) *adj.* violent

violō, -āre, -āvī, -ātum *v.t.* violate, injure, mar; profane, stain

vīpera, -ae *nf.* viper, serpent

vir, virī *nm.* man, male human being; husband; hero

virectum, -ī *nnt.* grassy area

vireo, -ēre, ---, --- *v.i.* be green, put forth leaves; flourish

virga, -ae *nf.* twig, stick, sapling, rod, wand

virgātus, -a, -um *adj.* made of twigs; striped

virginālis, -is, -e *adj.* of a maiden, maidenly

virgineus, -a, -um *adj.* of a maiden, maidenly

virginitās, -ātis *nf.* virginity

virgō, virginis *nf.* virgin, maiden, unmarried woman

virgultum, -ī *nnt.* thicket

viridāns (viridant-) *adj.* green

viridis, -is, -e *adj.* green grassy; mossy; fresh, vigorous

viriditās, ātis *nf.* green color, greenness; freshness, vigor

virīlis, -is, -e *adj.* manly; heroic; full-grown, mature; bold, noble

virtūs, -ūtis *nf.* valor, manliness, bravery, heroism; virtue, excellence

vīrus, -ī *nnt.* potent juice, medicinal liquid; poison, venom; slime

vīs (vim acc.; **vī** abl.) *nf.* (*irreg.*) power, strength, force, violence; injury;
vīrēs, -ium *nf./pl.* strength, power; powers, forces

vīscus, -eris *nnt.* flesh, viscera, entrails (*usu. pl.*)

visitō, -āre, -āvī, -ātum *v.t.* visit; see often

vīsō, -ere, vīsī, vīsum *v.t.* view, go to see, examine, look at

vīsum, -ī *nnt.* sight, spectacle; omen

vīsus, -ūs *nm.* sight, vision; gaze; omen; appearance, aspect

vīta, -ae *nf.* life, breath of life; soul; shade, spirit; mode of life

vītālis, -is, -e *adj.* of life, vital

vitiō, -āre, -āvī, -ātum *v.t.* corrupt, flaw, taint

vitiōsus, -a, -um (w. comp. + sup.) *adj.* full of faults, defective; wicked, vicious, evil

vītis, -is *nf.* vine; centurion's staff

vitium, -ī *nnt.* flaw, taint, defect

vītō, -āre, -āvī, -ātum *v.t.* avoid, shun

vitricus, -ī *nm.* stepfather

vitrum, -ī *nnt.* glass; woad (*a dye plant*)

vitta, -ae *nf.* ribbon, band; fillet

vitula, -ae *nf.* calf, heifer

vitulīna, -ae *nf.* veal

vitulus, -ī *nm.* calf, young bull

vituperō, -āre, -āvī, --- *v.t.* injure; find fault with, reproach, disparage

vīvidus, -a, -um *adj.* lively, vigorous, active, full of life

vīvō, -ere, vīxī, victum *v.i.* live, be alive; remain, keep alive

vīvus, -a, -um *adj.* live, lifelike; growing; natural; flowing, perennial; solid

vix *adv.* hardly, with difficulty, scarcely; (*of time*) no sooner

vixdum *adv.* scarcely yet, but just

vōcālis, -is, -e *adj.* uttering sounds, vocal, speaking, singing

vōciferor, vōciferārī, vōciferātus sum *v.d.i.t.* cry out, shout, exclaim

vocō, -āre, -āvī, -ātum *v.t.* call, summon, call together; pray for, invoke; call by name

vōcula, -ae *nf.* weak voice, small voice

volātilis, -is, -e *adj.* flying, winged

volātus, -ūs *nm.* flight; flight of birds

volēns (volent-) *adj.* willing, glad; well-wishing, kindly, propitious

volitō, -āre, -āvī, -ātum *v.i.* fly, flit about

volō, -āre, -āvī, -ātum *v.i.* fly, flit about, rush

volō, velle, voluī, --- *v.i.* wish, want, be willing (+ infv.); will, intend; claim, assert

volsella, -ae *nf.* tweezers, pinchers

voltur, volturis *nm.* vulture

voltus (vultus), -ūs *nnt.* look, facial expression, appearance

volūbilis, -is, -e *adj.* winding, twisting

volucer, volucris, volucre *adj.* flying, winged; rapid, swift; fleeting;
volucer, volucris *nf.* bird

volūmen, -inis *nnt.* roll, coil, fold, band wound round

voluntārius, -a, -um *adj.* voluntary, willing, of one's free will, intentional;
willful

voluntās, -ātis *nf.* will, wish, desire, pleasure

voluptās, -ātis *nf.* pleasure, enjoyment, delight

volvō, -ere, volvī, volūtum *v.t.* roll, roll down, roll over, roll up; toss;
unroll, disclose; revolve, spin; turn over in the mind, ponder

vomica, -ae *nf.* boil, sore, ulcer

vomō, -ere, -uī, -itum *v.t.* throw up, vomit

vorāgō, -inis *nf.* chasm, abyss, whirlpool

vorō, -āre, -āvī, -ātum *v.t.* swallow, devour, engulf

vortex, -icis *nm.* whirlpool

vōs *pron.* you (pl.)

vōtum, -ī *nnt.* desire, prayer, vow; votive offering

voveō, -ēre, vōvī, vōtum *v.t.* vow, dedicate; pray for

vōx, vōcis *nf.* voice; cry; note, tone, sound; word, words, language, speech

vulgāris, -is, -e *adj.* of the multitude, common, low, mean; vulgar

vulgō (volgō), -āre, -āvī, -ātum *v.t.* spread abroad, publish, make known

vulgus (volgus), -ī *nnt.* the crowd, populace, people, the mass, the common herd; **vulgō** *adv.* generally, commonly, everywhere

vulnerō (volnerō), -āre, -āvī, -ātum *v.t.* shoot, hit, wound

vulnus (volnus), -eris *nnt.* injury, wound

vulpēs, -is *nf.* fox

vultur, -uris *nm.* vulture

vultus (voltus), -ūs *nnt.* look, facial expression; appearance

X

xystus, -ī *nm.* avenue, garden walk, promenade, walk-way; open portico

Z

zōthēca, -ae *nf.* alcove, small private chamber

English–Latin
Dictionary

A

a, an *art.* (*not expressed in Latin*)
abacus *n.* abacus, -ī *m.*
abandon *v.t.* relinquō, -linquere, -līquī, -līctum
abbreviate *v.t.* praecīdō, -cīdere, -cīdī, -cīsum
abbreviation *n.* contrāctiō, -ōnis *f.*
abdomen *n.* abdōmen, -inis *nt.*
ability *n.* facultās, -ātis *f.*
able, be ~ *v.i.* possum, posse, potuī, --- (+ *infv.*); **not to be ~** *v.i.* nequeō, -quīre, -quīvī (-iī), -itum (+ infv.)
abnormal *adj.* mīrus, -a, -um
abortion *n.* abortiō, -ōnis *f.*
about *adv.* ferē (*postpos.*); *prep.* (~ *time;* ~ *place*) circa (+ acc.); (*concerning*) dē (+ abl.)
above *adv.* suprā; *prep.* (*on top of*) suprā (+ acc.); *prep.* (*over*) super (+ acc. *or* + abl.)
absence *n.* absentia, -ae *f.*
absent *adj.* absēns, -entis; **be ~** *v.i.* absum, abesse, āfuī, āfutūrus
absolute *adj.* absolūtus, -a, -um
absorb *v.t.* combibō, -bibere, -bibī, ---
absurd *adj.* absurdus, -a, -um
abundance *n.* abundantia, -ae *f.*
abundant *adj.* largus, -a, -um
abuse *v.i.* abūtor, abūtī, abūsus sum (+ abl.)
abusive *adj.* contumēliōsus, -a, -um
academic *adj.* scholasticus, -a, -um
academy *n.* schola, -ae *f.*
accelerate *v.i.* accelerō, -celerāre, -celerāvī, -celerātum
accent *n.* vōx, vōcis *f.*
accept *v.t.* accipiō, -cipere, -cēpī, -ceptum; *v.t.* recipiō, -cipere, -cēpī, -ceptum
acceptance *n.* acceptiō, -ōnis *f.*
access *n.* aditus, -ūs *m.*
accident *n.* cāsus, -ūs *m.*
accidental *adj.* fortuītus, -a, -um
accommodate *v.d.t.* mōrigeror, mōrigerārī, mōrigerātus sum
accommodation *n.* reconciliātiō, -ōnis *f.* (*agreement*)
accompany *v.d.t.* comitor, comitārī, comitātus sum

accomplice *n.* socius, -ī *m.*; *n.* socia, -ae *f.*
accomplish *v.t.* cōnficiō, -ficere, -fēcī, -fectum
accomplishment *n.* cōnfectiō, -ōnis *f.*
according to *prep.* dē, ex (+ abl.)
account *n.* ratiō, -ōnis *f.* (*reckoning; bank ~*); **on ~ of** *prep.* ob, propter (+ acc.)
accountant *n.* scrība, -ae *m.*
accounting *n.* ratiō, -ōnis *f.*
accumulate *v.t.* cumulō, -āre, -āvi, -ātum
accurate *adj.* vērus, -a, -um
accusation *n.* accūsātiō, -ōnis *f.*
accuse *v.t.* accūsō, -cūsāre, -cūsāvī, -cūsātum
accustom, be ~ed *v.i.* soleō, -ēre, solitus sum (+ infv.)
ache *n.* dolor, -ōris *m.*; *v.i.* doleō, -ēre, -uī, ---
achieve *v.t.* cōnficiō, -ficere, -fēcī, -fectum (*finish*)
achievement *n.* rēs gesta, reī gestae *f.*
acid *adj.* acerbus, -a, -um
acknowledge *v.d.t.* fateor, fatērī, fassus sum (*admit*)
acknowledgement *n.* cōnfessiō, -ōnis *f.* (*admission*)
acquaint *v.t.* cōgnōscō, -gnōscere, -gnōvī, -gnitum (*~ oneself with*)
acquaintance *n.* familiāris, -is *m/f.*
acquire *v.t.* adquīrō, -quīrere, -quīsīvī, -quīsītum
acquisition *n.* quaestus, -ūs *m.*
across *adv. use verb compounded with the pref.* trāns-; *prep.* trāns (+ acc.), per (+ acc.)
act *n.* rēs gesta, reī gestae *f.* (*deed*); *n.* actus, -ūs *m.* (*of a play*); *v.i.* agō, agere, ēgī, āctum
action *n.* āctiō, -ōnis *f.*
active *adj.* agilis, -is, -e
activity *n.* celeritās, -ātis *f.* (*quickness*); *n.* industria, -ae *f.* (*industry*)
actor *n.* histriō, -ōnis *m.*
actual *adj.* vērus, -a, -um
acute *adj.* acūtus, -a, -um (*of the senses: penetrating, sharp*); *adj.* ācer, ācris, ācre (*shrewd; of diseases: severe*)
adapt *v.t.* accommodō, -commodāre, -commodāvī, -commodātum
add *v.t.* addō, -dere, -didī, -ditum; **~ up** *v.t.* computō, -putāre, -putāvī, -putātum
addition *n.* adiectiō, -ōnis *f.*
additional *adj.* novus, -a, -um; *adj.* additus, -a, -um

address *n.* ōrātiō, -ōnis *f.* (*speech*); *n.* īnscrīptiō, -ōnis *f.* (*of a letter*); *v.d.t.* adloquor, -loquī, -locūtus sum (*speak to*)

adequate *adj.* satis (indecl., + gen.) (*sufficient*); *adj.* idōneus, -a, um (*suitable*)

adhere *v.i.* inhaereō, -haerēre, -haesī, -haesum (+ dat. *or* + **ad** + acc. *or* + **in** + abl.)

adhesive *adj.* tenāx, tenācis

adjacent *adj.* contiguus, -a, -um; *adj.* fīnitimus, -a, -um

adjoin *v.i.* iaceō, -ēre, iacuī, ---

adjust *v.t.* aptō, -āre, -āvī, -ātum (*adapt*); *v.t.* ōrdinō, -āre, -āvī, -ātum (*set in order*)

administer *v.t.* prōcūrō, -cūrāre, -cūrāvī, -cūrātum (*manage an estate, province, etc.*); *v.t.* administrō, -ministrāre, -ministrāvī, -ministrātum (*manage public affairs*)

administration *n.* prōcūrātiō, -ōnis *f.* (*of an estate, province, etc.*); *n.* administrātiō, -ōnis *f.* (*of public affairs*)

admirable *adj.* mīrābilis, -is, -e

admiral *n.* praefectus classis, praefectī classis *m.*

admire *v.d.t.* mīror, mīrārī, mīrātus sum

admission *n.* accessus, -ūs *m.* (*entrance*)

admit *v.t.* admittō, -mittere, -mīsī, -missum (*allow access*); *v.t.* concēdō, -cēdere, -cessī, -cessum (*concede*); *v.d.t.* fateor, fatērī, fassus sum (*confess*)

adolescent *n.* adulēscēns, -entis *m/f.*; *adj.* adulēscēns, -entis

adopt *v.t.* adoptō, -optāre, -optāvī, -optātum (~ *a child*); *v.t.* approbō, -probāre, -probāvī, -probātum (~ *a resolution*)

adoption *n.* adoptiō, -ōnis *f.*

adore *v.t.* colō, colere, coluī, cultum

adult *adj.* adultus, -a, -um; *n.* adultus, -ī *m.*

advance *n.* prōgressus, -ūs *m.*; *v.d.i.* prōgredior, prōgredī, prōgressus sum (*go forward*); *v.t.* prōmoveō, -movēre, -mōvī, -mōtum (*carry forward*)

advantage *n.* commodum, -ī *nt.*

adventurous *adj.* ausus, -a, -um

adverb *n.* adverbium, -ī *nt.*

adversary *n.* adversārius, -ī *m.*

advertise *v.t.* prōscrībō, -scrībere, -scrīpsī, -scrīptum (*publish a notice*); *v.t.* nūntiō, -āre, -āvī, -ātum (*inform*)

advertisement *n.* prōscrīptiō, -ōnis *f.*

advice *n.* cōnsilium, -ī *nt.*

advise *v.t.* suādeō, -ēre, suāsī, suāsum (+ dat. of person *or* + acc. + infv. *or* + **ut** or **nē** + subjv. of course advised)

adviser/advisor *n.* suāsor, -ōris *m.*

aedile *n.* aedīlis, -is *m.*

aerial *adj.* aethereus, -a, -um

affair *n.* rēs, reī *f.*

affect *v.t.* afficiō, -ficere, -fēcī, -fectum (*influence*); *v.t.* commoveō, -movēre, mōvī, -mōtum (*move emotionally*); *v.t.* simulō, -āre, -āvī, -ātum (*make a show of*)

affection *n.* amor, -ōris *m.*

affectionate *adj.* amāns, -antis

affirm *v.t.* adfirmō, -firmāre, -firmāvī, -firmātum

affirmation *n.* adfirmātiō, -ōnis *f.*

afflict *v.t.* afflīctō, -flīctāre, -flīctāvī, -flīctātum

affliction *n.* dolor, -ōris *m.*

afraid *adj.* timidus, -a, -um; **be ~ of** *v.t., v.i.* timeō, -ēre, timuī, ---

after *adv.* post, posteā; *prep.* post (+ acc.) (*in ref. to place, time*); *prep.* secundum (+ acc.) (*following in rank*)

afternoon *adj.* postmerīdiānus, -a, -um

afterward *adv.* post, posteā

again *adv.* rūrsum, rūrsus (*once more*); *adv.* iterum (*a second time*)

against *prep.* contrā (+ acc.)

age *n.* aetās, -ātis *f.*

agenda *n.* agenda, -ōrum *nt./pl.*

agent *n.* prōcūrātor, -ōris *m.*

aggravate *v.t.* aggravō, -gravāre, -gravāvī, -gravātum (*make worse*); *v.t.* vexō, -āre, -āvī, -ātum (*annoy*)

aggressive *adj.* hostīlis, -is, -e (*hostile*); *adj.* vehemēns, -entis (*forceful*)

agile *adj.* agilis, -is, -e

agitate *v.t.* agitō, -āre, -āvī, -ātum (*shake*); *v.t.* sollicitō, -āre, -āvī, -ātum (*worry; disturb*); *v.t.* vexō, -āre, -āvī, -ātum (*annoy*); *v.t.* perturbō, -turbāre, -turbāvī, -turbātum

ago *adv.* abhinc (+ acc., rarely + abl.); **a long time ~** *adv.* prīdem; **a short time ~** *adv.* nōn prīdem

agony *n.* dolor, -ōris *m.*

agree *v.t., v.i.* cōnsentiō, -sentīre, -sēnsī, -sēnsum; **~ with** (+ dat. *or* + **cum** + abl.); **~ upon** *v.t.* cōnstituō, -stituere, -stituī, -stitūtum; **it is agreed** *v.i.* cōnstat, cōnstāre, cōnstitit, --- (imp., + acc. + infv.)

agreeable *adj.* grātus, -a, -um

agreement *n.* pactum, -ī *n.* (*pact*); *n.* cōnsēnsus, -ūs *m.* (*unanimity*)
agricultural *adj.* rūsticus, -a, -um
agriculture *n.* agrīcultūra, -ae *f.*
ahead *adv. use compound verb with* prae- *or* prō-
aid *n.* auxilium, -ī *nt.; v.t.* adiuvō, -iuvāre, -iūvī, -iūtum
aim *n.* prōpositum, -ī *nt.* (*purpose*); *v.t.* intendō, -tendere, -tendī, -tēnsum
air *n.* āēr, āeris *m.* (*atmosphere near the earth*); *n.* aethēr, -eris *m.* (*upper air*)
alarm *n.* clāmor, -ōris *m.* (*loud noise*); *n.* terror, -ōris *m.* (*fear*)
alone *adj.* sōlus, -a, -um
along *adv.* porrō, prōtinus; *prep.* praeter (+ acc.)
aloud *adv.* clārē
alphabet *n.* elementa, -ōrum *nt./pl.*
already *adv.* iam
also *adv.* quoque
altar *n.* āra, -ae *f.*
alter *v.t.* mūtō, -āre, -āvī, -ātum
alteration *n.* mūtātiō, -ōnis *f.*
although *conj.* quamquam, cum (+ subjv.)
altitude *n.* altitūdō, -inis *f.*
altogether *adv.* omnīnō
always *adv.* semper
a.m. *adj.* ante merīdiem
amaze *v.t.* obstupefaciō, -facere- fēcī, -factum
amazing *adj.* mīrus, -a, -um
ambassador *n.* lēgātus, -ī *m.*
ambiguous *adj.* dubius, -a, -um
ambition *n.* glōria, -ae *f.*
ambitious *adj.* cupidus, -a, -um
amendment *n.* ēmendātiō, -ōnis *f.*
amid *prep.* inter (+ acc.)
among *prep.* inter (+ acc.)
ample *adj.* amplus, -a, -um
amplify *v.t.* amplificō, -ficāre, -ficāvī, -ficātum
amputate *v.t.* amputō, -āre, -āvī, -ātum
amuse *v.t.* dēlectō, -āre, -āvī, -ātum
amusement *n.* dēlectātiō, -ōnis *f.*
an *art. not expressed in Latin*
analogy *n.* similitūdō, -inis *f.*
analysis *n.* explicātiō, -ōnis *f.*

analyze *v.t.* explicō, -plicāre, -plicāvī, -plicātum
anarchy *n.* licentia, -ae *f.*
anatomy *n.* anatomia, -ae *f.*
ancestors *n./pl.* maiōrēs, -um *m./pl.*
anchor *n.* ancora, -ae *f.; v.i.* stō, stāre, stetī, statum
ancient *adj.* antīquus, -a, -um; *adj.* vetus, veteris; *adj.* prīscus, -a, -um
and *conj.* et; **~ also** *conj.* atque; **~ so** *conj.* itaque; **~ so forth** *conj.* et
  cētera
anecdote *n.* fābula, -ae *f.*
angel *n.* angelus, -ī *m.*
anger *n.* īra, -ae *f.; v.t.* inrītō, -rītāre, -rītāvī, -rītātum
angle *n.* angulus, -ī *m.*
angry *adj.* īrātus, -a, -um; **be(come) ~,** *v.d.i.* īrāscor, īrāscī, īrātus sum
anguish *n.* angor, -ōris *m.*
animal *n.* animal, -ālis *nt.* (*any living thing, including mankind*); *n.* bēstia, -ae
  f. (*creature without reason*)
ankle *n.* tālus, -ī *m.*
announce *v.t.* nūntiō, -āre, -āvī, -ātum
announcement *n.* prōnūntiātiō, -ōnis *f.*
annoy *v.t.* vexō, -āre, -āvī, -ātum
annoyance *n.* molestia, -ae *f.*
annual *adj.* annuus, -a, -um
annul *v.t.* abrogō, -rogāre, -rogāvī, -rogātum
anonymous *adj.* sine nōmine
another *adj.* alius, alia, aliud (*another of many*); *adj.* alter, altera, alterum
  (*other of two*)
answer *n.* respōnsum, -ī *nt.; v.t.* respondeō, -spondere, -spondī, -spōnsum
  (*verbal ~*); *v.t.* rescrībō, -scrībere, -scrīpsī, -scrīptum (*written ~*)
ant *n.* formīca, -ae *f.*
anticipate *v.t.* exspectō, -spectāre, -spectāvī, -spectātum (*expect*); *v.t.*
  praevertō, -vertere, -vertī, -versum (*forestall*); *v.t.* praesūmō, -sūmere,
  -sūmpsī, -sūmptum (*take or do before the proper time*)
anticipation *n.* exspectātiō, -ōnis *f.*
antique *adj.* antīquus, -a, -um
anxiety *n.* cūra, -ae *f.*
anxious *adj.* anxius, -a, -um
any *adj.* ūllus, -a, -um
anybody *pron.* quisquam, quaequam, quidquam; *pron.* quis (after **sī, nisi,
  num, nē**)

anyone *pron.* quisquam, quaequam, quidquam; *pron.* quis (after **sī, nisi, num, nē**)

anything *pron.* quidquam; *pron.* quid (after **sī, nisi, num, nē**)

anywhere *adv.* usquam (*at any place*); *adv.* quōquam (*to any place*)

apart *adv.* seorsum, seorsus

apartment *n.* conclāve, -is *nt.*

apathetic *adj.* languidus, -a, -um

apologize *v.i.* excūsō, -cūsāre, -cūsāvī, -cūsātum (+ refl. pron. if apologizing for oneself; + **dē** for the thing apologized for)

apology *n.* excūsātiō, -ōnis *f.* (*excuse*); *n.* dēfēnsiō, -ōnis *f.* (*defense*)

apparatus *n.* apparātus, -ūs *m.*

apparel *n.* vestis, -is *f.*

apparent *adj.* manifestus, -a, -um; **be ~** *v.i.* appāreō, -pārēre, -pāruī, -pāritum; **make ~** *v.t.* patefaciō, -facere, -fēcī, -factum

appeal *v.t.* appellō, -pellāre, -pellāvī, -pellātum (*plead; refer to a higher authority*); *v.t.* obsecrō, -secrāre, -secrāvī, -secrātum (*entreat*)

appear *v.i.* appāreō, -pārēre, -pāruī, -pāritum (*be evident*); *v.i.* videor, vidērī, vīsus sum (*seem*)

appearance *n.* adventus, -ūs *m.* (*arrival*); *n.* aspectus, -ūs *m.* (*the manner of appearance*); *n.* speciēs, -ēī *f.* (*outward appearance; apparition*)

appendix *n.* appendix, -icis *f.*

appetite *n.* famēs, -is *f.*

applaud *v.t.* plaudō, -ere, plausī, plausum

applause *n.* plausus, -ūs *m.*

apple *n.* mālum, -ī *nt.*; **~ tree** *n.* mālus, -ī *f.*

application *n.* petītiō, -ōnis *f.* (*request*)

apply *v.t.* adhibeō, -hibēre, -hibuī, -hibitum (*devote attention*)

appoint *v.t.* cōnstituō, -stituere, -stituī, -stitūtum (*settle, establish*); *v.t.* dēsīgnō, -sīgnāre, -sīgnāvī, -sīgnātum (*appoint to public office*); *v.t.* praepōnō, -pōnere, -posuī, -positum (+ dat.) (*place or set over as commander, etc.*)

appointment *n.* cōnstitūtum, -ī *nt.* (*agreement*); *n.* mūnus, -eris *nt.* (*office; duty*)

appraisal *n.* aestimātiō, -ōnis *f.*

appreciate *v.t.* aestimō, -āre, -āvī, -ātum

appreciation *n.* aestimātiō, -ōnis *f.*

approach *n.* adventus, -ūs *m.*; *v.i.* appropinquō, -propinquāre, -propinquāvī, -propinquātum (+ dat.)

appropriate *adj.* idōneus, -a, -um (+ dat.)

approval *n.* approbātiō, -ōnis *f.*

approve *v.t.* approbō, -probāre, -probāvī, -probātum

approximate *adj.* proximus, -a, -um

April *adj.* Aprīlis, -is, -e (*usu. w.* **mēnsis**); *n.* Aprīlis, -is *m.*

apt *adj.* idōneus, -a, um (+ *dat.*) (*appropriate*); *adj.* prōnus, -a, -um (+ **ad** or **in** + acc. *or* + dat.) (*inclined to*)

aptitude *n.* habilitās, -ātis *f.*

aquatic *adj.* aquātilis, -is, -e

aqueduct *n.* aquaeductus, -ūs *m.*

arbitrary *adj.* libīdinōsus, -a, -um

arch *n.* arcus, -ūs *m.*

architect *n.* architectus, -ī *m*; *n.* architectōn, -onis *m.*

architectural *adj.* architectonicus, -a, -um

architecture *n.* architectūra, -ae *f.*

archive *n.* tabulārium, -ī *nt.*

arctic *adj.* septentriōnālis, -is, -e

area *n.* ārea, -ae *f.*

argue *v.t.* disputō, -putāre, -putāvī, -putātum

argument *n.* disputātiō, -ōnis *f.*

arise *v.i.* surgō, surgere, surrēxī, surrēctum (*of heavenly bodies; of rising from bed*); *v.d.i.* orior, orīrī, ortus sum (*of heavenly bodies; of coming into existence*)

arithmetic *n.* arithmētica, -ae *f.*

arm *n.* bracchium, -ī *nt.*

armpit *n.* āla, -ae *f.*

army *n.* exercitus, -ūs *m.*

aroma *n.* odor, -ōris *m.*

around *adv.* circā, circum; *prep.* circum (+ acc.), circā (+ acc.)

arrange *v.t.* ōrdinō, -āre, -āvī, -ātum (*put in proper order*); *v.t.* cōnstituō, -stituere, -stituī, -stitūtum (*decide*)

arrangement *n.* ōrdō, -inis *f.*

arrest *v.t.* comprehendō, -prehendere, -prehendī, -prehēnsum (*seize*); *v.t.* sistō, -ere, stitī, statum (*stop*)

arrival *n.* adventus, -ūs *m.*

arrive *v.i.* adveniō, -venīre, -vēnī, -ventum (*reach*); *v.i.* perveniō, -venīre, -vēnī, -ventum (+ **ad** + acc.) (*come to the end of a journey*)

arrogance *n.* superbia, -ae *f.*

arrogant *adj.* superbus, -a, -um

arrow *n.* sagitta, -ae *f.*

art *n.* ars, artis *f.* (*skill; work of art*); *n.* artificium, -ī *nt.* (*practice of a craft*)
artery *n.* artēria, -ae *f.*
article *n.* rēs, reī *f.*
artificial *adj.* artificiōsus, -a, -um
artisan *n.* opifex, -ficis *m./f.*
artist *n.* artifex, -ficis *m.*
artistic *adj.* artifex, artificis
as *adv.* sīcut; ~ ... **so** *adv.* sīcut ... ita; ~ **though** *adv.* tamquam, quasi;
    ~ **long as** *conj.* dum; ~ **to** *prep.* dē (+ abl.)
ash *n.* cinis, cineris *m.*; *n.* fraxinus, -ī *f.* (*bot.*)
ashamed, be ~ *v.i.* pudet, pudēre, puduit (*imp.*) (+ acc. of person affected
    + gen. of the cause of shame)
aside *adv.* seorsum, seorsus
ask *v.t.* rogō, -āre, -āvī, -ātum; ~ **advice** *v.t.* cōnsulō, -sulere, -suluī, -sultum
    (+ acc.)
asleep *adj.* dormiēns, -entis
aspect *n.* aspectus, -ūs *m.*
assault *n.* oppūgnātiō, -ōnis *f.* (*attack on a city or place*); *n.* impetus, -ūs *m.*
    (*attack by a person, troop, or disease*); *v.t.* oppūgnō, -pūgnāre, -pūgnāvī,
    -pūgnātum (*attack a city or place*); *v.d.t.* adorior, adorīrī, adortus sum
    (*attack a person*)
assemble *v.t.* convocō, -vocāre, -vocāvī, -vocātum; *v.i.* conveniō, -venīre,
    -vēnī, -ventum
assembly *n.* coitus (coetus), -ūs *m.*
assert *v.t.* adfirmō, -firmāre, -firmāvī, -firmātum
assertion *n.* adfirmātiō, -ōnis *f.*
assign *v.t.* attribuō, -tribuere, -tribuī, -tribūtum
assist *v.t.* adiuvō, -iuvāre, -iūvī, -iūtum
assistance *n.* auxilium, -ī *nt.*
assistant *n.* adiūtor, -ōris *m.*; *n.* adiūtrīx, -īcis *f.*
associate *n.* sodālis, -is *m./f.*; *v.t.* coniungō, -iungere, -iūnxī, -iūnctum
association *n.* conlēgium, -ī *nt.* (*guild; fraternity; college*); *n.* sociētās, -ātis
    f. (~ *for trading purposes; political league*); *n.* sodālitās, -ātis *f.* (~ *of any
    kind, especially for religious purposes*)
assume *v.t.* sūmō, -sūmere, -sūmpsī, -sūmptum
assurance *n.* fidūcia, -ae *f.*
assure *v.t.* cōnfirmō, -firmāre, -firmāvī, -firmātum
asthma *n.* dyspnoea, -ae *f.*
asthmatic *adj.* asthmaticus, -a, -um

astonish *v.t.* obstupefaciō, -facere, -fēcī, -factum
astray *adj.* vagus, -a, -um (*wandering*); *adj.* āmissus, -a, -um (*lost*); **lead ~**
 v.t. sēdūcō, -dūcere, -dūxī, -ductum; **go ~** *v.i.* errō, -āre, -āvī, -ātum
astringent *adj.* astrictōrius, -a, -um
astrology *n.* astrologia, -ae *f.*
astronomy *n.* astrologia, -ae *f.*
astute *adj.* callidus, -a, -um
asylum *n.* refugium, -ī *nt.*
at *prep.* ad (+ acc.), apud (+ acc.) *For names of cities, towns, and small is-*
 lands, use locative case. For time expressions, e.g. "at the first hour," use
 the abl. case.; **~ midday** *adv.* ad merīdiem; **~ present** *adv.* nunc;
 ~ first *adv.* prīmō; **~ last** *adv.* postrēmō; **~ home** *adv.* domī
athlete *n.* āthlēta, -ae *m./f.*
atmosphere *n.* āēr, āeris *m.*
atom *n.* atomus, -ī *m.*
atrium *n.* ātrium, -ī *nt.*
attach *v.t.* adfigō, -figere, -fīxī, -fixum
attack *n.* oppūgnātiō, -ōnis *f.* (*assault on a city or place*); *n.* impetus, -ūs *m.*
 (*assault by a person, troop, or disease*); *v.t.* oppūgnō, -pūgnāre, -pūgnāvī,
 -pūgnātum (*assault a city or place*); *v.d.t.* adorior, adorirī, adortus sum
 (*assault a person*)
attempt *n.* cōnātus, -ūs *m.; v.d.t.* cōnor, cōnārī, cōnatus sum
attend *v.d.t.* comitor, comitārī, comitātus sum (*accompany*); *v.i.* adsum,
 adesse, adfuī, adfutūrus (*attend a gathering*); **~ to** *v.t.* cūrō, -āre, -āvī,
 -ātum (*take care of*); *v.t.* animadvertō, -vertere, -vertī, -versum (*pay
 attention to*)
attendance *n.* praesentia, -ae *f.*
attendant *n.* appāritor, -ōris *m.*
attention *n.* intentiō, -ōnis *f.*
attentive *adj.* attentus, -a, -um
attitude *n.* animus, -ī *m.*
attorney *n.* advocātus, -ī *m.*
attract *v.t.* attrahō, -trahere, -trāxī, -trāctum
attraction *n.* inlecebra, -ae *f.* (*charm*)
attractive *adj.* venustus, -a, -um
attribute *n.* nātūra, -ae *f.; v.t.* attribuō, -tribuere, -tribuī, -tribūtum
auction *n.* auctiō, -ōnis *f.; v.t.* auctiōne vēndō, -ere, -didī, -ditum
audience *n.* audītōrēs, -um *m./pl.* (*listeners*); *n.* admissiō, -ōnis *f.* (*formal
 interview*)

augment *v.t.* augeō, -ēre, auxī, auctum

augur *n.* augur, auguris *m./f.*

augury *n.* augurium, -ī *nt.*

August *adj.* Sextīlis, -is, -e (*usu. w.* **mēnsis**) (*later renamed* Augustus, -a, -um *in honor of the emperor*)

aunt *n.* amita, -ae *f.* (*paternal* ~); *n.* mātertera, -ae *f.* (*maternal* ~)

authentic *adj.* certus, -a, -um

author *n.* auctor, -ōris *m.* (*originator*); *n.* scrīptor, -ōris *m.* (*writer*)

authority *n.* auctōritās, -ātis *f.* (*influence*); *n.* potestās, -ātis *f.* (*power*)

authorize *v.t.* potestātem/auctōritātem dō, dare, dedī, datum (+ dat. of person authorized)

autumn *n.* autumnus, -ī *m.*; *adj.* autumnus, -a, -um

auxiliaries *n./pl.* auxilia, -ōrum *nt./pl.*

avenue *n.* via, -ae *f.* (*street*); *n.* xystus, -ī *m.* (*garden walk*)

avoid *v.t.* vītō, -āre, -āvī, -ātum

awake *v.d.i.* expergīscor, expergīscī, experrēctus sum

award *n.* pretium, -ī *nt.*; *v.t.* dō, dare, dedī, datum (*give, bestow*); *v.t.* adiūdicō, -iūdicāre, -iūdicāvī, -iūdicātum (*adjudge as due*)

aware *adj.* gnārus, -a, -um (+ gen.); **be(come) ~** *v.t.* sentiō, -īre, sēnsī, sēnsum

away *adv. use verb compounded with the pref.* ā-, ab-; **~ from** *prep.* ā, ab (+ abl.)

awful *adj.* malus, -a, -um (*bad*); *adj.* dīrus, -a, -um (*dreadful*)

awkward *adj.* inhabilis, -is, -e (*clumsy*); *adj.* invenustus, -a, -um (*inelegant*)

axe *n.* secūris, -is *f.*

axis *n.* axis, -is *m.*

axle *n.* axis, -is *m.*

B

baby *n.* īnfāns, īnfantis *m./f.*

back *n.* tergum, -ī *nt.*

backbone *n.* spīna, -ae *f.*

backward(s) *adv.* retrō, retrōrsum

bacon *n.* lārdum, -ī *nt.*

bad *adj.* malus, -a, -um (*not good; evil; malformed; adverse*); *adj.* aeger, aegra, aegrum (*ill*); *adj.* noxius, -a, -um (+dat.) (*harmful*); *adj.* pluvius, -a, -um (*of rainy weather*); *adj.* ventōsus, -a, -um (*of windy weather*); **~ly** *adv.* male; **rather ~ly** *adv.* pēius; **very ~ly** *adv.* pessimē

badge *n.* sīgnum, -ī *nt.*
bag *n.* saccus, -ī *m.*
baggage *n.* impedīmenta, -ōrum *nt./pl.*
bail *n.* vadimōnium, -ī *nt.*
bake *v.t.* coquō, -ere, coxī, coctum
baker *n.* pīstor, -ōris *m.*
balance *n.* trutina, -ae *f.* (*of a scale*); *n.* reliquum, -ī *nt.* (*remainder of a sum*)
bald *adj.* calvus, -a, -um
ball *n.* pila, -ae *f.*
band *n.* fascia, -ae *f.* (*bandage*); *n.* manus, -ūs *f.* (*a group united for a purpose*)
bandage *n.* fascia, -ae *f.*
bank *n.* rīpa, -ae *f.* (*of a lake or river*); *n.* argentāria , -ae *f.* (*place for money*)
banker *n.* argentārius, -ī *m.*
banner *n.* vexillum, -ī *nt.*
banquet *n.* cēna, -ae *f.*; *n.* epulae, -ārum *f./pl.* (*religious banquets*)
baptism *n.* baptisma, -atis *nt.*
baptize *v.t.* baptīzō, -āre, -āvī, -ātum
bar *n.* claustra, -ōrum *nt./pl.*
barbarian *n.* barbarus, -ī *m.*; *n.* barbara, -ae *f.*; *adj.* barbarus, -a, -um
barber *n.* tōnsor, -ōris *m.*
barbershop *n.* tōnstrīna, -ae *f.*
bare *adj.* nūdus, -a, -um
bargain *n.* pactum, -ī *nt.* (*agreement*)
bark *n.* lātrātus, -ūs *m.* (*of a dog*); *n.* cortex, -icis *m./f.* (*bot.*)
barley *n.* hordeum, -ī *nt.*
barracks *n.* castra, -ōrum *nt./pl.*
barrel *n.* cūpa, -ae *f.*
barren *adj.* sterilis, -is, -e
barrier *n.* saeptum, -ī *nt.*
base *n.* basis, -is *f.*
basilica *n.* basilica, -ae *f.*
basin *n.* pelvis, -is *f.*
basis *n.* basis, -is *f.*
basket *n.* corbis, -is *m./f.*
bat *n.* clāva, -ae *f.* (*club*); *n.* vespertīliō, -ōnis *m.* (*zool.*)
bath *n.* balneum, -ī *nt.* (*private ~*); *n.* thermae, -ārum *f./pl.* (*public ~*)
bathe *v.t.* lavō, -āre, lāvī, lautum; *v.d.i.* lavor, -ārī, lautus sum
bathtub *n.* alveus, -ī *m.*
batter *v.t.* percutiō, -cutere, -cussī, -cussum

battle *n.* pūgna, -ae *f.*; *n.* proelium, -ī *nt.*; *v.t.* pūgnō, -āre, -āvī, -ātum; *v.d.i.* proelior, proeliārī, proeliātus sum (+ **cum** + abl. *or* + **inter** + acc.)

bay *n.* sinus, -us *m.* (*a body of water*); *n.* laurus, -ī *f.* (*bot.*); *n.* laurea, -ae *f.* (*bot.*)

be *v.i.* sum, esse, fuī, futūrum

beach *n.* lītus, -oris *nt.*

beak *n.* rōstrum, -ī *nt.*

beam *n.* tīgnum, -ī *nt.* (*arch.*); *n.* radius, -ī *m.* (*ray of light*)

bean *n.* faba, -ae *f.*; *n.* phasēlus, -ī *m.* (*kidney bean*)

bear *n.* ursus, -ī *m.*; *n.* ursa, -ae *f.*; *v.t.* ferō, ferre, tulī, lātum (*carry*); *v.t.* gīgnō, -ere, genuī, genitum (~ *children*); *v.d.t.* patior, patī, passus sum (*endure*)

bearing *n.* habitus, -ūs *m.* (*attitude*)

beast *n.* bēstia, -ae *f.* (*especially wild*); *n.* ferae, -ārum *f./pl.* (*wild beasts, especially game beasts*)

beat *n.* ictus, -ūs *m.* (*of music; pulse*); *v.t.* verberō, -āre, -āvī, -ātum (*strike*); *v.t.* superō, -āre, -āvī, -ātum (*overcome*)

beautiful *adj.* pulcher, pulchra, pulchrum; *adj.* venustus, -a, -um (*elegant*); *adj.* amoenus, -a, -um (*pleasantness of scenery*)

beauty *n.* pulchritūdō, -inis *f.*; *n.* venustās, -ātis *f.* (*grace, elegance*); *n.* amoenitās, -ātis *f.* (*pleasantness of scenery*)

because *conj.* quod, quia ; ~ **of** *prep.* propter (+ acc.), ob (+ acc.)

become *v.i.* fīō, fierī, factus sum (*irreg.*)

bed *n.* lectus, -ī *m.*; *n.* alveus, -ī *m.* (*of a river*); *n.* ārea, -ae *f.* (*of a garden*); **go to ~** *v.i.* cubitum eō, īre, iī (īvī), itum

bedroom *n.* cubiculum, -ī *nt.*

bee *n.* apis, apis *f.*; ~**hive** *n.* alveus, -ī *m.*; ~ **swarm** *n.* exāmen, exāminis *nt.*

beef *n.* būbula, -ae *f.*

beer *n.* cervisia, -ae *f.*

beet *n.* bēta, -ae *f.*

beetle *n.* scarabaeus, -ī *m.*

before *adv.* anteā (*of time*), ante (*of time; of location*); *prep.* ante (+ acc.)

beg *v.d.t.* precor, precārī, precātus sum (+ acc. of person begged or thing begged for *or* + **ab, dē,** or **ex** + abl. of person begged *or* + **ut** or **nē** + subjv.); *v.t.* ōrō, -āre, -āvī, -ātum; (+ acc. of person begged or thing begged for *or* + **ab, dē,** or **ex** + abl. of person begged *or* + **ut** or **nē** + subjv.); *v.t.* petō, -ere, -īvī, -ītum (+ acc. of person begged or thing begged for *or* + **ab, dē,** or **ex** + abl. of person begged *or* + **ut** or **nē** + subjv.); *v.t.* rogō, -āre, -āvī, -ātum (+ acc. of person begged or thing begged for *or* + **ab, dē,** or **ex** + abl. of person begged *or* **ut** or **nē** + subjv.); *v.i.* mendīcō, -āre, -āvī, -ātum (*ask for money*)

beggar *n.* mendīcus, -ī *m.*

begin *v.t., v.i.* incipiō, -cipere, -cēpī, -ceptum; *v.d.t.; v.d.i.* ordior, ordīrī, orsus sum; **have begun, began** *v.t.* coepī, coepisse, coeptum (*def.*)

beginner *n.* tīrō, -ōnis *m.*

behalf, on ~ of *prep.* prō (+ abl.)

behave *v.t.* gerō, gerere, gessī, gestum (+ refl. pron.)

behavior *n.* mōrēs, mōrum *m./pl.*

behind *adv.* pōne, post; *prep.* pōne (+ acc.), post (+ acc.)

behold *v.t.* spectō, -āre, -āvī, -ātum

being, human ~ *n.* homō, -inis *m/f.*

belief *n.* fidēs, -eī *f.* (*confidence*); *n.* opīniō, -ōnis *f.* (*opinion*)

believe *v.t.* crēdō, -dere, -didī, -ditum (+ dat. of person or thing believed *or* + acc. + infv. of situation, circumstance, etc. believed)

bell *n.* tintinnābulum, -ī *nt.*

belly *n.* venter, ventris *m.*

belong *v.i.* pertineō, -tinēre, -tinuī, --- (+ **ad** + acc.) (*concern; pertain to*)

belongings *n./pl.* Use nt. pl. of poss. adjs., e.g. mea, tua, sua.

below *adv.* subter, īnfrā; *prep.* īnfrā (+ acc.); *prep.* sub (+ acc. when motion is implied; + abl. when rest is implied)

belt *n.* cingulum, -ī *nt.; n.* zōna, -ae *f.*

bench *n.* subsellium, -ī *nt.*

bend *v.t.* flectō, flectere, flexī, flectum

beneath *adv.* subter, īnfrā; *prep.* īnfrā (+ acc.), sub (+ acc. when motion is implied; + abl. when rest is implied)

beneficial *adj.* ūtilis, -is, -e (*useful; profitable; advantageous*); *adj.* salūtāris, -is, -e (*healthful; salutary*)

benefit *n.* beneficium, -ī *nt.; v.i.* prōsum, prōdesse, prōfuī, prōfutūrum (+ dat. of the beneficiary)

benign *adj.* benīgnus, -a, -um

bent *adj.* curvus, -a, -um

berry *n.* bāca, -ae *f.*

beside *prep.* ad (+ acc.), iūxtā (+ acc.), prope (+ acc.)

besides *adv.* praetereā

best *adj.* optimus, -a, -um; *adv.* optimē

bet *n.* pīgnus, -oris *nt.* (*stake*); *v.t.* pīgnore certō, -āre, -āvī, -ātum

betray *v.t.* prōdō, -dere, -didī, -ditum

better *adj.* melior, melius; *adv.* melius

between *prep.* inter (+ acc.)

beverage *n.* pōtiō, -ōnis *f.*

beware *v.t.* caveō, -ēre, cāvī, cautum (+ **ut** or **nē** + subjv.)
beyond *adv.* ūltrā, suprā; *prep.* trāns (+ acc.)
Bible *n.* biblia, bibliōrum *nt./pl*; *n.* biblia, -ae *f.*
big *adj.* mágnus, -a, -um; *adj.* ingēns, ingentis
bill *n.* rōstrum, -ī *nt.* (*of bird*); *n.* rogātiō, -ōnis *f.* (*of legislation*)
bind *v.t.* adligō, -ligāre, -ligāvī, -ligātum; ~ **together** *v.t.* cōnstringō, -stringere, -strinxī, -strictum
biography *n.* vīta, -ae *f.*
bird *n.* avis, -is *f.*; *n.* volucer, volucris *f.*
birth *n.* ortus, -ūs *m.*
birthday *n.* nātālis, -is *m.*
biscuit *n.* buccelātum, -ī *nt.*
bit *n.* frēnum, -ī *nt.* (*for horse*); *n.* frūstum, -ī *nt.* (*piece*)
bite *n.* morsus, -ūs *m.*; *v.t.* mordeō, -ēre, momordī, morsum
bitter *adj.* amārus, -a, -um (*sour*); *adj.* acerbus, -a, -um (*sharp, severe*)
black *adj.* āter, ātra, ātrum (*dead* ~); *adj.* niger, nigra, nigrum (*glossy* ~); ~ **and blue** *adj.* līvidus, -a, -um
blackberry *n.* rubus, -ī *m.*
bladder *n.* vēsīca, -ae *f.*
blade *n.* herba, -āe *f.* (*of grass*); *n.* palma, -ae *f.* (*of an oar*); *n.* lāmina, -ae *f.* (*of a knife, sword, etc.*)
blame *n.* culpa, -ae *f.*; *v.t.* reprehendō, -prehendere, -prehendī, -prehēnsum
blanket *n.* lōdix, lōdīcis *f.*
blast *n.* flātus, -us *m.*
blaze *n.* flamma, -ae *f.*
bleak *adj.* frīgidus, -a, -um (*cold*); *adj.* inhospitus, -a, -um (*unwelcoming*)
bleed *v.i.* sanguinem effundō, -fundere, -fūdī, -fūsum
bless *v.t.* beō, -āre, -āvī, -ātum
blessing *n.* benedictiō, -ōnis *f.*
blind *adj.* caecus, -a, -um
blindness *n.* caecitās, -ātis *f.*
blink *v.i.* nictō, -āre, -āvī, -ātum
block *n.* stīpes, -itis *m.*
blond *adj.* flāvus, -a, -um
blood *n.* sanguis, sanguinis *m.*
bloom *v.i.* flōreō, -ēre, flōruī, ---
blossom *n.* flōs, flōris *m.*
blow *v.t.* flō, flāre, flāvī, flātum
blue *adj.* caeruleus, -a, -um

blunt

blunt *adj.* hebes, hebetis
blush *v.i.* ērubēscō, ērubēscere, ērubuī, ---
board *n.* tabula, -ae *f.* (*plank*); *n.* conlēgium, -ī *nt.* (*body of officials*)
boat *n.* linter, lintris *f.*; *n.* scapha, -ae *f.*
body *n.* corpus, corporis *nt.*; **~ of men** *n.* manus, -ūs *f.*
boil *n.* vomica, -ae *f.*; *v.t.* fervefaciō, -facere, -fēcī, -factum
bold *adj.* audāx, audācis
bolt *n.* claustra, -ōrum *nt* /*pl*
bone *n.* os, ossis *nt.*
book *n.* liber, librī *m.*
bookcase *n.* pēgma, -atis *nt.*
bookseller *n.* bibliopōla, -ae *m.*
boot *n.* calceus, -ī *m.*; *n.* caliga, -ae *f.* (*military*)
border *n.* margō, -inis *m./f.* (*edge*); *n.* finēs, -ium *m./pl.* (*country*)
born *adj.* nātus, -a, -um; *v.d.i.* nāscor, nāscī, nātus sum
both *adj./pl.* ambō, ambae, ambō (*two together*); *adj.* uterque, utraque,
utrumque (*each of two; separately*); **both ... and** *conj.* et ... et, cum
... tum
bottle *n.* ampulla, -ae *f.*
bottom *n.* fundus, -ī *m.*
bounce *v.i.* exsiliō, -silīre, -siluī, ---
box *n.* arca, -ae *f.*; *v.i.* pūgnīs certō, -āre, -āvī, -ātum
boy *n.* puer, puerī *m.*
brave *adj.* fortis, -is, -e
bread *n.* pānis, -is *m.*
break *n.* intervāllum, -ī *nt.* (*gap, pause*); **~ of day** *n.* prīma lūx, prīmae lūcis *f.*;
v.t. frangō, -ere, frēgī, frāctum; **~ a promise** *v.t.* fallō, -ere, fefellī, falsum
breakfast *n.* ientāculum, -ī *nt.*
breeze *n.* aura, -ae *f.*
bribe *n.* pretium, -ī *nt.*
brief *adj.* brevis, -is, -e
bright *adj.* clārus, -a, -um (*shining*); *adj.* sollers, sollertis (*clever*)
brilliant *adj.* splendidus, -a, -um (*shining*); *adj.* sollers, sollertis (*skillful*)
bring *v.t.* adferō, -ferre, attulī, adlātum; **~ about** *v.t.* efficiō, -ficere, -fēcī,
-fectum; **~ back** *v.t.* referō, -ferre, rettulī, relātum
bronze *n.* aes, aeris *nt.*; *adj.* aēneus, -a, -um
broth *n.* iūs, iūris *nt.*
brother *n.* frāter, frātris *m.*; **full ~** *n.* germānus, -ī *m.*
brush *n.* pēnicillus, -ī *m.*

brutal *adj.* ferus, -a, -um
bubble *n.* bulla, -ae *f.*
bucket *n.* hama, -ae *f.*; *n.* situla, -ae *f.*
bulb *n.* bulbus, -ī *m.*
bulla *n.* bulla, -ae *f.*
bullet *n.* glāns, glandis *f.*
bundle *n.* fascis, -is *m.*
buoy *n.* cortex, corticis *m./f.*
burn *v.t.* ūrō, -ere, ussī, ustum
bury *v.t.* sepeliō, -pelīre, -pelīvī (-peliī), -pultum
business *n.* negōtium, -ī *nt.*; *n.* rēs, reī *f.* (*matter; affair*)
busy *adj.* occupātus, -a, -um (+ abl. *or* + **in** + abl.)
but *conj.* sed; ~ **if** *conj.* sīn; ~ **on the other hand** *conj.* at (*denoting transition*)
butterfly *n.* pāpiliō, -ōnis *m.*
buy *v.t.* emō, -ere, ēmī, ēmptum
buyer *n.* ēmptor, -ōris *m.*
by *prep.* ā, ab (+ abl.) (*agent*); prope (+ acc.) (*near*); *if expressing instrument or means, use abl. case.*

C

cabbage *n.* brassica, -ae *f.*
cable *n.* ancorāle, -is *nt.*
cage *n.* cavea, -ae *f.*
cake *n.* placenta, -ae *f.*; *n.* crūstulum, -ī *nt.*
calculate *v.t.* computō, -putāre, -putāvī, -putātum
calculation *n.* computātiō, -ōnis *f.*
calculator *n.* abacus, -ī *m.* (*counting table*)
calendar *n.* fāstī, -ōrum *m./pl.*
calf *n.* sūra, -ae *f.* (*of leg*); *n.* vitulus, -ī *m.*, vitula, -ae *f.* (*young cow*)
call *v.t.* vocō, -āre, -āvī, -ātum (*summon*); *v.t.* appellō, -pellāre, -pellāvī, -pellātum (*name*); *v.t.* nōminō, -āre, -āvī, -ātum (*name*); ~ **together** *v.t.* convocō, -vocāre, -vocāvī, -vocātum
calm *n.* tranquillitās, -ātis *f.*; *adj.* tranquillus, -a, -um; *v.t.* sēdō, -āre, -āvī, -ātum
camel *n.* camēlus, -ī *m./f.*
camp *n.* castra, castrōrum *nt./pl.*; **pitch** ~ *v.t.* castra pōnō, -ere, posuī, positum; **break** ~ *v.t.* castra moveō, -ēre, mōvī, mōtum
can *verbal aux.* possum, posse, potuī, --- (+ infv.)
canal *n.* fossa, -ae *f.*

cancel *v.t.* retrāctō, -trāctāre, -trāctāvī, -trāctātum
cancer *n.* cancer, cancrī *m.*
candid *adj.* candidus, -a, -um
candidate *n.* candidātus, -ī *m.*
candle *n.* candēla, -ae *f.*
cane *n.* harūndō, -inis *f.* (*bot.*); *n.* baculum, -ī *nt.* (*staff*)
canvas *n.* carbasus, -ī *f.* (*cloth; sail*)
capable *adj.* capāx, capācis
cape *n.* cucullus, -ī *m.*
capital *n.* caput, capitis *nt.* (*chief city; money*)
captain *n.* centuriō, -ōnis *m.* (*of infantry*); *n.* praefectus, -ī *m.* (*of navy*); *n.* magister, magistrī *m.* (*of merchant marine*)
care *n.* cūra, -ae *f.*; **free from ~** *adj.* sēcūrus, -a, -um; **~ for, ~ about** *v.i.* cūrō, -āre, -āvī, -ātum
careful *adj.* dīligēns, -entis
careless *adj.* neglegēns, -entis (*neglectful; inattentive*); *adj.* sēcūrus, -a, -um (*free from care*)
carnival *n.* feriae, -ārum *f./pl.*
carry *v.t.* ferō, ferre, tulī, lātum; *v.t.* portō, -āre, -āvī, -ātum; **~ across** *v.t.* trānsportō, -portāre, -portāvī, -portātum; **~ off** *v.t.* auferō, -ferre, abstulī, ablātum; **~ out** *v.t.* exportō, -portāre, -portāvī, -portātum
cart *n.* plaustrum, -ī *nt.*
carve *v.t.* sculpō, -ere, sculpsī, sculptum (*sculpt*); *v.t.* scindō, -ere, scidī, scissum (*cut meat*)
carving *n.* sculptūra, -ae *f.* (*sculpture*)
case *n.* causa, -ae *f.* (*legal action*); *n.* thēca, -ae *f.* (*envelope; hull; sheath*)
cashier *n.* dispēnsātor, -ōris *m.*
cask *n.* cūpa, -ae *f.*
cast *n.* iactus, -ūs *m.*; *v.t.* coniciō,-icere, -iēcī, -iectum
castle *n.* castellum, -ī *nt.*
casual *adj.* fortuītus, -a, -um
cat *n.* fēlēs, -is *f.*
catalog *n.* index, indicis *m./f.*
catch *v.t.* capiō, -ere, cēpī, captum; *v.t.* fallō, -ere, fefellī, falsum (*ensnare*)
cattle *n.* bovēs, -um *m./pl.*; **~ herd** *n.* pecus, -oris *nt.*
cause *n.* causa, -ae *f.*; *v.t.* efficiō, -ficere, -fēcī, -fectum
caution *n.* cautiō, -ōnis *f.*
cautious *adj.* cautus, -a, -um
cavalry *n.* equitēs, -um *m./pl.*; **~ soldier** *n.* eques, equitis *m.*

cave *n.* spēlunca, -ae *f.*

cease *v.t., v.i.* dēsinō, -sinere, dēstitī, dēsitum; *v.t.* dēsisto, -sistere, -stitī, -stitum (*doesn't finish*)

cedar *n.* cedrus, -ī *f.*

ceiling *n.* lacūnar, -āris *nt.*

celebrate *v.t.* celebrō, -āre, -āvī, -ātum

celebration *n.* celebrātiō, -ōnis *f.*

cell *n.* cella, -ae *f.*

cellar *n.* fornix, fornicis *m.*

cemetery *n.* sepulcrētum, -ī *nt.*

censor *n.* cēnsor, -ōris *m.*

center *n.* centrum, -ī *nt.;* **in the ~** *adj.* medius, -a, -um

centurion *n.* centuriō, -ōnis *m.*

century *n.* saeculum, -ī *nt.* (*period of time*); *n.* centuria, -ae *f.* (*military unit*)

cereal *n.* frūmentum, -ī *nt.*

ceremony *n.* caerimōnia, -ae *f.*

certain *adj.* certus, -a, -um (*definite; unavoidable*); *adj.* manifestus, -a, -um (*evident*); *adj.* fidus, -a, -um (*trustworthy*); **a ~ person** *adj.* quīdam, quaedam, quoddam; **a ~ person** *pron.* quīdam, quaedam, quiddam

certify *v.t.* cōnfirmō, -firmāre, -firmāvī, -firmātum

chain *n.* catēna, -ae *f.*

chair *n.* sella, -ae *f.*

chalk *n.* crēta, -ae *f.*

challenge *v.t.* prōvocō, -vocāre, -vocāvī, -vocātum

chamber *n.* cubiculum, -ī *nt.*

champion *n.* prōpūgnātor, -ōris *m.*

chance *n.* cāsus, -ūs *m.;* **by ~** *adv.* forte

change *n.* permūtātiō, -ōnis *f.; v.t.* permūtō, -mūtāre, -mūtāvī, -mūtātum

changeable *adj.* mūtābilis, -is, -e

channel *n.* canālis, -is *m.*

chaotic *adj.* cōnfūsus, -a, -um

chapel *n.* aedicula, -ae *f.*

chapter *n.* caput, capitis *nt.*

character *n.* ingenium, -ī *nt.* (*nature*); *n.* mōrēs, mōrum *m./pl.* (*manner of life*)

charge *n.* impetus, -ūs *m.* (*attack*); *v.t.* invādō, -vādere, -vāsī, -vāsum (*attack*); *v.t.* mandō, -dāre, -dāvī, -dātum (*entrust*); *v.t.* accūsō, -āre, -āvī, -ātum (*accuse*); **put in ~** *v.t.* praeficiō, -ficere, -fēcī, -fectum (+ acc. for person *or* + dat. for thing); **be in ~** *v.i.* praesum, praeesse, praefuī, praefutūrus (+ dat.)

charm

charm *n.* carmen, -inis *nt.* (*incantation*); *n.* fascinum, -ī *nt.* (*amulet; a bewitching*); *n.* venustās, -ātis *f.* (*comeliness; grace*)
charter *n.* pactum, -ī *nt.* (*agreement*)
chase *n.* vēnātiō, -ōnis *f.* (*hunting*); *v.d.t.* vēnor, vēnārī, vēnātus sum (*hunt*); *v.t.* sequor, sequī, secūtus sum (*pursue*)
chat *n.* sermō, sermōnis *m.*
chatter *n.* garrulitās, -ātis *f.*; *v.i.* garriō, -īre, -īvī (-iī), -ītum
cheap *adj.* vilis, -is, -e
check *n.* impedīmentum, -ī *nt.* (*hindrance*); *v.t.* impediō, -pedīre, -pedīvī, -pedītum (*hinder*); *v.t.* cōnfirmō, -firmāre, -firmāvī, -firmātum (*corroborate*)
cheek *n.* gena, -ae *f.*
cheese *n.* cāseus, -ī *m.*
cherish *v.t.* foveō, -ēre, fōvī, fōtum
cherry *n.* cerasus, -ī *f.*
chest *n.* pectus, pectoris *nt.* (*upper body*); *n.* arca, -ae *f.* (*container*)
chick(en) *n.* pullus, -ī *m.*
chief *n.* prīnceps, -cipis *m.*; *adj.* prīnceps, -cipis
child *n.* puer, puerī *m.*; *n.* puella, -ae *f.*
childhood *n.* pueritia, -ae *f.*
childish *adj.* puerīlis, -is, -e
children *n./pl.* līberī, -ōrum *m.*
chill *n.* frīgus, -oris *nt.*; *v.t.* refrīgerō, -frīgerāre, -frīgerāvī, -frīgerātum
chilly *adj.* frīgidus, -a, -um
chin *n.* mentum, -ī *nt.*
chip *n.* assula, -ae *f.*
chisel *n.* scalprum, -ī *nt.*; *v.t.* scalpō, -ere, scalpsī, scalptum
choice *n.* dēlectus, -ūs *m.*
choir *n.* chorus, -ī *m.*
choke *v.t.* suffōcō, -fōcāre, -fōcāvī, -fōcātum
choose *v.t.* dēligō, -ligere, -lēgī, -lēctum
chop *v.t.* caedō, -ere, cecīdī, caesum
chorus *n.* chorus, -ī *m.*
Christian *n.* Christiānus, -ī *m.*; *n.* Christiāna, -ae *f.*; *adj.* Christiānus, -a, -um
Christmas *n.* nātīvitās Christī, nātīvitātis Christī *f.*
chronic *adj.* longinquus, -a, -um
church *n.* ecclēsia, -ae *f.*
cinder *n.* cinis, cineris *m.*
cinnamon *n.* cinnamōmum (cinnamum, cinnamon), -ī *nt.*

circle *n.* orbis, -is *m.*
circuit *n.* circuitus, -ūs *m.*
circulate *v.t.* circummittō, -mittere, -mīsī, -missum
circumference *n.* ambitus, -ūs *m.*
circumstance *n.* rēs, reī *f.*
cite *v.t.* prōferō, -ferre, -tulī, -lātum
citizen *n.* cīvis, -is *m./f.*
city *n.* urbs, urbis *f.*
civilization *n.* cultus, -ūs *m.*
claim *v.t.* postulō, -āre, -āvī, -ātum
clap *v.t.* plaudō, -ere, plausī, plausum
class *n.* ordō, ordinis *m.* (*social* ~; *political* ~); *n.* genus, generis *nt.* (*sort; stock*)
claw *n.* unguis, -is *m.*
clay *n.* argilla, -ae *f.*
clean *adj.* pūrus, -a, -um (*unmixed*); *adj.* mundus, -a, -um (*neat; elegant*);
 v.t. purgō, -āre, -āvī, -ātum
clear *adj.* clārus, -a, -um; *adj.* manifestus, -a, -um; *adj.* serēnus, -a, -um
 (~ *weather*); *v.t.* purgō, -āre, -āvī, -ātum (*of an accusation*); **be** ~ *v.i.*
 appāret, appārēre, appāruit, --- (*imp.*) (+ infv.)
clergy *n.* clēricī, -ōrum *m./pl.*
clergyman *n.* clēricus, -ī *m.*
clerk *n.* scrība, -ae *m.*
clever *adj.* callidus, -a, -um
client *n.* cliēns, clientis *m.* (*personal dependent*)
cliff *n.* scopulus, -ī *m.*
climate *n.* caelum, -ī *nt.*
climax *n.* gradātiō, -ōnis *f.* (*rhetorical* ~)
climb *n.* ascensus, -ūs *m.*; *v.t.* ascendō, -scendere, -scendī, -scensum
cling *v.i.* adhaereō, -haerēre, -haesī, -haesum (+ dat.)
clip *v.t.* tondeō, -ēre, totondī, tonsum
clock *n.* hōrologium, -ī *nt.*
close *adj.* propinquus, -a, -um (*near*); *adj.* densus, -a, -um (*thick*); *adv.* iūxtā,
 prope; *prep.* iūxtā (+ acc.), prope (+ acc.); *v.t.* claudō, -ere, clausī, clausum
closed *adj.* clausus, -a, -um
cloth *n.* textilis, -is *nt.*
clothe *v.t.* vestiō, -īre, -īvī (-iī), -ītum
clothes *n.* vestis, -is *f.*
clothing *n.* vestīmentum, -ī *nt.*
cloud *n.* nūbēs, -is *f.*

cloudy *adj.* nūbilus, -a, -um
clown *n.* scurra, -ae *m.*
club *n.* fustis, -is *m.* (*cudgel*); *n.* sodālitās, -ātis *f.* (*association*)
clue *n.* indicium, -ī *nt.*
cluster *n.* corona, -ae *f.* (*crowd of people*); *n.* racēmus, -ī *m.* (*bunch of grapes*); *v.i.* confluō, -fluere, -flūxī, ---
clutch *v.t.* prehendō, -hendere, -hendī, -hēnsum
coach *n.* vehiculum, -ī *nt.*
coal *n.* carbō, -ōnis *m.*
coarse *adj.* incultus, -a, -um (*uncouth*); *adj.* rudis, -is, -e (*unfinished*); *adj.* crassus, -a, -um (*not fine in texture*)
coast *n.* lītus, -oris *nt.*
coat *n.* vellus, -eris *nt.* (*wool*); *n.* pellis, -is *f.* (*animal's pelt*)
cobweb *n.* arānea, -ae *f.*
cock *n.* gallus, -ī *m.*
code *n.* lēgēs, -um *f./pl.* (~ *of law*)
coffin *n.* sarcophagus, -ī *m.*
cohort *n.* cohors, cohortis *f.*
coil *n.* spīra, -ae *f.*
coin *n.* nummus, -ī *m.*
coincide *v.i.* congruō, -gruere, -gruī, ---
cold *n.* frīgus, -oris *nt.*; *adj.* frīgidus, -a, -um; *adj.* gelidus, -a, -um
collar *n.* monīle, -is *nt.* (*jewelry*); *n.* collāre, -is *nt.* (*dog's ~; prisoner's ~*)
collect *v.t.* colligō, -ligere, -lēgī, -lēctum
collection *n.* congeriēs, -ēī *f.*
college *n.* collēgium, -ī *nt.* (*official board*)
collide *v.t., v.i.* cōnflīgō, -flīgere, -flīxī, -flīctum
collision *n.* concursus, -ūs *m.*
colon *n.* cōlon (cōlum), -ī *nt.*(*anat.*)
colonel *n.* praefectus, -ī *m.*
colony *n.* colōnia, -ae *f.*
color *n.* color, -ōris *m.*; **of the same ~** *adj.* concolor, -ōris
column *n.* columna, -ae *f.*
comb *n.* pecten, -inis *m.*; *v.t.* pectō, -ere, pexī, pectum (pectitum)
combination *n.* coniūnctiō, -ōnis *f.*
combine *v.t.* coniungō, -iungere, -iūnxī, -iūnctum
come *v.i.* veniō, -īre, vēnī, ventum; **~ together** *v.i.* conveniō, -venīre, -vēnī, -ventum; **~ to pass** *v.i.* accidit, -cidere, -cidit, --- (*imp.*)
comedy *n.* cōmoedia, -ae *f.*

comfort *n.* cōnsōlātiō, -ōnis *f.* (*consolation*); *v.t.* cōnsōlor, cōnsōlārī, cōnsōlātus sum

comfortable *adj.* commodus, -a, -um

comic *adj.* cōmicus, -a, -um (*pertaining to comedy*); *adj.* ridiculus, -a, -um (*ridiculous*)

command *n.* imperium, -ī *nt.* (*right of commanding*); *n.* iussum, -ī *nt.* (*an order*); **be in ~** *v.i.* praesum, -esse, -fuī, --- (+ dat.)

commence *v.t.* incipiō, -cipere, -cēpī, -ceptum

comment *n.* dicta, -ōrum *nt./pl.*; *v.t.* explicō, -plicāre, -plicāvī, -plicātum

commentary *n.* commentārius, -ī *m.*

commerce *n.* commercium, -ī *nt.*

commission *n.* mandātum, -ī *nt.* (*task*)

committee *n.* cōnsilium, -ī *nt.*

common *adj.* commūnis, -is, -e

communicate *v.t.* commūnicō, -mūnicāre, -mūnicāvī, -mūnicātum

communication *n.* commūnicātiō, -ōnis *f.*

communion *n.* eucharistia, -ae *f.* (*ecclesiastical*)

compact *n.* pactum, -ī *nt.*; **form a ~** *v.d.i.* pacīscor, pacīscī, pactus sum

companion *n.* comes, comitis *m./f.*; *n.* sodālis, -is *m./f.*

companionship *n.* sodālitās, -ātis *f.*; *n.* societās, -ātis *f.*

company *n.* societās, -ātis *f.* (*business*); manipulus, -ī *m.* (*military unit*)

compare *v.t.* comparō, -parāre, -parāvī, -parātum

comparison *n.* comparātiō, -ōnis *f.*

compartment *n.* cella, -ae *f.*

compass *n.* circuitus, -ūs *m.*

compatible *adj.* conveniēns, -ientis

competence *n.* facultās, -ātis *f.*

competent *adj.* perītus, -a, um

competition *n.* certāmen, -inis *nt.*

complain *v.d.t.* queror, querī, questus sum (+ acc. + infv.); *v.d.t., v.d.i.* conqueror, conquerī, conquestus sum (*v.d.t.* + acc.; *v.d.i.* + **dē** + abl.)

complaining *adj.* querulus, -a, -um

complaint *n.* questus, -ūs *m.*

complete *adj.* perfectus, -a, -um; *v.t.* cōnficiō, -ficere, -fēcī, -fectum; *v.t.* perficiō, -ficere, -fēcī, -fectum; *v.t.* compleō, -plēre, -plēvī, -plētum

complicate *v.t.* impediō, -pedīre, -pedīvī, -peditum

complicated *adj.* involūtus, -a, -um

compliment *n.* blandīmenta, -ōrum *nt./pl.*; *v.d.t.* blandior, blandīrī, blandītus sum

compluvium *n.* compluvium, -ī *nt.*
comply *v.i.* concēdō, -cēdere, -cessī, -cessum (+ dat.)
compose *v.t.* compōnō, -pōnere, -posuī, -positum
composition *n.* scriptūra, -ae *f.*
compound *adj.* multiplex, -plicis
compromise *v.t.* compōnō, -pōnere, -posuī, -positum (*settle*); *v.t.* impediō, -pedīre, -pedīvī, -pedītum (*entangle; embarrass*)
conceal *v.t.* cēlō, -āre, -āvī, -ātum
conceit *n.* arrogantia, -ae *f.*
concentrate *v.i.* conveniō, -venīre, -vēnī, -ventum
concept *n.* nōtiō, -ōnis *f.*
concern *n.* sollicitūdō, -inis *f.* (*worry*); *n.* cūra, -ae *f.* (*interest*); *n.* rēs, reī *f.* (*affair*); *v.t.* pertineō, -tinēre, -tinuī, --- (+ **ad** + acc.) (*refer to*); **be ~ed about** *v.i.* interest, interesse, interfuit, --- (*imp.*) (+ gen. of person concerned *or* + **meā, tuā, suā,** etc. *or* + **ad** + acc. of thing concerned *or* + **ut** or **nē** + subjv.)
concerning *prep.* dē (+ abl.)
concert *n.* concentus, -ūs *m.*
concession *n.* concessiō, -ōnis *f.*
concise *adj.* brevis, -is, -e
condemn *v.t.* damnō, -āre, -āvī, -ātum
condition *n.* status, -ūs *m.* (*state*); *n.* condiciō, -ōnis *f.* (*stipulation*)
condole *v.t., v.i.* doleō, -ēre, doluī, -itum
conduct *n.* mōrēs, mōrum *m./pl.* (*behavior*); *n.* administrātiō, -ōnis *f.* (*management*); *v.t.* administrō, -ministrāre, -ministrāvī, -ministrātum (*manage*); *v.t.* dūcō, -ere, dūxī, ductum (*lead*)
conductor *n.* dux, ducis *m./f.* (*leader*)
cone *n.* cōnus, -ī *m.*
confess *v.d.t.* fateor, fatērī, fassus sum; *v.d.t.* cōnfiteor, cōnfitērī, cōnfessus sum
confession *n.* cōnfessiō, -ōnis *f.*
confidence *n.* fidēs, -eī *f.*
confirm *v.t.* affirmō, -firmāre, -firmāvī, -firmātum (*maintain; aver*); *v.t.* sanciō, -īre, sānxī, sānctum (*ratify*); *v.t.* cōnfirmō, -firmāre, -firmāvī, -firmātum (*strengthen*)
confirmation *n.* affirmātiō, -ōnis *f.* (*asseveration*); *n.* sānctiō, -ōnis *f.* (*inviolable ~*); *n.* cōnfirmātiō, -ōnis *f.* (*a strengthening*)
conflict *n.* certāmen, -inis *nt.* (*battle*); *n.* dissēnsiō, -ōnis *f.* (*difference of opinion*)

confuse *v.t.* cōnfundō, -fundere, -fūdī, -fūsum
confusion *n.* cōnfūsiō, -ōnis *f.*
congratulate *v.d.t.* grātulor, grātulārī, grātulātus sum (+ dat.)
congratulation *n.* grātulātiō, -ōnis *f.*
congress *n.* conventus, -ūs *m.*; *n.* concilium, -ī *nt.*
conjunction *n.* coniūnctiō, -ōnis *f.*
connect *v.t.* coniungō, -iungere, -iūnxī, -iūnctum
connection *n.* coniūnctiō, -ōnis *f.* (*a joining*); *n.* adfinitās, -ātis *f.* (*an association through marriage*)
conquer *v.t.* vincō, -ere, vīcī, victum; *v.t.* superō, -āre, -āvī, -ātum
conqueror *n.* victor, -ōris *m.*
conscience *n.* cōnscientia, -ae *f.*
conscientious *adj.* dīligēns, -entis (*careful*); *adj.* religiōsus, -a, -um (*religiously scrupulous*)
conscious *adj.* cōnscius, -a, -um
consent *n.* cōnsēnsus, -ūs *m.*; *v.t.* cōnsentiō, -sentīre, -sēnsī, -sēnsum
consequence *n.* ēventus, -ūs *m.*; **it is of ~** *v.i.* interest, interesse, interfuit, --- (*imp.*) (+ gen. of person or **meā, tuā, suā**, etc. *or* + subjv. or rel. clause + **ut** or **nē** *or* + **ad** + acc.); **it is of no ~** *v.i.* nīl interest, interesse, interfuit, --- (*imp.*) (+ gen. of person or **meā, tuā, suā**, etc. *or* + subjv. or rel. clause + **ut** or **nē** *or* + **ad** + acc.)
conserve *v.t.* servō, -āre, -āvī, -ātum
consider *v.d.t.* meditor, meditārī, meditātus sum (*think over*); *v.t.* dēlīberō, -līberāre, -līberāvī, -līberātum (*deliberate*); *v.t.* dūcō, -ere, duxī, ductum (*reckon; calculate; esteem*)
consideration *n.* dēlīberātiō, -ōnis *f.* (*thought*); *n.* respectus, -ūs *m.* (*regard for a person*)
consist, ~ of *v.i.* cōnstō, -stāre, -stitī, -stātum (+ abl. *or* + **ex** or **in** + abl.)
consolation *n.* sōlācium, -ī *nt.*; *n.* cōnsōlātiō, -ōnis *f.*
console *v.t.* cōnsōlō, -sōlāre, -sōlāvī, -sōlātum
constant *adj.* cōnstāns, -antis (*unchanging*); *adj.* continuus, -a, -um (*incessant*); *adj.* fidēlis, -is, -e (*faithful*)
constantly *adv.* semper
constellation *n.* sīdus, -eris *nt.*; *n.* signum, -ī *nt.*
constitute *v.t.* compōnō, -ponere, -posuī, -positum (*make up; compose*); *v.t.* statuō, -ere, statuī, statūtum (*establish*); *v.t.* creō, -āre, -āvī, -ātum (*appoint*)
consul *n.* cōnsul, -sulis *m.*
consulate *n.* cōnsulātus, -ūs *m.*

consult *v.t.* cōnsulō, -sulere, -suluī, -sultum; *v.t.* cōnsultō, -sultāre, -sultāvī, -sultātum

consume *v.t.* cōnsūmō, -sūmere, -sūmpsī, -sūmptum

consumer *n.* cōnsumptor, -ōris *m.*

consumption *n.* tābēs, -is *f.* (*tuberculosis*)

contact *n.* contactus, -ūs *m.*

contain *v.t.* capiō, -ere, cēpī, captum; *v.t.* contineō, -tinēre, -tinuī, -tentum

contaminate *v.t.* contāminō, -tāmināre, -tāmināvī, -tāminātum (*defile; pollute*); *v.t.* polluō, -ere, polluī, pollūtum (*desecrate; violate*)

contend *v.i.* contendō, -tendere, -tendī, -tentum

content *adj.* contentus, -a, -um; *v.t.* satisfaciō, -facere, -fēcī, -factum

contest *n.* certāmen, -inis *nt.*; *v.t.* contendō, -tendere, -tendī, -tentum

continent *n.* continēns, -ntis *f.*

continue *v.t.* extendō, -tendere, -tendī, -tentum (-tensum); *v.t.* continuō, -tinuāre, -tinuāvī, -tinuātum

continuous *adj.* continuus, -a, -um (*joining*); *adj.* perpetuus, -a, -um (*uninterrupted*)

contract *n.* pactum, -ī *nt.*; *v.t.* contrahō, -trahere, -trāxī, -trāctum

contrary *adj.* contrārius, -a, -um

contribute *v.t.* cōnferō, -ferre, -tulī, collātum

contribution *n.* collātiō, -ōnis *f.*

control *n.* potestās, -ātis *f.* (*power*); *n.* temperantia, -ae *f.* (*self-control*); *v.t.* regō, regere, rēxī, rēctum (*govern*); *v.t.* coerceō, -ercēre, -ercuī, -citum (*restrain*)

controller *n.* moderātor, -ōris *m.*

convene *v.t.* convocō, -vocāre, -vocāvī, -vocātum

convenience *n.* commoditās, -ātis *f.*

convention *n.* conventus, -ūs *m.* (*meeting*); *n.* pactum, -ī *nt.* (*agreement*); *n.* mōs, mōris *m.* (*custom*)

conversation *n.* sermō, -ōnis *m.*

convert *v.t.* convertō, -vertere, -vertī, -versum (*alter; change*); *v.t.* commūtō, -mūtāre, -mūtāvī, -mūtātum (*exchange*)

convey *v.t.* portō, -āre, -āvi, -ātum; *v.t.* ferō, ferre, tulī, lātum

cook *n.* coquus, -ī *m.*; *v.t.* coquō, -ere, coxī, coctum

cool *adj.* frīgidus, -a, -um; *v.t.* refrīgerō, -frīgerāre, -frīgerāvi, -frīgerātum

copper *n.* aes, aeris *nt.*

copy *v.d.t.* imitor, imitārī, imitātus sum (*resemble; act like*); *v.t.* trānscrībō, -scribere, -scrīpsī, -scrīptum (*make a written copy*)

coral *n.* coralium, -ī *nt.*

cordially *adv.* benignē
core *n.* medulla, -ae *f.* (*medulla; pith*)
cork *n.* cortex, corticis *m./f.*
corn *n.* frūmentum, -ī *nt.* (*grain in general*)
corner *n.* angulus, -ī *m.*
corporation *n.* collēgium, -ī *nt.*
corpse *n.* cadāver, -eris *nt.*
correct *adj.* ēmendātus, -a, -um (*faultless*); *adj.* rēctus, -a, -um (*proper*); *adj.* vērus, -a, -um (*true*); *v.t.* corrigō, -rigere, -rēxī, -rēctum (*amend*); *v.t.* ēmendō, -mendāre, -mendāvī, -mendātum (*amend*); *v.t.* pūniō, -īre, -īvī, -ītum (*punish*)
correction *n.* ēmendātiō, -ōnis *f.* (*improvement*); *n.* poena, -ae *f.* (*punishment*)
correspond *v.t.* rescrībō, -scrībere, -scrīpsī, -scrīptum (*write*); *v.i.* congruō, -gruere, -gruī, --- (*conform; be similar*)
correspondence *n.* litterae, -ārum *f./pl.*
corridor *n.* andrōn, -ōnis *m.*
corrupt *adj.* corruptus, -a, -um; *v.t.* corrumpō, -rumpere, -rūpī, -ruptum; *v.t.* vitiō, -āre, -āvī, -ātum
corruption *n.* corruptiō, -ōnis *f.*
cost *n.* pretium, -ī *nt.; v.i.* cōnstō, -stāre, -stitī, -stātum (+ abl. *or* + gen. of price)
costume *n.* vestītus, -ūs *m.*
cot *n.* lectulus, -ī *m.*
cottage *n.* casa, -ae *f.*
cotton *n.* gossypiōn, gossypiī *nt.*
couch *n.* lectus, -ī *m.*
cough *n.* tussis, -is *f.; v.i.* tussiō, -īre, -īvī, ---
could (*past of can*) use perfect or imperfect of **possum**
council *n.* concilium, -ī *nt.*
count *n.* numerus, -ī *m.; v.t.* numerō, -āre, -āvī, -ātum
counter *n.* mēnsa, -ae *f.* (*table*); *n.* abacus, -ī *m.* (*calculator*)
counterfeit *adj.* falsus, -a, -um
country *n.* rūs, rūris *nt.* (*countryside*); *n.* patria, -ae *f.* (*native land*); *adv.* **in the ~** rūrī
couple *n.* pār, paris *nt.; n.* coniugēs, -um *m./pl.* (*married couple*)
courage *n.* animus, -ī *m.*
courageous *adj.* fortis, -is, -e
course *n.* ratiō, -ōnis *f.* (*plan of proceeding*); *n.* mēnsa, -ae *f.* (*of dinner*); *n.* cursus, -ūs *m.* (*motion*); *adv.* **of ~** *adv.* certē

court *n.* rēgia, -ae *f.* (*royal* ~); *n.* tribūnal, -ālis *nt.* (*place of judgment*)
courtesy *n.* cōmitās, -ātis *f.*; *n.* urbānitās, -ātis *f.*
courtyard *n.* ārea, -ae *f.*
cousin *n.* cōnsōbrīnus, -ī *m.*, cōnsōbrīna, -ae *f.* (*maternal* ~); *n.* patruēlis, -is *m./f.* (*paternal* ~)
cover *n.* tegmen, -inis *nt.*; *n.* perfugium, -ī *nt.* (*shelter*); *n.* speciēs, -ēī *f.* (*pretense*); *v.t.* tegō, -ere, tēxī, tēctum (*overspread*); *v.t.* prōtegō, togere, -tēxī, -tēctum (*protect*); *v.t.* vēlō, -āre, -āvī, -ātum (*wrap; veil*)
cow *n.* vacca, -ae *f.*
cowardly *adj.* ignāvus, -a, -um
crab *n.* cancer, cancrī *m.*
crack *n.* rīma, -ae *f.* (*fissure*); *n.* fragor, -ōris *m.* (*loud noise*); *v.t.* frangō, -ere, frēgī, frāctum
cracker *n.* crustulum, -ī *nt.*
cradle *n.* cūnae, -ārum *f./pl.*
craft *n.* dolus, -ī *m.* (*cunning*); *n.* ars, artis *f.* (*skill*); *n.* scapha, -ae *f.* (*boat*)
craftsman *n.* artifex, artificis *m.*
crane *n.* grūs, gruis *m./f.* (*zool.*); *n.* tollēnō, -ōnis *m.* (*machine*)
crash *n.* fragor, -ōris *m.*; *v.t.* ēlīdō, -līdere, -līsī, -līsum
crawl *v.i.* rēpō, -ere, rēpsī, rēptum (*of animals and people*); *v.i.* serpō, -ere, serpsī, serptum (*of animals, particularly serpents*)
crazy *adj.* īnsānus, -a, -um
crease *n.* rūga, -ae *f.*
create *v.t.* creō, -āre, -āvī, -ātum
creation *n.* mundus, -ī *m.* (*world*)
creature *n.* animal, -ālis *nt.*
credit *n.* fidēs, -ēī *f.* (*belief; honor*); *v.t.* crēdō, -dere, -didī, -ditum (+ dat.) (*believe*)
creditor *n.* crēditor, -ōris *m.*
creep *v.i.* rēpō, -ere, rēpsī, rēptum (*of animals and people*); *v.i.* serpō, -ere, serpsī, serptum (*of animals, particularly serpents, and other things*)
crescent *adj.* lūnātus, -a, -um
crest *n.* crista, -ae *f.* (*of bird; of helmet*)
crew *n.* nautae, -ārum *m./pl.* (*of ship*); *n.* grex, gregis *m.* (*group*)
cricket *n.* cicāda, -ae *f.* (*tree insect*); *n.* gryllus, -ī *m.* (*ground insect*)
crime *n.* scelus, -eris *nt.*
criminal *adj.* scelestus, -a, -um
crippled *adj.* claudus, -a, -um (*lame*); *adj.* dēbilis, -is, -e (*disabled or weak in mind or body*)

crisis *n.* discrīmen, -inis *nt.*

criticism *n.* iūdicium, -ī *nt.* (*evaluation*)

criticize *v.t.* reprehendō, -hendere, -hendī, -hēnsum (*find fault*); *v.t.* iūdicō, -dicāre, -dicāvī, -dicātum (*judge*)

crooked *adj.* prāvus, -a, -um

crop *n.* messis, -is *f.*

cross *n.* crux, crucis *f.*; *v.t.* obsistō, -sistere, -stitī, -stitum (*oppose*); ~ **out** *v.t.* dēleō, -ēre, -ēvī, -ētum ; ~ **over** *v.i.* trānseō, -īre, -īvī (-iī), -itum

crossroad *n.* compitum, -ī *nt.*

crouch *v.i.* subsīdō, -sīdere, -sēdī, -sessum

crow *n.* cornīx, cornīcis *f.*

crowd *n.* turba, -ae *f.*; *n.* vulgus, -ī *m.*

crowded *adj.* cōnfertus, -a, -um (*crammed; dense*); *adj.* celeber, celebris, celebre (*frequented; thronged*)

crown *n.* diadēma, -atis *nt.* (*royal ~*); *n.* corōna, -ae *f.* (*chaplet; wreath*)

crude *adj.* crūdus, -a, -um (*raw; unripe; unprepared*); *adj.* incultus, -a, -um (*untilled; uncouth*); *adj.* rudis, -is, -e (*unfinished; unskilled*)

cruel *adj.* crūdēlis, -is, -e (*hard-hearted; merciless*); turbidus, -a, -um (*of weather: harsh*)

cruise *n.* nāvigātiō, -ōnis *f.*

crumb *n.* mīca, -ae *f.*

crumble *v.t.* friō, -āre, -āvī, -ātum

crush *v.t.* obterō, -terere, -trīvī, -trītum

crust *n.* crusta, -ae *f.*

cry *n.* clāmor, -ōris *m.* (*loud exclamation*); *n.* plōrātus, -ūs *m.* (*cry of distress*); *n.* vāgītus, -ūs *m.* (*infant's wail*); *v.t.* clāmō, -āre, -āvī, -ātum (*shout*); *v.t.* lacrīmō, -āre, -āvī, -ātum (*weep*)

crystal *n.* crystallum, -ī *nt.*

cub *n.* catulus, -ī *m.*

cuff *n.* alapa, -ae *f.* (*a slap*)

cultivate *v.t.* colō, -ere, coluī, cultum (~ *the land, the mind, etc.*)

cultivation *n.* cultūra, -ae *f.* (*of soil, mind, etc.*)

culture *n.* cultūra, -ae *f.* (*of soil, mind, etc.*)

cup *n.* pōculum, -ī *nt.*

cupboard *n.* armārium, -ī *nt.*

curb *n.* frēnum, -ī *nt.* (*horse bit*); *n.* crepīdō, -inis *f.* (*street; pier*); *v.t.* coerceō, -ercēre, -ercuī, -ercitum (*restrain*); *v.t.* frēnō, - āre, -āvī, -ātum (~ *horses*)

cure *n.* sānātiō, -ōnis *f.* (*act of curing*); *n.* remedium, -ī *nt.* (*that which cures*); *v.t.* cūrō, - āre, -āvī, -ātum

curious *adj.* cūriōsus, -a, -um (*inquisitive*); *adj.* avidus, -a, -um (+ gen.)
(*eager to know, etc.*); *adj.* novus, -a, -um (*strange*)
curl *n.* cincinnus, -ī *m.*; *v.t.* crispō, - āre, -āvī, -ātum
curly *adj.* crispus, -a, -um
currency *n.* monēta, -ae *f.* (*money*)
current *n.* flūmen, flūminis *nt.* (*of river*); *n.* aestus, -ūs *m.* (*of ocean*); *n.*
aura, -ae *f.* (*of air*); *adj.* ūsitātus, -a, -um (*in general use*); *adj.* vulgāris,
-is, -e (*generally received*); **be ~** *v.i.* viqeō, -ēre, viquī, ---
curse *n.* exsecrātiō, -ōnis *f.* ; *v.d.t.* exsecror, exsecrārī, exsecrātus sum
curtain *n.* vēlum, -ī *nt.*; *n.* aulaeum, -ī *nt.* (*an elaborate hanging*)
curve *n.* sinus, -ūs *m.*
cushion *n.* pulvīnus, -ī *m.*
custom *n.* cōnsuētūdō, -inis *f.* (*habitual using and doing*); *n.* mōs, mōris *m.*
(*especially, a habitual practice of a nation or community*)
customer *n.* ēmptor, -ōris *m.*
customs *n.* vectīgal, -ālis *nt.*
cut *n.* incīsiō, -ōnis *f.* (*incision*); *n.* ictus, -ūs *m.* (*stroke; wound*); *v.t.* caedo,
-ere, cecīdī, caesum (*hew; cut down; kill*); *v.t.* seco, secāre, secuī, sectum
(*~ with knife, scalpel, razor; divide*)
cycle *n.* orbis, -is *m.*
cylinder *n.* cylindrus, -drī *m.*

D

dad(dy) *n.* tata, -ae *m.*
daily *adj.* quotīdiānus, -a, um; *adv.* quotīdiē
dam *n.* mōlēs, -is *f.* (*structure*); *n.* agger, aggeris *m.* (*structure*); *n.* māter,
mātris *f.* (*female animal*)
damage *n.* damnum, -ī *nt.*; *v.t.* laedō, -ere, laesī, laesum
damn *v.t.* damnō, -āre, -āvī, -ātum
damp *adj.* ūmidus, -a, -um
dampen *v.t.* ūmectō, -āre, -āvī, -ātum (*moisten*); *v.t.* imminuō, -minuere,
-minuī, -minūtum (*depress spirits/mind*)
dance *n.* saltātiō, -ōnis *f.*; *v.i.* saltō, -āre, -āvī, -ātum
danger *n.* perīculum, -ī *nt.*
dangerous *adj.* perīculōsus, -a, -um
dare *v.t.* prōvocō, -vocāre, -vocāvī, -vocātum; *v.i., v.t.* audeo, -ēre, ausus sum
daring *adj.* audāx, audācis
dark *adj.* obscūrus, -a, -um (*without light; unintelligible*)

darken *v.t.* obscūrō, -āre, -āvī, -ātum
darkness *n.* obscūritās, -ātis *f.* (*state of ~*); *n.* tenebrae, -ārum *f.pl.* (*shadows*)
darn *v.t.* sarciō, -īre, sarsī, sartum
dash *n.* impetus, -ūs *m.* (*a rush*); *n.* nōn nihil (+ gen.) (*small amount*)
date *n.* diēs, diēī *m./f.* (*time of an event*); *n.* tempus, temporis *nt.* (*time*);
   out of ~ *adj.* obsolētus, -a, -um
daughter *n.* filia, -ae *f.*
daughter-in-law *n.* nurus, -ūs *f.*
dawn *n.* (prīma) lūx, (prīmae) lūcis *f.*; **it is ~** *v.i.* lūcēscit, -ere, lūxit, --- (*imp.*)
day *n.* diēs, diēī *m./f.*; **on the previous ~** *adv.* prīdiē
dead *adj.* mortuus, -a, -um
deaf *adj.* surdus, -a, -um
deal *n.* aliquantum, -ī *nt.*; **~ with a person/thing** *v.t.* trāctō, -āre, -āvī,
   -ātum; **~ in** *v.d.t.* negōtior, negōtiārī, negōtiātus sum
dealer *n.* mercātor, -ōris *m.*
dear *adj.* cārus, -a, -um (*beloved; expensive*)
death *n.* mors, mortis *f.*
debate *n.* contrōversia, -ae *f.*; *v.t.* disputō, -putāre, -putāvī, -putātum
debt *n.* aes aliēnum, aeris aliēnī *nt.*
decay *n.* tābēs, -is *f.*; *v.i.* tābēscō, -ere, tābuī, ---
deceit *n.* fraus, fraudis *f.* (*deceitful action*); *n.* fallācia, -ae *f.* (*deceitful words*)
deceive *v.t.* dēcipiō, -cipere, -cēpī, -ceptum; *v.t.* fallō, -ere, fefellī, falsum
December *adj.* December, Decembris (*usu. w.* **mēnsis**); *n.* December, Decembris *m.*
decent *adj.* honestus, -a, -um
deception *n.* fraus, fraudis *f.*
decide *v.t.* dēcernō, -cernere, -crēvī, -crētum ; *v.t.* diiūdicō, -iūdicāre, -iūdicāvī, -iūdicātum (*judicial*)
decision *n.* sententia, -ae *f.*; *n.* dēcrētum, -ī *nt.* (*especially judicial, legislative*); *n.* cōnstantia, -ae *f.* (*firmness of purpose*)
decisive *adj.* certus, -a, -um
deck *n.* nāvis cōnstrāta, nāvis cōnstrātae *f.*
declaration *n.* professiō, -ōnis *f.*
declare *v.t.* dēclārō, -clārāre, -clārāvī, -clārātum (*make known*); *v.t.* affirmō, -firmāre, -firmāvī, -firmātum (*assert strongly*)
decline *n.* dēminūtiō, -ōnis *f.*; *v.t.* recūsō, -cūsāre, -cūsāvī, -cūsātum; *v.i.* dēficiō, -ficere, -fēcī, -fectum
decorate *v.t.* exōrnō, -ōrnāre, -ōrnāvī, -ōrnātum

decoration *n.* ōrnātiō, -ōnis *f.* (*act of decorating*); *n.* ōrnāmentum, -ī *nt.*
(*ornament*)
decrease *n.* imminūtiō, -ōnis *f.*; *v.t.* minuō, -ere, -uī, -ūtum; *v.i.* dēcrēscō,
-crēscere, -crēvī, -crētum
dedicate *v.t.* dēdicō, -dicāre, -dicāvī, -dicātum
dedication *n.* dēdicātiō, -ōnis *f.*
deed *n.* factum, -ī *nt.* (*act*); *n.* tabula, -ae *f.* (*legal document*)
deem *v.t.* iūdicō, -dicāre, -dicāvī, -dicātum; *v.t.* exīstimō, -īstimāre, -īstimāvī,
-īstimātum
deep *adj.* altus, -a, -um; *adj.* gravis, -is, -e (*of sounds*)
deer *n.* cervus, -ī *m.*, cerva, -ae *f.*
default *n.* inopia, -ae *f.*
defeat *n.* clādēs, -is *f.*; *v.t.* vincō, -ere, vīcī, victum; *v.t.* superō, -āre, -āvī, -ātum
defect *n.* vitium, -ī *nt.*
defend *v.t.* dēfendō, -fendere, -fendī, -fēnsum
defendant *n.* reus, -ī *m.*, rea, -ae *f.*
defense *n.* dēfēnsiō, -ōnis *f.*
defer *v.t.* differō, -ferre, distulī, dīlātum (*postpone*); ~ **to** *v.i.* cēdō, -ere,
cessī, cessum (+ *dat.*)
define *v.t.* circumscrībō, -scrībere, -scrīpsī, -scrīptum (*fix limits*); *v.t.* dēfiniō,
-finīre, -finīvī, -finītum (*give a definition of*)
definite *adj.* dēfinītus, -a, -um
definition *n.* dēfinītiō, -ōnis *f.*
definitive *adj.* dēfinītīvus, -a, -um
defy *v.t.* prōvocō, -vocāre, -vocāvī, -vocātum
degree *n.* gradus, -ūs *m.*
delay *n.* mora, -ae *f.*; *v.d.t.* moror, morārī, morātus sum; *v.d.i.* cunctor,
cunctārī, cunctātus sum
delete *v.t.* dēleō, -ēre, -ēvī, -ētum
deliberate *adj.* cōnsīderātus, -a, -um
delicacy *n.* tenuitās, -ātis *f.* (*fineness of texture*); *n.* ēlegantia, -ae *f.* (*fineness
of taste*); *n.* suāvitās, -ātis *f.* (*flavor*)
delicate *adj.* tenuis, -is, -e (*fineness of texture*); *adj.* ēlegāns, -antis (*fineness
of taste*); *adj.* imbēcillus, -a, -um (*of health*)
delight *n.* voluptās, -ātis *f.*
deliver *v.t.* trādō, -dere, -didī, -ditum (*hand over*); *v.t.* līberō, -āre, -āvī,
-ātum (*free*)
delivery *n.* līberātiō, -ōnis *f.* (*act of freeing*); *n.* partus, -ūs *m.* (*childbirth*)
demand *n.* postulātiō, -ōnis *f.*; *v.t.* postulō, -āre, -āvī, -ātum

demonstrate *v.t.* dēmonstrō, -monstrāre, -monstrāvī, -monstrātum
den *n.* specus, -ūs *m./nt.*
denarius *n.* dēnārius, -ī *m.*
dense *adj.* dēnsus, -a, -um (*thick*); *adj.* stolidus, -a, -um (*stupid*)
density *n.* dēnsitās, -ātis *f.*
deny *v.d.t.* īnfitior, īnfitiārī, īnfitiātus sum (*disown*); *v.t.* negō, -āre, -āvī, -ātum (+ acc. + infv.) (*refute; say that . . . not*)
depart *v.i.* discēdō, -cēdere, -cessī, -cessum
department *n.* mūnus, -eris *nt.* (*post; function*)
departure *n.* discessus, -ūs *m.*
depend *v.i.* dēpendeō, -pendēre, -pendī, -pēnsum (*hang down*); *v.d.i.* nītor, nītī, nīxus (nīsus) sum (+ **in** + abl *or* + abl.) (*rely on*)
dependent *n.* cliēns, clientis *m.*
depict *v.t.* pingō, -ere, pīnxī, pictum
deport *v.t.* dēportō, -portāre, -portāvī, -portātum; *v.t.* gerō, -ere, gessī, gestum (+ refl. pron.) (*conduct oneself*)
depress *v.t.* premō, -ere, pressī, pressum (*press down*); *v.t.* frangō, -ere, frēgī, fractum (*depress someone's spirits*)
depressed *adj.* pressus, -a, -um (*pressed down*); *adj.* trīstis, -is, -e (*dejected*)
depression *n.* trīstitia, -ae *f.*
deprive *v.t.* prīvō, -āre, -āvī, -ātum (+ abl. of thing deprived of)
depth *n.* altitūdō, -inis *f.*
deputy *n.* prōcūrātor, -ōris *m.*
derive *v.t.* dēdūcō, -dūcere, -dūxī, -ductum
descend *v.i.* dēscendō, -scendere, -scendī, -scēnsum
descent *n.* dēscēnsus, -ūs *m.* (*slope*); *n.* irruptiō, -ōnis *f.* (*attack*)
describe *v.t.* dēscrībō, -scrībere, -scrīpsī, -scrīptum
description *n.* dēscrīptiō, -ōnis *f.*
desert *n.* sōlitūdō, -inis *f.* (*wilderness*); *v.t.* dēserō, -serere, -seruī, -sertum (*abandoning by soldiers*); *v.i.* trānseō, -īre, -īvī (-iī), -itum (*abandon*)
deserve *v.t.* commereō, -merēre, -meruī, -meritum
design *n.* dēscrīptiō, -ōnis *f.* (*drawing*); *n.* cōnsilium, -ī *nt.* (*purpose*); *v.t.* dēsignō, -signāre, -signāvī, -signātum
designate *v.t.* dēsignō, -signāre, -signāvī, -signātum
designer *n.* fabricātor, -ōris *m.*
desirable *adj.* optābilis, -is, -e
desire *n.* cupiditās, -ātis *f.* (*craving*); *n.* vōtum -ī *nt.* (*thing desired*); *v.t.* cupiō, cupere, cupīvī, cupītum
desk *n.* scrīnium, -ī *nt.*

despair *n.* dēsperātiō, -ōnis *f.*; *v.i.* dēspērō, -spērāre, -spērāvī, -spērātum
dessert *n.* bellāria, -ōrum *nt./pl.*
destiny *n.* fātum, -ī *nt.*
destroy *v.t.* perdō, -ere, -didī, -ditum
destruction *n.* perniciēs, -ēī *f.*
detach *v.t.* dēfringō, -fringere, -frēgī, -frāctum (*break off*); *v.t.* disiungō, -iungere, -iūnxī, -iūnctum (*separate*)
detain *v.t.* teneō, -ēre, tenuī, tentum
detect *v.t.* dēprehendō, -prehendere, -prehēndī, -prehēnsum
detection *n.* dēprehensiō, -ōnis *f.*
determination *n.* iūdicium, -ī *nt.* (*judicial decision*); *n.* cōnstantia, -ae *f.* (*resolve*)
determine *v.t.* iūdicō, -dicāre, -dicāvī, -dicātum (*judge*); *v.t.* statuō, statuere, statuī, statūtum (+ *infv.*) (*decide*)
determined *adj.* certus, -a, um
develop *v.t.* explicō, -plicāre, -plicāvī, -plicātum (*explain in words or actions*)
development *n.* auctus, -ūs *m.* (*growth; increase*)
deviation *n.* dēclīnātiō, -ōnis *f.*
device *n.* īnsigne, -is *nt.* (*emblem*); *n.* dolus, -ī *m.* (*contrivance*)
devil *n.* diabolus, -ī *m.*
devout *adj.* pius, -a, -um
dew *n.* rōs, rōris *m.*
diagonal *adj.* diagonālis, -is, -e
dial *n.* sōlārium, -ī *nt.* (*sundial*)
dialect *n.* dialectus, -ī *m.*
dialogue *n.* sermō, -ōnis *m.*
diameter *n.* diametros, -ī *f.*
diamond *n.* adamas, -antis *m.* (*precious stone*); *n.* scutula, -ae *f.* (*~ shape*)
diary *n.* diārium, -ī *nt.*
dictate *v.t.* dictō, -āre, -āvī, -ātum (*say what another is to repeat in speech or writing*); *v.t.* imperō, -āre, -āvī, -ātum (+ *infv. or* + **ut** *or* **nē** + *subjv.*) (*order*)
dictator *n.* dictātor, -ōris *m.*
dictionary *n.* glossārium, -ī *nt.*
die *n.* tessera, -ae *f.* (*gaming piece*); *v.d.i.* morior, morī, mortuus sum (*cease to live*); *v.i.* cadō, -ere, cecidī, cāsum
diet *n.* victus, -ūs *m.* (*food in general; prescribed food*)
differ *v.i.* differō, -ferre, distulī, dīlātum (+ *abl. of respect*) (*be unlike*); *v.i.* discrepō, -crepāre, -crepuī, --- (*disagree in opinion*)

difference *n.* dissimilitūdō, -inis *f.* (*state of being unlike*); *n.* dissēnsiō, -ōnis *f.* (*difference in opinion*); **it makes a ~ (it matters)** *v.i.* interest, interesse, interfuīt, --- (+ gen. of person concerned *or* + abl. f. sg. of poss. adj.) (*imp. v.*)

different *adj.* dīversus, -a, -um; *adj.* dissimilis, -is, -e (+ gen. *or* + dat. *or* + **inter sē**)

difficult *adj.* difficilis, -is, e

difficulty *n.* difficultās, -ātis *f.*; **be in ~** *v.i.* labōrō, -āre, -āvī, -ātum

dig *v.t.* fodiō, -ere, fōdī, fossum

digest *v.t.* concoquo, -coquere, -cōxī, -coctum

dignified *adj.* gravis, -is, -e

dignity *n.* dignitās, -ātis *f.*

diligent *adj.* dīligēns, -entis

dim *v.t.* obscūrō, -āre, -āvī, -ātum

diminish *v.t.* minuō, -ere, -uī, -ūtum

dine *v.i.* cēnō, -āre, -āvī, -ātum

dining room *n.* trīclīnium, -ī *nt.*

dinner *n.* cēna, -ae *f.*

dip *v.t.* mergō, -ere, mersī, mersum

direct *adj.* rectus, -a, -um; **direct** *v.t.* dīrigō, -rigere, -rēxī, -rēctum (*regulate; direct one's course*); *v.t.* iubeō, -ēre, iussī, iussum (+ acc. + infv.) (*order*)

direction *n.* regiō, -ōnis *f.* (*line of observation*); *n.* cursus, -ūs *m.* (*line of motion*); *n.* administrātiō, -ōnis *f.* (*management*)

directly *adv.* rectā (*straight forward*); *adv.* statim (*immediately*)

director *n.* cūrātor, -ōris *m.*

dirt *n.* sordēs, -ium *f./pl.*

dirty *adj.* sordidus, -a, -um; **be ~** *v.i.* sordeō, -ēre, ---, ---

disagree *v.i.* dissentiō, -sentīre, -sēnsī, -sēnsum

disagreement *n.* dissēnsiō, -ōnis *f.*

disappear *v.d.i.* dīlābor, dīlābī, dīlapsus sum

disappoint *v.d.t.* frustror, frustrārī, frustrātus sum

disaster *n.* clādēs, -is *f.*

discipline *n.* disciplīna, -ae *f.* (*any training or instruction*); *n.* castīgātiō, -ōnis *f.* (*punishment*)

discover *v.t.* aperiō, -īre, aperuī, apertum (*reveal*); *v.t.* inveniō, -venīre, -vēnī, -ventum (*find out*)

discreet *adj.* cautus, -a, -um

discriminate *v.i.* diiūdicō, -iūdicāre, -iūdicāvī, -iūdicātum

discuss *v.t.* dispūtō, -pūtāre, -pūtāvī, -pūtātum
discussion *n.* dispūtātiō, -ōnis *f.*
disease *n.* morbus, -ī *m.*
disgrace *n.* dēdecus, -oris *nt.*
disguise *n.* vestis, -is *f.*
disgust *n.* fastīdium, -ī *nt.*
disgusting *adj.* foedus, -a, -um
dish *n.* patina, -ae *f.*
dishonest *adj.* fraudulentus, -a, -um
dishonesty *n.* fraus, fraudis *f.*
dislike *v.i.* abhorreō, -horrēre, -horruī, --- (+ **ā/ab** + abl.)
dismiss *v.t.* dīmittō, -mittere, -mīsī, -missum
disobey *v.i.* nōn pāreō, -ēre, pāruī, pāritum (+ dat.)
display *n.* ostentus, -ūs *m.*; *v.t.* ostentō, -āre, -āvī, -ātum
displease *v.t.* offendō, -fendere, -fendī, -fēnsum
dispose *v.t.* dispōnō, -pōnere, -posuī, -positum (*arrange*); ~ **of** *v.t.* exuō, -uere, -uī, -ūtum (*lay aside; cast off*); ~ **of** *v.t.* vendō, -ere, -didī, -ditum (*sell*)
dispute *n.* contrōversia, -ae *f.*
disregard *n.* neglegentia, -ae *f.* (*heedlessness*); *v.t.* neglegō, -glegere, -glēxī, -glēctum
distance *n.* spatium, -ī *nt.*; **at a** ~ *adv.* procul
distant *adj.* longinquus, -a, -um; **be** ~ *v.i.* absum, -esse, āfuī, āfutūrum
distill *v.t.* stillō, -āre, -āvī, -ātum
distinct *adj.* alius, alia, aliud (*different*); *adj.* clārus, -a, -um (*clear*)
distinction *n.* distinctiō, -ōnis *f.* (*act of distinguishing between things*); *n.* discrīmen, -inis *nt.* (*distinction between things*); *n.* honōs, honōris *m.* (*mark of honor*)
distinguish *v.t.* distinguō, -stinguere, -stinxī, -stinctum (*mark as different*); *v.t.* sēcernō, -cernere, -crēvī, -crētum (*distinguish between things*); *v.t.* decorō, -āre, -āvī, -ātum (*honor*)
distort *v.t.* dētorqueō, -torquēre, -torsī, -tortum
distract *v.t.* distrahō, -trahere, -trāxī, -trāctum
distress *n.* miseria, -ae *f.* (*suffering*); *n.* angustiae, -ārum *f./pl.* (*financial difficulty*)
distribute *v.t.* distribuō, -tribuere, -tribuī, -tribūtum
distribution *n.* distribūtiō, -ōnis *f.*
district *n.* rēgiō, -ōnis *f.*
distrust *n.* diffīdentia, -ae *f.*; *v.i.* diffīdō, -fīdere, -fīsus sum (+ dat.)

disturb *v.t.* turbo, -āre, -āvī, -ātum
ditch *n.* fossa, -ae *f.*
dive *v.i.* mergō, -ere, mersī, mersum (+ ref. pron.)
diverse *adj.* alius, alia, aliud
divide *v.t.* dīvidō, -videre, -vīsī, -vīsum
division *n.* dīvīsiō, -ōnis *f.* (*act of dividing*)
divorce *n.* dīvortium, -ī *nt.*
dizziness *n.* vertīgō, -inis *f.*
dizzy *adj.* vertīginōsus, -a, -um
do *verbal aux. not expressed in Latin*
dock *n.* nāvālia, -ium *nt./pl.*
doctor *n.* medicus, -ī *m.*
dog *n.* canis, -is *m./f.*
doll *n.* pūpa, -ae *f.*
dolphin *n.* delphīnus, -ī *m.*
domain *n.* regnum, -ī *nt.* (*kingdom*)
dome *n.* tholus, -ī *m.*
domestic *adj.* domesticus, -a, -um
dominate *v.d.t.* dominor, dominārī, dominātus sum
domination *n.* dominātiō, -ōnis *f.*
donate *v.t.* dōnō, -āre, -āvī, -ātum
donation *n.* dōnum, -ī *nt.*
door *n.* iānua, -ae *f.*
doorman *n.* iānitor, -ōris *m.*
dot *n.* punctum, -ī *nt.*
double *adj.* duplex, -plicis (*twofold*); *adj.* duplus, -a, -um (*twice as much*)
doubt *v.t.* dubitō, -āre, -āvī, -ātum
doubtful *adj.* dubius, -a, -um
dove *n.* columba, -ae *f.*
down *n.* plūma, -ae *f.* (*feathers*); *n.* lānūgō, -inis *f.* (*fine hair*)
dowry *n.* dōs, dōtis *f.*
dozen *n.* duodecim *num.* (*indecl.*)
draft *n.* aura, -ae *f.* (*breeze*); *n.* haustus, -ūs *m.* (*a drink*)
drag *v.t.* trahō, -ere, trāxī, trāctum; **~ away** *v.t.* abstrahō, -trahere, - trāxī, -trāctum; **~ forth** *v.t.* extrahō, -trahere, - trāxī, -tractum
dragon *n.* dracō, -ōnis *m.*
drain *n.* cloāca, -ae *f.*; *v.t.* siccō, -āre, -āvī, -ātum
drama *n.* fābula, -ae *f.*

draw *v.t.* trahō, -ere, trāxī, trāctum (*pull*); *v.t.* dēstringō, -stringere, -strinxī, -strictum (*draw a weapon*); ~ **apart** *v.t.* dīdūcō, -dūcere, -dūxī, -ductum; ~ **out** *v.t.* extrahō, -trahere, -trāxī, -trāctum; ~ **tight** *v.t.* addūcō, -dūcere, -dūxī, -ductum; ~ **a picture** *v.t.* dēscrībō, -scrībere, -scrīpsī, -scrīptum; ~ **up troops** *v.t.* īnstruō, -struere, -strūxī, -strūctum; ~ **up a document or draft** *v.t.* scrībō, scrībere, scrīpsī, scrīptum

drawing *n.* pictūra, -ae *f.*

dread *n.* formīdō, -inis *f.*; *v.t.* formīdō, -āre, -āvī, -ātum

dreadful *adj.* dīrus, -a, -um

dream *n.* somnium, -ī *nt.*; *v.t.* somniō, -āre, -āvī, -ātum

dreary *adj.* vastus, -a, -um

dress *n.* vestis, -is *f.* (*clothes*); *n.* habitus, -ūs *m.* (*style of dress*); *v.t.* vestiō, -īre, -īvī, -ītum (*put on clothing*); *v.t.* cōmō, -ere, cōmpsī, cōmptum (*style hair*); *v.t.* cūrō, -āre, -āvī, -ātum (*care for a wound*)

drift *n.* agger, -eris *m.* (*heap*)

drill *n.* terebra, -ae *f.*; *v.t.* terebrō, -āre, -āvī, -ātum (*pierce*); *v.t.* exerceō, -ercēre, -ercuī, -ercitum (*train troops*)

drink *n.* pōtiō, -ōnis *f.*; *v.t.* bibō, -ere, bibī, bibitum

drive *v.t.* agō, ere, ēgī, actum (*impel*); ~ **away** *v.t.* abigō, -igere, -ēgī, -actum; ~ **back** *v.t.* repellō, -pellere, reppulī, repulsum ; ~ **forward**, ~ **out** *v.t.* expellō, -pellere, -pulī, -pulsum ; ~ **together** *v.t.* cōgō, -ere, coēgī, coāctum

driver *n.* agitātor, -ōris *m.*

drop *v.i.* stillō, -āre, -āvī, -ātum (*fall in drops*); *v.t.* dēmittō, -mittere, -mīsī, -missum (*let fall*); *v.d.i.* dēlābor, dēlābī, dēlāpsus sum

drown *v.t.* mergō, -ere, mersī, mersum

drug *n.* medicāmentum, -ī *nt.*

drum *n.* tympanum, -ī *nt.*

drunk *adj.* ēbrius, -a, -um

dry *adj.* siccus, -a, -um; *v.t.* siccō, -āre, -āvī, -ātum

duck *n.* anās, anātis *f.*

due *adj.* dēbitus, -a, -um

dull *adj.* hebes, hebetis (*of sharp instruments; of the mind; of the senses*); *adj.* nūbilus, -a, -um (*of sky; of weather*)

dumb *adj.* hebes, hebetis (*dull-witted*)

dung *n.* stercus, -oris *nt.*

during *prep.* per (+ acc.), inter (+ acc.)

dusk *n.* crepusculum, -ī *nt.*

dust *n.* pulvis, pulveris *m.*; *v.t.* dētergeō, -tergere, -tersī, -tersum

dusty *adj.* pulverulentus, -a, -um
duty *n.* officium, -ī *nt.*
dwell *v.i.* habitō, -āre, -āvī, -ātum
dwelling *n.* sēdēs, -is *f.*
dye *v.t.* tingō (tinguō), -ere, tinxī, tinctum
dying *adj.* moriēns, -ientis

E

each *n. adj.* uterque, utraque, utrumque (*of two*); *pron.* quisque, quaeque,
    quidque (*of three or more*); *adj.* quisque, quaeque, quodque (*of three or
    more*); **on/from ~ side** *adv.* utrimque; **in ~ direction** *adv.* utrōque
eager *adj.* avidus, -a, -um (usually + gen.) (*desirous*); *adj.* ācer, ācris, ācre
    (*impetuous*)
eagle *n.* aquila, -ae *f.*
ear *n.* auris, -is *f.* (*anat.*); *n.* spīca, -ae *f.* (*of grain*)
early *adj.* mātūtīnus, -a, -um (*in the morning*); *adj.* novus, -a, -um (*begin-
    ning*); *adj.* antīquus, -a, -um (*of early date*); **~ in the morning** *adv.*
    māne
earn *v.i.* mereō, -ēre, meruī, meritum
earnest *adj.* intentus, -a, -um (*eager*); *adj.* sērius, -a, -um (*serious*)
earnings *n.* quaestus, -ūs *m.*
earrings *n.* inaurēs, -ium *f./pl.*
earth *n.* terra, -ae *f.*
earthquake *n.* tremor, -ōris *m.*
easily *adv.* facile
east *n.* oriēns, orientis *m.*; *adj.* orientālis, -is, -e
eastern *adj.* orientālis, -is, -e
easy *adj.* facilis, -is, -e
eat *v.t.* edō, -ere, ēdī, ēsum
eccentric *adj.* mīrus, -a, -um
echo *n.* resonō, -sonāre, -sonāvī, -sonātum
economical *adj.* parcus, -a, -um
economy *n.* parsimōnia, -ae *f.* (*frugality*)
edge *n.* margō, -inis *m./f.*
edible *adj.* esculentus, -a, -um
edict *n.* ēdictum, -ī *nt.*
edit *v.t.* ēdō, -dere, -didī, -ditum
edition *n.* ēditiō, -ōnis *f.*

educate *v.t.* ēducō, -ducāre, -ducāvī, -ducātum (*rear; bring up*); *v.t.* īnstituō, -stituere, -stituī, -stitūtum (*train in a branch of knowledge*)

education *n.* ēducātiō, -ōnis *f.* (*the rearing of a child*); *n.* disciplīna, -ae *nf.* (*course of training*)

eel *n.* anguilla, -ae *f.*

effect *n.* effectus, -ūs *m.*

effective *adj.* efficax, efficācis

effort *n.* cōnātus, -ūs *m.*

egg *n.* ōvum, -ī *nt.*

eight *num.* octō (*indecl.*)

eighteen *num.* duodēvīgintī (*indecl.*)

eighteenth *adj.* duodēvīcēsimus, -a, -um

eighth *adj.* octāvus, -a, -um

eighty *num.* octōgintā (*indecl.*)

either *conj.* aut; ~ ... or *conj.* aut ... aut

elbow *n.* cubitum, -ī *nt.*

elderly *adj.* senex, senis

elect *v.t.* creō, -āre, -āvī, -ātum

election *n.* ēlectiō, -ōnis *f.*

elegant *adj.* ēlegāns, -antis

element *n.* elementum, -ī *nt.*

elementary *adj.* prīmus, -a, -um (*constituent*)

elephant *n.* elephās, -antis *m.*; *n.* elephantus, -ī *m.*

eleven *num.* ūndecim (*indecl.*)

eleventh *adj.* ūndecimus, -a, -um

eliminate *v.t.* āmoveō, -movēre, -mōvī, -mōtum

else *adj.* alius, alia, aliud; *adv.* praetereā

embark *v.t.* impōnō, -pōnere, -posuī, -positum

embarrass *v.t.* perturbō, -turbāre, -turbāvī, -turbātum

embassy *n.* lēgātiō, -ōnis *f.*

emblem *n.* signum, -ī *nt.*

embrace *n.* amplexus, -ūs *m.*

embroider *v.t.* pingō, -ere, pinxī, pictum

emerge *v.i.* ēmergō, -mergere, -mersī, -mersum

emergency *n.* tempus, -oris *nt.*

emigrant *n.* ēmigrāns, -antis *m./f.*

emigrate *v.i.* ēmigrō, -migrāre, -migrāvī, -migrātum

emit *v.t.* ēmittō, -mittere, -mīsī, -missum

emotion *n.* mōtus, -ūs *m.*

emperor *n.* imperātor, -ōris *m.*
emphasis *n.* vīs, vim (acc.), vī (abl.) *f.* (*def. n.*)
emphasize *v.t.* premō, -ere, pressī, pressum
empire *n.* imperium, -ī *nt.*
employ *v.d.i.* ūtor, ūtī, ūsus sum (+ abl.) (*use*)
employment *n.* ūsus, -ūs *m.* (*act of using*); *n.* quaestus, -ūs *m.* (*occupation*)
empty *adj.* vacuus, -a, -um (*unoccupied*); *adj.* inānis, -is, -e (*without effect*);
    v.t. vacuēfaciō, -facere, -fēcī, -factum
enable *v.t.* efficiō, -ficere, -fēcī, -fectum (+ **ut** clause)
enclose *v.t.* saepiō, -īre, saepsī, saeptum (*enclose with a fence*); *v.t.* inclūdō,
    -clūdere, -clūsī, -clūsum (*put something inside another*)
enclosure *n.* saeptum, -ī *nt.*
encounter *n.* congressus, -ūs *m.*; *v.t.* incidō, -cidere, -cidī, -cāsum (+ **in** +
    acc.) (*meet unexpectedly*); *v.d.i.* congredior, congredī, congressus sum
    (~ *with hostility*)
encourage *v.d.t.* hortor, hortārī, hortātus sum
end *n.* finis, -is *m.*; *v.t.* finiō, -īre, -īvī, -ītum ; *v.i.* dēsinō, -sinere, dēsiī,
    dēsitum
ending *n.* exitus, -ūs *m.*
endorse *v.t.* approbō, -probāre, -probāvī, -probātum
endurance *n.* patientia, -ae *f.*
endure *v.d.t.* patior, patī, passus sum (*submit to*); *v.i.* dūrō, -āre, -āvī, -ātum
    (*last*)
enemy *n.* hostis, -is *m./f.* (*of the state*); *n.* inimīcus, -ī *m.*; *n.* inimīca, -ae *f.*
energetic *adj.* strēnuus, -a, -um
energy *n.* vīs, vim (acc), vī (abl.) *f.* (*def. n.*)
engagement *n.* spōnsiō, -ōnis *f.* (*legal, religious or formal pact*); *n.* pugna, -ae
    f. (*battle*)
engrave *v.t.* scalpō, -ere, scalpsī, scalptum
engraving *n.* scalptūra, -ae *f.*
enjoy *v.d.i.* fruor, fruī, fructus sum (+ abl.) (*receive pleasure from*)
enjoyment *n.* dēlectātiō, -ōnis *f.* (*sense of pleasure*)
enlarge *v.t.* amplificō, -ficāre, -ficāvī, -ficātum
enormous *adj.* ingēns, -entis (*huge*); *adj.* immānis, -is, -e (*large and terrible*)
enough *adj.* satis (+ gen.) *nt.* (*indecl.*); *adv.* satis
enquire *v.t.* quaerō, -ere, quaesīvī, quaesītum
ensure *v.t.* caveō, -ēre, cāvī, cautum (+ **nē** + subjv.)
enter *v.t.* referō, -ferre, rettūlī, relātum (*write down*); *v.i.* intrō, -āre, -āvī,
    -ātum (*come in*)

enterprise *n.* inceptum, -ī *nt.*
entertain *v.t.* dēlectō, -āre, -āvī, -ātum (*amuse*); *v.t.* hospitiō excipiō, -cipere, -cēpī, -ceptum (*receive as guests*)
entertaining *adj.* festīvus, -a, -um
entertainment *n.* dēlectātiō, -ōnis *f.* (*amusement*); *n.* hospitium, -ī *nt.* (*reception of guests*)
enthusiasm *n.* studium, -ī *nt.*
entire *adj.* tōtus, -a, -um
entrance *n.* ingressiō, -ōnis *f.* (*act of entering*); *n.* aditus, -us *m.* (*place of entrance*)
entrust *v.t.* committō, -mittere, -mīsī, -missum
entry *n.* ingressiō, -ōnis *f.* (*act of entering*); *n.* aditus, -ūs *m.* (*place of entrance*)
envelop *v.t.* involvō, -volvere, -volvī, -volūtum
envelope *n.* involūcrum, -ī *nt.*
envious *adj.* invidus, -a, -um
environs *n.* vicinia, -ae *f.*
envy *n.* invidia, -ae *f.*; *v.i.* invideō, -vidēre, -vīdī, -vīsum (+ dat.)
epidemic *n.* pestilentia, -ae *f.*
epilepsy *n.* morbus sacer, morbī sacrī *m.*
equal *adj.* pār, paris (*corresponding to; matching*); *adj.* aequus, -a, -um (*having the same dimensions*); *v.t.* aequō, -āre, -āvī, -ātum
equality *n.* aequum, -ī *nt.*
equestrian order *n.* equitēs, -um *m./pl.*
equip *v.t.* īnstruō, -struere, -strūxī, -strūctum
equipment *n.* īnstrūmentum, -ī *nt.*
equity *n.* aequitās, -ātis *f.*
era *n.* tempus, -oris *nt.*
erase *v.t.* dēleō, -ēre, -ēvī, -ētum
erect *adj.* ērēctus, -a, -um; *v.t.* tollō, -ere, sustulī, sublātum (*raise high*); *v.t.* exstruō, -struere, -strūxī, -strūctum (*build*)
error *n.* error, -ōris *m.*
escape *n.* effugium, -ī *nt.*; *v.t., v.i.* effugiō, -fugere, -fūgī, ---
escort *n.* comitātus, -ūs *m.*; *v.d.t.* comitor, comitārī, comitātus sum
especially *adv.* praecipuē (*use with with single words*); *adv.* praesertim (*use with clauses*)
essay *n.* cōnātus, -ūs *m.* (*attempt*); *n.* libellus, -ī *m.* (*treatise*)
essence *n.* nātūra, -ae *f.*
establish *v.t.* stabiliō, -āre, -āvī, -ātum (*make firm*); *v.t.* īnstituō, -stituere, -stituī, -stitūtum (*institute*)

estate *n.* fundus, -ī *m.*

estimate *n.* aestimātiō, -ōnis *f.*

et cetera *n.* et cētera *nt./pl.*

eternal *adj.* aeternus, -a, -um

ethical *adj.* mōrālis, -is, -e

evacuate *v.t.* vacuēfaciō, -facere, -fēcī, -fectum (*make empty*); *v.t.* dēdūcō, -dūcere, -dūxī, -ductum (*withdraw people from*)

eve *n.* vesper, vesperī *m.* (*evening*)

even *adj.* aequus, -a, -um; *adv.* etiam; **not ~** *adv.* nē quidem

evening *n.* vesper, vesperī *m.* (*dusk*); **in the ~** *adv.* vesperī, vespere

event *n.* ēventus, -ūs *m.*

ever *adv.* umquam (*when preceded by a negative except in direct and indirect questions*); *adv.* quandō (*when preceded by* **sī** *or interrogatives*)

every *adj.* quisque, quaeque, quodque (*used singly, i.e. "every fourth year"*); *adj.* omnis, -is, -e (*used when "every" means "all," i.e. "of every kind"*); **~ day** *adv.* quotīdiē

everybody *pron.* quisque, quaeque, quidque (*used in singular only*); *pron.* omnis, -is, -e (*used when "every" means "all"*)

everyone *pron.* quisque, quaeque, quidque

everything *pron.* quidque

everywhere *adv.* ubīque

evidence *n.* testimōnium, -ī *nt.*

evident *adj.* apertus, -a, -um

evil *n.* malum, -ī *nt.*; *adj.* malus, -a, -um

exact *adj.* subtīlis, -is, -e

exaggerate *v.t.* augeō, -ēre, auxī, auctum

examination *n.* investīgātiō, -ōnis *f.* (*search*); *n.* interrogātiō, -ōnis *f.* (*cross-examination of witnesses*)

examine *v.t.* investīgō, -vestīgāre, -vestīgāvī, -vestīgātum (*search into*); *v.t.* interrogō, -rogāre, -rogāvī, -rogātum (*inquire by questioning*)

example *n.* exemplum, -ī *nt.*

exceed *v.t.* excēdō, -cēdere, -cessī, -cessum

excellent *adj.* optimus, -a, -um

except *conj.* nisi; *prep.* praeter (+ acc.)

exception *n.* exceptiō, -ōnis *f.*

excess *n.* nimium *nt.* (*indecl.*) (+ gen.); *n.* intemperantia, -ae *f.* (*over-indulgence*)

exchange *v.t.* mūtō, -āre, -āvī, -ātum

excite *v.t.* excitō, -citāre, -citāvī, -citātum

excitement *n.* commōtiō, -ōnis *f.*

exclaim *v.t.* clāmō, -āre, -āvī, -ātum

exclude *v.t.* exclūdō, -clūdere, -clūsī, -clūsum

excuse *v.t.* excūsō, -cūsāre, -cūsāvī, -cūsātum (*give an excuse*); *v.t.* ignōscō, -nōscere, -nōvī, -nōtum (+ dat.) (*forgive*)

execute *v.d.t.* exsequor, exsequī, exsecūtus sum (*fulfill; carry out*); *v.t.* necō, -āre, -āvī, -ātum (*kill*)

exempt *v.t.* līberō, -āre, -āvī, -ātum (+ abl. of thing exempted from)

exemption *n.* immūnitās, -ātis *f.*

exhale *v.i.* exhālō, -hālāre, -hālāvī, -hālātum

exhausted *adj.* dēfessus, -a, -um

exhibit *v.t.* expōnō, -pōnere, -posuī, -positum (*bring out to view*); *v.t.* praestō, -stāre, -stitī, -stitum (-stātum) (*evince; manifest*)

exile *n.* exsul, -sulis *m./f.* (*of a person*); *n.* exsilium (exilium), -ī *nt.* (*banishment*); *v.t.* exterminō, -termināre, -termināvī, -terminātum

exist *v.i.* sum, esse, fuī, futūrum

existence *n.* vīta, -ae *f.* (*life*)

expand *v.t.* dīlātō, -lātāre, -lātāvī, -lātātum

expect *v.t.* exspectō, -spectāre, -spectāvī, -spectātum

expectation *n.* exspectātiō, -ōnis *f.*

expel *v.t.* expellō, -pellere, -pulī, -pulsum

expense *n.* impēnsa, -ae *f.*

expensive *adj.* sūmptuōsus, -a, -um

experience *n.* ūsus, -ūs *m.*; *v.d.t.* experior, experīrī, expertus sum

expert *adj.* callidus, -a, -um

explain *v.t.* explicō, -plicāre, -plicāvī, -plicātum

explanation *n.* explicātiō, -ōnis *f.*

explode *v.t.* dīrumpō, -rumpere, -rūpī, -ruptum (*burst, break*); *v.t.* refūtō, -fūtāre, -fūtāvī, -fūtātum (*discredit*)

explore *v.t.* explōrō, -āre, -āvī, -ātum

explosion *n.* ēruptiō, -ōnis *f.*

export *v.t.* exportō, -portāre, -portāvī, -portātum

expose *v.t.* expōnō, -pōnere, -posuī, -positum (*place out; exhibit*); *v.t.* nūdō, -āre, -āvī, -ātum (*lay bare*)

express *v.t.* exprimō, -primere, -pressī, -pressum

extend *v.t.* extendō, -tendere, -tendī, -tentum (-tensum)

extension *n.* prōpāgātiō, -ōnis *f.*

external *adj.* externus, -a, -um

extinguish *v.t.* exstinguō, -stinguere, -stīnxī, -stīnctum

extra *adv.* praetereā
extract *v.t.* extrahō, -trahere, -trāxī, -tractum
extraordinary *adj.* insolitus, -a, -um
extreme *adj.* extrēmus, -a, -um (*farthest*); *adj.* summus, -a, -um (*exceeding usual limits*)
eye *n.* oculus, -ī *m.*
eyeball *n.* pūpula, -ae *f.*
eyebrow *n.* supercilium, -ī *nt.*
eyelash *n.* palpebra, -ae *f.*
eyelid *n.* palpebra, -ae *f.*

F

fabric *n.* textum, -ī *nt.* (*cloth*); *n.* aedificium, -ī *nt.* (*arch.*)
façade *n.* frōns, frōntis *f.*
face *n.* faciēs, -ēī *f.* (*of human*); *n.* ōs, ōris *nt.* (*of animal; of human*); *n.* vultus, -ūs *nt.* (*countenance; features*)
facilitate *v.t.* facilius reddō, -dere, -didī, -ditum
facility *n.* facilitās, -ātis *f.* (*readiness*); *n.* facultās, -ātis *f.* (*possibility of something being done*)
fact *n.* rēs, reī *f.*; **in ~** *adv.* quidem
factory *n.* officīna, -ae *f.*
faculty *n.* facultās, -ātis *f.* (*ability to do something*)
fade *v.i.* palleō, -ēre, palluī, --- (*lose color*); *v.i.* dēflōrēscō, -flōrēscere, -flōruī, --- (*wither*)
fail *v.i.* dēficiō, -ficere, -fēcī, -fectum (*be wanting*); *v.i.* dēsum, -esse, -fuī, --- (*be lacking*); *v.i.* concidō, -cidere, -cidī, --- (*be defeated or unsuccessful*)
failure *n.* dēfectus, -ūs *m.* (*of supply*)
faint *adj.* dēfessus, -a, -um (*weary*); *adj.* hebes, hebetis (*of the senses; of colors*); *adj.* dēmissus, -a, -um (*timid*); *v.d.i.* dēfatīgor, dēfatīgārī, dēfatīgātus sum (*be tired out*); *v.d.i.* collābor, collābī, collapsus sum (*swoon*)
fair *n.* nundinae, -ārum *f./pl.*; *adj.* pulcher, pulchra, pulchrum (*pretty*); *adj.* serēnus, -a, -um (*of weather*); *adj.* aequus, -a, -um (*equitable*)
faith *n.* fidēs, -eī *f.*
faithful *adj.* fidēlis, -is, -e
fall *n.* autumnus, -ī *m.*; *v.i.* cadō, -ere, cecidī, cāsum (*drop; decline*); *v.i.* occidō, -cidere, -cidī, -cāsum (*perish*)
false *adj.* falsus, -a, -um
falsify *v.t.* corrumpō, -rumpere, -rūpī, -ruptum

fame *n.* fāma, -ae *f.*

familiar *adj.* familiāris, -is, -e

family *n.* familia, -ae *f.*

famous *adj.* clārus, -a, -um

fan *n.* flābellum, -ī *nt.* (*device for moving air*)

far *adj.* longīnquus, -a, -um; *adv.* procul; **as ~ as** *adv.* usque (ad); **how ~** *adv.* quoad

faraway *adv.* longē

fare *n.* cibus, -ī *m.* (*food*); *n.* vectūra, -ae *f.* (*money for transport*)

farm *n.* fundus, -ī *m.*

farmer *n.* agricola, -ae *m.*

farsighted *adj.* providus, -a, -um (*prudent*)

fascinate *v.t.* fascinō, -āre, -āvī, -atum (*bewitch*); *v.t.* teneō, -ēre, tenuī, tentum (*captivate*)

fascination *n.* fascinātiō, -ōnis *f.* (*bewitchment*); *n.* blanditiae, -ārum *f./pl.* (*captivation*)

fashion *n.* mōs, mōris *m.* (*prevailing custom*)

fast *n.* iēiūnium, -ī *nt.*; *adj.* celer, celeris, celere

fasten *v.t.* figō, -ere, fixī, fixum (*nail down*); *v.t.* alligō, -līgāre, -ligāvī, -ligātum (*tie down; tie to*)

fat *n.* adeps, -ipis *m./f.*; *adj.* pinguis, -is, -e

fatal *adj.* fātālis, -is, -e

father *n.* pater, patris *m.*

father-in-law *n.* socer, socerī *m.*

fatty *adj.* pinguis, -is, -e

fault *n.* culpa, -ae *f.*

faulty *adj.* mendōsus, -a, -um

favor *n.* favor, -ōris *mn.* (*good will*); gratia, -ae *f.* (*a favor done*); *v.i.* faveō, -ēre, fāvī, fautum (+ dat.)

favorite *adj.* grātus, -a, -um

fear *n.* metus, -ūs *m.*; *v.t.* metuō, -ere, -uī, -ūtum

feast *n.* epulae, -ārum *f./pl.*

feather *n.* penna, -ae *f.*

February *adj.* Februārius, -a, -um (*usu. w.* **mēnsis**); *n.* Februārius, -ī *m.*

fee *n.* mercēs, -ēdis *f.*

feed *v.t.* alō, alere, aluī, alitum (altum) (*~ humans*); *v.t., v.i.* pascō, -ere, pāvī, pastum (*~ animals*)

feel *v.t.* temptō, -āre, -āvī, -ātum (*touch; handle*); *v.t., v.i.* sentiō, -īre, sēnsī, sēnsum (*~ with the senses*)

feeling *n.* sēnsus, -ūs *m.*
fellow *adj.* socius, -a, -um
female *n.* fēmina, -ae *f.*; *adj.* fēmineus, -a, -um
feminine *adj.* fēmineus, -a, -um
fence *n.* saepēs, -is *f.*
ferment *v.t.* fermentō, -āre, -āvī, -ātum
fern *n.* filix, filicis *f.*
fertile *adj.* fertilis, -is, -e
festival *n.* fēriae, -ārum *f./pl.*
fever *n.* febris, -is *f.*
few *adj.* paucus, -a, -um
fiber *n.* fibra, -ae *f.*
field *n.* ager, agrī *m.* (*of farm*); *n.* campus, -ī *m.* (*open country*)
fierce *adj.* atrōx, atrōcis
fifteen *num.* quīndecim (*indecl.*)
fifteenth *adj.* quīntus decimus, quīnta decima, quīntum decimum
fifth *adj.* quīntus, -a, -um
fiftieth *adj.* quīnquāgēsimus, -a, -um
fifty *num.* quīnquāgintā (*indecl.*)
fig *n.* ficus, -ī *f.*
fight *n.* pugna, -ae *f.*; *v.t.* pugnō, -āre, -āvī, -ātum
figure *n.* figūra, -ae *f.* (*mold; form; image*); *v.t.* fingō, -ere, finxī, fictum
　　(*fashion; make*)
file *n.* līma, -ae *f.* (*tool*); *n.* ordō, -inis *f.* (*a line; a rank*); *v.t.* līmō, -āre, -āvī,
　　-ātum
fill *v.t.* compleō, -plēre, -plēvī, -plētum
filter *n.* cōlum, -ī *nt.*
filthy *adj.* sordidus, -a, -um (*dirty*); *adj.* obscēnus, -a, -um (*offensive*)
final *adj.* extrēmus, -a, -um; **~ly** *adv.* postrēmō
find *v.t.* inveniō, -venīre, -vēnī, -ventum; **~ out** *v.t.* reperiō, -perīre, -perī,
　　-pertum
fine *n.* multa, -ae *f.*; *adj.* subtīlis, -is, -e (*~ texture*); *adj.* pulcher, pulchra,
　　pulchrum (*~ appearance*)
finger *n.* digitus, -ī *m.*
finish *v.t.* cōnficiō, -ficere, -fēcī, -fectum (*accomplish*)
fire *n.* ignis, -is *m.* (*the element ~*); *n.* incendium, -ī *nt.* (*a conflagration*);
　　set on ~ *v.t.* incendō, -cendere, -cendī, -censum
firm *adj.* firmus, -a, -um
first *adj.* prīmus, -a, -um; **at ~** *adv.* prīmō

fish *n.* piscis, -is *m.*; *v.t.* piscor, piscārī, piscātus sum
fisherman *n.* piscātor, -ōris *m.*
fishing *n.* piscātus, -ūs *m.*
fist *n.* pugna, -ae *f.*
fit *v.t.* aptō, -āre, -āvī, -ātum
five *num.* quīnque (*indecl.*)
fix *v.t.* figō, -ere, fīxī, fīxum (*make fast*); *v.t.* cōnstituō, -stituere, -stituī, -stitūtum (*appoint; settle; erect*)
fixed *adj.* certus, -a, -um
flag *n.* vexillum, -ī *nt.*
flame *n.* flamma, -ae *f.*
flap *n.* lacinia, -ae *f.* (*of cloth*)
flash *n.* fulgor, -ōris *m.*; *v.i.* fulgeō, -ēre, fulsī, ---
flat *adj.* campester, campestris, campestre (*level*); *adj.* vapidus, -a, -um (*insipid*)
flatter *v.d.t.* adūlor, adūlārī, adūlātus sum
flavor *n.* sapor, -ōris *m.*
flaw *n.* vitium, -ī *nt.*
flea *n.* pūlex, pūlicis *m.*
flee *v.i.* fugiō, -ere, fūgī, fūgitum
fleet *n.* classis, -is *f.*
flesh *n.* carō, carnis *f.*
flight *n.* volātus, -ūs *m.* (*of birds*); *n.* fuga, -ae *f.* (*escape*); *n.* scālae, -ārum *f./pl.* (*of stairs*)
float *v.i.* fluitō, -āre, -āvī, -ātum
flock *n.* grex, gregis *m.*
flood *n.* dīluvium, -ī *nt.* (*inundation*); *n.* flūmen, -inis *nt.* (*an outpouring of tears, etc.*)
floor *n.* solum, -ī *nt.* (*ground floor*); *n.* contignātiō, -ōnis *f.* (*floors above the ground floor*)
flour *n.* farīna, -ae *f.*
flow *n.* flūmen, -minis *nt.*; *v.i.* fluō, -ere, flūxī, flūxum
flower *n.* flōs, flōris *m.*
fluent *adj.* cōpiōsus, -a, -um
fluid *n.* hūmor, -ōris *m.*; *adj.* fluidus, -a, -um
fly *n.* musca, -ae *f.* (*insect*); *v.i.* volō, -āre, -āvī, -ātum
foam *n.* spūma, -ae *f.*
fog *n.* cālīgō, -inis *f.*
foggy *adj.* cālīginōsus, -a, -um

fold *n.* sinus, -ūs *m.* (*of a garment; of land*); *v.t.* complicō, -plicāre, -plicāvī, -plicātum

follow *v.d.i.* sequor, sequī, secūtus sum

following *adj.* sequēns, -entis

fond *adj.* amō, -āre, -āvī, -ātum

food *n.* cibus, -ī *m.*

fool *n.* stultus, -ī *m.*

foolish *adj.* stultus, -a, -um

foot *n.* pēs, pedis *m.*; **on ~** *adj.* pedester, pedestris, pedestre

for *conj.* nam; enim (enim *follows the first word in its clause*); *prep.:* usually the dative case for indirect objects; *prep.* prō (+ abl.) (*in place of; on behalf of; in proportion to; in return for*); *prep.* propter (+ acc.) (*because of*); **~ a length of time** *Use acc. for extent of time;* **~ a price** *Use abl. for definite prices; for indefinite prices, use gen. of an adj. denoting quantity, e.g. "of small account,"* parvī

forbid *v.t.* vetō, -āre, -uī, -itum

forbidden *adj.* vetitus, -a, -um

force *n.* vīs, vim (acc.), v ī (abl.) *f.* (*def. n.*); *n.* cōpiae, -ārum *f./pl.* (*military troops*); *v.t.* cōgō, -ere, coēgī, coāctum

forces (military) *n.* vīrēs, -ium *f./pl.*

ford *n.* vadum, -ī *nt.*

forearm *n.* bracchium, -ī *nt.*

forehead *n.* frōns, frontis *f.*

foreign *adj.* externus, -a, -um (*of another country*); *adj.* peregrīnus, -a, -um (*from abroad*)

foreigner *n.* peregrīnus, -ī *m.*; *n.* peregrīna, -ae *f.*

foresight *n.* prōvidentia, -ae *f.*

forest *n.* silva, -ae *f.*

forever *adv.* semper

forget *v.d.i.* oblīvīscor, oblīvīscī, oblītus sum (+ gen.)

forgive *v.t.* ignoscō, -noscere, -nōvī, -nōtum (+ dat. of person forgiven *or* + acc. of thing forgiven *or* + **quod** clause)

fork *n.* furca, -ae *f.* (*pitchfork*); *n.* bivium, -ī *nt.* (*of a road*)

form *n.* forma, -ae *f.*; *v.t.* formō, -āre, -āvī, -ātum (*shape*); *v.t.* ineō, -īre, -īvī (-iī), -ītum (*conceive; enter upon*)

former *adj.* prior, prius (*earlier*); *adj.* prīstinus -a, -um (*original*); **the ~** *adj.* ille, illa, illud ; **~ly** *adv.* quondam

formula *n.* formula, -ae *f.*

fort *n.* castellum, -ī *nt.*

fortieth *adj.* quadrāgēsimus, -a, -um
fortress *n.* castellum, -ī *nt.*
fortunate *adj.* fēlīx, fēlīcis; **~ly** *adv.* fēlīciter
fortune *n.* fortūna, -ae *f.*
forty *num.* quadrāgintā (*indecl.*)
forum *n.* forum, -ī *nt.*
forward *adv.* porrō (*frequently expressed by* prō- *compounded in a verb*)
foster *v.t.* foveō, -ēre, fōvī, fōtum; **~ child** *n.* alumnus, -ī *m.*, alumna, -ae *f.*
found *v.t.* condō, -dere, -didī, -ditum
foundation *n.* fundāmentum, -ī *nt.*
founder *n.* conditor, -ōris *m.*
fountain *n.* fōns, fōntis *m.*
four *num.* quattuor (*indecl.*)
fourteen *num.* quattuordecim (*indecl.*)
fourteenth *adj.* quārtus decimus, quārta decima, quārtum decimum
fourth *adj.* quārtus, -a, -um
fowl *n.* avis, avis *f.* (*bird*); *n.* gallīna, -ae *f.* (*domesticated ~*)
fox *n.* vulpēs, -is *f.*
fraction *n.* pars, partis *f.*
fragile *adj.* fragilis, -is, -e
frame *n.* compāgēs, -is *f.* (*structure*); *n.* forma, -ae *f.* (*that which shapes*); *n.* animus, -ī *m.* (*temper of mind*); *v.t.* formō, -āre, -āvī, -ātum
frantic *adj.* āmēns, -entis
fraud *n.* fraus, fraudis *f.*
free *adj.* līber, lībera, līberum (*having freedom; exempt from*); *adj.* vacuus, -a, -um (*at leisure*); *adj.* grātuītus, -a, -um (*without cost*); *v.t.* līberō, -āre, -āvī, -ātum
freedom *n.* lībertās, -ātis *f.* (*political ~*); *n.* vacātiō, -ōnis *f.* (*release from; exemption*)
freeze *v.t.* gelō, -āre, -āvī, -ātum; *v.i.* rigēscō, -ere, riguī, ---
freight *n.* onus, oneris *nt.*
frequency *n.* crēbritās, -ātis *f.*
frequent *adj.* crēber, crēbra, crēbrum; **~ly** *adv.* crēbrō
fresh *adj.* recēns, -entis (*new*); *adj.* integer, integra, integrum (*not tired out*)
Friday *n.* diēs Veneris, diēī Veneris *m.*
friend *n.* amīcus, -ī *m.*; *n.* amīca, -ae *f.*; **~ly** *adj.* amīcus, -a, -um
friendship *n.* amīcitia, -ae *f.*
fright *n.* terror, -ōris *m.*
frighten *v.t.* terreō, -ēre, terruī, territum

frightening *adj.* terribilis, -is, -e
frog *n.* rāna, -ae *f.*
from, away ~ *prep.* ā, ab (+ abl.); **down ~** *prep.* dē (+ abl.); **~ out of** *prep.* ē, ex (+ abl.)
front *n.* frōns, frōntis *f.*; **in ~ of** *prep.* prō (+ abl.)
frontier *n.* fīnēs, -ium *m./pl.*
frost *n.* gelum, -ī *nt.*
frostbitten *adj.* ambustus, -a, -um
frozen *adj.* rigidus, -a, -um
fruit *n.* frūctus, -ūs *m.*
frustrate *v.d.t.* frustror, frustrārī, frustrātus sum (*bring to naught*)
frustration *n.* frustrātiō, -ōnis *f.*
fry *v.t.* frīgō, -ere, frixī, frictum
frying pan *n.* sartāgō, -inis *f.*
fuel *n.* lignum, -ī *nt.* (*firewood*)
fugitive *adj.* profugus, -a, -um
full *adj.* plēnus, -a, -um (*filled with; complete*); *adj.* satur, satura, saturum (*satiated*); *adj.* integer, integra, integrum (*complete*); *adj.* crēber, crēbra, crēbrum (*crowded*)
function *n.* officium, -ī *nt.* (*duty*)
funeral *n.* fūnus, -eris *nt.*
fungus *n.* fungus, -ī *m.*
funny *adj.* rīdiculus, -a, -um
fur *n.* pilus, -ī *m.*
furious *adj.* īrātus, -a, -um
furnace *n.* fornāx, -ācis *f.*
furnish *v.t.* praebeō, -bēre, -buī, -bitum (+ dat. of person *or* + acc. of thing) (*supply*); *v.t.* ōrnō, -āre, -āvī, -ātum (*equip*)
furniture *n.* supellex, supellectilis *f.*
further *adv.* praetereā
future *n.* futūrum, -ī *nt.*

G

gain *n.* lucrum, -ī *nt.*; *v.d.t.* lucror, lucrārī, lucrātus sum (*make a profit*); *v.t.* acquīrō, -quīrere, -quīsīvī, -quīsītum (*obtain*)
gall *n.* fel, fellis *nt.*
gallery *n.* porticus, -ūs *f.*
gallop, at a ~ *adv.* equō citātō

game *n.* lūdus, -ī *m.* (*amusement*); *n.* ferae, -ārum *f./pl.* (*hunted animals*)

gang *n.* grex, gregis *m.* (*company*); *n.* caterva, -ae *f.* (*armed group*)

gap *n.* lacūna, -ae *f.*

garbage *n.* quisquiliae, -ārum *f./pl.*

garden *n.* hortus, -ī *m.*

gardener *n.* holitor, -ōris *m.*

gargle *v.i.* gargarīzō, -āre, -āvī, -ātum

garlic *n.* alium, -ī *nt.*

garment *n.* vestīmentum, -ī *nt.*

gas *n.* vapor, -ōris *m.*

gate *n.* porta, -ae *f.* (*city-gate; of camp*); *n.* iānua, -ae *f.* (*of house*)

gather *v.d.i.* congredior, congredī, congressus sum

gay *adj.* fēstus, -a, -um (*happy; festive*); *adj.* flōridus, -a, -um (*brightly colored*)

gear *n.* īnstrūmenta, -ōrum *nt./pl.*

gem *n.* gemma, -ae *f.*

gender *n.* genus, -eris *nt.*

general *n.* dux, ducis *m./f.*; *n.* imperātor, -ōris *m.*; *adj.* generālis, -is, -e (*not specific*); *adj.* commūnis, -is, -e (*common*); **in ~** *adv.* generātim

generally *adv.* generātim (*universally*); *adv.* plērumque (*for the most part*)

generate *v.t.* generō, -āre, -āvī, -ātum

generation *n.* genus, -eris *nt.* (*off-spring*); *n.* saeculum, -ī *nt.* (*a successive step in natural descent*); *n.* prōcreātiō, -ōnis *f.* (*act of begetting or producing*)

generous *adj.* generōsus, -a, -um

genital *adj.* genitālis, -is, -e; **~s** *n./pl.* genitālia, -um *nt./pl.*

genius *n.* ingenium, -ī *nt.* (*power of the mind*); *n.* facultās, -ātis *f.* (*natural capability or talent*)

gentle *adj.* lēnis, -is, -e (*mild; gradual*)

geography *n.* geōgraphia, -ae *f.*

germ *n.* germen, -inis *nt.* (*embryo plant*)

gesture *n.* gestus, -ūs *m.*

get *v.d.t.* adipīscor, adipīscī, adeptus sum (*acquire*); **~ something done** *v.t.* cūrō, -āre, -āvī, -ātum (+ acc. + gerv.); **~ to a place** *v.i.* adveniō, -venīre, -vēnī, -ventum; **~ up** *v.i.* surgō, surgere, surrēxī, surrēctum; **~ together** *v.t.* cōgō, cōgere, coēgī, coāctum; **~ together** *v.d.i.* congredior, congredī, congressus sum (+ refl. pron.)

ghost *n.* umbra, -ae *f.*

giant *adj.* immānis, -is, -e

gift *n.* dōnum, -ī *nt.* (*a present*); *n.* facultās, -ātis *f.* (*natural talent*)

gild *v.t.* inaurō, -aurāre, -aurāvī, -aurātum

gills *n./pl.* branchiae, -ārum *f./pl.*

girl *n.* puella, -ae *f.* (*female child*); *n.* virgō, -inis *f.* (*unmarried ~*)

girlfriend *n.* puella, -ae *f.*

give *v.t.* dō, dare, dedī, datum (*present*); *v.t.* trādō, -dere, -didī, -ditum
    (*hand over*); **~ back, ~up** *v.t.* remittō, -mittere, -mīsī, -mīssum

glad *adj.* laetus, -a, -um; **be ~** *v.i.* gaudeō, -ēre, gāvīsus sum; **be ~ that** *v.i.*
    gaudeō, -ēre, gāvīsus sum (+ *quod* clause)

gladiator *n.* gladiātor, -ōris *m.*

glance *v.i.* aspiciō, -spicere, -spexī, -spectum (*look at quickly*); *v.i.* stringō,
    -ere, strinxī, strictum (*touch lightly*)

gland *n.* glāns, glandis *f.*

glare *n.* fulgor, -ōris *m.* (*bright light*); *v.i.* torvīs oculīs aspiciō, -spicere, -spexī,
    -spectum (*cast a fierce look*); *v.i.* fulgeō, -ēre, fulsī, --- (*shine brightly*)

glass *n.* vitrum, -ī *nt.*

globe *n.* globus, -ī *m.*

gloom *n.* cālīgō, -inis *f.*

gloomy *adj.* tenebricōsus, -a, -um (*dark; shadowy*); *adj.* trīstis, -is, -e (*sad*)

glory *n.* glōria, -ae *f.*

glow *n.* ārdor, -ōris *m.*; *v.i.* candeō, -ēre, canduī, ---

glue *n.* glūten, -inis *nt.*; *v.t.* glūtinō, -āre, -āvī, -ātum

go *v.i.* eō, īre, īvī (iī), itum (*irreg.*); **~ away** *v.i.* abeō, -īre, -īī (-īvī), -itum;
    ~ up *v.i.* ascendō, -scendere, -scendī, -scēnsum; **~ down** *v.i.* dēscendō,
    -scendere, -scendī, -scēnsum; **going to** *Use first periphrastic conjugation*

goal *n.* mēta, -ae *f.* (*~ post*)

goat *n.* caper, caprī *m.*; *n.* capra, -ae *f.*

god *n.* deus, -ī *m.*

goddess *n.* dea, -ae *f.*

gold *n.* aurum, -ī *nt.*

golden *adj.* aureus, -a, -um

good *adj.* bonus, -a, -um; *n.* bonum, -ī *nt.* (*the opposite of evil*); *n.*
    commodum, -ī *nt.* (*advantage*); *n.* salūs, -ūtis *f.* (*welfare*)

good-bye *v.i.* valē!, valēte! (*impv. sg., pl.*)

goods *n./pl.* bona, -ōrum *nt./pl.*

goose *n.* anser, anseris *m.*

gospel *n.* ēvangelium, -ī *nt.*

gossip *n.* rūmor, -ōris *m.*; *v.i.* garriō, -īre, -īvī, -ītum

govern *v.t.* imperō, -āre, -āvī, -ātum

government *n.* imperium, -ī *nt.* (*supreme power*); *n.* administrātiō, -ōnis *f.*
    (*act or function of governing*)

governor *n.* gubernātor, -ōris *m.* (*one having highest power over a state*);
    n. praefectus, -ī *m.* (*~ of a Roman province*)
grace *n.* grātia, -ae *f.* (*favor*); *n.* venustās, -ātis *f.* (*beauty; gracefulness*);
    n. venia, -ae *f.* (*pardon*)
graceful *adj.* venustus, -a, -um
gracious *adj.* benignus, -a, -um
grade *n.* gradus, -ūs *m.*
qradually *adv.* paulātim
graft *v.t.* īnserō, -serere, -sēvī, -sertum
grain *n.* grānum, -ī *nt.*
grammar *n.* grammatica, -ae *f.*
grand *adj.* grandis, -is, -e
granddaughter *n.* neptis, -is *f.*
grandfather *n.* avus, -ī *m.*
grandmother *n.* avia, -ae *f.*
grandson *n.* nepōs, -ōtis *m.*
grant *n.* concessiō, -ōnis *f.*; *v.t.* concēdō, -cēdere, -cessī, -cessum
grape *n.* ūva, -ae *f.*; **~vine** *n.* vītis, -is *f.*
grasp *v.t.* comprehendō, -prehendere, -prehendī, -prehensum
grass *n.* grāmen, -inis *nt.*
grasshopper *n.* grillus (gryllus), -ī *m.*
grateful *adj.* grātus, -a, -um
gratitude *n.* grātia, -ae *f.*
grave *n.* sepulcrum, -ī *nt.*; *adj.* gravis, -is, -e (*weighty*); *adj.* sevērus, -a, -um
    (*solemn; stern*)
gravity *n.* gravitās, -ātis *f.* (*importance*); *n.* sevēritās, -ātis *f.* (*solemnity*)
gray *adj.* cānus, -a, -um
grease *n.* adeps, adipis *m./f.*
great *adj.* magnus, -a, -um; **so ~ as** *adj.* tantus, -a, -um ... quantus, -a, -um
great-grandfather *n.* proavus, -ī *m.*
great-grandmother *n.* proavia, -ae *f.*
greatness *n.* magnitūdō, -inis *f.*
green *adj.* viridis, -is, -e
greet *v.t.* salūtō, -āre, -āvī, -ātum
greeting *n.* salūtātiō, -ōnis *f.*
grief *n.* dolor, dolōris *m.*
grievance *n.* querella, -ae *f.* (*complaint*); *n.* iniūria, -ae *f.* (*wrong done*)
grieve *v.t., v.i.* doleō, -ēre, doluī, -itum
grill *v.t.* torreō, -ēre, torruī, tostum

grind *v.t.* molo, -ere, -uī, -itum (~ *grain*); ~ **down** *v.t.* opprimō, -primere, -pressī, -pressum

grip *v.t.* arripiō, -ripere, -ripuī, -reptum

groan *n.* gemitus, -ūs *m.*; *v.i.* gemō, -ere, -uī, -itum

groin *n.* inguen, inguinis *nt.*

ground *n.* humus, -ī *f.* (*soil*); *n.* locus, -ī *m.* (*place of action*); *n.* causa, -ae *f.* (*reason, cause for action*)

groundwork *n.* substructiō, -ōnis *f.*

group *n.* globus, -ī *m.*

grow *v.t.* colō, -ere, coluī, cultum (*cultivate*); *v.i.* crescō, -ere, crēvī, crētum (*increase in size*); *v.i.* fiō, fierī, factus sum (*become*)

growl *n.* fremitus, -ūs *m.*; *v.i.* fremō, -ere, -uī, -itum

grown-up *adj.* adultus, -a, -um

growth *n.* incrēmentum, -ī *nt.*

guarantee *n.* fidēs, -eī *f.*; *v.t.* intercēdō, -cēdere, -cessī, -cessum

guard *n.* custōdia, -ae *f.* (*protection*); *n.* custōs, -ōdis *m./f.* (*protector*); *n.* praesidium, -ī *nt.* (*military*); *v.t.* custōdiō, -īre, -īvī, -ītum

guardianship *n.* tūtēla, -ae *f.* (*legal ~ of a minor or a woman*)

guess *n.* coniectūra, -ae *f.*; *v.i.* coniciō, -icere, -iēcī, -iectum

guest *n.* hospes, -itis *m.* (*in a house*); *n.* hospita, -ae *f.* (*in a house*); *n.* convīva, -ae *m./f.* (*dinner ~*)

guide *n.* dux, ducis *m./f.*; *v.t.* dūcō, -ere, dūxī, ductum

guild *n.* collēgium, -ī *nt.*

guilt *n.* scelus, -eris *nt.*

guilty *adj.* sōns, sontis

gulf *n.* sinus, -ūs *m.* (*a bay*); *n.* gurges, -itis *m.* (*abyss*)

gum *n.* gingīva, -ae *f.* (*of the mouth*); *n.* gummis, -is *f.* (*substance*)

gust *n.* flāmen, -inis *nt.*

gutter *n.* fossa, -ae *f.*

H

habit *n.* cōnsuētūdō, -inis *f.*; **be in the** ~ *v.i.* sōleō, -ēre, solitus sum

hair *n.* capillus, -ī *m.*

hairdresser *n.* tonsor, -ōris *m.* (*barber*); *n.* ōrnātrīx, ōrnātrīcis *f.* (*for women*)

half *n.* dīmidium, -ī *nt.*; *adj.* dīmidius, -a, -um

hall *n.* ātrium, -ī *nt.*

ham *n.* perna, -ae *f.*

hammer *n.* malleus, -ī *m.*; *v.t.* tundō, -ere, tutudī, tūnsum

hamper *n.* quālus, -ī *m.*; *v.i.* impediō, -pedīre, -pedīvī, -pedītum
hand *n.* manus, -ūs *f.*
hand down/over *v.t.* trādō, -dere, -didī, -ditum
handkerchief *n.* sudārium, -ī *nt.*
handle *n.* ansa, -ae *f.*
handsome *adj.* pulcher, pulchra, pulchrum
handy *adj.* habilis, -is, -e
hang *v.t.* suspendō, -pendere, -pendī, -pēnsum; *v.i.* pendeō, -ēre,
 pependī, ---
happen *v.i.* accidit, -cidere, -cidit, --- (*imp.*); *v.i.* fit, fierī, factum est (*imp.*)
happiness *n.* fēlīcitās, -ātis *f.*
happy *adj.* beātus, -a, -um
harass *v.t.* vexō, -āre, -āvī, -ātum
harassment *n.* vexātiō, -ōnis *f.*
harbor *n.* portus, -ūs *m.*
hard *adj.* dūrus, -a, -um (*not soft; distressing*); *adj.* difficilis, -is, -e (*difficult*)
harden *v.i.* dūrēscō, -ere, dūruī, ---
hardly *adv.* vix
hardness *n.* dūritia, -ae *f.* (*physical*); *n.* inīquitās, -ātis *f.* (*difficulty*)
hardship *n.* labor, -ōris *m.*
hardware *n.* ferramenta, -ōrum *nt./pl.*
hardy *adj.* dūrus, -a, -um
hare *n.* lepus, leporis *m.*
harm *n.* damnum, -ī *nt.*; *v.i.* noceō, -ēre, nocuī, nocitum (+ dat.)
harmful *adj.* noxius, -a, -um
harmless *adj.* innocuus, -a, -um
harness *n.* ornāmenta, -ōrum *nt./pl.*; *v.t.* iungō, -ere, iunxī, iunctum
harp *n.* lyra, -ae *f.*
harsh *adj.* raucus, -a, -um (*of sounds*); *adj.* dūrus, -a, -um (*of temperament;
 of character*)
harvest *n.* messis, -is *f.*
haste *n.* celeritās, -ātis *f.*
hasty *adj.* praeceps, praecipitis
hat *n.* petasus, -ī *m.* (*broad-brimmed traveling ~*)
hatch *v.t.* excūdō, -cūdere, -cūdī, -cūsum (*~ from eggs*); *v.t.* māchinor,
 māchinārī, māchinātus sum (*~ a plan*)
hate *n.* odium, -ī *nt.*; *v.t.* ōdī, ōdisse, ōsūrum (*def.*)
have *v.t.* habeō, -ēre, habuī, habitum; *verbal aux. not expressed in Latin*;
 ~ to do something *v.t. use second periphrastic verb*; **~ a baby** *v.i.*

parturiō, -īre, -īvī, --- (*be pregnant*); ~ **a baby** *v.t.* pariō, -ere, peperī, partum (*give birth to*)

hawk *n.* accipiter, -cipitris *m.*

hay *n.* faenum, -ī *nt.*

hazard *n.* perīculum, -ī *nt.*

haze *n.* nebula, -ae *f.*

hazy *adj.* nebulōsus, -a, -um

he *pron.* is

head *n.* caput, capitis *nt.* (*of the body; top of anything; leader*); **be the ~ of something** *v.i.* praesum, -esse, -fuī, --- (+ *dat.*)

headquarters *n.* prīncipia, -um *nt./pl.*

heal *v.t.* sānō, -āre, -āvī, -ātum; *v.i.* sānescō, -ere, sānuī, --- (*of wounds*); *v.i.* convalēscō, -ere, -valuī, --- (*recover one's health*)

health *n.* sānitās, -ātis *f.* (*good ~*); *n.* salūs, -ūtis *f.* (*recovery from illness*)

healthy *adj.* sānus, -a, -um (*of persons*); *adj.* salūbris, salūbris, salūbre (*of places; of climates*)

heap *n.* cumulus, -ī *m.* (*pile with a rounded top*)

hear *v.t.* audiō, -īre, -īvī, -ītum

hearing *n.* audītus, -ūs *m.* (*sense of ~*); *n.* cōgnitiō, -ōnis *f.* (*legal ~*)

heart *n.* cor, cordis *nt.* (*anat.*); *n.* animus, -ī *m.* (*courage; sensibility*)

hearth *n.* focus, -ī *m.*

hearty *adj.* benignus, -a, -um (*welcoming*); *adj.* sincērus, -a, -um (*sincere*)

heat *n.* calor, -ōris *m.* (*opposite of cold*); *n.* fervor, -ōris *m.* (*glowing heat; heat of passion*); *v.t.* calefaciō, -facere, -fēcī, -factum

heaven *n.* caelum, -ī *nt.*

heavy *adj.* gravis, -is, -e (*having weight*); *adj.* maestus, -a, -um (*sad*); *adj.* tardus, -a, -um (*slow*)

hedge *n.* saepēs, -is *f.*

heel *n.* calx, calcis *f.*

height *n.* altitūdō, -inis *f.* (*elevation*); *n.* cacūmen, -inis *nt.* (*summit*)

heir *n.* hērēs, -ēdis *m./f.*

hell *n.* inferī, -ōrum *m./pl.* (*spirits of the underworld*)

hello *v.i.* salvē, salvēte (*impv. sg., pl.*)

helm *n.* gubernāculum, -ī *nt.*

helmet *n.* galea, -ae *f.* (*leather ~*); *n.* cassis, -idis *f.* (*metal ~*)

help *n.* auxilium, -ī *nt.*; *v.t.* iuvō, -āre, iūvī, iūtum

helper *n.* adiūtor, -ōris *m.*; *n.* adiūtrīx, -īcis *f.*

helpful *adj.* ūtilis, -is, -e

hem *n.* lacinia, -ae *f.*

hen *n.* gallīna, -ae *f.*

her *adj. Use gen. case of* ea. **~ own** *adj.* suus, -a, -um; *pron. Use dat., acc., or abl. case of* ea.

herd *n.* grex, gregis *m.*

here *adv.* hīc; **~ and there** *adv.* passim

hernia *n.* hernia, -ae *f.*

hero *n.* vir, virī *m.*

heroic *adj.* fortissimus, -a, -um

heron *n.* ardea, -ae *f.*

hers *pron. Use gen. case of* ea.

herself *refl. pron. Use forms of* sē; *use dem. pron.* ipsa

hesitate *v.t.* dubitō, -āre, -āvī, -ātum

hesitation *n.* dubitātiō, -ōnis *f.*

hiccup *n.* singultus, -ūs *m.; v.i.* singultiō, -īre, -īvī, ---

hide *n.* pellis, -is *f.; v.t.* abdō, -dere, -didī, -ditum

hidden *adj.* abditus, -a, -um

high *adj.* altus, -a, -um (*tall*); *adj.* magnus, -a, -um (**~ price**); **~er** *adj.* superior, superius; **~est** *adj.* summus, -a, -um

highway *n.* via, -ae *f.*

hill *n.* collis, -is *m.*

hilly *adj.* clīvōsus, -a, -um

him *pron. Use dat., acc., or abl. case of* is.

himself *refl. pron. Use forms of* sē; *for dem .adj. use* ipse

hinder *v.i.* obstō, -stāre, -stitī, -stātum (+ dat.)

hinge *n.* cardō, -inis *m.*

hint *v.i.* innuō, -nuere, -nuī, ---

hip *n.* coxa, -ae *f.*

hire *v.t.* condūcō, -dūcere, -dūxī, -ductum

his *pron. Use gen. of* is. **~ own** *adj.* suus, -a, -um

history *n.* historia, -ae *f.*

hit *n.* ictus, -ūs *m.* (*a blow*)

hive *n.* alveus, -ī *m.*

hoarse *adj.* raucus, -a, -um

hoe *n.* sarculum, -ī *nt.*

hoist *n.* tollēnō, -ōnis *m.; v.t.* tollō, -ere, sustulī, sublātum

hold *v.t.* teneō, -ēre, tenuī, tentum; *v.t.* possideō, -sidēre, -sēdī, -sessum (*occupy*); **~ a meeting** *v.t.* habeō, -ēre, -uī, -itum; **~ forth/out** *v.t.* porrigō, -rigere, -rēxī, -rēctum; **~ back/fast** *v.t.* retineō, -tinēre, -tinuī, -tentum

hole *n.* cavum, -ī *nt.*

holiday *n.* diēs festus, diēī festī *m.*; **holidays** *n./pl.* fēriae, -ārum *f./pl.*

holy day *n.* diēs festus, diēī festī *m.*

home *n.* domus, -ūs *f.*; **at ~** *adv.* domī; **from ~** *adv.* domō; **go ~** *adv.* domum

honest *adj.* probus, -a, -um

honesty *n.* probitās, -ātis *f.*

honey *n.* mel, mellis *nt.*

honor *n.* honōs (honor), -ōris *m.* (*reputation; award of distinction*); *n.* pudor, -ōris *m.* (*sense of propriety or right*); *n.* honestās, -ātis *f.* (*reputation for high conduct*); *v.t.* colō, -ere, coluī, cultum (*treat with respect*); *v.t.* honestō, -āre, -āvī, -ātum (*confer ~ upon*)

hood *n.* cucullus, -ī *m.* (*hooded garment*)

hook *n.* hāmus, -ī *m.*

hope *n.* spēs, speī *f.*; *v.t.* spērō, -āre, -āvī, -ātum

hopeful *adj.* spē plēnus, -a, -um

hopeless *adj.* spē carēns, -entis

horn *n.* cornū, -ūs *nt.* (*musical instrument; ~ of an animal*)

horrible *adj.* horribilis, -is, -e

horror *n.* horror, -ōris *m.*

hors-d'oeuvre *n.* gustus, -ūs *m.*

horse *n.* equus, -ī *m.*; *n.* equa, -ae *f.*; **on ~back** *adv.* in equō

hose *n.* tībiāle,-is *nt.* (*leggings*)

hospitable *adj.* hospitālis, -is, -e

hospital *n.* valētūdinārium, -ī *nt.*

hospitality *n.* hospitium, -ī *nt.*

host *n.* hospes, -itis *m.* (*giver of hospitality*); *n.* multitūdō, -inis *f.* (*large number*); *n.* cōpiae, -ārum *f./pl.* (*troops*)

hostage *n.* obses, -sidis *m./f.*

hostel *n.* hospitium, -ī *nt.*

hostess *n.* hospita, -ae *f.*

hostile *adj.* hostīlis, -is, -e

hot *adj.* calidus, -a, -um

hotel *n.* hospitium, -ī *nt.*

hour *n.* hōra, -ae *f.*

house *n.* domus, -ūs *f.*; **farm~** *n.* vīlla, -ae *f.*; **apartment ~** *n.* īnsula, -ae *f.*; **at the ~ of** *prep.* apud (+ acc.)

household *n.* domus, -ūs *f.*; *n.* familia, -ae *f.*

householder *n.* pater familiās, patris familiās *m.*

housewife *n.* māter familiās, mātris familiās *f.*

how *adv.* quōmodo (*in what way*); *adv.* quam (*to what degree*); **~ many** *indecl. adj.* quot; **~ much** *adv.* quantus, -a, -um; **~ often** *adv.* quotiēns

however *adv.* tamen; *conj.* autem

hug *n.* complexus, -ūs *m.*; *v.d.t.* amplector, amplectī, amplexus sum

huge *adj.* ingēns, -entis

human *adj.* hūmānus, -a, -um; **~ being** *n.* homō, hominis *m./f.*

humane *adj.* misericors, misericordis

humanity *n.* hūmānitās, -ātis *f.* (*humane feeling*)

humble *adj.* humilis, -is, -e

humid *adj.* ūmidus, -a, -um

humidity *n.* ūmor, -ōris *m.*

humor *n.* ingenium, -ī *nt.* (*inclination of mind*)

hump *n.* gibber, -eris *m.*

hundred *num.* centum (*indecl.*)

hundredth *adj.* centēsimus, -a, -um

hunger *n.* famēs, -is *f.*

hungry *adj.* ēsuriēns, -ientis; **be ~** *v.i.* ēsuriō, -īre, ---, -ītum

hunt *n.* vēnātiō, -ōnis *f.*; *v.d.t.* vēnor, vēnārī, vēnātus sum; **~ for** *v.i.* quaerō, -ere, quaesīvī, quaesītum

hunter *n.* vēnātor, -ōris *m.*

hurray *interj.* iō

hurry *n.* festīnātiō, -ōnis *f.*; *v.t.* rapiō, -ere, rapuī, raptum; *v.i.* festīnō, -āre, -āvī, -ātum

hurt *n.* vulnus, -eris *nt.*; *v.i.* noceō, -ēre, nocuī, nocitum (+ dat.); *v.i.* doleō, -ēre, doluī, ---

husband *n.* marītus, -ī *m.*

hut *n.* tugurium, -ī *nt.*

hymn *n.* carmen, -inis *nt.*

I

I *pron.* ego

ice *n.* glaciēs, -ēī *f.*

icy *adj.* gelidus, -a, -um

idea *n.* speciēs, -ēī *f.* (*conception*); *n.* imāgō, -inis *f.* (*mental image*); *n.* sententia, -ae *f.* (*thought*)

ideal *n.* speciēs, -ēī *f.*; *adj.* perfectus, -a, -um

identical *adj.* īdem, eadem, idem

identify *v.t.* agnōscō, -noscere, -nōvī, -nōtum (*recognize*)
idiotic *adj.* fatuus, -a, -um
idle *adj.* ōtiōsus, -a, -um (*at leisure*); *adj.* ignāvus, -a, -um (*slothful*)
if *conj.* sī; **~ not** *conj.* sī . . . nōn; **~ only** *conj.* dummodo (+ subjv.)
ignite *v.t.* accendō, -cendere, -cendī, -cēnsum; *v.i.* ārdēscō, -ere, arsī, ---
ignorance *n.* ignōrantia, -ae *f.*; *n.* īnscientia, -ae *f.*
ignorant *adj.* īnscius, -a, -um (+ gen. *or* rel. clause *or* acc. + infv.); *adj.*
　indoctus, -a, -um (*unlearned*); **to be ~** *v.i.* ignōrō, -āre, -āvī, -ātum (+
　rel. clause *or* acc. + infv.)
ignore *v.t.* neglegō, -glegere, -glexī, -glectum (*not pay attention to*); *v.d.t.*
　oblivīscor, oblivīscī, oblītus sum (*disregard*)
ill *adj.* aeger, aegra, aegrum; **be ~** *v.i.* aegrōtō, -āre, -āvī, -ātum
illegal *adj.* illicitus, -a, -um
illiterate *adj.* rudis, -is, -e
illness *n.* valētūdō, -inis *f.* (*state of ill health*); *n.* morbus, -ī *m.* (*disease*)
illusion *n.* error, -ōris *m.*
illustrate *v.t.* illūstrō, -āre, -āvī, -ātum (*explain*)
image *n.* effigiēs, -ēī *f.* (*a likeness or copy*); *n.* simulācrum, -ī *nt.* (*~ of a
　deity*); *n.* imāgō, -inis *f.* (*a likeness*)
imagination *n.* cōgitātiō, -ōnis *f.*
imagine *v.t.* concipiō, -cipere, -cēpī, -ceptum (*conceive with the mind*); *v.d.t.*
　opīnor, opīnārī, opīnātus sum (*think; suppose*)
imitate *v.d.t.* imitor, imitārī, imitātus sum
imitation *n.* imitātiō, -ōnis *f.* (*act of imitating*); *n.* imāgō, -inis (*thing pro-
　duced by imitation*)
immense *adj.* immēnsus, -a, -um
immoral *adj.* prāvus, -a, -um
immortal *adj.* immortālis, -is, -e (*deathless*); *adj.* aeternus, -a, -um
　(*eternal*)
impatient *adj.* impatiēns, -ientis (*unable to endure*); *adj.* avidus, -a, -um
　(*eager; greedy*)
imperfect *adj.* imperfectus, -a, -um
implement *n.* īnstrūmentum, -ī *nt.*
imply *v.t.* significō, -ficāre, -ficāvī, -ficātum
impolite *n.* inurbānus, -a, -um
import *v.t.* importō, -portāre, -portāvī, -portātum
importance *n.* mōmentum, -ī *nt.* (*consequence*)
important *adj.* gravis, -is, -e
impose *v.t.* impōnō, -pōnere, -posuī, -positum

impotent *adj.* īnfirmus, -a, -um (*weak; powerless*)
impress *v.t.* imprimō, -primere, -pressī, -pressum (*press upon*); *v.t.* permoveō, -movēre, -mōvī, -mōtum (*influence*)
imprint *v.t.* imprimō, -primere, -pressī, -pressum
imprison *v.t.* in carcerem coniciō, -icere, -iēcī, -iectum
improper *adj.* indecōrus, -a, -um
improve *v.t.* ēmendō, -mendāre, -mendāvī, -mendātum; *v.i.* melior fīō, fīērī, factus sum
impulse *n.* impulsus, -ūs *m.*
in *prep.* in (+ abl.); *for time when, use abl. of time when; for manner, use abl. of manner*; **come ~** *v.i.* intrō, -āre, -āvī, -ātum
inactive *adj.* iners, inertis
inaugurate *v.t.* inaugurō, -āre, -āvī, -ātum
inauguration *n.* cōnsecrātiō, -ōnis *f.*
incentive *n.* stimulus, -ī *m.*
inch *n.* digitus, -ī *m.*
inclination *n.* inclīnātiō, -ōnis *f.* (*act of bending; a propensity*); *n.* acclīvitās, -ātis *f.* (*a slope upward*)
incline *n.* clīvus, -ī *m.*; *v.i.* inclīnō, -clīnāre, -clīnāvī, -clīnātum
include *v.t.* inclūdō, -clūdere, -clūsī, -clūsum (*shut up/in*); *v.t.* habeō, -ēre, habuī, habitum (*contain*); *v.t.* adnumerō, -numerāre, -numerāvī, -numerātum (*reckon among*)
income *n.* vectīgal, -ālis *nt.*
incorrect *adj.* mendōsus, -a, -um
increase *n.* incrēmentum, -ī *nt.*; *v.t.* augeō, -ēre, auxī, auctum; *v.i.* crēscō, -ere, crēvī, crētum
indeed *adv.* quidem
independence *n.* lībertās, -ātis *f.*
independent *adj.* līber, lībera, līberum
index *n.* index, indicis *m./f.*
indicate *v.t.* indicō, -dicāre, -dicāvī, -dicātum (*point out*); *v.t.* significō, -ficāre, -ficāvī, -ficātum (*intimate*)
indifferent *adj.* sēcūrus, -a, -um (*not caring*); *adj.* indifferēns, -entis (*neither good nor bad*)
indignation *n.* indignātiō, -ōnis *f.*
indirect *adj.* vagus, -a, -um (*wandering*); *adj.* oblīquus, -a, -um (*covert*)
individual *n.* singulī, -ae, -a *pl.*; *adj.* singulī, -ae, -a *pl.*
industrious *adj.* industrius, -a, -um
industry *n.* industria, -ae *f.* (*activity*)

inexpensive *adj.* vīlis, -is, -e
infant *n.* īnfāns, -fantis *m./f.*; *adj.* īnfāns, -antis
infection *n.* contāgiō, -ōnis *f.*
inferior *adj.* īnferior, īnferius
inflame *v.t.* accendō, -cendere, -cendī, -cēnsum
inflammation *n.* īnflammātiō, -ōnis *f.*
inflation *n.* īnflātiō, -ōnis *f.*
influence *n.* vīs, vim (acc.), vī (abl.) *f.* (*def. n.*) (*power, force*); *n.* auctoritās, -ātis *f.* (*personal* ~); *v.t.* moveō, -ēre, mōvī, mōtum
inform *v.t.* certiōrem faciō, -ere, fēcī, factum
information *n.* nūntius, -ī *m.*
infringe *v.t.* rumpō, -ere, rūpī, ruptum
ingenious *adj.* sollers, sollertis
inhabit *v.t.* incolō, -colere, -coluī, -cultum
inhabitant *n.* incola, -ae *m./f.*
inherit *v.t.* per successiōnem accipiō, -cipere, -cēpī, -ceptum
inheritance *n.* hērēditās, -ātis *f.*
initial *adj.* prīmus, -a, -um
inject *v.t.* īnfundō, -fundere, -fūdī, -fūsum
injection *n.* īnfūsiō, -ōnis *f.* (*a pouring in*)
injure *v.i.* noceō, -ēre, nocuī, nocitum (+ dat.)
injured *adj.* laesus, -a, -um
injury *n.* vulnus, -eris *nt.* (*bodily harm*); *n.* iniūria, -ae *f.* (*wrong done to someone*); *n.* damnum, -ī *nt.* (*loss; damage*)
ink *n.* ātrāmentum, -ī *nt.*
inn *n.* caupōna, -ae *f.*
inner *adj.* interior, interius
innocent *adj.* īnsōns, insontis (*not guilty*); *adj.* innocuus, -a, -um (*doing no harm*)
inquire *v.i.* quaerō, -ere, quaesīvī, quaesītum
inquiry *n.* interrogātiō, -ōnis *f.* (*a question*); *n.* quaestiō, -ōnis *f.* (*investigation, often judicial*)
insane *adj.* īnsānus, -a, -um
insect *n.* īnsectum, -ī *nt.*
insert *v.t.* īnserō, -serere, -seruī, -sertum
inside *n.* interiōra, -um *nt./pl.*; *adj.* interior, interius
insist *v.i.* īnstō, -stāre, -stitī, -statum
insomnia *n.* īnsomnia, -ae *f.*
inspect *v.t.* īnspiciō, -spicere, -spēxī, -spectum

inspection *n.* īnspectiō, -ōnis *f.*
inspector *n.* cūrātor, -ōris *m.*
inspiration *n.* afflātus, -ūs *m.*
inspire *v.t.* iniciō, -icere, -iēcī, -iectum
install *v.t.* inaugurō, -augurāre, -augurāvī, -augurātum (*inaugurate*); *v.t.* cōnstituō, -stituere, -stituī, -stitūtum (*put in place*)
instance *n.* exemplum, -ī *nt.* (*an example*); **for ~** *adv.* exemplī causā
instant *adj.* praesēns, -entis (*imminent*); *adj.* intentus, -a, -um (*urgent*); **~ly** *adv.* statim
instead *adv.* potius; **~ of** *prep.* prō (+ *abl.*)
institute *v.t.* īnstituō, -stituere, -stituī, -stitūtum
instruct *v.t.* doceō, -ēre, docuī, doctum (*teach*); *v.t.* praecipiō, -cipere, -cēpī, -ceptum (+ *dat.* + **ut** or **nē**) (*command*)
instruction *n.* disciplīna, -ae *f.*
instrument *n.* īnstrūmentum, -ī *nt.*
insufficient *adj.* propter inōpiam (+ *gen.*)
insult *n.* contumēlia, -ae *f.*; *v.t.* contumēliam faciō, -ere, fēcī, factum
insure *v.t.* caveō, -ēre, cāvī, cautum (+ **nē**) (*make certain that*)
intelligence *n.* ingenium, -ī *nt.* (*quickness of mind*); *n.* nuntius, -ī *m.* (*information*)
intelligent *adj.* intelligēns, -entis
intend *v.t.* in animō habeō, -ēre, habuī, habitum
intense *adj.* ācer, ācris, ācre
intention *n.* cōnsilium, -ī *nt.*
interest *n.* bonum, -ī *nt.* (*advantage*); *n.* studium, -ī *nt.* (*attentiveness*); *n.* faenus, -oris *nt.* (*commercial ~*); **it is of ~ to** *v.i.* interest, interesse, interfuit (*imp. v.*) (+ *gen.* of person *or* + **meā, tuā, suā** *or* + substantive clause)
interior *adj.* interior, interius
internal *adj.* internus, -a, -um
interpreter *n.* interpres, -pretis *m./f.*
interrogate *v.t.* interrogō, -rogāre, -rogāvī, -rogātum
interrupt *v.t.* interpellō, -pellāre, -pellāvī, -pellātum
interruption *n.* interpellātiō, -ōnis *f.*
interval *n.* intervallum, -ī *nt.*
intervene *v.i.* intercēdō, -cēdere, -cessī, -cessum
interview *n.* congressus, -ūs *m.*
intestine *n.* intestīna, -ōrum *nt./pl.*
intimate *adj.* intimus, -a, -um

into *prep.* in (+ acc.)
introduce *v.t.* intrōdūcō, -dūcere, -dūxī, -ductum
introduction *n.* intrōductiō, -ōnis *f.*
invade *v.t.* invādō, -vādere, -vāsī, -vāsum
invasion *n.* incursiō, -ōnis *f.*
invent *v.t.* inveniō, -venīre, -vēnī, -ventum
invention *n.* inventum, -ī *nt.* (*thing invented*); *n.* inventiō, -onis *f.* (*faculty of invention*)
inventory *n.* inventārium, -ī *nt.*
investigate *v.d.t.* scrūtor, scrūtārī, scrūtātus sum
investigation *n.* investīgātiō, -ōnis *f.*
invitation *n.* invītātiō, -ōnis *f.*
invite *v.t.* invītō, -vītāre, -vītāvī, -vītātum
involve *v.t.* admisceō, -miscēre, -miscuī, -mixtum (*implicate*); *v.t.* contineō, -tinēre, -tinuī, -tentum (*comprise*); *v.t.* involvō, -volvere, -volvī, -volūtum (*wrap up; envelop*)
iron *n.* ferrum, -ī *nt.* (*metal*); *adj.* ferreus, -a, -um
irony *n.* īrōnīa, -ae *f.*
irrigate *v.t.* irrigō, -rigāre, -rigāvī, -rigātum
irrigation *n.* irrigātiō, -ōnis *f.*
island *n.* īnsula, -ae *f.*
isolate *v.t.* sēcernō, -cernere, -crēvī, -crētum
issue *n.* ēventus, -ūs *m.* (*result*); *n.* rēs, reī *f.* (*point; matter*); *v.t.* ēdō, -dere, -didī, -ditum
it *pron.* Use forms of id
itch *n.* prūrītus, -ūs *m.*; *v.i.* prūriō, -īre, -īvī, -ītum
item *n.* rēs, reī *f.*
its *adj.* Use gen. case of id; ~ **own** *adj.* suus, -a, -um
itself *refl. pron.* Use forms of sē; *dem. pron.* Use forms of ipsum
ivory *n.* ebur, -oris *nt.*; *adj.* eburneus, -a, -um
ivy *n.* hedera, -ae *f.*

J

jail *n.* carcer, -eris *m.*
January *adj.* Iānuārius, -a, -um (*usu. w.* **mēnsis**); *n.* Iānuārius, -ī *m.*
jar *n.* olla, -ae *f.*
jaw *n.* maxilla, -ae *f.*
jealous *adj.* invidus, -a, -um

jealousy *n.* invidia, -ae *f.*
jewel *n.* gemma, -ae *f.*
job *n.* opus, -eris *nt.* (*task*)
join *v.t.* iungō, -ere, iūnxī, iūnctum (*bring together*); *v.t.* adiungō, -iungere, -iunxī, -iūnctum (*bind; annex*)
joint *n.* articulus, -ī *m.*
joke *n.* iocus, -ī *m.; v.d.i.* iocor, iocārī, iocātus sum
journal *n.* diurnum, -ī *nt.*
journey *n.* iter, itineris *nt.;* **make a ~** *v.t.* iter faciō, -ere, fēcī, factum
joy *n.* gaudium, -ī *nt.*
judge *n.* iūdex, iūdicis *m.; v.t.* iūdicō, -dicāre, -dicāvī, -dicātum
judgment *n.* iūdicium, -ī *nt.*
jug *n.* urceus, -ī *m.*
juggler *n.* praestigiātor, -ōris *m.*
juice *n.* sūcus, -ī *m.*
July *adj.* lūlius, -a, -um; *n.* lūlius, -ī *m.* (*This month was originally called Quīntīlis, -is, -e but was renamed to honor Julius Caesar.*)
jumble *v.t.* misceō, -ēre, miscuī, mixtum
jump *n.* saltus, -ūs *m.; v.i.* saliō, -īre, saluī, saltum
junction *n.* coniūnctiō, -ōnis *f.*
June *adj.* lūnius, -a, -um (*usu. w.* **mēnsis**); *n.* lūnius, -ī *m.*
junior *adj.* minor, minus (*younger*)
just *adj.* iustus, -a, -um (*morally right*); *adj.* meritus, -a, -um (*deserved*); *adv.* modo (*a few moments ago*)
justice *n.* iūstitia, -ae *f.*
justification *n.* pūrgātiō, -ōnis *f.*
justify *v.t.* pūrgō, -āre, -āvī, -ātum
juvenile *adj.* iuvenīlis, -is, -e

K

keel *n.* carīna, -ae *f.*
keen *adj.* ācer, ācris, ācre
keep *v.t.* teneō, -ēre, tenuī, tenntum (*hold; retain*); *v.t.* servō, -āre, -āvī, -ātum (*preserve*); *v.t.* condo, -dere, didī, -ditum (*store up*); *v.t.* custōdiō, -īre, -īvī, -ītum (*guard*); *v.t.* alō, -ere, aluī, altum (alitum) (*raise animals*); **~ away** *v.t.* arceō, -ēre, arcuī, -itum
keeper *n.* custōs, -ōdis *m./f.*
kennel *n.* cūbīle, -is *nt.*

kernel *n.* nucleus, -ī *m.*
kettle *n.* olla, -ae *f.*
key *n.* clāvis, -is *f.*
kick *v.t.* calcitrō, -āre, -āvī, -ātum
kid *n.* puer, puerī *m.* (*male child*); *n.* puella, -ae *f.* (*female child*); *n.* haedus, -ī *m.* (*young goat*)
kidnapped *adj.* surreptus, -a, -um
kidneys *n.* rēnēs, rēnum *m./pl.*
kill *v.t.* interficiō, -ficere, -fēcī, -fectum
kind *n.* genus, -eris *nt.;adj.* benignus, -a, -um
kindle *v.t.* cōnflō, -flāre, -flāvī, -flātum
kindness *n.* benignitās, -ātis *f.*
king *n.* rēx, rēgis *m.*
kingdom *n.* rēgnum, -ī *nt.*
kiss *n.* osculum, -ī *nt.; v.d.t.* osculor, osculārī, osculātus sum
kitchen *n.* culīna, -ae *f.*
kite *n.* milvus, -ī *m.* (*zool.*)
kitten *n.* catulus, -ī *m.*
knapsack *n.* sarcina, -ae *f.*
knead *v.t.* subigō, -igere, -ēgī, -āctum
knee *n.* genū, genūs *nt.*
kneel *v.d.i.* genibus nītor, nītī, nīxus (nīsus) sum
knife *n.* culter, -trī *m.*
knight *n.* eques, -itis *m.* (*a social rank*)
knit *v.t.* texō, -ere, -uī, -tum (*weave; plait; braid*)
knock *n.* pulsātiō, -ōnis *f.; v.t.* pulsō -āre, -āvī, -ātum
knot *n.* nōdus, -ī *m.; v.t.* nōdō, -āre, -āvī, -ātum
know *v.t.* sciō, -īre, -īvī, -ītum (*know for a fact; know how to*); *v.t.* noscō, -ere, nōvī, nōtum (*be acquainted with, especially a person; have knowledge of*); **not ~** *v.t.* nesciō, -scīre, -scīvī, -scītum
knowledge *n.* scientia, -ae *f.*
knuckle *n.* articulus, -ī *m.*

L

label *n.* titulus, -ī *m.; v.t.* titulum adfīgō, -figere, -fīxī, -fīxum
labor *n.* labor, -ōris *m.* (*toil; exertion*); *n.* opus, -eris *nt.* (*work done*); *n.* partus, -ūs *m.* (*childbirth*); *v.t.* labōrō, -āre, -āvī, -ātum
laborer *n.* faber, fabrī *m.*

labyrinth *n.* labyrinthus, -ī *m.*
lace *n.* lōrum, -ī *nt. (strap); v.t.* nectō, -ere, nexuī (nexī), nexum
lack *n.* inopia, -ae *f.; v.i.* egeō, egēre, eguī, --- (+ abl.)
ladder *n.* scālae, -ārum *f./pl.*
ladle *n.* trulla, -ae *f.*
lady *n.* mātrōna, -ae *f. (married woman); n.* domina, -ae *f. (female head of household)*
lag *v.d.i.* moror, morārī, morātus sum
lake *n.* lacus, -ūs *m.*
lamb *n.* agnus, -ī *m.*
lame *adj.* claudus, -a, -um
lamp *n.* lucerna, -ae *f.*
land *n.* terra, -ae *f. (earth); n.* ager, agrī *m. (field; plot of land);* **native ~** *n.* patria, -ae *f.*
landing *n.* ēgressus, -ūs *m.*
landlord *n.* dominus, -ī *m. (of houses, estate, etc.); n.* caupō, -ōnis *m. (of an inn)*
landmark *n.* līmes, -itis *m. (boundary marker)*
lane *n.* sēmita, -ae *f.*
language *n.* lingua, -ae *f.*
lantern *n.* lanterna, -ae *f.*
lap *n.* gremium, -ī *nt.*
lapse *n.* error, -ōris *m. (mistake); n.* intervallum, -ī *nt. (interval); n.* lāpsus, -ūs *m. (gliding motion; slipping motion); v.d.i.* lābor, lābī, lāpsus sum *(slip; glide; pass away)*
lard *n.* lāridum (lārdum), -ī *nt.*
large *adj.* grandis, -is, -e; **~ly** *adv.* prōlixē
last *adj.* postrēmus, -a, -um *(hindmost);* **~ night** *adj.* superiōre nocte; **at ~** *adv.* postrēmō *(in order of happening),* dēmum *(finally; at length)*
latch *n.* ōbex, -icis *m./f. (bolt; bar); v.t.* obserō, -serāre, -serāvī, -serātum
late *adj.* sērus, -a, -um *(behind time); adv.* sērō *(behind time);* **~ly** *adv.* nūper *(recently)*
lathe *n.* tornus, -ī *m.*
Latin *adj.* Latīnus, -a, -um
latrine *n.* lātrīna, -ae *f.*
latter *adj.* posterior, posterius; **the ~** *adj., pron.* hic, haec, hoc
laugh *n.* rīsus, -ūs *m.; v.i.* rīdeō, -ēre, rīsī, rīsum
laughter *n.* rīsus, -ūs *m.*
launch *v.t.* contorqueō, -torquēre, -torsī, -tortum (-torsum) *(~ a missile); v.t.* dēdūcō, -dūcere, -dūxī, -ductum *(~ a boat)*

laundry *n.* fullōnica, -ae f.

lavish *adj.* prōfūsus, -a, -um (*generous*); *adj.* prōdigus, -a, -um (*wasteful*)

law *n.* lēx, lēgis f. (*a bill adopted; an enactment*); *n.* iūs, iūris nt. (*that which is right by its nature; the body of laws*); *n.* fās nt. (*indecl.*) (*divine law*)

lawful *adj.* lēgitimus, -a, -um

lawsuit *n.* līs, lītis f.

lawyer *n.* iūrisconsultus, -ī m.

lay *v.t.* pōnō, -ere, posuī, positum (*place; lay aside*); ~ **eggs** *v.t.* pariō, -ere, peperī, partum; ~ **a plan** *v.t.* cōnsilium capiō, -ere, cēpī, captum; ~ **waste** *v.t.* vāstō, -āre, -āvī, -ātum

lazy *adj.* ignāvus, -a, -um

lead *n.* plumbum, -ī nt.; *v.t.* dūcō, -ere, dūxī, ductum; ~ **the way** *v.t.* praeeō, -īre, -īvī, (-iī), -ītum

leader *n.* dux, ducis m./f.

leaf *n.* folium, -ī nt. (*bot.*); *n.* pāgina, -ae f. (*paper*)

leak *n.* rīma, -ae f.; *v.t., v.i.* perfluō, -fluere, -flūxī, -flūxum

lean *adj.* macer, macra, macrum; *v.d.i.* nītor, nītī, nīxus (nīsus) sum (*press upon*) (+ abl.); *v.i.* inclīnō, -clīnāre, -clīnāvī, -clīnātum (*slant*)

leap *n.* saltus, -ūs m.; *v.i.* saliō, -īre, saluī, saltum

learn *v.t.* discō, -ere, didicī, --- (*acquire knowledge*); *v.t.* cōgnoscō, -gnoscere, -gnōvī, -gnitum (*get information; become aware*)

learned *adj.* doctus, -a, -um

learner *n.* discipulus, -ī m.; *n.* discipula, -ae f.

lease *n.* conductiō, -ōnis f.; *v.t.* condūcō, -dūcere, -dūxī, -ductum

leash *n.* cōpula, -ae f.

least *adj.* minimus, -a, -um; *adv.* minimē; **at** ~ *adv.* saltem

leather *n.* corium, -ī nt.

leave *v.t.* discēdō, -cēdere, -cessī, -cessum (*go away*); *v.t.* relinquō, -linquere, -līquī, -līctum (*abandon; bequeath*); *v.t.* commendō, -mendāre, -mendāvī, -mendātum (*entrust*)

lecture *n.* audītiō, -ōnis f.

ledge *n.* pluteus, -ī m.

left *adj.* reliquus, -a, -um (*remaining*); *adj.* sinister, sinistra, sinistrum (*on the left*)

leg *n.* crūs, crūris nt.; *n.* tībia, -ae f. (*shin*)

legal *adj.* lēgitimus, -a, -um

legation *n.* lēgātiō, -ōnis f.

legend *n.* fābula, -ae f.

legion *n.* legiō, -ōnis f.

legionary *n.* legiōnārius, -ī *m.*
legitimate *adj.* lēgitimus, -a, um
leisure *n.* ōtium, -ī *nt.*
lend *v.t.* commodō, -modāre, -modāvī, -modātum (*supply*); *v.d.t.* faeneror, faenerārī, faenerātus sum (~ *at interest*)
length *n.* longitūdō, -inis *f.* (*distance*); *n.* longinquitās, -ātis *f.* (*time*)
lengthen *v.t.* extendō, -tendere, -tendī, -tentum (-tēnsum)
lentil *n.* lēns, lentis *f.*
lesion *n.* ulcus, ulceris *nt.*
less *adj.* minor, minus; *adv.* minus
lesson *n.* praeceptum, -ī *nt.*
let *v.t.* sinō, -ere, sīvī, situm (*allow*); *v.t.* locō, -āre, -āvī, -ātum (*lease; hire*); in an exhortation, use hortatory subjv.
letter *n.* littera, -ae *f.* (*alphabet*); *n.* litterae, -ārum *f./pl.* (*epistle*)
lettuce *n.* lactūca, -ae *f.*
level *adj.* plānus, -a, -um
lever *n.* vectis, -is *m.*
liable *adj.* obnoxius, -a, -um
liar *n.* mendāx, mendācis *m.*
libel *n.* calumnia, -ae *f.*; *v.d.t.* calumnior, calumniārī, calumniātus sum
liberal *adj.* līberālis, -is, -e
liberty *n.* lībertās, -ātis *f.*
library *n.* bibliothēca, -ae *f.*
license *n.* licentia, -ae *f.* (*unrestrained freedom*)
lid *n.* operculum, -ī *nt.*
lie *n.* mendācium, -ī *nt.*; *v.d.t.* mentior, mentīrī, mentītus sum (*utter falsehood*); *v.i.* iaceō, -ēre, iacuī, --- (*rest; recline*)
lieutenant *n.* lēgātus, -ī *m.*
life *n.* vīta, -ae *f.*
lifeless *adj.* inanimus, -a, -um (*of things naturally without life*); *adj.* mortuus, -a, -um (*dead*)
lifetime *n.* aetās, -ātis *f.*
lift *v.t.* tollō, -ere, sustulī, sublātum
light *n.* lūx, lūcis *f.* (*brightness; daylight*); *n.* lūmen, -inis *nt.* (*source of* ~); *adj.* illūstris, -is, -e (*full of* ~; *not darkened*); *adj.* levis, -is, -e (*not heavy*); *v.t.* illūminō, -lūmināre, -lūmināvī, -lūminātum (*illuminate*); *v.t.* incendō, -cendere, -cendī, -cēnsum (*set alight*)
lighten *v.t.* levō, -āre, -āvī, -ātum (*make less heavy*)
lighthouse *n.* pharus, -ī *m.*

lightning *n.* fulmen, -inis *nt.*

like *adj.* similis, -is, -e (*similar*) (+ dat.); *adj.* aequālis, -is, -e (*equal*); **~wise** *adv.* similiter; *v.t.* amō, -āre, -āvī, -ātum

limbs *n./pl.* artūs, -uum *m./pl.*

lime *n.* calx, calcis *f.* (*mineral*)

limit *n.* fīnis, -is *m.*

limp *v.i.* claudicō, -āre, -āvī, ---

line *n.* līnea, -ae *f.* (*string; limit; mark*); *n.* seriēs, -ēī *f.* (*row*); *n.* regiō, -ōnis *f.* (*direction*); *n.* versus, -ūs *m.* (*~ of poetry*); *n.* aciēs, -ēī *f.* (*~ of battle*)

linen *n.* linteum, linteī *nt.*

link *n.* ānulus, -ī *m.* (*of a chain*); *n.* vinculum, -ī *nt.* (*a bond*); *v.t.* cōnectō, -nectere, nexuī, nexum

lion *n.* leō, leōnis *m.*

lioness *n.* leaena, -ae *f.*

lip *n.* labrum, -ī *nt.*

liquid *n.* liquor, -ōris *m.*; *adj.* liquidus, -a, -um

list *n.* index, indicis *m.*

listen *v.t.* audiō, -īre, -īvī, -ītum

literature *n.* litterae, -ārum *f./pl.*

litter *n.* lectīca, -ae *f.* (*portable couch*); *n.* fētus, -ūs *m.* (*set of young animals*)

little *adj.* parvus, -a, -um; **a ~** *adv.* paulum

live *adj.* vīvus, -a, -um; *v.i.* vīvō, -ere, vīxī, vīctum (*be alive*); *v.i.* habitō, -āre, -āvī, -ātum (*dwell*)

lively *adj.* alacer, alacris, alacre

liver *n.* iecur, -oris *nt.*

lizard *n.* lacerta, -ae *f.*

load *n.* onus, oneris *nt.*; *v.t.* onerō, -āre, -āvī, -ātum

loaf *n.* pānis, -is *m.*

loan *n.* mūtuum, -ī *nt.*; *v.t.* commodō, -modāre, -modāvī, -modātum (*supply*); *v.d.t.* faeneror, faenerārī, faenerātus sum (*~ at interest*)

loaned *adj.* mūtuus, -a, -um

lobster *n.* locusta, -ae *f.*

lock *n.* claustra, -ōrum *nt./pl.*; *v.t.* occlūdō, -clūdere, -clūsī, -clūsum

locker *n.* armārium, -ī *nt.*

locust *n.* locusta, -ae *f.*

lodge *v.d.i.* dēversor, dēversārī, dēversātus sum

lodging *n.* dēversōrium, -ī *nt.*

loft *n.* cēnāculum, -ī *nt.* (*room under a roof*); *n.* faenīlia, -um *nt./pl.* (*hay~*)

log *n.* tignum, -ī *nt.*

logical *adj.* dialecticus, -a, -um
lone(ly) *adj.* sōlus, -a, -um
long *adj.* longus, -a, -um (*physical extension*); *adj.* diūturnus, -a, -um (*of ~ duration*); *adv.* diū; **~ for** *v.t.* dēsīderō, -āre, -āvī, -ātum
look *n.* aspectus, -ūs *m.* (*act of looking*); *n.* vultus, -ūs *nt.* (*a facial expression*); *n.* speciēs, -ēī *f.* (*appearance; semblance*); *v.i.* videor, vidērī, vīsus sum (*appear; seem*); **~ at** *v.i.* aspiciō, -spicere, -spēxī, -spectum
loom *n.* tēla, -ae *f.*
loop *n.* laqueus, -ī *m.*
loose *adj.* laxus, -a, -um
loosen *v.t.* laxō, -āre, -āvī, -ātum
lord *n.* dominus, -ī *m.*
lose *v.t.* āmittō, -mittere, -mīsī, -missum (*part with accidentally*); *v.t.* perdō, -dere, -didī, -ditum (*squander; forfeit*)
loss *n.* damnum, -ī *nt.*
lost *adj.* amissus, -a, -um (*missing; gone astray*); *adj.* perditus, -a, -um (*ruined; wasted*)
lot *n.* sors, sortis *f.* (*decision by drawing lots; fortune*); *n.* agellus, -ī *m.* (*section of land*)
loud *adj.* clārus, -a, -um; **~ly** *adv.* magnā vōce
lounge *n.* lectus, -ī *m.*
love *n.* amor, -ōris *m.*; *v.t.* amō, -āre, -āvī, -ātum; **fall in ~** *v.t.* adamō, -amāre, -amāvī, -amātum
lovely *adj.* venustus, -a, -um (*charming*); *adj.* amoenus, -a, -um (*of scenery*)
lover *n.* amāns, amantis *m./f.*
low *adj.* humilis, -is, -e (*short in height*); *adj.* gravis, -is, -e (*of sounds*); *adj.* vīlis, -is, -e (*of price*); *adj.* trīstis, -is, -e (*sad in spirit*); *adj.* turpis, -is, -e (*disgraceful; mean*)
lower *adj.* īnferior, īnferius (*further down*); *adj.* īnferus, -a, -um (*situated below*); **the ~ classes** *n.* vulgus, -ī *nt.*
lowest *adj.* īmus, -a, -um (*furthest down*)
loyal *adj.* fidēlis, -is, -e
loyalty *n.* fidēlitās, -ātis *f.*
luck *n.* cāsus, -ūs *m.* (*accident; chance*); *n.* sors, sortis *f.* (*good or bad ~*); **good ~** *n.* fēlicitās, -ātis *f.*; **~ily** *adv.* fēliciter
lucky *adj.* fēlīx, fēlīcis
luggage *n.* sarcinae, -ārum *f./pl.*
lump *n.* massa, -ae *f.*
lunar *adj.* lūnāris, -is, -e

lunatic *adj.* īnsānus, -a, -um
lunch *n.* prandium, -ī *nt.*; **have ~** *v.i.* prandeō, -ēre, prandī, pransum
lung *n.* pulmō, -ōnis *m.*
lust *n.* libīdō, -dinis *f.*
lustration *n.* lūstrātiō, -ōnis *f.*
luxurious *adj.* lūxuriōsus, -a, -um
luxury *n.* lūxuria, -ae *f.*
lye *n.* lixīvium, -ī *nt.*

M

machine *n.* māchina, -ae *f.*
machinery *n.* māchinātiō, -ōnis *f.*
mad *adj.* īrātus, -a, -um (*angry*); *adj.* īnsānus, -a, -um (*insane*)
madam *n.* domina, -ae *f.*
magazine *n.* horreum, -ī *nt.* (*warehouse*)
magic *n.* magica ars, magicae artis *f.*
magical *adj.* magicus, -a, -um
magician *n.* magus, -ī *m.*
magistrate *n.* magistrātus, -ūs *m.*
magnet *n.* magnēs, magnētis *m.*
magnetic *adj.* magnēticus, -a, -um
magnificent *adj.* magnificus, -a, -um
magnify *v.t.* amplificō, -ficāre, -ficāvī, -ficātum (*enlarge; make impressive*)
maid *n.* ancilla, -ae *f.*
mail *n.* lōrīca, -ae *f.* (*armor*)
main *adj.* prīmus, -a, -um; **~ly** *adv.* praecipuē
mainland *n.* continēns, -entis *f.*
maintain *v.t.* servo, -āre, -āvī, -ātum (*preserve*); *v.t.* alō, -ere, aluī, altum (alitum) (*support with the necessities of life*); *v.t.* contendō, -tendere, -tendī, -tentum (*support by argument*); *v.t.* retineō, -tinēre, -tinuī, -tentum (*hold out against attack; uphold*); *v.t.* sustineō, -tinēre, -tinuī, -tentum (*sustain; endure; nourish; support*)
majestic *adj.* augustus, -a, -um
majesty *n.* māiestās, -ātis *f.*
major *adj.* māior, maius
make *v.i.* faciō, -ere, fēcī, factum (*fashion; render*); *v.t.* creō, -āre, -āvī, -ātum (*appoint*); *v.t.* cōgō, -ere, coēgī, coāctum (*compel*); **~ war** *v.t.* bellum īnferō, -ferre, -tulī, -lātum

maker *n.* fabricātor, -ōris *m.*

make-up *n.* medicāmina faciēī, medicāminum faciēī *nt./pl.*

male *n.* mās, maris *m.*; *adj.* masculus, -a, -um

malignant *adj.* malignus, -a, -um (*evil*); *adj.* mortifer, -fera, -ferum (*deadly*)

man *n.* homō, -inis *m./f.* (*human being*); *n.* vir, virī *m.* (*male human being*)

manage *v.t.* cūrō, -āre, -āvī, -ātum (*attend to*); *v.t.* administrō, -ministrāre, -ministrāvī, -ministrātum (*superintend; rule; direct*)

management *n.* cūrātiō, -ōnis *f.*

manager *n.* cūrātor, -ōris *m.*

maneuver *v.t.* dēcurrō, -currere, -currī (-cucurrī), -cursum (*of troops*)

manhood *n.* pūbertās, -ātis *f.*

manifold *adj.* multiplex, -plicis

manipulate *v.t.* trāctō, -āre, -āvī, -ātum

mankind *n.* hominēs, -um *m./pl.*

manner *n.* modus, -ī *m.* (*way*); *n.* mōs, mōris *m.* (*custom*)

mansion *n.* domus, -ūs *f.*

manufacture *v.d.t.* fabricor, fabricārī, fabricātus sum

manure *n.* stercus, -oris *nt.*

manuscript *n.* liber, librī *m.*

many *adj.* multī, -ae, -a *pl.*(*a great number*); *adj.* complūrēs, complūrēs, complūra *pl.* (*a good many; several*); **as ~ as** *conj.* tot … quot; **so ~** *adj.* tot (*indecl.*); **how ~** *adj.* quot (*indecl.*)

map *n.* tabula, -ae *f.*

marble *n.* marmor, -oris *nt.*

march *v.i.* iter faciō, -ere, fēcī, factum

March *adj.* Mārtius, -a, -um (*usu. w.* **mēnsis**); *n* Mārtius, -ī *m.*

mare *n.* equa, -ae *f.*

margin *n.* margō, -inis *m./f.*

marine *adj.* marīnus, -a, -um

mark *n.* nota, -ae *f.*; *n.* indicium, -ī *nt*

market *n.* macellum, -ī *nt.*

marriage *n.* coniugium, -ī *nt.*; *n.* mātrimōnium, -ī *nt.* (*used only in reference to the wife*); **~ ceremony** *n.* nūptiae, -ārum *f./pl.*

married *adj.* nupta, -ae (*used only of the woman*)

marrow *n.* medulla, -ae *f.*

marry *v.t.* (uxōrem) dūcō, -ere, dūxī, ductum (*used only of the man*); *v.i.* nūbō, -ere, nūpsī, nūptum (+ *dat.*) (*used only of the woman*)

marsh *n.* palūs, -ūdis *f.*

marvelous *adj.* mīrus, -a, -um

masculine *adj.* virīlis, -is, -e (*manly*); *adj.* masculīnus, -a, -um (*male*)

mash *v.t.* contundō, -tundere, -tudī, -tūsum

mask *n.* persōna, -ae *f.*

mass *n.* mōlēs, -is *f.* (*a great bulk*); *n.* magnitūdō, -inis *f.* (*great number of people*); **the masses** *n./pl.* vulgus, -ī *nt./sg.*

massive *adj.* solidus, -a, -um

mast *n.* mālus, -ī *m.*

master *n.* dominus, -ī *m.* (~ *of a household or slaves*); *n.* magister, magistrī *m.* (*school* ~)

mat *n.* teges, -etis *f.*

match *n.* pār, paris *nt.* (*equal*); *n.* certāmen, -inis *nt.* (*a contest*)

material *n.* māteriēs, -ēī (māteria, -ae) *f.*

mathematics *n.* mathēmatica ars, mathēmaticae artis *f.*

matron *n.* mātrōna, -ae *f.*

matter *n.* māteriēs, -ēī (māteria, -ae) *f.* (*subject under discussion*); *n.* rēs, reī *f.* (*affair*)

mattress *n.* culcita, -ae *f.*

mature *adj.* adultus, -a, -um (*grown up*); *adj.* mātūrus, -a, -um (*ripe*)

maturity *n.* mātūritās, -ātis *f.*

maximum *n.* maximum, -ī *nt.*; *adj.* maximus, -a, -um

may (be permitted) *verbal aux.* licet, licēre, licuit (licitum est) (+ *dat.*) (*imp.*); *verbal aux.* (*if expressing contingency, or possibility, use subjv.*)

May *adj.* Māius, -a, -um (*usu. w.* **mēnsis**); *n.* Māius, -ī *m.*

maybe *adv.* fortasse

maze *n.* labyrinthus, -ī *m.*

me *pron.* Use dat., acc., or abl. case of ego.

meadow *n.* prātum, -ī *nt.*

meager *adj.* exiguus, -a, -um (*insufficient*); *adj.* macer, macra, macrum (*poor; barren*)

meal *n.* cēna, -ae *f.* (*repast*); *n.* farīna, -ae *f.* (*flour*)

mean *n.* mediocritās, -ātis *f.* (*moderateness*); *adj.* medius, -a, -um (*middle*); *adj.* humilis, -is, -e (*low in social rank*); *adj.* illīberālis, -is, -e (*ungenerous*)

meaning *n.* significātiō, -ōnis *f.*

means *n./pl.* facultās, -ātis *f.*; **by no** ~ *adv.* minimē

meantime (in the ~) *adv.* intereā

meanwhile *adv.* intereā

measure *n.* mensūra, -ae *f.* (*a standard quantity*); *n.* cōnsilium, -ī *nt.* (*plan of action*)

meat *n.* carō, carnis *f.*

mechanic *n.* opifex, opificis *m./f.*
medal *n.* īnsigne, -is *nt.*
medical *adj.* medicus, -a, -um
medicine *n.* medicīna, -ae *f.*
medium *adj.* mediocris, mediocris, mediocre (*middling; moderate*)
meet *v.t., v.i.* occurrō, -currere, -currī, -cursum (+ dat.) (*encounter*); *v.i.*
    conveniō, -venīre, -vēnī, -ventum (*assemble*)
meeting *n.* conventus, -ūs *m.*
mellow *adj.* mātūrus, -a, -um (*ripe*); *adj.* cōmis, -is, -e (*gentle; affable*)
melon *n.* pepō, -onis *m.*
melt *v.i.* liquēscō, -ere, licuī, ---
member *n.* sodālis, -is *m./f.* (*of an organization*); *n.* membrum, -ī *nt.* (*limb; part*)
membrane *n.* membrāna, -ae *f.*
memoir *n.* commentāriī, -ōrum *m./pl.*
memorize *v.t.* ēdiscō, -discere, -didicī, ---
memory *n.* memoria, -ae *f.*
menace *n.* minae, -ārum *f./pl.*
mend *v.t.* sarciō, -īre, -sarsī, -sartum; **be on the ~** *v.i.* convalēscō, -valēscere,
    -valuī, ---
mention *n.* mentiō, -ōnis *f.*; *v.t.* mentiōnem faciō, -ere, fēcī, factum (+ gen.)
merchandise *n.* merx, mercis *f.*
merchant *n.* mercātor, -ōris *m.*
merciful *adj.* misericors, -cordis
merciless *adj.* crūdēlis, -is, -e
mercy *n.* misericordia, -ae *f.*
merely *adv.* tantummodo
merit *n.* meritum, -ī *nt.*
merry *adj.* hilaris, -is, -e
mesh *n.* plaga, -ae *f.*
mess *n.* squālor, -ōris *m.*
message *n.* nūntius, -ī *m.*
messenger *n.* nūntius, -ī *m.*
metal *n.* metallum, -ī *nt.*
meter *n.* numerus, -ī *m.* (*of poetic*)
method *n.* ratiō, -ōnis *f.*
mid *adj.* medius, -a, -um
midday *n.* merīdiēs, -ēī *m.*
middle (of) *use adj.* medius, -a, -um
midnight (at ~) *adv.* mediā nocte

midwife *n.* obstetrīx, -īcis *f.*

might (*expressing contingency, or possibility*) *verbal aux.* (*use subjv.*)

migrate *v.i.* migrō, -āre, -āvī, -ātum

mild *adj.* mītis, -is, -e

mile *n.* mīlle passuum *nt.* (*indecl.*); **miles** *n.pl.* mīlia passuum, mīlium passuum *nt./pl.*

milestone *n.* mīlliārium, -ī *nt.*

military *n.* mīlitēs, -um *m./pl.*

milk *n.* lac, lactis *nt.*

mill *n.* mola, -ae *f.* (*hand ~*); *n.* pistrīnum, -ī *nt.* (*~ for crushing grain*)

miller *n.* molitor, -ōris *m.*

million *n.* deciēs (deciēns) centēna mīlia (*numerical adv.*)

mind *n.* mēns, mentis *f.* (*intellect*); *n.* sententia, -ae *f.* (*opinion; way of thinking*); *v.t.* cūrō, -āre, -āvī, -ātum (*attend to*); (**re**)**call to ~** *v.d.t.* recordor, recordārī, recordātus sum

mindful *adj.* memor, memoris

mine *n.* metallum, -ī *nt.*; *v.t.* effōdiō, -fōdere, -fōdī, -fossum; *poss. pron.* meus, -a, -um

mingle *v.d.i.* misceor, miscērī, mīxtus sum

minimum *n.* minimum, -ī *nt.*

minor *adj.* minor, minus

minority *n.* minor pārs, minōris partis *f.*

mint *n.* menta, -ae *f.* (*herb*); *n.* monēta, -ae *f.* (*coinage*)

minus *prep.* sine (+ abl.) (*without*)

minute *adj.* exiguus, -a, -um

miracle *n.* mīrāculum, -ī *nt.*

miraculous *adj.* mīrus, -a, -um (*wonderful; astonishing*)

mire *n.* lutum, -ī *nt.*

mirror *n.* speculum, -ī *nt.*

misadventure *n.* cāsus, -ūs *m.*

mischief *n.* damnum, -ī *nt.*

misdeed *n.* dēlictum, -ī *nt.*

misery *n.* miseria, -ae *f.*

misfortune *n.* adversum, adversī *nt.*

mislay *v.t.* āmittō, -mittere, -mīsī, -mīssum

miss *v.t.* nōn tangō, -ere, tetigī, tactum (*not touch a mark*); *v.t.* praetereō, -īre, -īvī (-iī), -itum (*pass by without noticing; omit*); *v.t.* dēsīderō, -āre, -āvī, -ātum (*feel the want of*)

missile *n.* tēlum, -ī *nt.*

mission *n.* lēgātiō, -ōnis *f.* (*delegation*); *n.* officium, -ī *nt.* (*special duty*)

mist *n.* nebula, -ae *f.*

mistake *n.* error, -ōris *m.*; *v.t.* errō, -āre, -āvī, -ātum; **be ~n** *v.d.i.* fallor, fallī, falsus sum

mistress *n.* domina, -ae *f.* (*of a household or slaves*)

mistrust *v.i.* diffidō, -fidere, -fīsus sum (+ dat.)

misunderstanding *n.* error, -ōris *m.*

mix *v.t.* misceō, -ēre, miscuī, mīxtum

mixed *adj.* mīxtus, -a, -um

mixture *n.* mistūra, -ae *f.*

moan *n.* gemitus, -ūs *m.*

mode *n.* modus, -ī *m.*

model *n.* exemplum, -ī *nt.*

modest *adj.* verēcundus, -a, -um

modification *n.* mūtātiō, -ōnis *f.*

moist *adj.* ūmidus, -a, -um

moisten *v.t.* rigō, -āre, -āvī, -ātum

moisture *n.* ūmor, -ōris *m.*

mold *n.* forma, -ae *f.* (*shape*); *n.* mūcor, -ōris *m.* (*fungal growth*); *v.t.* fingō, -ere, finxī, fictum (*shape*)

moment *n.* punctum, punctī *nt.* (*time*); *n.* mōmentum, -ī *nt.* (*importance*)

monarch *n.* rēx, rēgis *m.*

monarchy *n.* rēgnum, -ī *nt.*

monastery *n.* monastērium, -ī *nt.*

Monday *n.* diēs Lūnae, diēī Lūnae *m.*

money *n.* pecūnia, -ae *f.*

monk *n.* monachus, -ī *m.*

monkey *n.* sīmia, -ae *f.*

monopoly *n.* monopōlium, -ī *nt.*

monster *n.* mōnstrum, -ī *nt.*

monstrous *adj.* immānis, -is, -e

month *n.* mēnsis, -is *m.*

mood *n.* animus, -ī *m.* (*frame of mind*); *n.* modus, -ī *m.* (*grammar*)

moon *n.* lūna, -ae *f.*

mop *v.t.* dētergeō, -tergēre, -tersī, -tersum

moral *n.* mōrālis, -is, -e

more *adj.* plūs, plūris *nnt.* (+ gen.) (*of an amount, e.g.* **more wine**); *adj.* plūres, plūra (*to indicate more in number, e.g.* **more men**); *adv.* magis; **~ than** *conj.* magis quam

moreover *adv.* praetereā

morning *n.* manē *nt.* (*indecl.*); **in the ~** *adv.* māne; **early in the ~** *adv.* prīmā lūce

mortgage *n.* pignus, -ōris *nt.*

mosquito *n.* culex, culicis *m.*

most *adj.* plūrimus, -a, -um; *adv.* maximē; **~ly, for the ~ part** *adv.* plērumque; **-most** *suffix: use sup. form of adj. or adv.*

moth *n.* blatta, -ae *f.*

mother *n.* māter, mātris *f.*

mother-in-law *n.* socrus, -ūs *f.*

motion *n.* mōtus, -ūs *m.* (*a movement*); *n.* impetus, -ūs *m.* (*impulse*); *n.* rōgātiō, -ōnis *f.* (*proposed law*); *n.* sententia, -ae *f.* (*formal proposal in a meeting*)

motive *n.* causa, -ae *f.*

mount *v.t.* ascendō, -scendere, -scendī, -scēnsum

mountain *n.* mōns, montis *m.*

mourn *v.t.* lūgeō, -ēre, lūxī, lūctum

mourning *n.* lūctus, -ūs *m.*; **dressed in ~** *adj.* pullātus, -a, -um

mouse *n.* mūs, mūris *m./f.*

mouth *n.* ōs, ōris *nt.*

move *v.t., v.i.* moveō, -ēre, mōvī, mōtum

much *adj.* multus, -a, -um; *adv.* multum; **so ~ as** *adj.* tantus, -a, -um . . . quantus, -a, -um; *adv.* tantum . . . quantum; **how ~** *adj.* quantus, -a, -um; *adv.* quantum; **so ~** *adj.* tantus, -a, -um; *adv.* tantum; **too ~** *adj.* nimius, -a, -um; *adv.* nimis, nimium

mud *n.* lutum, -ī *nt.*

muffle *v.t.* involvō, -volvere, -volvī, -volūtum (*wrap up*)

mug *n.* pōculum, -ī *nt.*

multiplication *n.* multiplicātiō, -ōnis *f.*

multiply *v.t.* multiplicō, -plicāre, -plicāvī, -plicātum (*mathematics*)

municipality *n.* mūnicipium, -ī *nt.*

murder *n.* nex, necis *f.*; *v.t.* necō, -āre, -āvī, -ātum

murderer *n.* interfector, -ōris *m.*

muscle *n.* musculus, -ī *m.*

muscular *adj.* lacertōsus, -a, -um

mushroom *n.* fungus, -ī *m.*

music *n.* mūsica, -ae *f.* (*art of music*); *n.* cantus, -ūs *m.* (*music sung or played*)

musician *n.* mūsicus, -ī *m.*; *n.* tībīcen, -inis *m.* (*flautist; piper*); *n.* fidicen, -inis *m.* (*lyre-player*)

must *verbal aux.* necesse est, esse, fuit (*imp. v.*) (+ infv.); oportet, oportēre, oportuit (*imp. v.*) (+ acc. of person + infv.)
mustard *n.* sināpi, -is *nt.*
mute *adj.* mūtus, -a, -um
mutiny *n.* sēditiō, -ōnis *f.*
mutual *adj.* mūtuus, -a, -um
muzzle *n.* ōs, ōris *nt.*
my *adj.* meus, -a, -um
myself *dem.pron.* ipse, ipsa; *pron.* Use forms of ego.
mystery *n.* mystērium, -ī *nt.* (*secret thing*)
myth *n.* fābula, -ae *f.*

N

nail *n.* clāvus, -ī *m.* (*metal*); *n.* unguis, -is *m.* (*finger~*; *toe~*); *v.t.* figō, -ere, fīxī, fīxum
naïve *adj.* simplex, -plicis
naked *adj.* nūdus, -a, -um
name *n.* nōmen, -inis *nt.*; *v.t.* nōminō, -āre, -āvī, -ātum; **first ~** *n.* praenōmen, -inis *nt.*; **~ of the gens** *n.* nōmen, -inis *nt.*; **~ of the family** *n.* cognōmen, -inis *nt.*
nanny *n.* nūtrīx, nūtrīcis *f.*
napkin *n.* mappa, -ae *f.*
narcotic *adj.* somnifer, somnifera, somniferum
narrate *v.t.* narrō, -āre, -āvī, -ātum
narrator *n.* narrātor, -ōris *m.*
narrow *adj.* angustus, -a, -um
nasty *adj.* foedus, -a, -um
nation *n.* gēns, gentis *f.*; *n.* nātiō, -ōnis *f.* (*tribe*); *n.* populus, -ī *m.* (*a people; an organized community*)
native *n.* indigena, -ae *m./f.*; *adj.* indigena, -ae; **~ land** *n.* patria, -ae *f.*
natural *adj.* nātūrālis, -is, -e; **~ly** *adv.* nātūrāliter
naughty *adj.* improbus, -a, -um
nausea *n.* nausea, -ae *f.*
naval *adj.* nāvālis, -is, -e
navel *n.* umbilīcus, -ī *m.*
navigate *v.t.* nāvigō, -igāre, -igāvī, -igātum
navigation *n.* nāvigātiō, -ōnis *f.*
navy *n.* classis, -is *f.*

near *adj.* propinquus, -a, -um; *prep.* prope (+ acc.)
nearby *adj.* propinquus, -a, -um; *adv.* prope
neat *adj.* comptus, -a, -um
necessarily *adv.* necessāriō
necessary *adj.* necessārius, -a, -um; **it is ~** *v.i.* necesse est, esse, fuit (*imp. v.*) (w. dat. of person + infv.)
necessity *n.* necessitās, -ātis *f.* (*unavoidability*); *n.* egestās, -ātis *f.* (*want, need*)
neck *n.* collum, -ī *nt.* (*human, animal, jar*); *n.* angustiae, -ārum *f./pl.* (*land*)
necklace *n.* monīle, -is *nt.*
need *n.* usus, -ūs *m.* (*want, necessity*); *n.* ēgestās, -ātis *f.*, paupertās, -ātis *f.* (*poverty*); *v.i.* opus est, esse, fuit (*imp. v.*) (+ abl. of thing needed)
needle *n.* acus, -ūs *f.*
needless *adj.* inūtilis, -is, -e; **~ly** *adv.* nēquīquam
negation *n.* negātiō, -ōnis *f.*
neglect *v.t.* neglegō, -legere, -lēxī, -lēctum
negotiate *v.i.* agō, -ere, ēgī, actum
neighbor *n.* vīcīnus, -ī *m.*, vīcīna, -ae *f.*
neighborhood *n.* vīcīnitās, -ātis *f.*
neither *adj., pron.* neuter, neutra, neutrum; *conj.* neque (nec); **~ ... nor** *conj.* neque (nec) ... neque (nec)
nephew *n.* nepōs, -ōtis *m.*
nerve *n.* nervus, -ī *m.* (*biol.*); *n.* audācia, -ae *f.* (*boldness*)
nervous *adj.* trepidus, -a, -um
nest *n.* nīdus, -ī *m.*
net(work) *n.* rēte, -is *nt.*
neuter *adj.* neuter, neutra, neutrum
never *adv.* numquam
nevertheless *adv.* nihilōminus
new *adj.* novus, -a, -um; **~ly** *adv.* nūper; **What's ~?** Quid novī?
news *n.* nuntius, -ī *m.*
newspaper *n.* acta diurna, actōrum diurnōrum *nt./pl.*
next *adj.* proximus, -a, -um (+ dat.); *adv.* proximē; **~ day** *adv.* postrīdiē; **~ to** *prep.* iuxtā (+ acc.)
nice *adj.* iūcundus, -a, -um (*pleasant, delicious*); *adj.* subtīlis, -is, -e (*precise, discriminating*); *adj.* fastīdiōsus, -a, -um (*fussy; selective*)
niece *n.* fratris (sorōris) filia, -ae *f.*
night *n.* nox, noctis *f.*; **by ~** *adv.* nocte, noctū; **at ~** *adv.* nocte, noctū; **spend the ~** *v.i.* pernoctō, -noctāre, -noctāvī, -noctātum

nimble *adj.* pernīx, -nīcis
nine *num.* novem (*indecl.*)
nineteen *num.* ūndēvīgintī (*indecl.*)
nineteenth *adj.* ūndēvīcēsimus, -a, -um
ninety *num.* nōnāgintā (*indecl.*)
ninth *adj.* nōnus, -a, -um
no *adj.* nūllus, -a, -um; *adv.* nōn
nobility *n.* nōbilitās, -ātis *f.* (*the aristocracy*)
noble *n.* nōbilis, nōbilis *m./f.*; *adj.* nōbilis, -is, -e (*of high rank*); *adj.* honestus, -a, -um (*of high character*)
nobody *pron.* nēmō, -inis *m./f.*
noise *n.* strepitus, -ūs *m.*
noisy *adj.* raucus, -a, -um
nomadic *adj.* vagus, -a, -um
nominate *v.t.* nōminō, -āre, -āvī, -ātum
nomination *n.* nōminātiō, -ōnis *f.*
none *adj.* nūllus, -a, -um; *pron.* nēmō, -inis *m./f.*; *pron.* nihil *nt.*, nīl *nt.* (*indecl.*)
nonsense *n.* nūgae, -ārum *f./pl.*
noon *n.* merīdiēs, -ēī *m.*; **at ~** *adv.* merīdiē
no one *pron.* nēmō, -inis *m./f.*
nor *conj.* neque (nec)
normal *adj.* solitus, -a, -um (*usual*); **~ly** *adv.* plērumque
north *n.* septentriō, -ōnis *m.*; *adj.* septentriōnālis, -is, -e
northeast *n.* inter septentriōnālem et orientem
northern *adj.* septentriōnālis, -is, -e
northwest *n.* inter septentriōnālem et occāsum sōlis
nose *n.* nāsus, -ī *m.*
nostril *n.* nāris, -is *f.*
not *adv.* nōn (*generally with indv. mood*); *adv.* nē (*generally with subjv. mood*); **~ even** nē ... quidem
note *n.* nota, -ae *f.*; *v.t.* notō, -āre, -āvī, -ātum
notebook *n.* pugillārēs, -ium *m./pl.*
nothing *n.* nihilum, -ī *nt.*; *n.* nihil, nīl *nt.* (*indecl.*)
notice *n.* notātiō, -ōnis *f.* (*an observing*); *n.* prōscrīptiō, -ōnis *f.* (*public notification*); *v.t.* animadvertō, -vertere, -vertī, -versum
notification *n.* dēnūntiātiō, -ōnis *f.*
notify *v.t.* dēnūntiō, -nūntiāre, -nūntiāvī, -nūntiātum
notion *n.* nōtiō, -ōnis *f.* (*conception of a thing*)
notorious *adj.* nōtus, -a, -um (*well-known in good or bad sense*)

noun *n.* nōmen, -inis *nt.*
nourish *v.t.* nūtriō, -īre, -īvī, -ītum
nourishment *n.* alimenta, -ōrum *nt./pl.*
novel *adj.* novus, -a, -um
novelty *n.* novitās, -ātis *f.*
November *adj.* Novembris, Novembre (*usu. w.* **mēnsis**); *n.* November, -bris *m.*
now *adv.* nunc (*at the present time*); **~ and then** *adv.* interdum; **by ~,**
    ~ already *adv.* iam; **~ ... ~** modo ... modo
nowadays *adv.* hodiē
nowhere *adv.* nūsquam
noxious *adj.* noxius, -a, -um
nozzle *n.* nāsus, -ī *m.*
nude *adj.* nūdus, -a, -um
nudity *n.* nūditās, -ātis *f.*
null *adj.* irritus, -a, -um (*invalid*)
nullify *v.t.* īnfirmō, -firmāre, -firmāvī, -firmātum
numb *adj.* torpēns, -entis
number *n.* numerus, -ī *m.*
numerous *adj.* multī, -ae, -a *pl.* (*many*); *adj.* frequēns, -entis (*a consider-able number*)
nun *n.* monacha, -ae *f.*
nurse *n.* nūtrīx, -īcis *f.* (*wet~*; *child's ~*); *v.t.* nūtriō, -īre, -īvī, -ītum (*suckle a baby*); *v.t.* assideō, -sidēre, -sēdī, -sessum (*care for the ill*)
nut *n.* nūx, nucis *f.*; **~shell** *n.* putāmen, -inis *nt.*
nymph *n.* nympha, -ae *f.*

O

oak *n.* quercus, -ūs *f.*
oar *n.* rēmus, -ī *m.*
oat *n.* avēna, -ae *f.*
oath *n.* iūs iūrandum, iūris iūrandī *nt.*; *n.* sacrāmentum, -ī *nt.* (*military ~ of allegiance*); **false ~** *n.* periūrium, -ī *nt.*; **take an ~** *v.t.* iūrō, -āre, -āvī, -ātum
obedience *n.* oboedientia, -ae *f.*
obedient *adj.* oboediēns, -ientis
obey *v.i.* pāreō, -ēre, pāruī, pāritum (+ dat.)
object *n.* prōpositum, -ī *nt.* (*aim*; *intention*); *v.t.* recūsō, -cūsāre, -cūsāvī, -cūsātum

obligation *n.* officium, -ī *nt.* (*obligatory or official service*); *n.* obligātiō, -ōnis *f.* (*legal obligation*)

oblige *v.t.* obligō, -ligāre, -ligāvī, -ligātum

oblong *adj.* oblongus, -a, -um

obscene *adj.* obscēnus, -a, -um

obscure *adj.* obscūrus, -a, -um; *v.t.* obscūrō, -āre, -āvī, -ātum

observation *n.* observātiō, -ōnis *f.* (*a noticing*); *n.* nōtātiō, -ōnis *f.* (*making careful notation*)

observe *v.t.* observō, -servāre, -servāvī, -servātum (*notice; attend to*); *v.t.* dīcō, -ere, dīxī, dictum (*remark; say*)

obstacle *n.* impedīmentum, -ī *nt.*

obstinate *adj.* pertināx, pertinācis

obstruct *v.i.* obstō, -stāre, -stitī, -stātum (+ dat. of person or thing obstructed)

obstruction *n.* impedīmentum, -ī *nt.*

obtain *v.d.t.* adipiscor, adipiscī, adeptus sum (*obtain through one's exertions*); *v.d.t.* nancīscōr, -nancīscī, nactus (nanctus) sum (*obtain by accident; light upon*)

obvious *adj.* manifestus, -a, -um

occasion *n.* occāsiō, -ōnis *f.*

occasionally *adv.* per occāsiōnem (*as opportunity affords*); *adv.* aliquandō (*from time to time*)

occult *adj.* occultus, -a, -um (*secret*)

occupation *n.* possessiō, -ōnis *f.* (*a possessing; a seizing*); *n.* quaestus, -ūs *m.* (*employment; trade*)

occupy *v.t.* occupō, -cupāre, -cupāvī, -cupātum (*seize; take possession; take up time; engross*); *v.t.* teneō, -ēre, tenuī, tentum (*be in possession of; hold*); *v.t.* compleō, -plēre, -plēvī, -plētum (*fill up a space or thing*)

occur *v.t.* incidō, -cidere, -cidī, -cāsum (*happen; arise; occur to the mind*)

occurrence *n.* rēs, reī *f.*

ocean *n.* ōceanus, -ī *m.*

October *adj.* Octōber, Octōbris, Octōbre (*usu. w.* **mēnsis**); *n. .* Octōber, -bris *m.*

odd *adj.* impār, imparis (*of numbers*); *adj.* īnsolitus, -a, -um (*strange; unusual*)

odor *n.* odor, -ōris *m.*

of *prep.* Generally, use the gen. case. To indicate the material from which something is made, use dē, ē, ex (+ abl.) To denote cause, e.g. "to die of a disease," use the abl. case

off *prep.* dē (+ abl.); *adv.* As part of a verbal idea, often expressed by a verb compounded with ab-, dē-, or ex-; **far ~** *adv.* procul

offend *v.t.* offendō, -fendere, -fendī, -fēnsum (*annoy*; *be displeasing to*); *v.t.* peccō, -āre, -āvī, -ātum (*commit a fault*; *transgress*)

offense *n.* facinus, -oris *nt.* (*crime*); *n.* iniūria, -ae *f.* (*wrong*; *insult*); *n.* impetus, -ūs *m.* (*attack*)

offensive *adj.* odiōsus, -a, -um

offer *n.* condiciō, -ōnis *f.*; *v.t.* offerō, -ferre, obtūlī, oblātum (*present*; *sacrifice*)

office *n.* officium, -ī *nt.* (*responsibility*; *special duty*); *n.* magistrātus, -ūs *m.* (*official or political position*)

officer *n.* praefectus, -ī *m.*

official *n.* praefectus, -ī *m.*

often *adv.* saepe

oil *n.* oleum, -ī *nt.*; *v.t.* ungō (unguō), -ere, unxī, ūnctum

oily *adj.* oleōsus, -a, -um

ointment *n.* unguentum, -ī *nt.*

OK *adv.* bene

old *adj.* senex, senis (*advanced in years*); *adj.* vetus, veteris (*not new*); ~ **age** *n.* senectūs, -ūtis *f.*; ~ **man** *n.* senex, senis *m.*; ~ **woman** *n.* anus, -ūs *f.*; (**three**) **years** ~ *adj.* (trēs) annōs nātus, -a, -um

olden, old-fashioned *adj.* prīscus, -a, -um

olive *n.* olea, -ae *f.*

omen *n.* ōmen, -inis *nt.*

omission *n.* praetermissiō, -ōnis *f.*

omit *v.t.* praetermittō, -mittere, -mīsī, -missum

on *prep.* in (+ abl.) (*location*; *place*); *prep.* dē (*concerning*; *about*); For time expressions, e.g. "on that day", use ablative of time.

once *adv.* semel; **at** ~ *adv.* statim (*immediately*), simul (*at the same time*)

one *adj.* ūnus, -a, -um; ~ **and the same** *adj.* īdem, eadem, idem; ~ **by** ~ *adj.* singulī, -ae, -a *pl.*; **a certain** ~ *pron.* quīdam, quaedam, quiddam; **the** ~ **... the other** alter (altera, alterum) ... alter (altera, alterum)

onion *n.* caepa, -ae *f.*; *n.* caepe, -is *nt.*

only *adj.* ūnicus, -a, -um (*no other like it*); *adj.* sōlus, -a, -um (*solitary*; *by oneself*); *adv.* sōlum; **not** ~ **... but also** nōn sōlum ... sed etiam

open *adj.* apertus, -a, -um; *v.t.* aperiō, -īre, aperuī, apertum; **be** ~ *v.i.* pateō, -ēre, patuī, ---

opening *n.* hiātus, -ūs *m.* (*aperture*); *n.* exordium, -ī *nt.* (*beginning*)

operate *v.i.* ūtor, ūtī, ūsus sum (+ abl.)

opinion *n.* sententia, -ae *f.* (*judgment*); *n.* opīniō, -ōnis *f.* (*belief*; *reputation*); **be of the** ~ *v.t.* cēnseō, -ēre, cēnsuī, cēnsum

opponent *n.* adversārius, -ī *m.*
opportunity *n.* occāsiō, -ōnis *f.*
oppose *v.t.* oppōnō, -pōnere, -posuī, -positum (*place against*); *v.d.t.*
  adversor, adversārī, adversātus sum (*resist*)
opposite *adj.* adversus, -a, -um (*placed in front of; opposed to*); *adj.*
  contrārius, -a, -um (*reverse*)
oppress *v.t.* premō, -ere, pressī, pressum (*weigh down; crush*); *v.t.* opprimō,
  -primere, -pressī, -pressum (*treat cruelly*)
oppression *n.* gravātiō, -ōnis *f.* (*a weighing down*); *n.* iniūria, -ae *f.* (*wrong
  done*)
oppressive *adj.* gravis, -is, -e
option *n.* optiō, -ōnis *f.*
or *conj.* aut, vel (*When the two alternative possibilities rule each other out,
  e.g. "It is either true or not," use aut. Use vel ("if you please") when there
  is more choice*); *conj.* an (*in alternative questions*); **whether ... ~** *conj.*
  utrum ... an (*in conditional sentences use* sīve ... sīve)
oracle *n.* ōrāculum, -ī *nt.*
orange *adj.* lūteus, -a, -um
orator *n.* ōrātor, -ōris *m.*
orchard *n.* pōmārium, -ī *nt.*
order *n.* iussum, -ī *nt.* (*command*); *n.* ordō, -inis *m.* (*arrangement; rank; social class*); *v.t.* iubeō, -ēre, iussī, iussum (+ acc. + infv.) (*command*); *v.t.*
  imperō, -āre, -āvī, -ātum (+ dat. + **ut/nē** + subv.) (*command*); *v.t.*
  dispōnō, -pōnere, -posuī, -positum (*arrange*); **~ of battle** *n.* aciēs, -ēī *f.*
ordinary *adj.* solitus, -a, -um
ore *n.* aes, aeris *nt.*
organ *n.* exta, -ōrum *nt./pl.* (*anat.*)
organization *n.* ordinātiō, -ōnis *f.* (*act of arranging; an arrangement*)
organize *v.t.* ordinō, -āre, -āvī, -ātum
origin *n.* orīgō, -inis *f.* (*source; start; lineage*); *n.* prīncipia, -ōrum *nt./pl.*
  (*foundations; principles; elements*)
original *adj.* prīstinus, -a, -um; *adv.* prīmum
ornament *n.* ōrnāmentum, -ī *nt.*
orphan *n.* orbus, -ī *m.*; *n.* orba, -ae *f.*
other *adj.* alter, altera, alterum (*of two only*); *adj.* alius, alia, aliud (*another*);
  the ~s *pron.* cēterī, -ae, -a *pl.*
otherwise *adv.* aliter
ought *v.i.* dēbeō, -ēre, debuī, dēbitum (*obligation*); *v.t.* oportet, oportēre,
  oportuit, --- (*imp.*) (+ acc. of person + infv., e.g. "I ought to go")

ounce *n.* uncia, -ae *f.*

our *adj.* noster, nostra, nostrum

ours *pron.* noster, nostra, nostrum

ourselves *adj. Use forms of* ipsī, ipsae *pl.; pron. Use forms of* nōs.

out(side) *adv.* forīs (*be outdoors*); *adv.* forās (*going outdoors*)

outcast *n.* exsul, exsulis *m./f.*

outcome *n.* ēventus, -ūs *m.*

outdoors *adv.* forīs (*be ~*); *adv.* forās (*going ~*)

outer *adj.* exterior, -ius

outlaw *n.* latrō, -ōnis *m.*

out of *prep.* ē, ex (+ abl.)

outside *adv.* extra; ~ **of** *prep.* extrā (+ abl.)

outskirts *n.* suburbānus, -a, -um

outstanding *adj.* praeclārus, -a, -um (*remarkable; excellent*)

oval *adj.* ōvātus, -a, -um

oven *n.* furnus, -ī *m.*

over *adv.* super; *prep.* super (+ acc. or abl.) (*above*); *prep.* trāns (+ acc.) (*across, e.g. "over the river"*); ~ **and above** *adv.* īnsuper

overcast *adj.* nūbilus, -a, -um

overlook *v.t.* ignōscō, -nōscere, -nōvī, -nōtum (+ dat. for person *or* + acc. for offense) (*excuse*); *v.t.* neglegō, -glegere, -glexī, -glectum (*neglect*); *v.t.* prōspiciō, -spicere, -spexī, -spectum (*have a view of*)

overtake *v.d.t.* cōnsequor, cōnsequī, cōnsecūtus sum (*catch up with*); *v.t.* superveniō, -venīre, -vēnī, -ventum (*come upon or take by surprise*)

owe *v.t.* dēbeō, -ēre, debuī, debitum

owing to *prep.* propter (+ acc.)

owl *n.* būbō, būbōnis *m.*

own (my, your, etc.) *adj. Use a poss. adj.* meus, tuus, suus, noster, vester; *v.t.* possideō, -sidēre, -sēdī, -sessum (*possess*); *v.d.t.* fateor, fatērī, fassus sum (*confess*)

owner *n.* dominus, -ī *m.*

ox *n.* bōs, bovis *m./f.*

oxen *n.* bovēs, bovum (boum) *m./f./pl.*

oyster *n.* ostrea, -ae *f.*

P

pace *n.* passus, -ūs *m.* (*step; unit of measurement*); *n.* gradus, -ūs *m.* (*gait*);
    v.i. incēdō, -cēdere, -cessī, -cessum
pack *v.t.* colligō, -ligere, -lēgī, -lectum
package *n.* sarcina, -ae *f.*
pagan *adj.* pāgānus, -a, -um
page *n.* pāgina, -ae *f.*
pail *n.* hama, -ae *f.*
pain *n.* dolor, -ōris *m.*; **cause ~** *v.i.* dolōrem faciō, -ere, fēcī, factum (+ dat.);
    feel ~ *v.i.* doleō, -ēre, doluī, -itum
painful *adj.* dolēns, -entis; **~ly** *adv.* cum dolōre
painless *adj.* sine dolōre
paint *n.* pigmentum, -ī *nt.*; *v.t.* pingō, -ere, pinxī, pictum
painter *n.* pictor, -ōris *m.*
painting *n.* pictūra, -ae *f.* (*art of painting*)
pair *n.* pār, paris *nt.*
palace *n.* rēgia, -ae *f.*
pale *adj.* pallidus, -a, -um; **be ~** *v.i.* palleō, -ēre, palluī, ---
pall *n.* pallium, -ī *nt.* (*funeral covering*)
palm *n.* palma, -ae *f.* (*of hand*); **~ tree** *n.* palma, -ae *f.* (*bot.*)
pan *n.* patina, -ae *f.*; **frying ~** *n.* sartāgō, -inis *f.*
panic *n.* pavor, -ōris *m.*
pant *v.i.* anhēlō, -āre, -āvī, -ātum
pantry *n.* penāria, penāriae *f.*
paper *n.* charta, -ae *f.* (*sheet of ~*)
papyrus *n.* papyrus, -ī *m./f.*
parade *n.* pompa, -ae *f.*
paragraph *n.* caput, capitis *nt.*
parallel *adj.* parallēlus, -a, -um
paralysis *n.* paralysis, -is *f.*
parasite *n.* parasītus, -ī *m.* (*sycophant*)
parasitic *adj.* parasīticus, -a, -um
parcel *n.* fasiculus, -ī *m.*
parchment *n.* membrāna, -ae *f.*
pardon *n.* venia, -ae *f.*; *v.t.* īgnōscō, -gnōscere, -gnōvī, -gnōtum (*overlook;
    forgive*); *v.t.* condōnō, -dōnāre, -dōnāvī, -dōnātum (+ acc. of offence +
    dat. of person)

parent *n.* parēns, parentis *m./f.*

park *n.* hortī, -ōrum *m./pl.*

parrot *n.* psittacus, -ī *m.*

parsley *n.* apium, -ī *nt.*

part *n.* pars, partis *f.* (*portion*); *n.* persōna, -ae *f.* (*character in a play*); *n.* officium, -ī *nt.* (*duty*); *v.t.* sēparō, -parāre, -parāvī, -parātum (*sever; separate*); *v.i.* discēdō, -cēdere, -cessī, -cessum (*depart; part company*); **take ~ in** *v.i.* intersum, -esse, -fuī, --- (+ dat. *or* **in** + abl.)

partial *adj.* studiōsus, -a, -um

participate *v.i.* intersum, -esse, -fuī, --- (+ dat. *or* **in** + abl.)

particle *n.* particula, -ae *f.*

particular *adj.* proprius, -a, -um (*individual*); *adj.* praecipuus, -a, -um (*special; outstanding*); **~ly** *adv.* magnopere (*very much*)

partition *n.* partītiō, -ōnis *f.* (*act of dividing*); *n.* pariēs, -ētis *m.* (*wall*)

partner *n.* socius, -ī *m.*

party *n.* convīvium, -ī *nt.* (*dinner ~*); *n.* partēs, -ium *f./pl.* (*political faction*)

pass *v.t.* praetereō, -īre, -iī (-īvī), -itum (*~ by*); **~ away** *v.i.* ēvānēscō, -vānēscere, -vānuī, --- (*disappear*); **~ time** *v.t.* agō, -ere, ēgī, āctum

passage *n.* trānsitus, -ūs *m.* (*act of ~*); *n.* iter, itineris *nt.* (*path of access*); *n.* locus, -ī *m.* (*section of a book*)

passenger *n.* vector, -ōris *m.*

passion *n.* studium, -ī *nt.* (*enthusiasm; application to learning*); *n.* cupiditās, -ātis *f.* (*a longing; a desire*); *n.* libīdō, -inis *f.* (*inordinate desire; sensuality*); *n.* īra, -ae *f.* (*violent anger*)

passionate *adj.* fervidus, -a, -um (*ardent*); *adj.* īrācundus, -a, -um (*hot-headed: angry*)

passive *adj.* iners, -ertis (*inactive*); *adj.* obnoxius, -a, -um (*submissive*)

password *n.* tessera, -ae *f.*

past *n.* praeteritia, -ōrum *nt./pl.*; *adj.* praeteritus, -a, -um; *prep.* praeter (+ acc.) (*beyond*)

pastime *n.* lūdus, -ī *m.*

pastry *n.* crustum, -ī *nt.*

pasture *n.* pāstus, -ūs *m.*

patch *n.* pannus, -ī *m.*; *v.t.* sarciō, -īre, sarsī, sartum

path *n.* sēmita, -ae *f.*

pathetic *adj.* flēbilis, -is, -e

patience *n.* patientia, -ae *f.*

patient *n.* aeger, aegrī *m.*; *n.* aegra, -ae *f.*; *adj.* patiēns, -ientis

patrician *adj.* patricius, -a, -um

patrimony *n.* patrimōnium, -ī *nt.*

patrol *n.* circuitō, -ōnis *f.* (*act of patrolling*); *n.* circitōrēs, -um *m./pl.*; *v.i.* circumeō, -īre, -īvī (-iī), -itum

patron *n.* patrōnus, -ī *m.*; **~ess** *n.* patrōna, -ae *f.*

pattern *n.* exemplum, -ī *nt.*

paunch *n.* venter, ventris *m.*

pause *n.* intermissiō, -ōnis *f.*; *v.t., v.i.* intermittō, -mittere, -mīsī, -missum

pave *v.t.* sternō, -ere, strāvī, strātum

pavement *n.* pavīmentum, -ī *nt.*

pavilion *n.* pāpiliō, -ōnis *m.*

paw *n.* pēs, pedis *m.*

pawn *n.* pignus, -oris (-eris) *nt.* (*for a pledge; for security*)

pay *n.* stīpendium, -ī *nt.*; *v.t.* persolvō, -solvere, -solvī, -solūtum; **~ attention to** *v.t.* colō, -ere, coluī, cultum; **~ a penalty** *v.t.* poenam dō, dare, dedī, datum

payment *n.* solūtiō, -ōnis *f.* (*act of paying*); *n.* pensiō, -ōnis *f.* (*sum of money*)

pea *n.* pĭsum, -ī *nt.*

peace *n.* pāx, pācis *f.*

peaceful *adj.* tranquillus, -a, -um

peach *n.* mālum Persicum, mālī Persicī *nt.*

peacock *n.* pāvō, -ōnis *m.*

peak *n.* cacūmen, -inis *nt.* (*mountain*); *n.* apex, apicis *m.* (*the point or summit of anything*)

pear *n.* pirum, -ī *nt.*

pearl *n.* margarīta, -ae *f.*

peasant *n.* rusticus, -ī *m.*

pebble *n.* lapillus, -ī *m.*

pedestrian *adj.* pedester, pedestris, pedestre

peel *n.* tunica, -ae *f.*; *v.t.* cutem detrahō, -trahere, -trāxī, -tractum

pen *n.* stilus, -ī *m.* (*writing instrument*); *n.* saeptum, -ī *nt.* (*enclosure*)

penalty *n.* poena, -ae *f.*

penetrate *v.i.* penetrō, -āre, -āvī, -ātum

penis *n.* pēnis, -is *m.*

penknife *n.* scalprum, -ī *nt.*

penny *n.* as, assis *m.* (*smallest Roman coin*)

people *n.* populus, -ī *m.* (*nation*); *n.* hominēs, -um *m./pl.* (*persons*); **common ~** *n.* plēbs, plēbis (plēbēs, plebēī) *f.*

pepper *n.* piper, piperis *nt.*

perceive *v.t.* sentiō, -īre, sēnsī, sēnsum

perfect *adj.* perfectus, -a, -um

perform *v.t.* perficiō, -ficere, -fēcī, -fectum (*carry out: accomplish*); **~ a play** *v.t.* agō, -ere, ēgī, āctum

performance *n.* functiō, -ōnis *f.* (*accomplishment of a task*)

perfume *n.* unguentum, -ī *nt.*

perhaps *adv.* fōrtasse

peril *n.* perīculum, -ī *nt.*

period *n.* aetās, -ātis *f.* (*space of time*); *n.* fīnis, -is *m.* (*termination*); *n.* periodus, -ī *f.* (*a complete sentence*); *n.* punctum, -ī *nt.* (*a mark*)

perish *v.i.* pereō, -īre, -īvī (-iī), -itum

permanent *adj.* perennis, -is, -e

permit *v.t.* sinō, -ere, sīvī, situm

persist *v.i.* perstō, -stare, -stitī, -stātum

person *n.* homō, -inis *m./f.*

personal *adj.* prīvātus, -a, -um

perspective *n.* scēnographia, -ae *f.*

perspiration *n.* sūdor, -ōris *m.*

perspire *v.i.* sūdō, -āre, -āvī, -ātum

persuade *v.i.* persuādeō, -suādēre, -suāsī, -suāsum (+ dat.)

persuasion *n.* persuāsiō, -ōnis *f.*

pester *v.t.* sollicitō, -āre, -āvī, -ātum

pestilence *n.* pestilentia, -ae *f.*

pet *n.* dēlīciae, -ārum *f./pl.* (*sweetheart*)

petty *adj.* parvus, -a, -um (*insignificant*); *adj.* angustus, -a, -um (*narrow*)

phantom *n.* simulācrum, -ī *nt.*

pheasant *n.* phāsiānus, -ī *m.*

phenomenon *n.* rēs, reī *f.*

philosophy *n.* philosophia, -ae *f.*

phlegm *n.* pītuīta, -ae *f.*

phrase *n.* locūtiō, -ōnis *f.*

physical *adj.* physicus, -a, -um (*pertaining to nature*)

physician *n.* medicus, -ī *m.*

pick *v.t.* legō, -ere, lēgī, lēctum (*select; pull off*); **~ up** *v.t.* tollō, -ere, sustulī, sublātum

pickle *n.* muria, -ae *f.*

picture *n.* pictūra, -ae *f.*; *v.t.* verbīs dēpingō, -pingere,-pinxī, -pictum

piece *n.* pars, partis *f.* (*a small bit*); *n.* frustum, -ī *nt.* (*small bit of food*); *n.* frāgmentum, -ī *nt.* (*a part broken off*); **cut into ~s** *v.t.* concīdō, -cīdere, -cīdī, -cīsum; **break into ~s** *v.t.* comminuō, -minuere, -minuī, minūtum

pierce *v.t.* perforō, -forāre, -forāvī, -forātum (*bore through*); *v.t.* trānsfigō, -figere, -fixī, -fixum (*wound*)

piety *n.* piētās, -ātis *f.*

pig *n.* sūs, suis *m./f.*

pigeon *n.* columbus, -ī *m.*; *n.* columba, -ae *f.*

pile *n.* acervus, -ī *m.* (*heap*); *n.* rogus, -ī *m.* (*funeral pyre*); *n.* sublica, -ae *f.* (*stake*); *n.* agger, aggeris *m.* (~ *of rubbish, stone, etc.; dike; dam; rampart*); *n.* villus, -ī *m.* (*nap of cloth*); *v.t.* cumulō, -āre, -āvī, -ātum

pill *n.* pilula, -ae *f.*

pillage *v.d.t.* populor, populārī, populātus sum

pillar *n.* columna, -ae *f.*

pillow *n.* pulvīnus, -ī *m.*

pilot *n.* gubernātor, -ōris *m.* (*of a boat*)

pimple *n.* pustula, -ae *f.*

pin *n.* acus, -ūs *f.*

pincers *n.* forceps, -cipis *m./f.*

pinch *v.t.* vellicō, -āre, -āvī, -ātum (*nip with fingers*); *v.t.* ūrō, -ere, ussī, ustum (*hurt by pinching or being too small*)

pine *n.* pīnus, -ūs (-ī) *f.* (*bot.*)

pint *n.* sextārius, -ī *m.*

pious *adj.* pius, -a, -um

pipe *n.* tubus, -ī *m.* (*tube*); *n.* canālis, -is *m.* (*drainage* ~); *n.* fistula, -ae *f.* (*musical instrument*)

pirate *n.* pīrāta, -ae *m.*

pit *n.* puteus, -ī *m.* (*hole*); *n.* nucleus, -ī *m.* (*kernel*)

pitcher *n.* urceus, -ī *m.* (*container*)

pity *n.* misericordia, -ae *f.*; *v.i.* miseret, miserēre, miseruit, --- (*imp.*) (+ acc. of person pitying + gen. of object)

place *n.* locus, -ī *m.* (in pl., locī for individual places; loca *nt./pl.* for connected places, e.g. a region); *v.t.* pōnō, -ere, posuī, positum; ~ **before/over/in command** *v.t.* praepōnō, -pōnere, -posuī, -positum; ~ **between** *v.t.* interpōnō, -pōnere, -posuī, -positum; ~ **upon** *v.t.* impōnō, -pōnere, -posuī, -positum; **in** ~ **of** *prep.* prō (+ abl.)

plague *n.* pestilentia, -ae *f.*; *v.t.* vexō, -āre, -āvī, -ātum

plain *n.* campus, -ī *m.*; *adj.* aequus, -a, -um (*level*); *adj.* simplex, -plicis (*unadorned; artless*); *adj.* manifestus, -a, -um (*apparent*); *adj.* sincērus, -a, -um (*frank*)

plan *n.* cōnsilium, -ī *nt.* (*project*); *n.* forma, -ae *f.* (*design of a building, etc.*); *v.t.* cōgitō, -āre, -āvī, -ātum

planet *n.* stella (errāns); *n.* stellae (errantis) *f.*

plank *n.* tabula, -ae *f.*

plant *n.* planta, -ae *f.*; *v.t.* serō, -ere, sēvī, satum (*plant; sow*); *v.t.* statuō, -ere, statuī, statūtum (*set up in a place*)

plaster *n.* gypsum, -ī *nt.*

plate *n.* lāmina, -ae *f.* (*thin layer of metal*); *n.* patina, -ae *f.* (*dish*); *n.* argentum, -ī *nt.* (*silver ~*)

platform *n.* suggestus, -ūs *m.*

play *n.* lūdus, -ī *m.* (*game; sport*); *n.* fābula, -ae *f.* (*theater*); *n.* alea, -ae *f.* (*gambling*); *v.t.* lūdō, -ere, lūsī, lūsum (*take recreation; gamble; trifle with*); *v.t.* canō, -ere, cecinī, cantum (*~ a musical instrument*); *v.t.* agō, -ere, ēgī, āctum (*~ a part*)

player *n.* lūsor, -ōris *m.* (*gambler*); *n.* histriō, -ōnis *m.* (*actor*). For one playing a musical instrument, see translations with the instrument entry.

plea *n.* petītiō, -ōnis *f.* (*judicial*); *n.* excūsātiō, -ōnis *f.* (*excuse*); *n.* prex, precis *f.* (*entreaty*)

plead *v.i.* (causam) ōrō, -āre, -āvī, -ātum (*plead a case in court*); *v.i.* excūsō, -cūsāre, -cūsāvī, -cūsātum (*offer as an excuse*); *v.i.* obsecrō, -secrāre, -secrāvī, -secrātum (*supplicate*)

pleasant *adj.* iūcundus, -a, -um (*agreeable*); *adj.* amoenus, -a, -um (*of scenery*)

please *v.i.* placeō, -ēre, placuī, placitum (+ dat.) (*give pleasure to*); *v.i.* libet, libēre, libuit (libitum est) (*imp.*) (*it pleases; it seems good to*); *v.i.* placet, placēre, placuit (placitum est) (*imp.*) (+ dat. of person); **if you ~** sī libet, sī placet

pleasure *n.* voluptās, -ātis *f.* (*enjoyment*); *n.* arbitrium, -ī *nt.* (*will; liking*)

plebeian *n.* plēbēius, -ī *m.*; **~ order** *n.* plēbs, plēbis (plēbēs, -eī) *f.*

plebiscite *n.* plēbiscītum, -ī *nt.*

plenty *n.* cōpia, -ae *f.*

plot *n.* coniūrātiō, -ōnis *f.* (*conspiracy*); *n.* agellus, -ī *m.* (*amount of land*); *n.* argūmentum, -ī *nt.* (*~ of a play*); *v.t.* coniūrō, -iūrāre, -iūrāvī, -iūrātum

plow *n.* arātrum, -ī *nt.*; *v.t.* arō, -āre, -āvī, -ātum

plug *v.t.* obtūrō, -āre, -āvī, -ātum

plum *n.* prūnum, -ī *nt.*

plumber *n.* plumbārius, -ī *m.*

plume *n.* penna, -ae *f.*

plump *adj.* pīnguis, -is, -e (*chubby*); *adj.* nitidus, -a, -um (*in good condition; sleek*)

plunder *n.* praeda, -ae *f.*; *v.d.t.* praedor, praedārī, praedātus sum

plunge *v.i.* mergō, -ere, mersī, mersum

p.m. *adj.* post merīdiem

pod *n.* siliqua, -ae *f.*

poem *n.* poēma, -atis *nt.*

poet *n.* poēta, -ae *m.*

poetry *n.* versūs, -uum *m./pl.*

point *n.* acūmen, -inis *nt.* (*tip*); *n.* caput, capitis *nt.* (*main line of reasoning*); *n.* quaestiō, -ōnis *f.* (*matter of dispute*); *n.* rēs, reī *f.* (*position; situation*); **~ out** *v.t.* mônstrō, -āre, -āvī, -ātum

pointed *adj.* praeacūtus, -a, -um

poison *n.* venēnum, -ī *nt.*; *v.t.* venēnō, -āre, -āvī, -ātum

poisonous *adj.* venēnātus, -a, -um

pole *n.* asser, asseris *m.* (*long staff*); *n.* polus, -ī *nt.* (*~ of the earth*)

police *n.* vigilēs, -ium *m./pl.*

policy *n.* ratiō, -ōnis *f.* (*plan*)

polish *n.* nītor, -ōris *m.* (*sheen*); *v.t.* poliō, -īre, -īvī, -ītum

polite *adj.* cōmis, -is, -e

political *adj.* cīvīlis, -is, -e

politics *n.* rēs pūblica; *n.* reī pūblicae *f.*

poll *n.* suffrāgium, -ī *nt.*

pollute *v.t.* polluō, -ere, polluī, pollūtum

polluted *adj.* pollūtus, -a, -um

pollution *n.* colluviō, -ōnis *f.*

pond *n.* stagnum, -ī *nt.*

pool *n.* lacūs, -ūs *m.*

poor *adj.* pauper, paupera, pauperum (*not wealthy*); *adj.* miser, misera, miserum (*pitiable*)

populace *n.* vulgus, -ī *nt.*

popular *adj.* populāris, -is, -e (*of the people*); **the ~ party** *n.* populārēs, -ium *m./pl.*

pore *n.* forāmen, -inis *nt.*

pork *n.* suilla, -ae *f.*

port *n.* portus, -ūs *m.*

porter *n.* iānitor, -ōris *m.* (*doorkeeper*)

portico *n.* porticus, -ūs *f.*

portrait *n.* imāgō, -inis *f.*

position *n.* situs, -ūs *m.* (*place; site*); *n.* sententia, -ae *f.* (*opinion*); *n.* status, -ūs *m.* (*social rank*)

positive *adj.* certus, -a, -um (*certain; sure*)

possess *v.t.* habeō, -ēre, habuī, habitum

possession *n.* possessiō, -ōnis *f.*; **take ~ of** *v.d.i.* potior, potīrī, potītus sum (+ abl. *or* + gen.)

possible *adj.* Use the verb possum; **it is ~ that** fierī potest ut (+ subjv.); **as ... as ~** quam (+ sup. adj. *or* + adv.)

possibly *adv.* fierī potest ut (+ subjv.)

post *n.* postis, -is *m.*; *n.* statiō, -ōnis *f.* (*military station*); *n.* praesidium, -ī *nt.* (*garrison; camp*); *n.* cursus pūblicus, cursūs pūblicī *m.* (*government system for communications*); *v.t.* dispōnō, -ponere, -posuī, -positum (*station troops*); *v.t.* prōpōnō, -pōnere, -posuī, -positum (*hang a notice*)

posterity *n.* posterī, -ōrum *m./pl.*

postpone *v.t.* differō, -ferre, distulī, dīlātum

pot *n.* olla, -ae *f.*

pottery *n.* fictilia, -um *nt./pl.*

pouch *n.* sacculus, -ī *m.*

pound *n.* lībra, -ae *f.*; *v.t.* tundō, -ere, tutudī, tunsum (tūsum)

pour *v.t.* fundō, -ere, fūdī, fūsum; *v.i.* fluō, -ere, flūxī, fluxum

powder *n.* pulvis, pulveris *m.*

power *n.* potestās, -ātis *f.* (*control; legal authority*); *n.* vīs, vim (acc.), vī (abl.) *f.* (*def. n.*); *n.* vīrēs, -ium *f.* (*irreg.*) (*vigor; in pl., military forces or strength*); *n.* imperium, -ī *nt.* (*jurisdiction; chief military command*); *n.* facultās, -ātis *f.* (*ability*); **heavenly ~** *n.* nūmen, -inis *nt.*

powerful *adj.* potēns, -entis (*having power or influence*); *adj.* validus, -a, -um (*physically strong; effective*)

practical *adj.* prūdēns, -entis (*sensible*); **~ly** *adv.* paene (*almost*)

practice *n.* ūsus, -ūs *m.*; *v.t.* exerceō, -ēre, -ercuī, -ercitum (*exercise; train*)

praetor *n.* praetor, -ōris *m.*

praise *n.* laus, laudis *f.*; *v.t.* laudō, -āre, -āvī, -ātum

praiseworthy *adj.* laudābilis, -is, -e

pray (for) *v.d.t.* precor, precārī, precātus sum (+ acc. of person addressed + acc. of thing prayed for *or* + **ut** or **nē** + subjv.)

prayer *n.* prex, precis *f.* (*usually used in the plural*)

precarious *adj.* incertus, -a, -um

precede *v.t.* praeeō, -īre, -īvī (-iī), -itum (*lead the way*)

precise *adj.* dēfīnītus, -a, -um

predict *v.t.* praedīcō, -dīcere, -dīxī, -dictum

prefer *v.t.* praepōnō, -pōnere, -posuī, -positum (*put one person/thing before another*); *v.t.* mālō, mālle, māluī, --- (*irreg.*) (+ infv.) (*like to do better*)

pregnant *adj.* gravidus, -a, -um

prepare *v.i.* parō, -āre, -āvī, -ātum (+ infv.)

preposition *n.* praepositiō, -ōnis *f.*

prescribe *v.t.* praescrībō, -scrībere, -scrīpsī, -scrīptum

present *n.* dōnum, -ī *nt.* (*gift*); *n.* praesentia, -ōrum *nt./pl.* (~ *circumstances*); *adj.* praesēns, -entis; *v.t.* dōnō, -āre, -āvī, -ātum (*give*); *v.t.* offerō, -ferre, obtulī, oblātum (*bring before; offer; inflict*); *v.t.* intrōdūcō, -dūcere, -dūxī, -ductum (*bring forward; introduce*); **be ~** *v.i.* adsum, -esse, -fuī, ---; **~ly** *adv.* mox

preserve *v.t.* servō, -āre, -āvī, -ātum (*keep safe*); *v.t.* condiō, -īre, -īvī, -ītum (*conserve; put up*)

press *n.* prēlum, -ī *nt.* (*for wine or oil*); *v.t.* premō, -ere, pressī, pressum (*apply physical pressure*); *v.t.* īnstō, -stāre, -stitī, -statum (*urge*)

pressure *n.* pressūra, -ae *f.* (*physical ~*)

prestige *n.* fāma, -ae *f.*

pretty *adj.* pulcher, pulchra, pulchrum (*attractive*); *adv. For adverbial use, e.g. "pretty easy," use comp. adj. form.*

prevail *v.t.* vincō, -ere, vīcī, victum (*overcome; succeed*); **~ upon** *v.t.* addūcō, -dūcere, -dūxī, -ductum (+ **ad** or **in** + acc. *or* + **ut** clause)

prevent *v.t.* prohibeō, -hibēre, -hibuī, -hibitum (+ infv.) (*restrain; prohibit; forbid*); *v.t.* impediō, -pedīre, -pedīvī, -pedītum (+ acc., or **ā/ab** or abl. *or* **nē** or **quin** or **quōminus** + subj. *or* infv.) (*hinder, obstruct, impede*)

previous *adj.* proximus, -a, -um

prey *n.* praeda, -ae *f.*; **~ upon** *v.d.t.* praedor, praedārī, praedātus sum

price *n.* pretium, -ī *nt.*; **at a high ~** magnī (pretiī); **at a low ~** parvī (pretiī)

priceless *adj.* pretiōsissimus, -a, -um

pride *n.* superbia, -ae *f.*

priest(ess) *n.* sacerdōs, -ōtis *m./f.*

primary *adj.* prīncipālis, -is, -e (*first*); *adj.* praecipuus, -a, -um (*chief*)

prime *adj.* optimus, -a, -um *m.*

prince *n.* rēx, rēgis *m.*; *n.* rēgulus, -ī *m.*

princess *n.* rēgīna, -ae *f.* (*a ruler*); *n.* rēgis fīlia, rēgis fīliae *f.* (*king's daughter*)

principal *adj.* praecipuus, -a, -um

principle *n.* īnstitūtum, -ī *nt.* (*rule for conduct*)

print *v.t.* imprimō, -primere, -pressī, -pressum (*imprint*)

prison *n.* carcer, carceris *m.*

prisoner *n.* reus, -ī *m.*, rea, -ae *f.* (*legal ~*); *n.* captīvus, -ī *m.*, captīva, -ae *f.* (*~ of war*)

private *adj.* sēcrētus, -a, -um (*secluded*); *adj.* prīvātus, -a, -um (*not of a* *public character*); *adj.* proprius, -a, -um (*one's own*); **~ property** *n.* rēs familiāris, reī familiāris *f.*

privilege *n.* iūs, iūris *nt.*

prize *n.* praemium, -ī *nt.*

probable *adj.* vērī similis, -is, -e

probably *adv.* vērī similiter

problem *n.* quaestiō, -ōnis *f.*

procedure *n.* ratiō, -ōnis *f.*

proceed *v.i.* pergō, -ere, perrēxī, perrēctum (*go ahead*); *v.t.* agō, -ere, ēgī, actum (*act*)

process *n.* ratiō, -ōnis *f.*

procession *n.* pompa, -ae *f.*

proclaim *v.t.* ēdīcō, -dīcere, -dīxī, -dictum (*announce; make public*); *v.t.* patefaciō, -facere, -fēcī, -factum (*reveal*)

produce *v.t.* prōferō, -ferre, -tulī, -lātum (*bring forward*); *v.t.* pariō, -ere, peperī, partum (*give birth; bear offspring*); *v.t.* efficiō, -ficere, -fēcī, -fectum (*cause*)

profession *n.* mūnus, -eris *nt.* (*employment*); *n.* professiō, -ōnis *f.* (*declaration*)

profit *n.* lucrum, -ī *nt.*; *v.i.* prōsum, prōdesse, prōfuī, --- (+ dat. *or* + infv.)

profound *adj.* altus, -a, -um (*deep*); *adj.* doctus, -a, -um (*learned*)

progress *n.* iter, itineris *nt.* (*journey*); *n.* prōgressus, -ūs *m.* (*improvement*); *v.d.i.* prōgredior, prōgredī, prōgressus sum

prohibit *v.t.* veto, -āre, -uī, -itum (+ infv. + acc.)

prohibition *n.* interdictum, -ī *nt.*

project *n.* cōnsilium, -ī *nt.*

promenade *n.* ambulatiō, -ōnis *f.* (*a walking about*); *n.* xystus, -ī *m.* (*a walkway*)

promise *n.* prōmissum, -ī; *v.d.t.* polliceor, pollicērī, pollicitus sum (+ acc. + infv.); **break a ~** *v.t.* fallō, -ere, fefellī, falsum

pronounce *v.t.* prōnūntiō, -nūntiāre, -nūntiāvī, -nūntiātum (*state; declare*); *v.t.* ēnūntiō, -nūntiāre, -nūntiāvī, -nūntiātum (*articulate*)

pronunciation *n.* locūtiō, -ōnis *f.*

proof *n.* indicium, -ī *nt.* (*evidence*); *n.* experientia, -ae *f.* (*test; trial; experiment*)

propel *v.t.* prōpellō, -pellere, -pulī, -pulsum

proper *adj.* decōrus, -a, -um (*seemly; right*); *adj.* proprius, -a, -um (*one's own*); *adj.* aptus, -a, -um (*fit; suitable*)

property *n.* bona, -ōrum *nt./pl.* (*what is possessed*); *n.* rēs familiāris, reī familiāris *f.* (*private ~*)

prophecy *n.* ōrāculum, -ī *nt.*

prophesy *v.i.* praedīcō, -dīcere, -dīxī, -dictum

prophet *n.* vātes, -is *m./f.*

proposal *n.* condiciō, -ōnis *f.*

propose *v.t.* in animō habeō, -ēre, habuī, habitum (*have in mind*); *v.t.* ferō, ferre, tulī, lātum (*make a motion*)

proprietor *n.* dominus, -ī *m.*

prose *n.* ōrātiō solūta, ōrātiōnis solūtae *f.*

prospective *adj.* futūrus, -a, -um

prosper *v.i.* flōreō, -ēre, flōruī, ---

prosperity *n.* rēs secundae, rērum secundārum *f./pl.*

prosperous *adj.* secundus, -a, -um

prostitute *n.* scortum, -ī *nt.*

protect *v.d.t.* tueor, tuērī, tūtus sum

protection *n.* praesidium, -ī *nt.*

protest *v.d.t.* obtestor, obtestārī, obtestātus sum (*make a solemn declaration; call as witness*); ~ **against** *v.t.* intercēdō, -cēdere, -cessī, -cessum (*oppose; withstand*)

proud *adj.* superbus, -a, -um

prove *v.t.* probō, -āre, -āvī, -ātum; ~ **oneself** *v.t.* praebeō, -bēre, -buī, -bitum (+ refl. pron.)

proverb *n.* prōverbium, -ī *nt.*

provide *v.t.* parō, -āre, -āvī, -ātum (*gather beforehand*); *v.t.* praebeō, -bēre, -buī, -bitum (*supply*); **provide against** *v.t.* caveō, -ēre, cāvī, cautum (+ **nē** + subjv.)

provided that (**not**) *conj.* (dum)modo (nē) (+ subjv.)

province *n.* prōvincia, -ae *f.*

prudent *adj.* prōvidus, -a, -um

public *adj.* pūblicus, -a, -um (*not private; relating to the state*); *adj.* nōtus, -a, -um (*generally known*)

publicity *n.* celebritās, -ātis *f.*

publish *v.t.* efferō, -ferre, extulī, ēlātum (*make public*); *v.t.* ēdō, -ere, -didī, -ditum (~ *a book, etc.*)

pull *v.t.* trahō, -ere, trāxī, trāctum (*drag*); *v.t.* carpō, -ere, carpsī, carptum (*pluck*); ~ **down** *v.t.* ēvertō, -vertere, -vertī, -versum

pulley *n.* trochlea (troclea), -ae *f.*

pulse *n.* pulsus, -ūs *m.*

pump *n.* antlia, -ae *f.*; *v.t.* exhauriō, -haurīre, -hausī, -haustum

pumpkin *n.* pepō, -onis *m.*

punch *n.* ictus, -ūs *m.* (*a blow*); *v.t.* percutiō, -cutere, -cussī, -cussum (*hit*)

punctuate *v.t.* interpungō, -pungere, -punxī (-pupugī), -pūnctum
punctuation *n.* interpūnctiō, -ōnis *f.*
puncture *n.* pūnctum, -ī *nt.*
punish *v.t.* pūniō, -īre, -īvī, -ītum
punishment *n.* poena, -ae *f.*
pupil *n.* discipulus, -ī *m.*; *n.* discipula, -ae *f.*
puppet *n.* pūpa, -ae *f.*
puppy *n.* catulus, -ī *m.*
purchase *n.* ēmptiō, -ōnis *f.* (*act of purchasing*); *n.* merx, mercis *f.* (*thing bought*); *v.t.* emō, -ere, ēmī, ēmptum
pure *adj.* pūrus, -a, -um (*physically and morally innocent*); *adj.* castus, -a, -um (*chaste*); *adj.* merus, -a, -um (*unmixed; undiluted*)
purification *n.* purgātiō, -ōnis *f.* (*physical cleaning*); *n.* lūstrātiō, -ōnis *f.* (*religious rite*)
purify *v.t.* purgō, -āre, -āvī, -ātum (*purge; cleanse of dirt*); *v.t.* lūstrō, -āre, -āvī, -ātum (~ *with religious ceremony*)
purple *adj.* purpureus, -a, -um
purpose *n.* prōpositum, -ī *nt.* (*end proposed or desired*); **on** ~ *adv.* cōnsultō
purse *n.* marsūpium, -ī *nt.*
pursue *v.d.t.* sequor, sequī, secūtus sum
pus *n.* pūs, pūris *nt.*
push *n.* impulsus, -ūs *m.*; *v.t.* impellō, -pellere, -pulī, -pulsum (*thrust away*)
put *v.t.* pōnō, -ere, posuī, positum; ~ **on clothes** *v.t.* induō, -duere, -duī, -dūtum; ~ **out** *v.t.* exstinguō, -stinguere, -stīnxī, -stīnctum (*extinguish*)
puzzle *n.* nōdus, -ī *m.* (*a knotty point*); *v.t.* cōnfundō, -fundere, -fūdī, -fūsum
pyramid *n.* pȳramis, -idis *f.*

Q

quack *n.* circūlātor, -ōris *m.* (*fake doctor*)
quaestor *n.* quaestor, -ōris *m.*
quail *n.* coturnīx, coturnīcis *f.*
quaint *adj.* mīrus, -a, -um (*unusual*); *adj.* antīquus, -a, -um (*old-fashioned*)
qualified *adj.* aptus, -a, -um
qualify *v.t.* īnstruō, -struere, -strūxī, -strūctum
quality *n.* aestimātiō, -ōnis *f.* (*value*); *n.* nātūra, -ae *f.* (*natural property*)
qualm *n.* cōnscientia, -ae *f.* (*conscience*); *n.* nausea, -ae *f.* (*physical sensation*)
quantity *n.* cōpia, -ae *f.* (*large* ~); *n.* numerus, -ī *m.* (*amount*)

quarrel *n.* iurgium, -ī *nt.*; *v.i.* iurgō, -āre, -āvī, -ātum
quarry *n.* praeda, -ae (*prey*); *n.* lapicīdīnae, -ārum *f./pl.* (*excavation*)
quart *n.* duo sextāriī, duorum sextāriōrum *m./pl.*
quarter *n.* quārta pars, quārtae partis *f.* (*one-fourth part*); *n.* regiō, -ōnis *f.*
   (*region*)
queasy *adj.* nauseāns, -antis
queen *n.* rēgīna, -ae *f.*
queer *adj.* īnsolitus, -a, -um (*unusual*)
query *n.* quaestiō, -ōnis *f.*; *v.t.* quaerō, -ere, quaesīvī, quaesītum
question *v.t.* rogō, -āre, -āvī, -ātum
quick *adj.* celer, celeris, celere (*swift*); *adj.* vīvus, -a, -um (*alive*); *adj.* agilis,
   -is, -e (*active; nimble; prompt*); *adj.* acūtus, -a, -um (*~-witted*)
quiet *n.* quiēs, -ētis *f.*; *adj.* tacitus, -a, -um (*silent*); *adj.* tranquillus, -a, -um
   (*calm; still; undisturbed*); *v.i.* quiēscō, -ere, quiēvī, quiētum (*rest; keep ~;*
   be at peace)
quilt *n.* strāgulum, -ī *nt.*
quit *v.i.* dēcēdō, -cēdere, -cessī, -cessum (*withdraw; resign*); *v.i.* dēsistō,
   -sistere, -stitī, -stitum (+ infv.) (*cease*)
quite *adv.* omnīnō (*completely*); *adv.* satis (*fairly*)
quota *n.* rāta pars, rātae partis *f.*
quote *v.t.* prōferō, -ferre, -tulī, -lātum

R

rabbit *n.* cunīculus, -ī *m.*
race *n.* cursus, -ūs *m.* (*contest of running*); *n.* genus, -eris *nt.* (*family; stock*);
   v.i. certō, -āre, -āvī, -ātum
racetrack *n.* stadium, -ī *nt.*
rack *n.* tormentum, -ī *nt.* (*instrument of torture*)
racket *n.* strepitus, -ūs *m.* (*noise*)
radiance *n.* fulgor, -ōris *m.*
radiant *adj.* radiāns, -antis
radiate *v.i.* fulgeō, -ēre, fulsī, ---
radical *adj.* novārum rērum cupidus, -a, -um (*politics*); *adj.* innātus, -a, -um
   (*original; innate*)
radius *n.* radius, -ī *m.*
raft *n.* ratis, -is *f.*
rag *n.* pannus, -ī *m.*
rage *n.* īra, -ae *f.*

ragged *adj.* pannōsus, -a, -um

raid *n.* incursiō, -ōnis *f.*; *v.t.* incursō, -cursāre, -cursāvī, -cursātum

rail *n.* longurius, -ī *m.*

railing *n.* saepimentum, -ī *nt.*

rain *n.* pluvia, -ae *f.* (*gentle* ~); *n.* imber, imbris *m.* (*heavy* ~); *v.i.* pluit,
   pluere, pluit, --- (*imp.*)

rainbow *n.* arcus, -ūs *m.*

rainy *adj.* pluvius, -a, -um

raise *v.t.* tollō, -ere, sustulī, sublātum (*lift up; exalt*); *v.t.* exstruō, -struere,
   -strūxī, -strūctum (*build; erect*); *v.t.* ēvehō, -vehere, -vexī, -vectum (*elevate in rank or position*); *v.t.* augeō, -ēre, auxī, auctum (*increase*); *v.t.*
   excitō, -citāre, -citāvī, -citātum (*stir up emotions*); *v.t.* cōnscrībō,
   -scrībere, -scrīpsī, -scrīptum (*collect; enlist*); ~ **children** *v.t.* ēducō,
   -ducāre, -ducāvī, -ducātum

raisin *n.* acinus passus, acinī passī *m.*

rake *n.* rastrum, -ī *nt.*; *v.t.* rādō, -ere, rāsī, rāsum

rally *v.i.* convalēscō, -valēscere, -valuī, --- (*regain health or strength*);
   ~ **troops** *v.t.* restituō, -stituere, -stitī, -stitūtum

ramble *v.d.i.* vagor, vagārī, vagātus sum

rampart *n.* agger, aggeris *m.*

rancid *adj.* rancidus, -a, -um

random *adj.* fōrtuītus, -a, -um

range *n.* ordō, -inis *m.* (*line; row*); *n.* iactus, -ūs *m.* (*reach of a missile*);
   mountain ~ *n.* montēs, -ium *m./pl.*

rank *n.* ordō, -inis *m.* (*row; line of soldiers; class*); **high** ~ *n.* dignitās, -ātis *f.*;
   v.t. numerō, -āre, -āvī, -ātum

ransack *v.t.* dīripiō, -ripere, -ripuī, -reptum

ransom *n.* pretium, -ī *nt.* (*money paid*); *n.* redēmptiō, -ōnis *f.* (*act of* ~); *v.t.*
   redimō, -imere, -ēmī, -ēmptum

rape *n.* raptus, -ūs *m.*; *v.t.* vim offerō, offerre, obtulī, oblātum (+ dat. Of
   person raped)

rapid *adj.* rapidus, -a, -um

rare *adj.* rārus, -a, -um

rash *n.* ēruptiō, -ōnis *f.;adj.* temerārius, -a, -um

rashness *n.* temeritās, -ātis *f.*

rat *n.* mūs, mūris *m./f.*

rate *n.* pretium, -ī *nt.* (*price*)

rather *adv.* magis; *adv.* To express degree, e.g. "rather slowly," use comp. adj.
   or adv.

ratification *n.* sanctiō, -ōnis *f.*

ratify *v.t.* sanciō, -īre, sānxī, sānctum

rational *n.* ratiōne praeditus, -a, -um

rations *n./pl.* cibāria, -ōrum *nt./pl.*

ravine *n.* vallis (vallēs) arta, vallis artae *f.*

raw *adj.* crūdus, -a, -um (*uncooked; unhealed*); *adj.* rudis, -is, -e
(*inexperienced*)

ray *n.* radius, -ī *m.*

razor *n.* novācula, -ae *f.*

reach *n.* trāctus, -ūs *m.* (*region; territory*); *n.* iactus, -ūs *m.* (*reach of a
missile*); *n.* captus, -ūs *m.* (*capacity of mind*); *v.i.* pertineō, -tinēre, -tinuī,
--- (*extend*); *v.i.* perveniō, -venīre, -vēnī, -ventum (*arrive*)

read *v.t.* legō, -ere, lēgī, lectum

reader *n.* lector, -ōris *m.*

reading *n.* lectiō, -ōnis *m.*

ready *adj.* parātus, -a, -um; **be ~** *v.i.* praestō sum, esse, fuī, futūrus

real *adj.* vērus, -a, -um; **~ly** *adv.* vērē

reality *n.* rēs, reī *f.*

realize *v.t.* intellegō, -legere, -lēxī, -lēctum

reap *v.t.* metō, -ere, messuī, messum

reappear *v.i.* redeō, -īre, -īvī (-iī), -itum

rear *n.* tergum, -ī *nt.*; *adj.* novissimus, -a, um (*of an army on the march or
engaged in battle*)

reason *n.* ratio, -ōnis *f.* (*rational faculty of the mind; good reason or argument*); *n.* causa, -ae *f.* (*cause*); *v.d.i.* ratiōcinor, ratiōcinārī, ratiōcinātus
sum

reasonable *adj.* prūdēns, -entis (*judicious*); *adj.* aequus, -a, -um (*fair;
equitable*)

reassure *v.t.* cōnfirmō, -firmāre, -firmāvī, -firmātum

rebel *adj.* rebellis, -is, -e; *v.i.* rebellō, -bellāre, -bellāvī, -bellātum

rebellion *n.* rebelliō, -ōnis *f.*

rebuff *v.t.* repellō, -pellere, reppulī, repulsum

recall *v.t.* revocō, -vocāre, -vocāvī, -vocātum

receipt *n.* acceptiō, -ōnis *f.* (*act of receiving*); *n.* acceptum, -ī *nt.* (*payment*)

receive *v.t.* accipiō, -cipere, -cēpī, -ceptum (*accept; take into possession; ~ a
guest*)

receiver *n.* receptor, -ōris *m.*

recent *adj.* recēns, -entis; **~ly** *adv.* nūper

reception *n.* aditus, -ūs *m.* (*access*); *n.* hospitium, -ī *nt.* (*~ of guests*)

reciprocity *n.* vicissitūdō, -inis *f.*

recite *v.t.* recitō, -āre, -āvī, -ātum

reckon *v.t.* numerō, -āre, -āvī, -ātum

recognition *n.* cognitiō, -ōnis *f.*

recognize *v.t.* cognōscō, -gnōscere, -gnōvī, -gnitum

recommend *v.t.* commendō, -mendāre, -mendāvī, -mendātum

recommendation *n.* commendātiō, -ōnis *f.*

recompense *n.* praemium, -ī *nt.; v.d.t.* remūneror, remūnerārī, remūnerātus sum

reconcile *v.t.* reconciliō, -conciliāre, -conciliāvī, -conciliātum

reconciliation *n.* reconciliātiō, -ōnis *f.*

record *n.* monumentum, -ī *nt.* (*tradition*; *chronicle*; *monument*); **public ~s** *n./pl.* tabulae, -ārum *f./pl.; v.t.* referō, -ferre, rettulī, relātum

recover *v.t.* recipiō, -cipere, -cēpī, -ceptum

recreation *n.* requiēs, -ētis *f.* (*relaxation*)

recruit *n.* tīrō, -ōnis *m.; v.t.* cōnscrībō, -scrībere, -scrīpsī, -scrīptum

recuperate *v.i.* convalēscō, -valēscere, -valuī, ---

recurrence *n.* reditus, -ūs *m.*

red *adj.* rūfus, -a, -um

reddish *adj.* subrūfus, -a, -um

redness *n.* rubor, -ōris *m.*

reduce *v.t.* minuō, -ere, -uī, -ūtum (*make small*; *weaken*); *v.t.* redigō, -igere, -ēgī, -āctum (*compel*; *subdue*)

reduction *n.* dēminūtiō, -ōnis *f.* (*diminution*); *n.* expugnātiō, -ōnis *f.* (*subjugation*)

reed *n.* harundō, -inis *f.*

refer *v.t.* referō, -ferre, rettulī, relātum

reference *n.* ratiō, -ōnis *f.*

refill *v.t.* repleō, -plēre, -plēvī, -plētum

refine *v.t.* pūrgō, -āre, -āvī, -ātum (*purify*); *v.t.* poliō, -īre, -īvī, -ītum (*polish*; *improve*)

reflect *v.t.* reddō, -dere, -didī, -ditum (~ *light*); **~ on** *v.d.t., v.d.i.* meditor, meditārī, meditātus sum

reform *v.t.* reficiō, -ficere, -fēcī, -fectum (*make or form anew*); *v.t.* corrigō, -rigere, -rēxī, -rēctum (*amend*)

refresh *v.t.* recreō, -creāre, -creāvī, -creātum

refuge *n.* perfugium, -ī *nt.;* **take ~ in** *v.i.* cōnfugiō, -fugere, -fūgī, --- (+ **in** or **ad** + acc.)

refugee *n.* profugus, -ī *m.*

refund *v.t.* reddō, -dere, -didī, -ditum
refusal *n.* repulsa, -ae *f.*
refuse *n.* pūrgāmentum, -ī *nt.*; *v.t.* negō, -āre, -āvī, -ātum (*deny a request*);
    v.t. recūsō, -āre, -āvī, -ātum (*reject an offer*); *v.i.* nōlō, nōlle, nōluī, ---
    (*be unwilling*)
regard *n.* ratiō, -ōnis *f.* (*consideration*); *n.* honōs (honor), -ōris *m.* (*esteem*);
    v.d.t. intueor, intuērī, intuitus sum (*look upon; consider*); **~ as** *v.t.* dūcō,
    -ere, dūxī, ductum
regarding *prep.* dē (+ abl.)
region *n.* regiō, -ōnis *f.*
register *n.* tabulae pūblicae, tabulārum pūblicārum *f./pl.*; *v.t.* perscrībō,
    -scrībere, -scrīpsī, -scrīptum
regret *n.* dēsīderium, -ī *nt.*; *v.t.* paenitet, paenitēre, paenituit, --- (*imp.*) (+
    acc. of person + gen. of thing)
regular *adj.* certus, -a, -um (*consistent*); *adj.* ūsitātus, -a, -um (*usual*)
regulation *n.* ordinātiō, -ōnis *f.* (*act of arranging*); *n.* praeceptum, -ī *nt.* (*rule*)
rehearse *v.t.* recitō, -āre, -āvī, -ātum (*practice reciting*)
reimburse *v.t.* rependō, -pendere, -pendī, -pēnsum
rein *n.* hābēna, -ae *f.*
reject *v.t.* negō, -āre, -āvī, -ātum (*deny a request*); *v.t.* abiciō, -icere, -iēcī,
    -iectum (*cast off*)
rejection *n.* rēiectiō, -ōnis *f.*
relapse *v.d.i.* relābor, relābī, relapsus sum
relate *v.t.* nārrō, -āre, -āvī, -ātum
relation *n.* nārrātiō, -ōnis *f.* (*narrative*); *n.* propinquus, -ī *m.*, propinqua, -ae
    f. (*relative*); *n.* adfinis, -is *m./f.* (*relative by marriage*); *n.* cōgnātus, -ī *m.*,
    cōgnāta, -ae *f.* (*blood-relation*)
relationship *n.* propinquitās, -ātis *f.*
relative *n.* adfinis, -is *m./f.* (*~ by marriage*); *n.* cōgnātus, -ī *m.*, cōgnāta, -ae
    f. (*blood-relation*)
relax *v.i.* relanguēscō, -languēscere, -languī, ---
relaxation *n.* ōtium, -ī *nt.* (*leisure*); *n.* remīssiō, -ōnis *f.* (*abatement*)
release *n.* līberātiō, -ōnis *f.*; *v.t.* exsolvō, -solvere, -solvī, -solūtum
reliable *adj.* fīdus, -a, -um
relief *n.* levātiō, -ōnis *f.* (*alleviation*); *n.* auxilium, -ī *nt.* (*assistance*)
relieve *v.t.* levō, -āre, -āvī, -ātum (*alleviate*); *v.i.* succurrō, -currere, -currī,
    -cursum (+ dat.) (*assist*)
religion *n.* religiō, -ōnis *f.*
religious *adj.* religiōsus, -a, -um

rely *v.t.* cōnfīdō, -fīdere, -fīsus sum (+ dat. of person relied on *or* + abl. of thing relied on)

remain *v.i.* māneō, -ēre, mānsī, mānsum (*last; stay; tarry*); *v.i.* restō, -stāre, -stitī, --- (*be left over*)

remaining *adj.* reliquus, -a, -um

remark *n.* dicta, -ōrum *nt./pl.*; *v.i.* dīcō, -ere, dīxī, dictum

remedy *n.* remedium, -ī *nt.*; *v.t.* sānō, -āre, -āvī, -ātum

remember *v.t.* meminī, meminisse, --- (*def. v.*) (+ gen. or acc. of person or thing)

remind *v.t.* admoneō, -monēre, -monuī, -monitum

remit *v.t.* remittō, -mittere, -mīsī, -missum

remorse, feel ~ *v.t.* paenitet, paenitēre, paenituit, --- (*imp. v.*) (+ acc. of person feeling remorse + gen. of thing regretted)

remote *adj.* remōtus, -a, -um (*far away*); *adj.* ultimus, -a, -um (*farthest*)

remove *v.t.* removeō, -movēre, -mōvī, -mōtum

renew *v.t.* renovō, -novāre, -novāvī, -novatum

renewal *n.* renovātiō, -ōnis *f.*

renounce *v.t.* renūntiō, -nūntiāre, -nūntiāvī, -nūntiātum

renovate *v.t.* renovō, -novāre, -novāvī, -novatum

renovation *n.* renovātiō, -ōnis *f.*

rent *n.* scissūra, -ae *f.* (*tear*); *n.* vectīgal, -ālis *nt.* (*payment for occupation or use*); *v.t.* locō, -āre, -āvī, -ātum (*let out*); *v.t.* condūcō, -dūcere, -dūxī, -ductum (*hire*)

repair *v.t.* reficiō, -ficere, -fēcī, -fectum

repeat *v.t.* iterō, -āre, -āvī, -ātum

repel *v.t.* repellō, -pellere, reppulī, repulsum

repetition *n.* iterātiō, -ōnis *f.*

replace *v.t.* repōnō, -pōnere, -posuī, -positum (*put back*); *v.t.* substituō, -stituere, -stituī, -stitūtum (*put something in place of another*)

reply *n.* respōnsum, -ī *nt.*; *v.i.* respondeō, -spondēre, -spondī, -spōnsum

report *n.* renūntiātiō, -ōnis *f.* (*official announcement*); *n.* fāma, -ae *f.* (*rumor; reputation*); *n.* fragor, -ōris *m.* (*loud noise*); *v.t.* renūntiō, -nūntiāre, -nūntiāvī, -nūntiātum

represent *v.t.* exprimō, -primere, -pressī, -pressum (*portray*); *v.t.* prōpōnō, -pōnere, -posuī, -positum (*point out*)

representative *n.* prōcūrātor, -ōris *m.* (*agent of another*)

repress *v.t.* cohibeō, -hibēre, -hibuī, -hibitum

reprimand *v.t.* reprehendō, -prehendere, -prehendī, -prehensum

reprisal *n.* tāliō, -ōnis *f.*

reproduce *v.t.* regenerō, -generāre, -generāvī, -generātum
republic *n.* rēspūblica, -ae *f.*
republican *adj.* populāris, -is, -e
reputation *n.* fāma, -ae *f.*
request *n.* precēs, -um *f./pl.; v.d.t.* precor, precārī, precātus sum
require *v.t.* poscō, -ere, poposcī, --- (*demand*); *v.t.* requīrō, -quīrere, -quīsīvī, -quīsītum (*need*)
rescue *n.* līberātiō, -ōnis *f.; v.t.* līberō, -āre, -āvī, -ātum (*deliver; release*); *v.t.* ēripiō, -ripere, -ripuī, -reptum (*snatch from*)
research *n.* investīgātiō, -ōnis *f.* (*inquiry*); *v.t.* investīgō, -vestīgāre, -vestīgāvī, -vestīgātum (*search into; discover*)
resemblance *n.* similitūdō, -inis *f.*
resemble *v.i.* similis, -is, -e sum, esse, fuī, --- (+ *dat.*)
resent *v.t.* aegrē ferō, -ferre, -tulī, -lātum
reserve *n.* subsidia, -ōrum *nt./pl.* (*troops*); *n.* pudor, -ōris *m.* (*sense of modesty; propriety*); *v.t.* servō, -āre, -āvī, -ātum
reserved *adj.* reconditus, -a, -um (*reticent*); *adj.* rēservātus, -a, -um (*kept back*)
reservoir *n.* lācus, -ūs *m.*
reside *v.i.* habitō, -āre, -āvī, -ātum
residence *n.* domus, -ūs *f.*
residue *n.* reliquiae, -ārum *f./pl.*
resign *v.t.* abdīcō, -dīcere, -dīxī, -dictum
resignation *n.* abdicātiō, -ōnis *f.* (*act of yielding*)
resigned, be ~ *v.i.* animō aequō sum, esse, fuī, --- (*be acquiescent*)
resin *n.* rēsīna, -ae *f.*
resist *v.i.* resistō, -sistere, -stitī, ---
respect *n.* honōs (*honor*), -ōris *m.; v.d.t.* vereor, verērī, veritus sum
respond *v.i.* respondeō, -spondēre, -spondī, -spōnsum
response *n.* respōnsum, -ī *nt.*
responsible *adj.* reus, -a, -um
rest *n.* quies, -ētis *f.* (*repose*); *v.i.* quiēscō, -ere, quiēvī, quiētum; **the ~** *adj.* cēterī, -ae, -a *pl.*(*the others*); *adj.* reliquus, -a, -um (*remainder*)
restless *adj.* inquiētus, -a, -um
restore *v.t.* reddō, -dere, -didī, -ditum (*give back*); *v.t.* rēstituō, -stituere, -stituī, -stitūtum (*reinstate; replace*)
restrain *v.t.* coerceō, -ercēre, -ercuī, -ercitum
restrict *v.t.* circumscrībō, -scrībere, -scrīpsī, -scrīptum
restriction *n.* modus, -ī *m.*

result *n.* ēventus, -ūs *m.*; **~ in** *v.i.* ēveniō, -venīre, -vēnī, -ventum

resume *v.t.* repetō, -petere, -petīvī, -petītum

retailer *n.* caupō, -ōnis *m.*

retain *v.t.* teneō, -ēre, tenuī, tentum

retire *v.i.* recēdō, -cēdere, -cessī, -cessum (*go back or away*)

retired *adj.* remōtus, -a, -um (*secluded*)

retribution *n.* poena, -ae *f.*

return *n.* reditus, -ūs *m.* (*journey back*); *n.* restitūtiō, -ōnis *f.* (*restoring*); *v.i.* redeō, -īre, -īvī (-iī), -itum (*come back*); *v.t.* reddō, -dere, -didī, -ditum (*give back*)

reveal *v.t.* patefaciō, -facere, -fēcī, -factum

revelation *n.* patefactiō, -ōnis *f.*

revenge *n.* ultiō, -ōnis *f.*; *v.d.t.* ulcīscor, ulcīscī, ultus sum

revenue *n.* vectīgal, -ālis *nt.*

revere *v.d.t.* revereor, -verērī, -veritus sum

reverent *adj.* pius, -a, -um

reverse *n.* contrārium, -ī *nt.* (*change to the opposite*); *n.* clādēs, -is *f.* (*military defeat*); *adj.* contrārius, -a, -um; *v.t.* invertō, -vertere, -vertī, -versum

review *n.* recognitiō, -ōnis *f.*; *v.t.* recēnseō, -cēnsēre, -cēnsuī, -cēnsum

revise *v.t.* recēnseō, -censēre, -censuī, -censum (*go over; examine*); *v.t.* corrigō, -rigere, -rēxī, -rēctum (*correct; amend*)

revive *v.t.* recreō, -creāre, -creāvī, -creātum

revoke *v.t.* abrogō, -rogāre, -rogāvī, -rogātum

revolt *n.* dēfectiō, -ōnis *f.*; *v.i.* dēficiō, -ficere, -fēcī, -fectum

revolution *n.* rēs novae, rērum novārum *f./pl.* (*political*); *n.* conversiō, -ōnis *f.* (*going or turning around*)

revolve *v.i.* revolvōr, revolvī, revolūtus sum

reward *n.* praemium, -ī *nt.*; *v.d.t.* remūneror, remūnerārī, remūnerātus sum

rhythm *n.* numerus, -ī *m.*

rib *n.* costa, -ae *f.*

ribbon *n.* vitta, -ae *f.*

rich *adj.* dīves, dīvitis

riches *n/pl.* dīvitiae, -ārum *f./pl.*

rickety *adj.* īnstabilis, -is, -e

riddle *n.* aenigma, -matis *nt.*

ride *v.t.* equitō, -āre, -āvī, -ātum (*on horseback*)

rider *n.* eques, equitis *m.*

ridge *n.* iugum, -ī *nt.* (*mountain ~*)

ridiculous *adj.* ridiculus, -a, -um
right *n.* fās *nt.* (*indecl.*) (*morally right*); *n.* iūs, iūris *nt.* (*justice*); *adj.* dexter, dextra (dextera), dextrum (*~ hand*); *adj.* rēctus, -a, -um (*correct*); **~ly** *adv.* rēctē (*correctly*)
rigid *adj.* rigidus, -a, -um
rim *n.* labrum, -ī *nt.*
rind *n.* crūsta, -ae *f.*
ring *n.* ānulus, -ī *m.*; *v.t., v.i.* tinniō, -īre, -īvī, ---
riot *n.* turba, -ae *f.*
rip *v.t.* scindō, -ere, scidī, scissum
ripe *adj.* mātūrus, -a, -um
rise *n.* ortus, -ūs *m.* (*ascending; origin*); *v.i.* surgō, surgere, surrēxī, surrēctum (*get up or stand up*); *v.d.i.* orior, orīrī, ortus sum (*become visible; spring from; start*)
risk *n.* perīculum, -ī *nt.*; *v.d.t., v.d.i.* perīclitor, perīclitārī, perīclitātus sum
rival *n.* aemulus, -ī *m.*; *v.d.t., v.d.i.* aemulor, aemulārī, aemulātus sum
rivalry *n.* aemulātiō, -ōnis *f.*
river *n.* flūmen, -inis *nt.*
road *n.* via, -ae *f.*
roar *n.* fremitus, -ūs *m.*; *v.i.* fremō, -ere, -uī, ---
roast *adj.* assus, -a, -um; *v.t.* torreō, -ēre, -uī, tostum
rob *v.t.* prīvō, -āre, -āvī, -ātum
robber *n.* latrō, -ōnis *m.*
robbery *n.* latrōcinium, -ī *nt.*
robe *n.* vestis, -is *f.*
rock *n.* saxum, -ī *nt.*; *v.t.* agitō, -āre, -āvī, -ātum
rocky *adj.* scopulōsus, -a, -um
rod *n.* virga, -ae *f.*
roll *n.* volūmen, -minis *nt.* (*scroll of writing*); *v.t.* volvō, -ere, volvī, volūtum
romance *n.* fābula, -ae *f.* (*love story*)
roof *n.* tēctum, -ī *nt.*
room *n.* spatium, -ī *nt.* (*space*); *n.* conclāve, -is *nt.* (*chamber*)
rooster *n.* gallus, -ī *m.*
root *n.* rādīx, -dīcis *f.*
rope *n.* fūnis, -is *m.*
rose *n.* rosa, -ae *f.*; *adj.* roseus, -a, -um; **~bush** *n.* rosa, -ae *f.*
rot *v.i.* pūtēscō, -ere, pūtuī, ---
rotten *adj.* pūtridus, -a, -um
rouge *n.* fūcus, -ī *m.*

rough *adj.* asper, aspera, asperum (*uneven; rugged; bumpy; harsh*); *adj.* horridus, -a, -um (*bristling*); *adj.* incultus, -a, -um (*unpolished; uneducated*); *adj.* rudis, -is, -e (*in a natural state; unpolished*); *adj.* procellōsus, -a, -um (*of weather*)

round *n.* rotundus, -a, -um

routine *n.* ūsus, -ūs *m.*

row *n.* ordō, -inis *m.* (*line*); *n.* turba, -ae *f.* (*riot*); *v.t., v.i.* rēmigō, -āre, -āvī, -ātum (~ *a boat*)

royal *adj.* rēgius, -a, -um (*kingly*); *adj.* rēgālis, -is, -e (*kingly; worthy of a king*)

rub *v.t.* fricō, -āre, fricuī, frictum; ~ **out** *v.t.* dēleō, -ēre, -ēvī, -ētum

ruby *n.* carbunculus, ī *m.*

rucksack *n.* sarcina, -ae *f.*

rudder *n.* gubernāculum, -ī *nt.*

rude *adj.* rudis, -is, -e (*unfinished; unpolished; ignorant*); *adj.* asper, aspera, asperum (*ill-mannered*)

rug *n.* strāgulum, -ī *nt.*

ruin *n.* exitium, -ī *nt.* (*utter destruction*); *n.* ruīnae, -ārum *f./pl.* (*broken or collapsed building/s*); *v.t.* perdō, -ere, -didī -ditum

rule *n.* praeceptum, -ī *nt.* (*regulation*); *n.* imperium, -ī *nt.* (*government*); *n.* norma, -ae *f.* (*standard*); *v.t.* regō, -ere, rēxī, rēctum

ruler *n.* rēctor, -ōris *m.* (*one who rules*); *n.* rēgula, -ae *f.* (*measuring implement*)

rumble *n.* murmur, murmuris *nt.*

rumor *n.* rūmor, -ōris *m.*

run *n.* cursus, -ūs *m.*; *v.i.* currō, -ere, cucurrī, cursum

runner *n.* cursor, -ōris *m.*

rush *n.* impetus, -ūs *m.* (*running; dash*); *n.* scirpus, -ī *m.* (*bot.*); *v.t.* ruō, -ere, ruī, rutum

rust *n.* rōbīgō, -inis *f.* (*metallic oxide; blight; smut*)

rustic *adj.* rusticus, -a, -um

rusty *adj.* aerūginōsus, -a, -um

rye *n.* secāle, -is *nt.*

S

sack *n.* saccus, -ī *m.*

sacred *adj.* sacer, sacra, sacrum

sacrifice *n.* sacrificium, -ī *nt.* (*act of formal dedication*); *n.* hostia, -ae *f.* (*victim*); *v.t.* immolō, -molāre, -molāvī, -molātum; *v.t., v.i.* sacrificō, -ficāre, -ficāvī, -ficātum

sad *adj.* trīstis, -is, -e
sadden *v.t.* contrīstō, -trīstāre, -trīstāvī, -trīstātum
saddle *v.t.* sternō, -ere, strāvī, stratum; **~ blanket** *n.* ephippium, -ī *nt.*
sadness *n.* trīstitia, -ae *f.*
safe *adj.* tūtus, -a, -um (*free from danger*); *adj.* incolumis, -is, -e (*unharmed; out of danger*)
safeguard *n.* mūnīmentum, -ī *nt.* (*defense; fortification*); *v.t.* praecaveō, -cavēre, -cāvī, -cautum
safety *n.* salŭs, -ŭtis *f.*
saffron *n.* crocus, -ī *m.*
said, it is ~ *v.* dīcitur, fertur, traditur (*imp.*)
sail *n.* vēlum, -ī *nt.; v.t., v.i.* nāvigō, -igāre, -igāvī, -igātum
sailing *n.* nāvigātiō, -ōnis *f.*
sailor *n.* nauta, -ae *m.*
saint *n.* sānctus, -ī *m.; n.* sāncta, -ae *f.*
sake, for the ~ of *prep.* grātiā (+ gen.) (*the object precedes the prep.*)
salad *n.* acētāria, -ōrum *nt./pl.*
salary *n.* mercēs, -ēdis *f.*
sale *n.* vēnditiō, -ōnis *f.* (*act of selling*); **for ~** *adj.* vēnālis, -is, -e
salesman *n.* vēnditor, -ōris *m.*
salmon *n.* salmō, -ōnis *m.*
salt *n.* sāl, salis *nt.*
salty *adj.* salsus, -a, -um
salute *v.t., v.i.* salūtō, -āre, -āvī, -ātum (*greet*)
salvation *n.* salŭs, -ŭtis *f.*
salve *n.* unguentum, -ī *nt.*
same *adj.* īdem, eadem, idem; **at the ~ time** *adv.* simul
sample *n.* exemplum, -ī *nt.*
sanctuary *n.* adytum, -ī *nt.* (*holy place*); *n.* refugium, -ī *nt.* (*place of refuge*)
sand *n.* harēna, -ae *f.*
sandal *n.* solea, -ae *f.*
sane *adj.* sānus, -a, -um
sanitary *adj.* pūrus, -a, -um (*clean*)
sap *n.* sūcus, -ī *m.*
sapphire *n.* sapphīrus, -ī *f.*
sardine *n.* sarda, -ae *f.*
satisfaction *n.* voluptās, -ātis *f.* (*state of being satisfied*); *n.* poena, -ae *f.* (*atonement for a crime*)
satisfactory *adj.* idōneus, -a, -um

satisfy *v.t.* expleō, -plēre, -plēvī, -plētum (*supply a natural desire or need*); *v.t.* satisfaciō, -facere, -fēcī, -factum (*please; indemnify*)

Saturday *n.* diēs Sāturnī, diēī Sāturnī *m.*

sauce *n.* iūs, iūris *nt.*

sausage *n.* farcīmen, -minis *nt.*

savage *adj.* ferus, -a, -um (*wild; fierce*); *adj.* immānis, -is, -e (*monstrous; uncivilized*)

save *v.t.* servō, -āre, -āvī, -ātum (*preserve from danger*); *v.t.* līberō, -āre, -āvī, -ātum (*rescue*)

saving *n.* conservatiō, -ōnis *f.* (*preservation*)

savior *n.* conservātor, -ōris *m.*

savor *n.* sapor, -ōris *m.*; *v.t.* sapiō, -ere, -ivī, ---

savory *n.* thymbra, -ae *f.*

saw *n.* serra, -ae *f.*; *v.t.* serrā secō, -āre, secuī, sectum

sawdust *n.* scobis, -is *f.*

say *v.t.* dīcō, -ere, dīxī, dictum (*express in words*); *v.t.* trādō, -dere, -didī, -ditum (*hand down by tradition; report*); **they ~** *v.i.* dīcunt, tradunt, ferunt; *v.i.* āiō (*def.*) (*used parenthetically*), inquam (*def.*) (*used to cite a direct quotation*)

saying *n.* dictiō, -ōnis *f.* (*act of speaking*); *n.* dictum, -ī *nt.* (*remark; comment*)

scab *n.* crusta, -ae *f.*

scaffold *n.* catasta, -ae *f.*

scale *n.* squāma, -ae *f.* (*of a fish; thin metallic plate*)

scales *n./pl.* trutina, -ae *f.*

scallop *n.* pecten, -inis *m.*

scandal *n.* opprobrium, -ī *nt.* (*offense*)

scandalous *adj.* prōbrōsus, -a, -um

scar *n.* cicātrīx, -trīcis *f.*

scarce *adj.* rārus, -a, -um

scare *v.t.* terreō, -ēre, terruī, territum

scarf *n.* fōcāle, -is *nt.* (*for the neck*)

scarlet *adj.* coccinus, -a, -um

scatter *v.t.* spargō, -ere, sparsī, sparsum; *v.i.* diffugiō, -fugere, -fūgī, ---

scene *n.* scaena, -ae *f.* (*theater*); *n.* spectāculum, -ī *n.* (*spectacle*)

scenery *n.* scaena, -ae *f.* (*theater*)

scent *n.* odor, -ōris *m.*; **get (a) ~ of** *v.t.* olfaciō, -facere, -fēcī, -factum

scheme *n.* cōnsilium, -ī *nt.*

scholar *n.* discipulus, -ī *m.*, discipula, -ae *f.* (*pupil*); *n.* vir doctus, virī doctī *m.* (*learned man*)

scholarship *n.* doctrīna, -ae *f.* (*learning*)
school *n.* lūdus, -ī *m.*
schoolchild *n.* discipulus, -ī *m.*; *n.* discipula, -ae *f.* (*pupil*)
schoolteacher *n.* magister, magistrī *m.*; *n.* magistra, -ae *f.*
science *n.* scientia, -ae *f.* (*knowledge in general*); *n.* ars, artis *f.* (*systematized knowledge*)
scissors *n/.pl.* forfex, -ficis *f.*
scold *v.t.* obiūrgō, -iūrgāre, -iūrgāvī, -iūrgātum
score *n.* summa, -ae *f.* (*total*); *n.* ratiō, -ōnis *f.* (*reckoning*)
scorn *n.* contemptiō, -ōnis *f.*; *v.t.* contemnō, -temnere, -tempsī, -temptum
scorpion *n.* scorpiō, -ōnis *m.*
scour *v.t.* tergeō, -ēre, tersī, tersum
scout *n.* explōrātor, -ōris *m.*; *v.d.t.* speculor, speculārī, speculātus sum
scrap *n.* frustum, -ī *nt.*
scrape *v.t.* rādō, -ere, rāsī, rāsum
scratch *v.t.* rādō, -ere, rāsī, rāsum
scream *v.i.* ululō, -āre, -āvī, -ātum
screen *v.t.* tegō, -ere, tēxī, tēctum
screw *n.* coclea, -ae *f.*
scribe *n.* scrība, -ae *m.*
scrub *v.t.* tergeō, -ēre, tersī, tersum
scruple *n.* scrūpulus, -ī *m.*
scrupulous *adj.* religiōsus, -a, -um
scrutinize *v.d.t.* scrūtor, scrūtārī, scrūtātus sum
scrutiny *n.* scrūtātiō, -ōnis *f.*
sculpt *v.t.* sculpō, -ere, sculpsī, sculptum
sculptor *n.* sculptor, -ōris *m.*
sculpture *n.* sculptūra, -ae *f.* (*act of sculpting*); *n.* signum, -ī *nt.* (*work made by a sculptor*)
scum *n.* spūma, -ae *f.*
scythe *n.* falx, falcis *f.*
sea *n.* mare, -is *nt.*
seacoast *n.* lītus, -oris *nt.*
seagull *n.* gavia, -ae *f.*
seal *n.* signum, -ī *nt.* (*impression on wax; signet*); *n.* phōca, -ae *f.* (*zool.*); *v.t.* signō, -āre, -āvī, -ātum (*make an impression in wax*); **~ up** *v.t.* obsignō, -signāre, -signāvī, -signātum
seam *n.* sūtūra, -ae *f.*

search *v.t.* explōrō, -āre, -āvī, -ātum (~ *out*); ~ **for** *v.t.* quaerō, -ere, quaesīvī, quaesītum

seasick *adj.* nauseabundus, -a, -um

seasickness *n.* nausea, -ae *f.*

season *n.* tempus, -oris *nt.* (*time of the year*); *v.t.* condiō, -īre, -īvī, -ītum

seat *n.* sēdēs, -is *f.*

seaweed *n.* alga, -ae *f.*

seclude *v.t.* sēclūdō, -clūdere, -clūsī, -clūsum

seclusion *n.* sōlitūdō, -inis *f.*

second *adj.* secundus, -a, -um (*in counting*); *adj.* alter, altera, alterum (*the other of two*); **a ~ time** *adv.* iterum

secret *adj.* arcānus, -a, -um; *n.* arcānum, -ī *nt.*

secretary *n.* scrība, -ae *m.*

section *n.* pars, partis *f.*

secular *adj.* profānus, -a, -um

secure *adj.* sēcūrus, -a, -um (*carefree*); *adj.* tūtus, -a, -um (*safe; certain*); *v.t.* mūniō, -īre, -īvī, -ītum (*make safe; fortify; defend*); *v.t.* cōnfirmō, -firmāre, -firmāvī, -firmātum (*strengthen; reinforce*)

security *n.* salūs, -ūtis *f.* (*freedom from danger*); *n.* sēcūritās, -ātis *f.* (*freedom from anxiety*); *n.* pignus, -noris (-neris) *nt.* (*pledge*)

sedate *adj.* sēdātus, -a, -um

seduce *v.t.* corrumpō, -rumpere, -rūpī, -ruptum

seduction *n.* corruptēla, -ae *f.*

see *v.t.* videō, -ēre, vīdī, vīsum

seed *n.* sēmen, -inis *nt.*

seek *v.t.* quaerō, -ere, quaesīvī, quaesītum

seem *v.i.* videor, vidērī, vīsus sum

seize *v.t.* rapiō, -ere, rapuī, raptum (*rush upon and grab*); *v.t.* occupō, -āre, -āvī, -ātum (*invade and take by force*); *v.t.* comprehendō, -prehendere, -prehendī, -prehēnsum (*grasp; lay hold of; capture*)

seizure *n.* comprehēnsiō, -ōnis *f.* (*grasping*); *n.* temptātiō, -ōnis *f.* (*illness*)

seldom *adv.* rārō

select *v.t.* legō, -ere, lēgī, lēctum

selection *n.* dēlectus, -ūs *m.*

self *pron.* ipse, ipsa, ipsum

self-control *n.* modestia, -ae *f.*

sell *v.t.* vēndō, -dere, -didī, -ditum

seller *n.* vēnditor, -ōris *m.*

senate *n.* senātus, -ūs *m.*

senator *n.* senātor, -ōris *m.*

send *v.t.* mittō, -ere, mīsī, missum; **~ for** *v.t.* arcessō, -ere, -īvī, -ītum

senior *adj.* māior, maius

sensation *n.* sēnsus, -ūs *m. (impression gained through the senses)*

sense *n.* sēnsus, -ūs *m. (impression gained through the senses)*; *n.* prūdentia, -ae *f. (soundness of judgment)*; *n.* sententia, -ae *f. (signification)*

sentence *n.* iūdicium, -ī *nt. (judicial decision)*; *v.t.* damnō, -āre, -āvī, -ātum

sentinel *n.* cūstōs, -ōdis *m./f.*

separate *adj.* sēparātus, -a, -um; **~ly** *adv.* sēparātim; *v.t.* sēparō, -parāre, -parāvī, -parātum *(part physically)*; *v.t.* discernō, -cernere, -crēvī, -crētum *(distinguish between)*

separation *n.* sēparātiō, -ōnis *f.*

September *adj.* September, -bris *(usu. w.* **mēnsis***)*; *n.* September, -bris *m.*

serene *adj.* serēnus, -a, -um

series *n.* seriēs, -em *(acc.)*, -ē *(abl.) f. (irreg.)*

serious *adj.* sevērus, -a, -um

servant *n.* minister, -strī *m.*; *n.* famulus, -ī *m.*, famula, -ae *f. (slave belonging to a household)*

serve *v.t.* ministrō, -āre, -āvī, -ātum *(attend on)*; *v.t.* mīlitō, -āre, -āvī, -ātum *(~ in the army)*; *v.i.* serviō, -īre, -īvī (-iī), -ītum *(labor for someone)*

service *n.* ministerium, -ī *nt. (labor performed)*; *n.* officium, -ī *nt. (helpful action)*; *n.* mīlitia, -ae *f. (military service)*

session *n.* conventus, -ūs *m. (judicial court meeting)*

set *adj.* status, -a, -um; *v.t.* statuō, -ere, statuī, statūtum *(place upright)*; *v.t.* pōnō, -ere, posuī, positum *(place)*

settle *v.t.* cōnstituō, -stituere, -stituī, -stitūtum *(put in a certain place; colonize; determine what is uncertain)*; *v.i.* cōnsīdō, -sīdere, -sēdī, -sessum *(take seats or an abode)*; *v.i.* sīdō, -ere, sīdī, --- *(sink down; alight)*

settlement *n.* pactum, -ī *nt. (agreement)*; *n.* dēductiō, -ōnis *f. (act of establishing a colony)*

seven *num.* septem *(indecl.)*

seventeen *num.* septemdecim *(indecl.)*

seventeenth *adj.* septimus decimus, septima decima, septimum decimum

seventh *adj.* septimus, -a, -um

seventy *num.* septuāgintā *(indecl.)*

several *adj.* nōnnūllī, -ae, -a *pl. (some)*; *adj.* aliquot (+ gen.) *(indecl.) (a considerable number of something)*

severe *adj.* sevērus, -a, -um *(austere; critical)*; *adj.* asper, aspera, asperum *(of weather)*

sew *v.t.* suō, -ere, suī, sūtum

sewer *n.* cloāca, -ae *f.* (*drain*)

sex *n.* sexus, -ūs *m.*

sexual intercourse *n.* coitus, -ūs *m.*

shabby *adj.* obsolētus, -a, -um (*worn out; poor; low*); *adj.* turpis, -is, -e (*disgraceful; dishonorable*)

shade *n.* umbra, -ae *f.*

shades, the *n./pl.* mānēs, -ium *m./pl.* (*spirits of the dead*)

shadow *n.* umbra, -ae *f.*

shady *adj.* umbrōsus, -a, -um

shaft *n.* sagitta, -ae *f.* (*of arrow*); *n.* hastīle, -is *nt.* (*of spear*); *n.* puteus, -ī *m.* (*of mine*)

shaggy *adj.* hirsūtus, -a, -um

shake *v.t.* concutiō, -cutere, -cussī, -cussum; *v.i.* tremō, -ere, -uī, --- ; **cause to ~** *v.t.* tremefaciō, -facere, -fēcī, -factum

shallow *adj.* vadōsus, -a, -um (*of physical things*); *adj.* levis, -is, -e (*of thought, intellect, etc.*)

sham *v.t.* simulō, -āre, -āvī, -ātum

shame *n.* pudor, -ōris *m.* (*sense of ~ or modesty*); *n.* dēdecus, -oris *nt.* (*disgrace; source of ~*); **feel ~** *v.i.* pudeō, -ēre, puduī, puditum (*often used impersonally with acc. of person feeling shame and gen. of thing/person causing shame, or infv..*)

shameful *adj.* turpis, -is, -e

shape *n.* fōrma, -ae *f.*; *v.t.* fōrmō, -āre, -āvī, -ātum

share *n.* pars, partis *f.*; *v.t.* partiō, -īre, -īvī, -ītum

shark *n.* pistrīx, -trīcis *f.*

sharp *adj.* acūtus, -a, -um (*finely pointed; of the senses and mental faculties*); *adj.* mordāx, mordācis (*biting*); *adj.* ācer, ācris, ācre (*severe; bitter*)

sharpen *v.t.* acuō, -ere, acuī, acūtum

shave *v.t.* rādō, -ere, rāsī, rāsum

she *pron.* ea

sheaf *n.* manipulus, -ī *m.* (*of hay or grain*); *n.* fascis, -is *m.* (*of twigs, straw, etc.*)

shear *v.t.* tondeō, -ēre, totondī, tonsum

shears *n./pl.* forfex, -ficis *f.*

shed *n.* tugurium, -ī *nt.*

sheep *n.* ovis, -is *f.*; **herd of ~** *n.* pecus, -udis *f.*

sheer *adj.* abruptus, -a, -um (*steep*); *adj.* merus, -a, -um (*pure; nothing but*)

sheet *n.* lōdīx, -dīcis *f.* (*covering for a bed*)

shelf

shelf *n.* pluteus, -ī *m.*
shell *n.* concha, -ae *f.* (*mollusk ~*); *n.* putāmen, -inis *nt.* (*nut~*)
shellfish *n.* concha, -ae *f.*
shepherd *n.* pāstor, -ōris *m.*
shield *n.* scūtum, -ī *nt.* (*oblong ~*); *n.* parma, -ae *f.* (*small, round cavalry ~*)
shift *n.* dolus, -ī *m.* (*trick; expedient*); *v.t.* mūtō, -āre, -āvī, -ātum (*alter*); *v.t.* moveō, -ēre, mōvī, mōtum (*move*)
shine *v.i.* fulqeō, -ēre, fulsī, ---
shining *adj.* nitēns, -entis
ship *n.* nāvis, -is *f.*
shirt *n.* subūcula, -ae *f.*
shiver *v.i.* horreō, -ēre, horruī, ---
shock *n.* impetus, -ūs *m.* (*running together in battle*); *n.* stupor, -ōris *m.* (*mental ~*)
shoe *n.* calceus, -ī *m.*
shoelace *n.* corrigia, -ae *f.*
shoot *v.t.* mittō, -ere, mīsī, missum (*let fly*); *v.t.* vulnerō, -āre, -āvī, -ātum (*wound*)
shop *n.* taberna, -ae *f.*; *v.t.* emō, -ere, ēmī, ēmptum
shopkeeper *n.* tabernārius, -ī *m.*
shore *n.* lītus, -oris *nt.*
short *adj.* brevis, -is, -e
shortage *n.* inopia, -ae *f.*
shorten *v.t.* contrahō, -trahere, -trāxī, -tractum
shortly *adv.* breviter (*in a few words*); *adv.* brevī (*in a short time*)
should *verbal aux.* Use subjv..
shoulder *n.* umerus, -ī *m.*
shove *v.t.* trūdō, -ere, trūsī, trūsum
shovel *n.* pāla, -ae *f.*
show *n.* spectāculum, -ī *nt.* (*exhibition*); *n.* ostentātiō, -ōnis *f.* (*display*); *n.* speciēs, -ēī *f.* (*superficial appearance; pretense*); *v.t.* monstrō, -āre, -āvī, -ātum (*point out*); *v.t.* praebeō, -bēre, -buī, -bitum (*present*); *v.t.* probō, -āre, -āvī, -ātum (*prove*)
shower *n.* imber, imbris *m.*; *v.t.* fundō, -ere, fūdī, fūsum (*pour*); *v.i.* pluit, pluere, pluit (*imp.*)
shrewd *adj.* acūtus, -a, -um
shrine *n.* sacellum, -ī *nt.*
shrink *v.t.* contrahō, -trahere, -trāxī, -tractum; ~ **from** *v.i.* refugiō, -fugere, -fūgī, --- (*recoil from*)

shut *v.t.* claudō, -ere, clausī, clausum
shuttle *n.* radius, -ī *m.*
shy *adj.* verēcundus, -a, -um
shyness *n.* verēcundia, -ae *f.*
sick *adj.* aeger, aegra, aegrum; **be ~** *v.i.* aegrōtō, -āre, -āvī, ---
sickness *n.* morbus, -ī *m.*
side *n.* latus, -eris *nt.* (*flank*); *n.* partēs, -ium *f./pl.* (*political faction*); **on this ~** *adv.* hinc; **on that ~** *adv.* illinc; **on/from both sides** *adv.* utrimque; **on all sides** *adv.* undique
sideways *adv.* in lātitūdinem
sieve *n.* crībrum, -ī *nt.*
sift *v.t.* crībrō, -āre, -āvī, -ātum
sigh *n.* suspīrium, -ī *nt.*; *v.i.* suspīrō, -āre, -āvī, -ātum
sight *n.* vīsus, -ūs *m.* (*act of seeing*); *n.* cōnspectus, -ūs *m.* (*view; range of ~*); *n.* spectāculum, -ī *nt.* (*spectacle*)
sign *n.* signum, -ī *nt.* (*mark; token; astronomical ~*); *n.* monstrum, -ī *nt.* (*portent*)
signal *n.* signum, -ī *nt.*
significance *n.* momentum, -ī *nt.* (*importance*); *n.* significātiō, -ōnis *f.* (*meaning*)
signify *v.t.* significō, -ficāre, -ficāvī, -ficātum
silence *n.* silentium, -ī *nt.*; *v.t.* comprimō, -primere, -pressī, -pressum
silent *adj.* tacitus, -a, -um (*not speaking*); *adj.* silēns, -entis; **be ~** *v.i.* taceō, -ēre, tacuī, tacitum
silk *n.* sēricum, -ī *nt.*
sill *n.* līmen, -inis *nt.*
silly *adj.* stultus, -a, -um
silver *n.* argentum, -ī *nt.*; *adj.* argenteus, -a, -um
silverware *n.* argentum, -ī *nt.*
similar *adj.* similis, -is, -e
similarity *n.* similitūdō, -inis *f.*
simple *adj.* simplex, -plicis
simulate *v.t.* simulō, -āre, -āvī, -ātum
simulation *n.* simulātiō, -ōnis *f.*
sin *n.* peccātum, -ī *nt.* (*moral wrong*); *n.* piāculum, -ī *nt.* (*pollution against the gods*); *v.i.* peccō, -āre, -āvī, -ātum
since *adv.* posteā; *conj.* cum (+ subjv.) (*because*)
sincere *adj.* sincērus, -a, -um
sincerity *n.* sincēritās, -ātis *f.*

sinew *n.* nervus, -ī *m.*

sing *v.t., v.i.* canō, -ere, cecinī, cantum

singer *n.* cantor, -ōris *m.*

singing *n.* cantus, -ūs *m.*

single *adj.* ūnus, -a, -um (*one*); *adj.* sōlus, -a, -um (*alone*); *adj.* simplex, -plicis (*not double*); *adj.* singulī, -ae, -a *pl.* (*one at a time; individual*); *adj.* caelebs, caelibis (*of unmarried men*); *adj.* innupta (*of unmarried woman*)

sinister *adj.* īnfaustus, -a, -um

sink *v.i.* mergō, -ere, mersī, mersum

sip *v.t.* lībō, -āre, -āvī, -ātum

sister *n.* soror, -ōris *f.*

sister-in-law *n.* glōs, glōris *f.*

sit *v.i.* sedeō, -ēre, sēdī, sessum

site *n.* situs, -ūs *m.*

situation *n.* situs, -ūs *m.* (*position*); *n.* status, -ūs *m.* (*circumstances*)

six *num.* sex (*indecl.*)

sixteen *num.* sēdecim (*indecl.*)

sixteenth *adj.* sextus decimus, sexta decima, sextum decimum

sixth *adj.* sextus, -a, -um

sixty *num.* sexāgintā (*indecl.*)

size *n.* magnitūdō, -inis *f.*

skeleton *n.* ossa, -ium *nt./pl.*

sketch *v.i.* adumbrō, -umbrāre, -umbrāvī, -umbrātum

skill *n.* sollertia, -ae *f.*

skillful *adj.* sollers, sollertis

skim *v.t.* dēspumō, -spumāre, -spumāvī, -spumātum (*remove scum*); *v.t.* percurrō, -currere, -cucurrī (currī), -cursum (*pass over rapidly*)

skin *n.* cutis, -is *f.* (*of human*); *n.* pellis, -is *f.* (*of animal*)

skinny *adj.* macer, macra, macrum

skip *v.i.* saliō, -īre, saluī, saltum

skull *n.* calvāria, -ae *f.*

sky *n.* caelum, -ī *nt.*

slack *adj.* remissus, -a, -um

slander *v.d.t.* calumnior, calumniārī, calumniātus sum

slanting *adj.* oblīquus, -a, -um

slap *n.* alapa, -ae *f.; v.t.* alapam dūcō, -ere, dūxī, ductum

slash *v.t.* caedō, -ere, cecīdī, caesum

slave *n.* servus, -ī *m.; n.* serva, -ae *f.*

slavery *n.* servitium, -ī *nt.*

sleep *n.* somnus, -ī *m.*; *v.i.* dormiō, -īre, -īvī, -ītum

sleepy *adj.* sēmisomnus, -a, -um

sleeves *n./pl.* manicae, -ārum *f./pl.*

slender *adj.* tenuis, -is, -e (*of form, texture, substance*); *adj.* gracilis, -is, -e (*of living bodies*)

slice *n.* frustum, -ī *nt.*; *v.t.* secō, -āre, secuī, sectum

slide *v.d.i.* lābor, lābī, lāpsus sum

slight *adj.* levis, -is, -e

slim *adj.* gracilis, -is, -e

sling *n.* funda, -ae *f.* (*weapon*)

slip *n.* lāpsus, -ūs *m.* (*act of slipping*); *n.* peccātum, -ī *nt.* (*error*); *n.* surculus, -ī *m.* (*bot.*); *v.d.i.* lābor, lābī, lāpsus sum

slipper *n.* solea, -ae *f.*

slippery *adj.* lūbricus, -a, -um

slope *n.* clīvus, -ī *m.*

sloppy *adj.* lutulentus, -a, -um (*muddy*)

slow *adj.* tardus, -a, -um

slug *n.* līmāx, līmācis *f.*

sluggish *adj.* piger, pigra, pigrum

small *adj.* parvus, -a, -um

smart *adj.* nitidus, -a, -um (*elegant; handsome*)

smell *n.* odōrātus, -ūs *m.* (*sense of smell*); *n.* odor, -ōris *m.* (*scent; stench*); *v.t.* olfaciō, -facere, -fēcī, -factum (*track by smell; perceive a smell*); *v.i.* oleō, -ēre, oluī, ---

smile *n.* rīsus, -ūs *m.*; *v.i.* rīdeō, -ēre, rīsī, rīsum

smith *n.* faber, fabrī *m.*

smoke *n.* fūmus, -ī *m.*; *v.i.* fūmō, -āre, -āvī, -ātum

smoky *adj.* fūmōsus, -a, -um

smooth *adj.* lēvis, -is, -e (*not rough*); *adj.* lēnis, -is, -e (*soft*)

snail *n.* coclea, -ae *f.*

snake *n.* anguis, -is *m./f.*

snarl *v.d.i.* ringor, ringārī, rictus sum

sneeze *n.* sternūmentum, -ī *nt.*; *v.i.* sternuō, -ere, sternuī, ---

snore *v.i.* stertō, -ere, -uī, ---

snort *v.i.* fremō, -ere, -uī, ---

snout *n.* rōstrum, -ī *nt.*

snow *n.* nīx, nivis *f.*; *v.i.* ningit (ninguit), ningēre, ninxit, --- (*imp.*)

snowy *adj.* niveus, -a, -um

so *adv.* sīc (*in this way*); *adv.* tam (*w. advs. and adjs.*) (*to such a degree*); *adv.* adeō (*w. verbs*); **and ~** *conj.* itaque; **~ far** *adv.* adhūc; **~ great** *adj.* tantus, -a, -um; **~ many** *adj.* tot (*indecl.*); **~ often** *adv.* totiēns; **~ that** *conj.* ut (+ subjv.); **~ that not** *conj.* ut nōn (*in clauses of result*), ut nē (*in substantive clauses of purpose*)

soak *v.t.* madefaciō, -facere, -fēcī, -factum; *v.i.* madeō, -ēre, maduī, ---

soaking *adj.* madidus, -a, -um

soap *n.* sāpō, -ōnis *m.*

soar *v.i.* subvolo, -are, -avī, -atum

sob *v.i.* singultō, -āre, -āvī, -ātum

social *adj.* commūnis, -is, -e (*shared in general*); *adj.* cīvīlis, -is, -e (*pertaining to public or political life*)

society *n.* societās, -ātis *f.* (*association*)

sock *n.* ūdō, -ōnis *m.*

soda *n.* nitrum, -ī *nt.* (*alkaline compound*)

sofa *n.* lectus, -ī *m.*

soft *adj.* mollis, -is, -e (*gentle; delicate; weak*); *adj.* lēnis, -is, -e (*mild*)

soil *n.* solum, -ī *nt.*

solar *adj.* sōlāris, -is, -e

soldier *n.* mīles, -itis *m./f.*

sole *n.* solum, -ī *nt.*; *adj.* sōlus, -a, -um

solemn *adj.* sollemnis, -is, -e (*pertaining to religious ceremonies, etc.*); *adj.* sērius, -a, -um (*serious*)

solid *adj.* solidus, -a, -um

solution *n.* solūtiō, -ōnis *f.* (*explication of problems*); *n.* dīlūtum, -ī *nt.* (*liquid*)

solve *v.t.* explicō, -plicāre, -plicāvī, -plicātum

somber *adj.* trīstis, -is, -e

some *adj.* aliquī, aliqua, aliquod

somebody *pron.* aliquis

somehow *adv.* nesciō quō modō

someone *pron.* aliquis

something *n.* nesciō quid *nt.* (*indecl.*)

sometime *adv.* aliquandō; **~s** *adv.* interdum

somewhat *adv.* aliquid

somewhere *adv.* alicubī

son *n.* fīlius, -ī *m.*

song *n.* cantus, -ūs *m.*

son-in-law *n.* gener, generī *m.*

soon *adv.* mox; **as ~ as** *conj.* simul ac; **as ~ as possible** *conj.* quam prīmum; **~ after** *adv.* paulō post

sorcerer *n.* venēficus, -ī *m.*

sorceress *n.* venēfica, -ae *f.*

sorcery *n.* venēficium, -ī *nt.*

sore *n.* ulcus, ulceris *nt.*; *adj.* ācer, ācris, ācre

sorrow *n.* dolor, -ōris *m.*

sorry, be ~ *v.i.* paenitet, paenitēre, paenituit, --- *(imp.)* (+ acc. of person + gen. of thing)

sort *n.* genus, -eris *nt.*; **of what ~?** quālis, -is, -e; *v.t.* dīgerō, -gerere, -gessī, -gestum

soul *n.* anima, -ae *f.* *(vital principle)*; *n.* animus, -ī *m.* *(rational principle)*

sound *n.* sonus, -ī *m.*; *adj.* sānus, -a, -um *(healthy)*; *adj.* altus, -a, -um *(of deep sleep; of deep learning)*; *adj.* firmus, -a, -um *(of arguments)*; *v.i.* sonō, -āre, -uī, -itum

soup *n.* iūs, iūris *nt.*

sour *adj.* acidus, -a, -um *(not sweet)*; *adj.* acerbus, -a, -um *(peevish)*

source *n.* orīgō, -inis *f.*

south *n.* merīdiēs, -ēī *f.*

southeast *n.* inter merīdiem et sōlis ortum

southern *adj.* merīdiānus, -a, -um

southwest *n.* inter occāsum sōlis et merīdiem

sovereign *n.* prīnceps, -cipis *m.*; *adj.* suprēmus, -a, -um

sow *v.t.* serō, -ere, sēvī, satum

space *n.* spatium, -ī *nt.*

spade *n.* pāla, -ae *f.*

spare *v.i.* parcō, -ere, pepercī (parsī), parsum (+ dat.)

spark *n.* scintilla, -ae *f.*

sparkle *v.i.* scintillō, -āre, -āvī, -ātum

speak *v.d.t., v.d.i.* loquor, loquī, locūtus sum *(converse)*; *v.i.* dīcō, -ere, dīxī, dictum *(make a speech; express ideas)*

speaker *n.* ōrātor, -ōris *m.*

special *adj.* praecipuus, -a, -um *(outstanding; chief)*; *adj.* pecūliāris, -is, -e *(of a particular person or group)*

specify *v.t.* dēnotō, -notāre, -notāvī, -notātum

specimen *n.* exemplum, -ī *nt.*

spectator *n.* spectator, -ōris *m.*

speech *n.* ōrātiō, -ōnis *f.* *(faculty of speaking; oration)*; **make a ~** ōrātiōnem habeō, -ēre, habuī, habitum

speed *n.* celeritās, -ātis *f.*

spell *n.* carmen, -inis *nt.*

spend *v.t.* impendō, -pendere, -pendī, -pensum (*of money*); *v.t.* agō, -ere, ēgī, actum (~ *life or time*); *v.t.* cōnsūmō, -sūmere, -sūmpsī, -sūmptum (*exhaust*); ~ **the night** *v.i.* pernoctō, -noctāre, -noctāvī, -noctātum

sphere *n.* sphaera, -ae *f.* (*globe*); *n.* prōvincia, -ae *f.* (*task; function*)

spice *n.* condimentum, -ī *nt.*

spicy *adj.* condītus, -a, -um

spider *n.* arānea, -ae *f.*; ~ **web** *n.* arānea, -ae *f.*

spill *n.* effūsiō, -ōnis *f.*; *v.t.* effundō, -fundere, -fūdī, -fūsum

spin *v.i.* neō, nēre, nēvī, nētum (*twist fibers*)

spine *n.* spīna, -ae *f.*

spiral *adj.* involūtus, -a, -um

spirit *n.* spīritus, -ūs *m.* (*disposition; high* ~); *n.* animus, -ī *m.* (*courage*)

spirits, the *n./pl.* mānēs, -ium *m./pl.* (*spirit of a deceased person; spirits of the dead in general*)

spit *v.t., v.i.* spuō, -ere, spuī, spūtum (*eject saliva*); *v.t.* trānsfigō, -figere, -fīxī, -fīxum (*pierce through*)

spite *n.* līvor, -ōris *m.*

splash *n.* aspergō, -inis *f.*; *v.t.* aspergō, -spergere, -spersī, -spersum

splint *n.* ferula, -ae *f.*; *n.* canālis, -is *m.*

splinter *n.* assula, -ae *f.*

spoil *v.t.* spoliō, -āre, -āvī, -ātum (*strip by violence; plunder*); *v.t.* corrumpō, -rumpere, -rūpī, -ruptum (*mar; ruin*); *v.d.i.* corrumpor, corrumpī, corruptus sum

spoils *n./pl.* spolia, -ōrum *nt./pl.*

spoke *n.* radius, -ī *m.*

sponge *n.* spongia (spongea), -ae *f.*

sponsor *n.* fautor, -ōris *m.*

spontaneously *adv.* sponte

spool *n.* fūsus, -ī

spoon *n.* coclear, -āris *nt.*

sport *n.* lūdus, -ī *m.*

spot *n.* macula, -ae *f.* (*stain*); *n.* locus, -ī *m.* (*place*); *v.t.* animadvertō, -vertere, -vertī, -versum (*notice*); *v.t.* maculō, -āre, -āvī, -ātum (*stain*)

spout *n.* ōs, ōris *nt.* (*of a vessel*); *n.* canālis, -is *m.* (*roof channel*)

sprain *v.t.* intorqueō, -torquēre, -torsī, -torsum

spray *n.* aspergō, -inis *f.*; *v.t.* aspergō, -spergere, -spersī, -spersum

spread *v.t.* pandō, -ere, pandī, passum (*unfold; lay open*); *v.t.* extendō, -tendere, -tendī, -tensum (tentum) (*stretch out; enlarge*); *v.t.* dīvulgō, -vulgāre, -vulgāvī, -vulgātum (*publish; divulge*); *v.i.* patēscō, -ēre, patuī, --- (*open out; extend*); *v.i.* crēscō, -ere, crēvī, crētum (*become more widely known*)

spring *n.* fons, fontis *m.* (*source of water*); *n.* vēr, vēris *nt.* (*season of the year*); *v.i.* crēscō, -ere, crēvī, crētum (*of plants, grow up*); *v.d.i.* orior, orīrī, ortus sum (*originate; arise*)

sprinkle *v.t.* aspergō, -spergere, -spersī, -spersum

sprout *n.* surculus, -ī *m.*; *v.i.* germinō, -āre, -āvī, -ātum

spur *n.* calcār, -āris *nt.*

spy *n.* explōrātor, -ōris *m.*; *v.i.* explōrō, -āre, -āvī, -ātum

squadron *n.* āla, -ae *f.*

square *adj.* quadrātus, -a, -um; *n.* quadrātum, -ī *nt.*; **market ~** *n.* forum, -ī *nt.*

squash *n.* cucurbita, -ae *f.* (*bot.*); *v.t.* obterō, -terere, -trīvī, -trītum

squinter *n.* strabō, -ōnis *m.*

squirrel *n.* sciūrus, -ī *m.*

stab *v.t.* cōnfodiō, -fodere, -fōdī, -fossum

stable *n.* stabulum, -ī *nt.*; *adj.* stabilis, -is, -e

stadium *n.* stadium, -ī *nt.* (*course for foot-racers*)

stage *n.* proscēnium, -ī *nt.* (*theater*)

stain *n.* macula, -ae *f.*; *v.t.* maculō, -āre, -āvī, -ātum

stainless *adj.* pūrus, -a, -um

stair *n.* gradūs, -uum *m./pl.*

staircase *n.* scālae, -ārum *f./pl.*

stake *n.* pālus, -ī *m.* (*post*); *n.* pignus, -oris (-eris) *nt.* (*pledge*)

stale *adj.* vetus, veteris (*old*); *adj.* mūcidus, -a, -um (*moldy or musty: of food and wine*)

stalk *n.* stirps, stirpis *m./f.*; *v.t.* vestīgō, -āre, -āvī, -ātum

stall *n.* stabulum, -ī *nt.* (*for animals*); *n.* taberna, -ae *f.* (*little shop*)

stammer *n.* haesitātiō, -ōnis *f.*; *v.t., v.i.* balbutiō, -īre, -īvī, -ītum

stamp *n.* signum, -ī *nt.* (*impression*); *n.* supplōsiō, -ōnis *f.* (*of the foot*); *v.t.* signō, -āre, -āvī, -ātum (*mark; imprint*); *v.t.* (pedem) supplōdō, -plōdere, -plōsī, --- (*~ with the foot*)

stand *n.* statiō, -ōnis *f.* (*standing place; position*); *v.i.* stō, -āre, stetī, statum (*be upright*); **~ upright** *v.t.* statuō, -ere, statuī, statūtum; **~ for office** *v.t.* petō, -ere, -īvī, -ītum; **~ fast** *v.i.* cōnsistō, -sistere, -stitī, -stitum

standard *n.* signum, -ī *nt.* (*of a military unit*); *n.* aquila, -ae *f.* (*legionary*); *n.* mēnsūra, -ae (*standard of measure*)

standard-bearer *n.* signifer, signiferī *m.* (*of a unit*); *n.* aquilifer, aquiliferī *m.* (*of a legion*)

star *n.* stella, -ae *f.*

starch *n.* amylum, -ī *nt.*

stare *v.d.i.* mīror, mīrārī, mīrātus sum

starfish *n.* stella, -ae *f.*

start *n.* initium, -ī *nt.* (*beginning*); *n.* prōfectiō, -ōnis *f.* (*beginning of a journey*); *v.t., v.i.* incipiō, -cipere, -cēpī, -ceptum (*begin*); ~ **out on a journey** *v.d.i.* prōficīscor, prōficīscī, prōfectus sum

starvation *n.* famēs, -is *f.*

state *n.* status, -ūs *m.* (*condition; status*); *n.* cīvitās, -ātis *f.* (*body of citizens*); *n.* magnificentia, -ae *f.* (*grandeur*); *adj.* pūblicus, -a, -um; *v.i.* dīcō, -ere, dīxī, dictum; **the Roman** ~ *n.* rēs pūblica, reī pūblicae *f.*

station *n.* ordō, -inis *f.* (*social rank*); *n.* statiō, -ōnis *f.* (*assigned post*); *v.t.* dispōnō, -pōnere, -posuī, -positum

stationary *adj.* immōbilis, -is, -e

statue *n.* statua, -ae *f.*

status *n.* ordō, -inis *f.* (*social rank*)

stay *n.* mānsiō, -ōnis *f.* (*residence*); *n.* mora, -ae *f.* (*delay*); *v.i.* maneō, -ēre, mānsī, mānsum (*abide*)

steady *adj.* immōbilis, -is, -e

steal *v.d.t.* fūror, fūrārī, fūrātus sum (*rob*); *v.i.* subrēpō, -rēpere, -rēpsī, -rēptum (*go stealthily*)

stealthily *adv.* furtim

steam *n.* vapor, -ōris *m.*

steer *v.t.* gubernō, -āre, -āvī, -ātum

stem *n.* caulis, -is *m.*

step *n.* gradus, -ūs *m.*; *v.d.i.* gradior, gradī, gressus sum

stepbrother *n.* filius vitricus, filiī vitricī *m.* (*paternal*); *n.* filius novercae, filiī novercae *m.* (*maternal*)

stepdaughter *n.* prīvigna, -ae *f.*

stepfather *n.* vitricus, -ī *m.*

stepmother *n.* noverca, -ae *f.*

stepsister *n.* filia vitricī, filiae vitricī *f.* (*paternal*); *n.* filia novercae, filiae novercae *f.* (*maternal*)

stepson *n.* prīvignus, -ī *m.*

sterile *adj.* sterilis, -is, -e

stern *n.* puppis, -is *f.* (*of a ship*); *adj.* dūrus, -a, -um

steward *n.* prōcūrātor, -ōris *m.* (*manager*); *n.* vīlicus, -ī *m.* (*caretaker of an estate*)

stick *n.* baculum, -ī *nt.*; *v.t.* figō, -ere, fīxī, fīxum (*attach; fasten*); *v.i.* haereō, -ēre, haesī, haesum (+ *dat.*) (*adhere to*)

sticky *adj.* tenax, tenācis

stiff *adj.* rigidus, -a, -um

stiffen *v.t.* dūrō, -āre, -āvī, -ātum; *v.i.* rigēscō, -ere, riguī, ---

still *adj.* tranquillus, -a, -um; *adv.* etiam (*besides*); *adv.* nihilōminus (*nevertheless*)

stimulant *n.* stimulus, -ī *m.*

stimulate *v.t.* stimulō, -āre, -āvī, -ātum

sting *n.* aculeus, -ī *m.*; *v.t.* pungō, -ere, pupugī, punctum

stir *v.t.* moveō, -ēre, mōvī, mōtum (*mix; agitate*); *v.t.* excitō, -citāre, -citāvī, -citātum (*rouse; incite*)

stock *n.* cōpia, -ae *f.* (*store; quantity*); *n.* pecus, pecoris *nt.* (*livestock*); *v.t.* īnstruō, -struere, -strūxī, -strūctum

stocking *n.* tībiāle, -is *nt.*

stomach *n.* stomachus, -ī *m.*

stone *n.* lapis, lapidis *m.* (*mineral*); *n.* gemma, -ae *f.* (*precious stone*)

stool *n.* scabellum, -ī *nt.*

stop *n.* mānsiō, -ōnis *f.* (*sojourn; stay*); *n.* fīnis, -is *m.* (*end*); *v.t.* occlūdō, -clūdere, -clūsī, -clūsum (*obstruct an aperture*); *v.i.* sistō, -ere, stitī, statum (*halt*)

store *n.* cōpia, -ae *f.* (*quantity; stock*); *v.t.* condō, -dere, -didī, -ditum

storeroom *n.* cella, -ae *f.*

stork *n.* cicōnia, -ae *f.*

storm *n.* tempestās, -ātis *f.*

stormy *adj.* turbulentus, -a, -um

story *n.* fābula, -ae *f.* (*tale*); *n.* tabulātum, -ī *nt.* (*of a building*); *n.* mendācium, -ī *nt.* (*lie*)

stout *adj.* corpulentus, -a, -um (*corpulent*); *adj.* fortis, -is, -e (*brave*)

straight *adj.* rēctus, -a, -um

strain *v.t.* cōlō, -āre, -āvī, -ātum (*filter*); *v.t.* contendō, -tendere, -tendī, -tentum (*strive*)

strainer *n.* cōlum, -ī *nt.*

strand *n.* lītus, lītoris *nt.* (*shore*)

strange *adj.* īnsolitus, -a, -um (*unusual*); *adj.* peregrīnus, -a, -um (*foreign; exotic*)

stranger *n.* advena, -ae *m./f.*

strangle *v.t.* strangulō, -āre, -āvī, -ātum

strap *n.* lōrum, -ī *nt.*

straw *n.* strāmentum, -ī *nt.*
strawberry *n.* fragum, -ī *nt.*
streak *n.* virga, -ae *f.*
stream *n.* rīvus,-ī *m.*
street *n.* via, -ae *f.*
strength *n.* vīrēs, -ium *f./pl.*
strengthen *v.t.* cōnfirmō, -firmāre, -firmāvī, -firmātum
stress *n.* vīs, vim (*acc.*), vī (*abl.*) *f.* (*def. n.*) (*emphasis*); *n.* sollicitūdō, -inis *f.* (*worry; anxiety*)
stretch *v.t.* tendō, -ere, tetendī, tentum (tēnsum)
strict *adj.* dīligēns, -entis (*exact*); *adj.* sevērus, -a, -um (*rigorous; stern*)
strike *v.t.* percutiō, -cutere, -cussī, -cussum
striking *adj.* īnsignis, -is, -e
string *n.* līnea, -ae *f.*
strip *n.* lacinia, -ae *f.*; *v.t.* spoliō, -āre, -āvī, -ātum
stripe *n.* clāvus, -ī *m.* (*colored vertical band on clothing*); *n.* verber, verberis *nt.* (*blow of a whip*)
striped *adj.* virgātus, -a, -um
strive *v.d.i.* nītor, nītī, nīxus (nīsus) sum
stroke *n.* ictus, -ūs *m.* (*blow*); *n.* fulmen, -inis *nt.* (*of lightning*); *n.* līnea, -ae *f.* (*in writing or painting*)
strong *adj.* validus, -a, -um (*well; effective*); *adj.* potēns, -entis (*able; powerful*); *adj.* firmus, -a, -um (*solid; firm, e.g. of hope, arguments, etc.*); *adj.* mūnītus, -a, -um (*fortified*); **be ~** *v.i.* valeō, -ēre, valuī, valitūrum
structure *n.* aedificium, -ī *nt.* (*building*); *n.* strūctūra, -ae *f.* (*building; arrangement of language*)
struggle *n.* certāmen, -inis *nt.*; *v.d.t.* lūctor, lūctārī, lūctātus sum; *v.i.* contendō, -tendere, -tendī, -tentum
stubborn *adj.* pertināx, -ācis
student *n.* discipulus, -ī *m.*; *n.* discipula, -ae *f.*
study *n.* studium, -ī *nt.* (*application*); *n.* cōgnitiō, -ōnis *f.* (*a ~ of something*); *v.i.* studeō, -ēre, studuī, --- (+ infv. and/or dat.)
stuff *n.* māteria, -ae *f.* (*substance*); *v.t.* farciō, -īre, farsī, fartum
stumble *v.i.* offendō, -fendere, -fendī, -fēnsum (*blunder*)
stun *v.t.* stupefaciō, -facere, -fēcī, -factum
stupid *adj.* stupidus, -a, -um
style *n.* stilus, -ī *m.* (*instrument for writing*); *n.* modus, -ī *m.* (*manner*)
subdue *v.t.* subiciō, -icere, -iēcī, -iectum
subject *n.* rēs, reī *f.* (*topic; ~ matter*)

submit *v.t.* referō, -ferre, retulī, relātum (*propose*); *v.i.* pāreō, -ēre, pāruī, pāritum (+ dat.) (*be subject to*)

subscribe *v.d.i.* adsentior, adsentīrī, adsēnsus sum (+ dat.) (*agree to*)

subscription *n.* subscriptiō, -ōnis *f.* (*act of signing under*); *n.* collātiō, -ōnis *f.* (*contribution*)

subsidy *n.* subsidium, -ī *nt.*

substance *n.* rēs, reī *f.* (*property*); *n.* māteria, -ae *f.* (*stuff*; *matter*); *n.* opēs, opum *f./pl.* (*wealth*)

substantial *adj.* magnus, -a, -um (*large*); *adj.* gravis, -is, -e (*important*)

substitute *n.* vicārius, -ī *m.*; **a ~ for** *prep.* prō (+ abl.); *v.t.* repōnō, -pōnere, -posuī, -positum

subtle *adj.* subtīlis, -is, -e (*fine*; *delicate*); *adj.* astūtus, -a, -um (*clever*)

subtract *v.t.* subtrahō, -trahere, -trāxī, -trāctum

suburban *adj.* suburbānus, -a, -um

succeed *v.i.* flōreō, -ēre, flōruī, --- (*of people: to prosper*); *v.i.* succēdō, -cēdere, -cessī, -cessum (*follow*; *prosper*)

success *n.* rēs secundae, rērum secundārum *f./pl.*

such *adj.* tālis, -is, -e; **~ ... as** tālis, -is, -e ... quālis, -is, -e

suck *v.t.* sūgō, -ere, sūxī, sūctum

sudden *adj.* subitus, -a, -um; **~ly** *adv.* subitō

suffer *v.d.i.* patior, patī, passus sum

suffice *v.i.* sufficiō, -ficere, -fēcī, -fectum

sufficient *adj.* satis (*adv.*) (+ partitive gen.)

suggest *v.t.* admoneō, -monēre, -monuī, -monitum

suggestion *n.* admonitiō, -ōnis *f.*

suit *n.* līs, lītis *f.* (*law~*); *v.t.* accommodō, -commodare, -commodāvī, -commodātum

suitable *adj.* aptus, -a, -um

suite *n.* comitātus, -ūs *m.* (*retinue*)

suitor *n.* procus, -ī *m.* (*wooer*); *n.* petītor, -ōris *m.* (*plaintiff*; *petitioner*; *candidate*)

sullen *adj.* trīstis, -is, -e

sum *n.* summa, -ae *f.*; **~ up** *v.t.* subdūcō, -ducere, -dūxī, -ductum (*calculate*)

summarize *v.t.* coartō (coarctō), -āre, -āvī, -ātum

summary *n.* epitomē, -ēs *f.*

summer *n.* aestās, -ātis *f.*; *adj.* aestīvus, -a, -um; **in ~** *adv.* aestāte

summit *n.* cacūmen, -inis *nt.*

sun *n.* sōl, sōlis *m.*

sunburnt *adj.* fuscus, -a, -um

Sunday *n.* diēs Sōlis, diēī Sōlis *m.*

sundial *n.* sōlārium, -ī *nt.*

sunny *adj.* aprīcus, -a, -um

sunrise *n.* sōlis ortus, sōlis ortūs *m.*

sunset *n.* sōlis occāsus, sōlis occāsūs *m.*

sunshine *n.* sōl, sōlis *m.*

superficial *adj.* levis, -is, -e

superior *adj.* superior, superius (*higher; better*); *adj.* melior, melius (*better*)

superstition *n.* superstitiō, -ōnis *f.*

superstitious *adj.* superstitiōsus, -a, -um

supervise *v.t.* prōcūrō, -cūrāre, -cūrāvī, -cūrātum

supervisor *n.* prōcūrātor, -ōris *m.*

supper *n.* cēna, -ae *f.*

suppliant *n.* supplex, -plicis *m./f.*

supplicate *v.i.* supplicō, -plicāre, -plicāvī, -plicātum (+ dat.)

supply *n.* cōpia, -ae *f.; v.t.* suppleō, -plēre, -plēvī, -plētum (*fill up*); *v.t.* praebeō, -bēre, -buī, -bitum (*furnish*)

support *n.* fulcīmentum, -ī *nt.* (*prop*); *n.* alimenta, -ōrum *nt./pl.* (*nourishment; maintenance*); *n.* subsidium, -ī *nt.* (*help*); *v.t.* sustineō, -tinēre, -tinuī, -tentum (*hold up*); *v.t.* alō, -ere, aluī, alitum (*maintain; nourish*); *v.t.* adiuvō, -iuvāre, -iūvī, -iūtum (*help*)

supporter *n.* adiūtor, -ōris *m.*

suppose *v.d.i.* opīnor, opīnārī, opīnātus sum

suppress *v.t.* supprimō, -primere, -pressī, -pressum

sure *adj.* certus, -a, -um (*certain; unavoidable; evident*); *adj.* tūtus, -a, -um (*safe*); *adj.* fidēlis, -is, -e (*faithful; trustworthy; trusted*); *adj.* firmus, -a, -um (*stable*)

surety *n.* vas, vadis *m.*

surf *n.* fluctus, -ūs *m.*

surface *n.* superficiēs, -ēī *f.*

surgeon *n.* medicus, -ī *m.*

surgery *n.* chiūrgia, -ae *f.*

surly *adj.* mōrōsus, -a, -um

surname *n.* cōgnōmen, -inis *nt.*

surpass *v.t.* superō, -āre, -āvī, -ātum

surplus *n.* cumulus, -ī *m.*

surprise *n.* mīrātiō, -ōnis *f.* (*feeling of surprise*); *v.t.* obstupefaciō, -facere, -fēcī, -factum (*astonish*); *v.t.* occupō, -āre, -āvī, -ātum (*take unawares*)

surprising *adj.* mīrus, -a, -um

surrender *n.* dēditiō, -ōnis *f.* (*capitulation*); *n.* trāditiō, -ōnis *f.* (*handing over of a town*); *v.t.* trādō, -dere, -didī, -ditum (*hand over*); *v.i.* cēdō, -ere, cessī, cessum (+ dat.) (*yield; abandon*)

surround *v.t.* cingō, -ere, cīnxī, cīnctum

surrounding *adj.* circumiectus, -a, -um

survive *v.i.* supersum, -esse, -fuī, ---

survivor *n.* superstes, -stitis *m./f.*

suspect *v.d.i.* suspicor, suspicārī, suspicātus sum

suspend *v.t.* suspendō, -pendere, -pendī, -pēnsum (*hang up; stop; interrupt*); *v.t.* intermittō, -mittere, -mīsī, -missum (*defer*); *v.t.* summoveō, -movēre, -mōvī, -mōtum (*remove from office*)

suspicion *n.* suspiciō, -ōnis *f.*

suspicious *adj.* suspiciōsus, -a, -um

sustain *v.t.* sustineō, -tinēre, -tinuī, -tentum

swallow *n.* hirundō, -dinis *f.* (*zool.*); *v.t.* vorō, -āre, -āvī, -ātum

swamp *n.* palus, palūdis *f.*

swan *n.* cygnus, -ī *m.*

swarm *n.* exāmen, -inis *nt.* (*of bees*); *n.* turba, -ae *f.* (*of people*)

swear *v.t.* iūrō, -āre, -āvī, -ātum; ~ **falsely** *v.t.* pēierō (pēiurō), -ierāre, -ierāvī, -ierātum

sweat *n.* sūdor, -ōris *m.*; *v.i.* sūdō, -āre, -āvī, -ātum

sweep *v.t.* verrō, -ere, verrī, versum

sweet *adj.* dulcis, -is, -e

sweeten *v.t.* dulcem reddō, -dere, -didī, -ditum

swell *n.* aestus, -ūs *m.* (*of the sea*); *v.i.* tumeō, -ēre, ---, ---

swelling *n.* tumor, -ōris *m.*

swift *adj.* celer, celeris, celere

swim *v.i.* natō, -āre, -āvī, -ātum

swimmer *n.* natātor, -ōris *m./f.*

swimming *n.* natātiō, -ōnis *f.*

swindle *v.t.* fraudō, -āre, -āvī, -ātum

swindler *n.* fraudātor, -ōris *m.*

swing *v.t., v.i.* oscillō, -āre, -āvī, -ātum

switch *n.* virga, -ae *f.* (*stick*); *v.t.* substituō, -stituere, -stituī, -ūtum (*substitute*)

sword *n.* gladius, -ī *m.*

syllable *n.* syllaba, -ae *f.*

symbol *n.* signum, -ī *nt.*

sympathetic *adj.* misericors, -cordis
sympathize *v.d.i.* miseror, miserārī, miserātus sum
sympathy *n.* misericordia, -ae *f.*
symptom *n.* indicium, -ī *nt.*
synagogue *n.* synagōga, -ae *f.*
syntax *n.* syntaxis, -is, *f.*
system *n.* ratiō, -ōnis *f.*
systematic *adj.* ordinātus, -a, -um

T

table *n.* mēnsa, -ae *f.*
tablecloth *n.* mantēle, -is *nt.*
tablet *n.* tabula, -ae *f.*
tack *n.* clāvulus, -ī *m.*
tactic *n.* rēs mīlitāris, reī mīlitāris *f.*
tail *n.* cauda, -ae *f.*
take *v.t.* capiō, -ere, cēpī, captum (*get possession of; conduct; lead*); *v.t.*
    rapiō, -ere, rapuī, raptum (*seize and carry off*); *v.t.* accipiō, -cipere, -cēpī,
    -ceptum (*receive; submit to*); *v.t.* conducō, -ducere, -dūxī, -ductum
    (*hire*); *v.t.* dēprehendō, -prehendere, -prehendī, -prehensum (*seize
    upon; over~*); *v.t.* ferō, ferre, tūlī, lātum (*~ up; carry*)
tale *n.* fābula, -ae *f.*
talent *n.* ingenium, -ī *nt.* (*ability*); *n.* talentum, -ī *nt.* (*unit of money; unit of
    weight*)
talented *adj.* ingeniōsus, -a, -um
talk *n.* sermō, -ōnis *m.*; *v.d.i.* loquor, loquī, locūtus sum
talkative *adj.* loquāx, loquācis
tall *adj.* prōcērus, -a, -um
tame *adj.* mansuētus, -a, -um; *v.t.* mansuēfaciō, -facere, -fēcī, -factum
tamper *v.t.* interveniō, -venīre, -vēnī, -ventum (*interfere*); *~* **with** *v.t.*
    temptō, -āre, -āvī, -ātum
tan *v.t.* perficiō, -ficere, -fēcī, -fectum (*of animal skins*); *v.i.* colōrō, -āre, -āvī,
    -ātum (*become darkened by the sun*)
tangle *v.t.* implicō, -plicāre, -plicāvī, -plicātum
tank *n.* lacus, -ūs *m.* (*cistern*)
tap *n.* levis plāga, levis plāgae *f.* (*a light hit*); *v.t.* leviter feriō, -īre, -īvī, -ītum
tar *n.* pix, picis *f.*
target *n.* scopus, -ī *m.*

tariff *n.* portōrium, -ī *nt.*

tart *adj.* acerbus, -a, -um

task *n.* opus, operis *nt.*

taste *n.* gustātus, -ūs *m.* (*sense of ~*); *n.* sapor, -ōris *m.* (*flavor*); *n.* gustus, -ūs *m.* (*nibble*); *n.* ēlegantia, -ae *f.* (*good style; discrimination*); *v.t.* gustō, -āre, -āvī, -ātum; *v.i.* sapiō, -ere, -īvī, ---

tavern *n.* caupōna, -ae *f.*

tax *n.* vectīgal, -ālis *nt.*

teach *v.t.* doceō, -ēre, docuī, doctum (w. acc. of person taught and subject taught)

teacher *n.* magister, magistrī *m.*; *n.* magistra, -ae *f.*

team *n.* iugālēs, -ium *m./pl.* (*of horses and oxen*)

tear *n.* lacrima, -ae *f.* (*of the eye*); *n.* scissūra, -ae *f.* (*rip*); *v.t.* scindō, -ere, scidī, scissum

tease *v.t.* vexō, -āre, -āvī, -ātum

tell *v.t.* nārrō, -āre, -āvī, -ātum (*relate*); *v.t.* iubeō, -ēre, iussī, iussum (*order*)

temper *n.* ingenium, -ī *nt.*

temperate *adj.* temperātus, -a, -um

temple *n.* aedis (aedēs), -is *f.* (*arch.*); *n.* templum, -ī *nt.* (*arch.*); *n.* tempus, -oris *nt.* (*anat.*)

temporary *adj.* temporārius, -a, -um

tempt *v.t.* temptō, -āre, -āvī, -ātum

temptation *n.* sollicitātiō, -ōnis *f.* (*act of tempting*)

ten *num.* decem (*indecl.*)

tenacious *adj.* tenāx, tenācis

tenant *n.* inquilīnus, -ī *m.*; *n.* inquilīna, -ae *f.*

tend *v.i.* pertineō, -tinēre, -tinuī, ---

tendency *n.* inclīnātiō, -ōnis *f.*

tender *adj.* tener, tenera, tenerum (*soft; gentle; sensitive*); *adj.* amāns, -antis (*loving*)

tendon *n.* nervus, -ī *m.*

tense *n.* tempus, -oris *nt.*; *adj.* tentus, -a, -um

tension *n.* intentiō, -ōnis *f.*

tent *n.* tabernāculum, -ī *nt.*

tentacle *n.* bracchium, -ī *nt.*

tenth *adj.* decimus, -a, -um

tepid *adj.* tepidus, -a, -um

term *n.* spatium, -ī *nt.* (*set period of time*); *n.* terminus, -ī *m.* (*limit*); *n.* verbum, -ī *nt.* (*word; expression*); *n.* condiciō, -ōnis *f.* (*condition*)

terminate *v.t.* terminō, -āre, -āvī, -ātum
terrestrial *adj.* terrestris, -is, -e
terrible *adj.* terribilis, -is, -e
terribly *adv.* atrōciter (*cruelly*)
terrific *adj.* terribilis, -is, -e
territory *n.* finēs, -ium *m./pl.*
terror *n.* terror, -ōris *m.*
test *n.* experīmentum, -ī *nt.* (*trial*); *v.t.* temptō, -āre, -āvī, -ātum
testify *v.d.i.* testor, testārī, testātus sum
testimony *n.* testimōnium, -ī *nt.*
text *n.* scrīptum, -ī *nt.*
textile *n.* textile, -is *nt.*
than *conj.* Use abl. of comparison or quam.
thank *v.t.* grātiās agō, -ere, ēgī, actum
thankful *adj.* grātus, -a, -um
thanks *n./pl.* grātia, -ae *f.*
that *adj., pron.* ille, illa, illud; is, ea, id
thaw *v.t.* solvō, -ere, solvī, solūtum
the *art.* not expressed in Latin
theater *n.* theātrum, -ī *nt.*
their *pron.* Use gen. pl. of ille, illa, illud *or* is, ea, id; **~ own** *adj.* suus, -a, -um
them *pron.* Use acc. pl. of of ille, illa, illud *or* is, ea, id
theme *n.* rēs, reī *f.*
themselves *refl. pron.* Use forms of sē; *pron.* ipsī, ipsae, ipsa
then *adv.* tum
theory *n.* ratiō, -ōnis *f.*
there *adv.* ibi; **~ is/are** *exp.* est/sunt
therefore *adv.* igitur
these *adj., pron.* hī, hae, haec
thesis *n.* rēs, reī *f.*
they *pron.* illī, illae, illa; *pron.* is, ea, id (*often expressed only by verb ending*)
thick *adj.* dēnsus, -a, -um (*closely packed*); *adj.* crassus, -a, -um (*of liquids and solid objects*)
thicken *v.t.* dēnsō, -āre, āvī, -ātum; *v.i.* concrēscō, -crēscere, -crēvī, -crētum
thickness *n.* crassitūdō, -inis *f.*
thief *n.* fūr, fūris *m.*
thigh *n.* femur, -oris (-inis) *nt.*
thin *adj.* tenuis, -is, -e
thing *n.* rēs, reī *f.* (*or use adj. as a substantive*)

think *v.i.* cōgitō, -āre, -āvī, -ātum (*ponder*); *v.i.* exīstimō, -āre, -āvī, -ātum
    (*believe; suppose*)
third *adj.* tertius, -a, -um
thirst *n.* sitis, -is *f.*
thirsty *adj.* sitiēns, -ientis; **be ~** *v.i.* sitiō, -īre, -īvī, ---
thirteen *num.* tredecim (*indecl.*)
thirteenth *adj.* tertius decimus, tertia decima, tertius decimus
thirty *num.* trīgintā (*indecl.*)
this *adj., pron.* hic, haec, hoc
thorn *n.* spīna, -ae *f.*
thoroughfare *n.* pervium, -ī *nt.*
those *adj., pron.* illī, illae, illa
though *conj.* quamquam, cum (+ subjv.)
thought *n.* cōgitātiō, -ōnis *f.*
thoughtful *adj.* prūdēns, -entis (*sensible*)
thousand *num.* mīlle (*indecl.*)
thousandth *adj.* mīllēsimus, -a, -um
thread *n.* līnum, -ī *nt.*
threat *n.* minae, -ārum *f./pl.*
threaten *v.d.i.* minor, minārī, minātus sum (+ dat. of person)
three *num.* trēs, tria
threshold *n.* līmen, -inis *nt.*
thrift *n.* frūgālitās, -ātis *f.*
thrifty *adj.* frūgālis, -is, -e
thrive *v.i.* vigeō, -ēre, viguī, ---
throat *n.* faucēs, -ium *f./pl.*
throb *v.i.* palpitō, -āre, -āvī, -ātum
throne *n.* solium, -ī *nt.*
through *prep.* per (+ acc.) (*of place or time*), propter (+ acc.) (*on account
    of*) (*for means or instrument, use abl.*)
throughout *adv.* penitus
throw *n.* iactus, -ūs *m.*; *v.t.* iaciō, -ere, iēcī, iactum; **~ away** *v.t.* abiciō,
    -icere, -iēcī, -iectum; **~ up** *v.t.* vomō, -ere, -uī, -itum (*vomit*)
thrust *v.t.* trūdō, -ere, trūsī, trūsum
thumb *n.* pollex, -licis *m.*
thunder *n.* tonitrus, -ūs *m.*
thunderstorm *n.* tonitrua et fulmina, tonitruum et fulminum *nt./pl.*
Thursday *n.* diēs Iōvis, diēī Iōvis *m.*
thyme *n.* thymum, -ī *nt.*

ticket *n.* tessera, -ae *f.*

tickle *v.t.* tītillō, -āre, -āvī, -ātum

tide *n.* aestus, -ūs *m.*

tidy *adj.* mundus, -a, -um

tie *n.* vinculum, -ī (*bond*); *v.t.* ligō, -āre, -āvī, -ātum

tiger *n.* tigris, -is (-idis) *m./f.*

tight *adj.* strictus, -a, -um

tighten *v.t.* stringō, -ere, strinxī, strictum

tile *n.* tēgula, -ae *f.*

timber *n.* māteria, -ae *f.*

time *n.* tempus, -oris *nt.*

timid *adj.* timidus, -a, -um

tin *n.* plumbum album, plumbī albī *nt.*

tingle *v.i.* formīcō, -āre, -āvī, -ātum

tint *n.* color, -ōris *m.*; *v.t.* imbuō, -buere, -buī, -būtum

tip *n.* apex, apicis *m.*; *v.t., v.i.* invertō, -vertere, -vertī, -versum (*incline*)

tiptoe *n.* suspēnsō gradū (*abl. of manner*)

tire *v.t.* fātīgō, -āre, -āvī, -ātum

tired *adj.* fatīgātus, -a, -um; **be ~** *v.i.* taedet, -ēre, taeduit (taesum est) (*imp.*) (+ acc. of person + gen. of thing)

tiredness *n.* fātīgātiō, -ōnis *f.*

tiresome *adj.* importūnus, -a, -um (*of persons*); *adj.* labōriōsus, -a, -um (*of things*)

tissue *n.* textile, -is *nt.* (*textile*)

title *n.* nōmen, -inis *nt.* (*name*); *n.* titulus, -ī *m.* (*inscription*)

to *prep.* ad (+ acc.)

toad *n.* būfō, -ōnis *m.*

today *adv.* hodiē

toe *n.* digitus, -ī *m.*

toga *n.* toga, -ae *f.*

together *adv.* simul

toil *n.* labor, -ōris *m.*; *v.t.* labōrō, -āre, -āvī, -ātum

toilet *n.* lātrīna, -ae *f.* (*privy*)

toilette *n.* cultus, -ūs *m.*

token *n.* signum, -ī *nt.*

tolerance *n.* patientia, -ae *f.*

tolerate *v.t.* tolerō, -āre, -āvī, -ātum

toll *n.* vectīgal, -ālis *nt.*

tomb *n.* sepulcrum, -ī *nt.*

tomorrow *adv.* crās

tone *n.* sonus, -ī *m.* (*character; style*)

tongs *n.* forceps, -cipis *m./f.*

tongue *n.* lingua, -ae *f.*

tonsils *n.* tonsillae, -ārum *f./pl.*

too *adv.* etiam (*also*); *adv.* nimis (*to an excessive degree*); *for sup. degree, use*
-issimus, -a, -um

tool *n.* īnstrūmentum, -ī *nt.*

tooth *n.* dēns, dentis *m.*

top *n.* culmen, -inis *nt.*; *adj.* summus, -a, -um

topic *n.* rēs, reī *f.*

torch *n.* taeda, -ae *f.*

torment *n.* cruciātus, -ūs *m.*; *v.t.* cruciō, -āre, -āvī, -ātum

torque *n.* torques (torquis), -is *m./f.* (*twisted neck-chain*)

torrent *n.* torrēns, torrentis *m.*

torture *n.* tormenta, -ōrum *nt./pl.* (*instruments of torture; pain*); *n.*
cruciātus, -ūs *m.* (*pain; extreme suffering*); *v.t.* excruciō, -āre, -āvī, -ātum

toss *v.t.* iactō, -āre, -āvī, -ātum

total *n.* summa, -ae *f.*; *adj.* tōtus, -a, -um; **~ly** *adv.* omnīnō

touch *n.* tactus, -ūs *m.*; *v.t.* tangō, -ere, tetigī, tāctum (*physically*); *v.t.*
commoveō, commovēre, commōvī, commōtum (*emotionally*)

touchy *adj.* īrācundus, -a, -um

tough *adj.* lentus, -a, -um (*not brittle*); *adj.* difficilis, -is, -e (*not easy*)

toughness *n.* dūritia, -ae *f.* (*hardness*)

tour *n.* peregrīnātiō, -ōnis *f.*; *v.t.* circumeō, -īre, -īvī (-iī), -itum

tow *v.t.* trahō, -ere, trāxī, trāctum

toward *prep.* adversum, adversus (+ acc.) (*motion towards*); *prep.* sub (+
acc.) (*of time, e.g. towards night*); *prep.* ergā (+ acc.) (*of feelings*)

tower *n.* turris, -is *f.*

town *n.* oppidum, -ī *nt.*

toy *n.* crepundia, -ōrum *nt./pl.*

trace *n.* vestīgium, -ī *nt.* (*footprint; mark; indication*); *v.t.* dēsignō, -signāre,
-signāvī, -signātum (*draw; mark out*); *v.t.* investīgō, -āre, -āvī, -ātum
(*track; discover*)

track *n.* vestīgium, -ī *n.* (*footprint; mark; indication*); *n.* callis, -is *m./f.*
(*path*); *v.t.* investīgō, -vestīgāre, -vestīgāvī, -vestīgātum

trade *n.* mercātūra, -ae *f.* (*commerce*); *n.* ars, artis *f.* (*occupation*); *v.d.t.*
commercor, commercārī, commercātus sum; *v.d.i.* mercor, mercārī,
mercātus sum

trader *n.* mercātor, -ōris *m.*

tradition *n.* memoria, -ae *f.*

traditional *adj.* antīquus, -a, -um

tragedy *n.* tragoedia, -ae *f.*

tragic *adj.* tragicus, -a, -um

trail *n.* vestīgia, -ōrum *nt./pl.* (*marks left behind*); *n.* callis, -is *m./f.* (*path*); *v.t.* trahō, -ere, trāxī, trāctum (*drag*)

train *n.* pompa, -ae *f.* (*retinue*); *n.* ordō, -inis *m.* (*succession of events, etc.*); *n.* impedīmenta, -ōrum *nt./pl.* (*baggage, etc. following an army*); *v.t.* īnstituō, -stituere, -stituī, -stitūtum (*educate*); *v.t.* exerceō, -ercēre, -ercuī, -ercitum (*drill to prepare for battle or contest*)

trainer *n.* aliptēs, -is *m.*, alipta, -ae *m.* (*of wrestlers*); *n.* lanista, -ae *m.* (*of gladiators*)

training *n.* disciplīna, -ae *f.* (*instruction*); *n.* exercitātiō, -ōnis *f.* (*physical ~*)

trait *n.* habitus, -ūs *m.*

traitor *n.* prōditor, -ōris *m.*

tranquil *adj.* tranquillus, -a, -um

tranquility *n.* tranquillitās, -ātis *f.*

transaction *n.* rēs, reī *f.*

transfer *v.t.* trānsferō, -ferre, -tulī, -lātum

transit *n.* trānsitus, -ūs *m.*

translate *v.d.t.* interpretor, interpretārī, interpretātus sum

translation *n.* interpretātiō, -ōnis *f.*

translator *n.* interpres, interpretis *m./f.*

transmit *v.t.* trānsmittō, -mittere, -mīsī, -missum

trap *n.* pedica, -ae *f.*; *v.t.* captō, -āre, -āvī, -ātum

trash *n.* quisquiliae, -ārum *f./pl.*

travel *v.d.i.* peregrīnor, peregrīnārī, peregrīnātus sum

traveler *n.* viātor, -ōris *m.*

tray *n.* ferculum, -ī *nt.*

treason *n.* māiestās, -ātis *f.*

treasure *n.* thēsaurus, -ī *m.*

treasurer *n.* aerāriī praefectus, aerāriī praefectī *m.*

treasury *n.* aerārium, -ī *nt.*

treat *v.t.* trāctō, -āre, -āvī, -ātum (*deal with; discuss*); *v.t.* cūrō, -āre, -āvī, -ātum (*care for medically*); *v.t.* agō, -ere, ēgī, actum (*carry on negotiations*)

treatise *n.* līber, librī *m.*

treatment *n.* trāctātiō, -ōnis *f.*

treaty *n.* foedus, -eris *nt.*

tree *n.* arbor, -oris *f.*
tremble *v.i.* tremō, -ere, -uī, ---
trench *n.* fossa, -ae *f.*
trespass *n.* peccātum, -ī *nt.* (*wrong-doing*)
trial *n.* experientia, -ae *f.* (*test*); *n.* cōnātus, -ūs *m.* (*attempt*); *n.* iūdicium, -ī *nt.* (*judicial ~*); **bring to ~** in iūdicium vōcō, -āre, -āvī, -ātum
triangle *n.* triangulum, -ī *nt.*
triangular *adj.* triangulus, -a, -um
tribe *n.* tribus, -ūs *f.*
tribunal *n.* tribūnal, -ālis *nt.*
tribune *n.* tribūnus plēbis, tribūnī plēbis *m.*
tribute *n.* tribūtum, -ī *nt.* (*tax*)
trick *n.* dolus, -ī *m.*; *v.t.* illūdō, -lūdere, -lūsī, -lūsum
trickle *v.i.* stīllō, -āre, -āvī, -ātum
trident *n.* tridēns, -dentis *m.*
trifles *n.* nūgae, -ārum *f./pl.*
trip *n.* iter, itineris *nt.* (*journey*)
tripod *n.* tripūs, -podis *m.*
triumph *n.* triumphus, -ī *m.*
trivial *adj.* levis, -is, -e
troop *n.* turma, -ae *f.*; **~s** *n.* cōpiae, -ārum *f./pl.*
trophy *n.* tropaeum, -ī *nt.*
tropical *adj.* aestuōsus, -a, -um
trouble *n.* labor, -ōris *m.* (*hardship*); *n.* sollicitūdō, -inis *f.* (*worry*); *v.t.* vexō, -āre, -āvī, -ātum (*annoy; harass*); *v.t.* sollicitō, -āre, -āvī, -ātum (*worry; disturb*)
troublesome *adj.* molestus, -a, -um (*annoying*); *adj.* gravis, -is, -e (*burdensome*); *adj.* incommodus, -a, -um (*inconvenient*)
trowel *n.* trulla, -ae *f.*
truce *n.* indūtiae, -ārum *f./pl.*
true *adj.* vērus, -a, -um (*not false; real; genuine*); *adj.* fidus, -a, -um (*faithful*)
truffle *n.* tūber, tūberis *nt.*
truly *adv.* vērē, vērō
trunk *n.* truncus, -ī *m.* (*bot.*); *n.* cista, -ae *f.* (*box*); *n.* proboscis, -scidis *f.* (*zool.*)
trust *n.* fidēs, -eī *f.* (*confidence; protection*); *v.i.* cōnfīdō, -fidere, -fīsus sum (+ *dat.* of persons *or* + *abl.* of things)
trustworthy *adj.* fidus, -a, -um
truth *n.* vēritās, -ātis *f.*
truthful *adj.* vērāx, -ācis

try *n.* cōnātus, -ūs *m.*; *v.d.t.* experior, experīrī, expertus sum (*make trial of*);
    v.d.t. cōnor, cōnārī, cōnātus sum (*attempt*); *v.t.* iūdicō, -dicāre, -dicāvī,
    -dicātum (*try judicially*)
tube *n.* tubus, -ī *m.*
Tuesday *n.* diēs Mārtis, diēī Mārtis *m.*
tug *v.t.* trahō, -ere, trāxī, trāctum
tumor *n.* tumor, -ōris *m.*
tumult *n.* tumultus, -ūs *m.*
tune *n.* cantus, -ūs *m.*
tunic *n.* tunica, -ae *f.*
tunnel *n.* cunīculus, -ī *m.*
turmoil *n.* turba, -ae *f.*
turn *n.* conversiō, -ōnis *f.* (*revolving*); *n.* flexus, -ūs *m.* (*bending*); *n.*
    vicissitūdō, -inis *f.* (*change in course of events*); *v.t.* vertō, -ere, versī,
    versum (*change; change direction*); *v.t.* volvō, -ere, volvī, volūtum (*cause
    to revolve*); *v.i.* convertō, -vertere, -vertī, -versum (+ refl. pron.) (*change
    one's direction*)
turtle *n.* tēstūdō, -inis *f.*
tutor *n.* magister, magistrī *m.*
tweezers *n.* volsella, -ae *f.*
twelfth *adj.* duodecimus, -a, -um
twelve *num.* duodecim (*indecl.*)
twentieth *adj.* vīcēsimus, -a, -um
twenty *num.* vīgintī (*indecl.*)
twice *adv.* bis
twig *n.* surculus, -ī *m.*
twilight *n.* crepusculum, -ī *nt.*
twin *adj.* geminus, -a, -um
twinge *n.* dolor, -ōris *m.*
twinkle *v.i.* micō, -āre, -uī, ---
twist *v.t.* torqueō, -ēre, torsī, tortum
two *num.* duo, duae, duo
type *n.* exemplar, -āris *nt.* (*model*); *n.* genus, -eris *nt.* (*class*)

U

ugly *adj.* dēfōrmis, -is, -e
ulcer *n.* ulcus, ulceris *nt.*
ultimate *adj.* ultimus, -a, -um

umbrella *n.* umbella, -ae *f.*

unable, be ~ *v.i.* nequeō, -quīre, -quīvī (-iī), -itum (+ infv.)

unacceptable *adj.* ingrātus, -a, -um

unaccountable *adj.* inexplicābilis, -is, -e

unanimous *adj.* concors, -cordis

unarmed *adj.* inermis, -is, -e

unauthorized *adj.* illicitus, -a, -um

unavenged *adj.* inultus, -a, -um

unavoidable *adj.* inēvītābilis, -is, -e

unaware *adj.* inscius, -a, -um

uncertain *adj.* incertus, -a, -um

uncle *n.* patruus, -ī *m.* (*paternal*); *n.* avunculus, -ī *m.* (*maternal*)

uncomfortable *adj.* incommodus, -a, -um

unconscious *adj.* inscius, -a, -um (*unaware*)

uncover *v.t.* retegō, -tegere, -tēxī, -tēctum

undamaged *adj.* integer, integra, integrum

undecided *adj.* incertus, -a, -um

under *adv.* īnfrā; *prep.* sub (+ abl. *or* + acc.)

undergo *v.d.t.* patior, patī, passus sum

underground *adj.* subterrāneus, -a, -um

underneath *prep.* īnfrā (+ acc.); *adv.* īnfrā

understand *v.t.* intellegō, -legere, -lēxī, -lēctum

understanding *n.* mēns, mentis *f.*

undertake *v.t.* suscipiō, -cipere, -cēpī, -ceptum

underwear *n.* subligāculum, -ī *nt.* (*breechcloth*)

undo *v.t.* solvō, -ere, solvī, solūtum (*unfasten; release*); *v.t.* īnfirmō, -firmāre, -firmāvī, -firmātum (*nullify*)

uneasiness *n.* sollicitūdō, -inis *f.*

uneasy *adj.* sollicitus, -a, -um

uneducated *adj.* indoctus, -a, -um

unemployed *adj.* ōtiōsus, -a, -um; **be ~** *v.i.* cessō, -āre, -āvī, -ātum

unequal *adj.* impār, imparis

unfair *adj.* inīquus, -a, -um

unfaithful *adj.* īnfidus, -a, -um

unfamiliar *adj.* mīrus, -a, -um (*unusual; uncommon*); *adj.* ignōtus, -a, -um (*unknown*)

unfasten *v.t.* solvō, -ere, solvī, solūtum

unfortunate *adj.* īnfēlīx, īnfēlīcis; **~ly** *adv.* īnfēlīciter

unfriendly *adj.* inimīcus, -a, -um

unguent *n.* unguentum, -ī *nt.*

unhappy *adj.* miser, misera, miserum

unhealthy *adj.* īnsalūbris, -is, -e (*causing illness*); *adj.* īnfirmus, -a, -um (*feeble*)

uniform *adj.* aequābilis, -is, -e

unimportant *adj.* levis, -is, -e

unintentional *adj.* nōn sponte

union *n.* coniūnctiō, -ōnis *f.* (*act of joining*); *n.* foedus, -eris *nt.* (*alliance*); *n.* concordia, -ae *f.* (*unanimity*)

unique *adj.* ūnicus, -a, -um

unite *v.t.* coniungō, -iungere, -iūnxī, -iūnctum

unity *n.* concordia, -ae *f.*

universal *adj.* commūnis, -is, -e

universe *n.* mundus, -ī *m.*

unknown *adj.* ignōtus, -a, -um

unless *conj.* nisi

unlike *adj.* dissimilis, -is, -e

unlikely *adj.* imprōvīsus, -a, -um

unload *v.t.* exonerō, -onerāre, -onerāvī, -onerātum (*free from a burden*); *v.t.* dēpōnō, -pōnere, -posuī, -positum (*put down a burden*)

unlucky *adj.* īnfēlīx, īnfēlīcis

unnecessary *adj.* supervacāneus, -a, -um

unpack *v.t.* exonerō, -onerāre, -onerāvī, -onerātum

unpleasant *adj.* iniūcundus, -a, -um

unpopular *adj.* invīsus, -a, -um

unrest *n.* inquiēs, -ētis *f.*

unsafe *adj.* perīculōsus, -a, -um

unsatisfactory *adj.* malus, -a, -um

unskilled *adj.* imperītus, -a, -um

unstable *adj.* īnstabilis, -is, -e

unsuccessful *adj.* īnfēlīx, īnfēlīcis

untie *v.t.* solvō, -ere, solvī, solūtum

until *conj.* dum, dōnec, quoad; *prep.* ad (+ acc.)

untrue *adj.* falsus, -a, -um

unwell *adj.* aeger, aegra, aegrum

unwrap *v.t.* ēvolvō, -volvere, -volvī, -volūtum (*unroll*); *v.t.* explicō, -plicāre, -plicāvī, -plicātum (*unfold*)

up *adv.* sursum; *prep. Usually expressed by a verbal prefix, e.g.* ad-, sub-, ex-; ~ **to** *adv.* usque ad (+ acc.)

upon *prep.* in (+ abl.); *prep.* super (+ acc.)
upper *adj.* superus, -a, -um
uproar *n.* tumultus, -ūs *m.*
upset *v.t.* ēvertō, -vertere, -vertī, -versum (*overturn*); *v.t.* commoveō, -movēre, -mōvī, -mōtum (*disquiet; disturb*)
upsetting *adj.* gravis, -is, -e (*distressing*)
upstream *adv.* adversō flūmine
upward(s) *adv.* sursum
urban *adj.* urbānus, -a, -um
urge *v.t.* īnstō, -stāre, -stitī, -stātum
urgent *adj.* gravis, -is, -e
urinary *adj.* ūrīnālis, -is, -e
urine *n.* ūrīna, -ae *f.*
urn *n.* urna, -ae *f.*
us *pron.* Use forms of nōs.
usage *n.* mōs, mōris *m.*
use *n.* ūsus, -ūs *m.*; *v.d.i.* ūtor, ūtī, ūsus sum (+ abl.)
used to *adj.* assuētus, -a, -um (+ dat.); *For verbal aux., use imperfect tense.*
useful *adj.* ūtilis, -is, -e
useless *adj.* inūtilis, -is, -e
usual *adj.* ūsitātus, -a, -um; **~ly** *adv.* ferē
utensils *n./pl.* ūtēnsilia, -ium *nt./pl.*
uterus *n.* uterus, -ī *m.*
utility *n.* ūtilitās, -ātis *f.* (*usefulness*)
utilize *v.d.t, v.d.i.* ūtor, ūtī, ūsus sum (+ abl.)
utmost *adj.* extrēmus, -a, -um
utter *adj.* tōtus, -a, -um; *v.t.* dīcō, -ere, dīxī, dictum

V

vacancy *n.* vacuum, -ī *nt.* (*emptiness*)
vacant *adj.* vacuus, -a, -um
vacuum *n.* vacuum, -ī *nt.* (*emptiness*)
vague *adj.* incertus, -a, -um
vain *adj.* inānis, -is, -e (*empty; worthless; fruitless*); *adj.* glōriōsus, -a, -um (*bragging; conceited*); **in ~** *adv.* frūstrā
valiant *adj.* fortis, -is, -e
valid *adj.* validus, -a, -um (*of arguments, reasons, etc.*); *adj.* ratus, -a, -um (*established by law*)

valley *n.* vallis, -is *f.*

valor *n.* virtūs, -ūtis *f.*

valuable *adj.* pretiōsus, -a, -um

value *n.* pretium, -ī *nt.* (*price*); *n.* aestimātiō, -ōnis *f.* (*estimated worth*); *v.t.* aestimō, -āre, -āvī, -ātum (*set a price on*); *v.t.* dīligō, -ligere, -lēxī, -lēctum (*esteem*)

vanish *v.i.* ēvānēscō, -vānēscere, -vānuī, ---

vapor *n.* vapor, -ōris *m.*

variable *adj.* varius, -a, -um

variation *n.* varietās, -ātis *f.*

variety *n.* varietās, -ātis *f.*

various *adj.* varius, -a, -um

vary *v.t.* variō, -āre, -āvī, -ātum

vase *n.* vās, vāsis *nt.*

vast *adj.* vastus, -a, -um

vault *n.* fornix, -icis *m.*

veal *n.* vitulīna, -ae *f.*

vegetable *n.* holus, holeris *nt.*

vegetation *n.* herbae, -ārum *f./pl.*

vehement *adj.* vehemēns, -entis

vehicle *n.* vehiculum, -ī *nt.*

veil *n.* palla, -ae *f.* (*woman's head veil*); **bridal ~** *n.* flammeum, -ī *nt.*; *v.t.* vēlō, -āre, -āvī, -ātum

vein *n.* vēna, -ae *f.*

venerate *v.d.t.* veneror, venerārī, venerātus sum

venereal *adj.* venereus, -a, -um

vengeance *n.* ultiō, -ōnis *f.*

venom *n.* venēnum, -ī *nt.*

vent *n.* spīrāculum, -ī *nt.*; *v.t.* aperiō, -īre, aperuī, apertum

ventilation *n.* ventilātiō, -ōnis *f.*

venture *n.* perīculum, -ī *nt.* (*risk*)

verb *n.* verbum, -ī *nt.*

verdict *n.* iūdicium, -ī *nt.*

verge *n.* margō, -inis *m./f.*

verification *n.* cōnfirmātiō, -ōnis *f.*

verify *v.t.* cōnfirmō, -firmāre, -firmāvī, -firmātum

versatile *adj.* versātilis, -is, -e

verse *n.* versus, -ūs *m.*

versus *prep.* contrā (+ acc.)

vertebra *n.* vertebra, -ae *f.*

vertical *adj.* dīrēctus, -a, -um

very *adv.* For adjs. and advs., use the sup. form.

vessel *n.* vās, vāsis *nt.* (*vase*); *n.* nāvis, -is *f.* (*ship*); **blood ~** *n.* artēria, -ae *f.* (*artery*), vēna, -ae *f.* (*vein*)

vestal virgin *n.* virgō Vestālis, virginis Vestālis *f.*

veteran *n.* veterānus, -ī *m.*; *adj.* veterānus, -a, -um

vial *n.* ampulla, -ae *f.*

vibrate *v.i.* vibrō, -āre, -āvī, -ātum

vice *n.* vitium, -ī *nt.*

vicinity *n.* vīcīnitās, -ātis *f.*

vicious *adj.* saevus, -a, -um

victim *n.* victima, -ae *f.* (*beast for sacrifice*); *n.* praeda, -ae *f.* (*prey*)

victory *n.* victōria, -ae *f.*

view *n.* aspectus, -ūs *m.* (*sense of sight*); *n.* sententia, -ae *f.* (*opinion; judgment*); *v.t.* vīsō, -ere, vīsī, vīsum

vigor *n.* vīs, vim (*acc.*), vī (*abl.*) *f.* (*def. n.*)

villa *n.* vīlla, -ae *f.*

village *n.* vīcus, -ī *m.*

vine *n.* vītis, -is *f.*

vinegar *n.* acētum, -ī *nt.*

vineyard *n.* vīnea, -ae *f.*

vintage *n.* vindēmia, -ae *f.*

violate *v.t.* violō, -āre, -āvī, -ātum

violation *n.* violātiō, -ōnis *f.* (*profanation; injury*)

violence *n.* violentia, -ae *f.*

violent *adj.* violentus, -a, -um

violet *n.* viola, -ae *f.*; *adj.* violāceus, -a, -um

virgin *n.* virgō, -inis *f.*

virginal *adj.* virginālis, -is, -e

virginity *n.* virginitās, -ātis *f.*

virtue *n.* virtus, -ūtis *f.*

visible *adj.* cōnspicuus, -a, -um

vision *n.* vīsus, -ūs *m.* (*sense of sight; thing seen*); *n.* simulacrum, -ī *nt.* (*apparition*)

visit *n.* salūtātiō, -ōnis *f.* (*ceremonial call*); *n.* mānsiō, -ōnis *f.* (*extended stay*); *v.t.* visitō, -āre, -āvī, -ātum (*go to see*); *v.t.* salūtō, -āre, -āvī, -ātum (*pay a call on*)

visitor *n.* salūtātor, -ōris *m.* (*one paying a call*); *n.* hospes, -itis *m./f.* (*guest*)

vital *adj.* vītālis, -is, -e
vivid *adj.* vīvidus, -a, -um
vocabulary *n.* cōpia verbōrum, cōpiae verbōrum *f.* (*stock of words*); *n.* index verbōrum, indicis verbōrum *m.* (*list of words*)
vocal *adj.* vōcālis, -is, -e
voice *n.* vōx, vōcis *f.*; *v.t.* dēclārō, -clārāre, -clārāvī, -clārātum
void *adj.* inānis, -is -e (*empty*); *adj.* irritus, -a, -um (*invalid; of no effect*)
volume *n.* volūmen, -inis *nt.* (*roll; scroll; book*); *n.* magnitūdō, -inis *f.* (*size*); *n.* cōpia, -ae *f.* (*quantity*)
voluntary *adj.* voluntārius, -a, -um
volunteer *n.* voluntārius, -ī *m.*
vomit *v.i.* vomō, -ere, -uī, -itum
vote *n.* suffrāgium, -ī *nt.*; *v.d.i.* suffrāgor, suffrāgārī, suffrāgātus sum
voter *n.* suffrāgātor, -ōris *m.*
voucher *n.* testis, -is *m./f.* (*witness*)
vow *n.* vōtum, -ī *nt.*; *v.t.* voveō, -ēre, vōvī, vōtum
vowel *n.* littera vōcālis, litterae vōcālis *f.*
voyage *n.* nāvigātiō, -ōnis *f.*; *v.i.* nāvigō, -igāre, -igāvī, -igātum
vulgar *adj.* vulgāris, -is, -e (*pertaining to the multitude or the vulgus*); *adj.* sordidus, -a, -um (*base; low*)

W

wade *v.i.* vadō trānseō, -īre, -īvī (-iī), -ītum
wag *v.t.* moveō, -ēre, mōvī, mōtum
wages *n.* mercēs, -ēdis *f.*
wagon *n.* plaustrum, -ī *nt.*
waist *n.* Use the *adj.* medius, -a, -um.
wait *n.* mora, -ae *f.*; *v.i.* maneō, -ēre, mānsī, mānsum; **~ for** *v.t.* exspectō, -spectāre, -spectāvī, -spectātum; **~ on** *v.t.* ministrō, -āre, -āvī, -ātum
waiter *n.* minister, ministrī *m.*
waitress *n.* ancilla, -ae *f.*
waive *v.t.* rēmittō, -mittere, -mīsī, -mīssum
wake *v.t.* excitō, -citāre, -citāvī, -citātum; **~ up** *v.d.i.* expergīscor, expergīscī, experrēctus sum
walk *n.* incessus, -ūs *m.* (*gait*); *n.* ambulātiō, -ōnis *f.* (*stroll; place for walking*); *v.i.* ambulō, -āre, -āvī, -ātum
walker *n.* pedes, -itis *m.*
wall *n.* mūrus, -ī *m.*

wallet *n.* pēra, -ae *f.*

walnut *n.* iūglāns, iūglandis *f.*

wand *n.* virga, -ae *f.*

wander *v.i.* errō, -āre, -āvī, -ātum

wandering *adj.* vagus, -a, -um

want *n.* pēnūria, -ae *f.*; *v.t.* dēsīderō, -āre, -āvī, -ātum (*long for*); *v.i.* careō, -ēre, caruī, caritūrum (+ abl.) (*be without*); *v.i.* volō, velle, voluī, --- (+ infv. or jussive subjv. clause *or* + acc. of thing desired) (*wish*); **be in ~ of** *v.i.* egeō, egēre, eguī , --- (+ abl. *or* + gen.)

war *n.* bellum, -ī *nt.*; **wage ~** *v.i.* bellum gerō, -ere, gessī, gestum

wardrobe *n.* vestiārium, -ī *nt.*

ware(s) *n.* merx, mercis *f.*

warehouse *n.* horreum, -ī *nt.*

warm *adj.* calidus, -a, -um

warmth *n.* calor, -ōris *m.*

warn *v.t.* moneō, -ēre, monuī, monitum

warning *n.* monitiō, -ōnis *f.*

warrant *n.* auctoritās, -ātis *f.*

wart *n.* verrūca, -ae *f.*

wash *v.t.* lavō, -āre, lāvī, lautum (lōtum)

wasp *n.* vespa, -ae *f.*

waste *n.* quisquiliae, -ārum *f./pl.* (*trash*); *n.* populātiō, -ōnis *f.* (*devastation; ravaging*); *v.t.* cōnsūmō, -sūmere, -sūmpsī, -sūmptum

wasteful *adj.* prōdigus, -a, -um

wasteland *n.* sōlitūdō, -inis *f.*

watch *n.* vigilia, -ae *f.* (*period of guard duty*); *n.* custōs, -ōdis *m./f.* (*guard*); *v.t.* observō, -servāre, -servāvī, -servātum (*observe; note*); **keep ~** *v.t., v.i.* vigilō, -āre, -āvī, -ātum

watchful *adj.* vigilāns, -antis

watchman *n.* custōs, -ōdis *m./f.*

water *n.* aqua, -ae *f.*; *v.t.* irrigō, -rigāre, -rigāvī, -rigātum

watery *adj.* aquārius, -a, -um

wave *n.* unda, -ae *f.*; *v.t.* agitō, -āre, -āvī, -ātum

waver *v.i.* fluctuō, -āre, -āvī, -ātum

wax *n.* cēra, -ae *f.*; *v.t.* cērō, -āre, -āvī, -ātum (*apply wax*); *v.i.* crēscō, -ere, crēvī, crētum (*increase*)

way *n.* via, -ae *f.* (*road; journey; manner*); *n.* modus, -ī *m.* (*manner*); **in the ~** *adj.* obvius, -a, -um; **lose one's ~** *v.i.* errō, -āre, -āvī, -ātum

wayward *adj.* pertināx, -ācis

we

we *pron.* nōs

weak *adj.* īnfirmus, -a, -um (*unhealthy; feeble*); *adj.* levis, -is, -e (*of character, arguments, etc.*)

weaken *v.t.* dēbilitō, -āre, -āvī, -ātum

weakness *n.* dēbilitās, -ātis *f.*

wealth *n.* dīvitiae, -ārum *f./pl.*

wealthy *adj.* dīves, dīvitis

weapon *n.* tēlum, -ī *nt.*

wear *v.t.* conterō, -terere, -trīvī, -trītum (*rub on*; ~ *away*; ~ *out*); *v.t.* gerō, -ere, gessī, gessum (~ *clothes*)

weary *adj.* fātigātus, -a, -um

weather *n.* tempestās, -ātis *f.*

weave *v.t.* texō, -ere, texuī, textum

weaver *n.* textor, -ōris *m.*

web *n.* tēla, -ae *f.*

wedding day *n.* diēs nūptiārum, diēī nūptiārum *m.*

wedge *n.* cuneus, -ī *m.*

Wednesday *n.* diēs Mercuriī, diēī Mercuriī *m.*

weed *n.* herba, -ae *f.*; *v.t.* ēruncō, -āre, -āvī, -ātum

weep *v.i.* lacrimō, -āre, -āvī, -ātum

weigh *v.t.* pendō, -ere, pependī, pēnsum

weight *n.* pondus, -eris *nt.*

weird *adj.* mīrus, -a, -um

welcome *n.* salūtātiō, -ōnis *f.*; *v.t.* accipiō, -cipere, -cēpī, -ceptum (*receive as one's guest*); *v.t.* salūtō, -āre, -āvī, -ātum (*greet*); **Welcome!** Salvē! (*sg.*), Salvēte (*pl.*)

welfare *n.* salūs, -ūtis *f.*

well *n.* puteus, -ī *m.*; *adj.* salvus, -a, -um; *adv.* bene; **be** ~ *v.i.* valeō, -ēre, valuī, valitum

west *n.* occidēns, -entis *m.*; *adj.* occidentālis, -is, -e; *adv.* ad occidentem

western *adj.* occidentālis, -is, -e

wet *adj.* madidus, -a, -um; *v.t.* madefaciō, -facere, -fēcī, -factum

whale *n.* bālaena, -ae *f.*

wharf *n.* nāvālia, -ium *nt./pl.*

what *adj.* qui, quae, quod; *pron.* quis, quis quid; ~ **sort of** *adj.* quālis, -is, -e

whatever *adj.* quisquis, quaeque, quodquod; *pron.* quisquis, quaeque, quicquid (quidquid)

wheat *n.* trīticum, -ī *nt.*

wheel *n.* rota, -ae *f.*

wheeze *n.* anhēlitus, -ūs *m.*; *v.i.* anhēlō, -āre, -āvī, -ātum
when *conj.* cum, ubi; *inter. adv.* quandō
whence *adv.* unde
where *adv.* ubi
wherever *adv.* ubicumque; *conj.* ubicumque
whether *conj.* num (*in indirect questions*); ~ ... or *conj.* utrum ... an;
  utrum ... -ne
which *adj.* uter, utra, utrum (*referring to two*); *adj.* quī, quae, quod (*referring to more than two*); *pron.* quī, quae, quod; ~ **way** *adv.* quā
whichever *adj.* quisquis, quaeque, quodquod; *pron.* quīcumque,
  quaecumque, quodcumque
while *conj.* dum; **for a ~** *adv.* paulisper
whip *v.t.* verberō, -āre, -āvī, -ātum
whirl *v.t.* torqueō, torquēre, torsī, tortum
whirlpool *n.* vortex, -icis *m.*
whisk *n.* scopula, -ae *f.*; *v.t., v.i.* verrō, -ere, verrī, versum (*sweep*); *v.t.* rapiō,
  -ere, rapuī, raptum (*snatch*)
whisper *n.* susurrus, -ī *m.*; *v.i.* susurrō, -āre, -āvī, -ātum
whistle *n.* fistula, -ae *f.* (*instrument*); *n.* sībulus, -ī *m.* (*act of whistling*); *v.i.*
  sībilō, -āre, -āvī, -ātum
white *adj.* albus, -a, -um
whiten *v.t.* dealbō, -albāre, -albāvī, -albātum
whither *adv.* quō
who *rel. pron.* quī, quae, quod; *inter. pron.* quis, quis, quid
whoever *pron.* quīcumque, quaecumque, quodcumque
whole *adj.* tōtus, -a, -um (*entire*); *adj.* integer, integra, integrum (*unhurt*)
wholesome *adj.* salūtāris, -is, -e
whom *pron.* Use dat., acc., or abl. case of quī, quae, quod
whose *pron.* Use gen. case of quī, quae, quod
why *adv.* cūr, quārē
wick *n.* filum, -ī *nt.*
wicked *adj.* improbus, -a, -um
wicker *adj.* crāticulus, -a, -um
wide *adj.* lātus, -a, -um
widen *v.t.* dīlātō, -lātāre, -lātāvī, -lātātum
widow *n.* vidua, -ae *f.*
widower *n.* (vir) viduus, (virī) viduī *m.*
width *n.* lātitūdō, -inis *f.*
wield *v.t.* trāctō, -āre, -āvī, -ātum

wife *n.* uxor, -ōris *f.*

wig *n.* capillāmentum, -ī *nt.*

wild *adj.* ferus, -a, -um

wilderness *n.* sōlitūdō, -inis *f.*

wildlife *n./pl.* ferae, -ārum *f./pl.*

will *n.* voluntās, -ātis *f. (volition; purpose); n.* testāmentum, -ī *nt. (legal document); v.i.* volo, velle, voluī, ---; *for verbal aux. use future tense.*

willing *adj.* libēns, libentis; **~ly** *adv.* libenter

willow *n.* salīx, salicis *f.*

win *v.d.t.* adipīscor, adipīscī, adeptus sum *(gain; secure); v.i.* vincō, -ere, vīcī, victum *(~ a victory)*

wind *n.* ventus, -ī *m.; v.t.* volvō, -ere, volvī, volūtum *(turn round)*

window *n.* fenestra, -ae *f.*

windy *adj.* ventōsus, -a, -um

wine *n.* vīnum, -ī *nt.*

wing *n.* āla, -ae *f.*

wink *n.* nictātiō, -ōnis *f.; v.i.* nictō, -āre, -āvī, -ātum

winner *n.* victor, -ōris *m.*

winter *n.* hiems, hiemis *f.*

wipe *v.t.* tergeō, -ēre, tersī, tersum

wire *n.* filum, -ī *nt.*

wisdom *n.* sapientia, -ae *f.*

wise *adj.* sapiēns, -entis

wish *n.* optātiō, -ōnis *f. (act of wishing); n.* optātum, -ī *nt. (thing wished for); n.* vōtum, -ī *nt. (prayer); v.t.* optō, -āre, -āvī, -ātum *(choose; prefer); v.i.* volō, velle, voluī, ---

wit *n.* ingenium, -ī *nt. (intellectual power); n.* facētiae, -ārum *f./pl. (humor)*

witch *n.* venēfica, -ae *f.*

with *prep.* cum (+ abl.) *In expression of "means," use abl. with no prep.*

withdraw *v.t.* subdūcō, -dūcere, -dūxī, -ductum; *v.i.* cēdō, -ere, cessī, cessum

withhold *v.t.* retineō, -tinēre, -tinuī, -tentum

within *adv.* intus; *prep.* intrā (+ acc.) *(of place or time). For time expressions, one may use abl. case and no prep.*

without *adv.* extra; *prep.* extrā (+ acc.) *(on the outside of); prep.* sine (+ abl.) *(expressing want or absence)*

withstand *v.i.* resistō, -sistere, -stitī, ---

witness *n.* testis, -is *m./f. (legal ~); n.* spectātor, -ōris *m. (observer; watcher); v.d.t.* testor, testārī, testātus sum *(for legal proceeding); v.t.* spectō, -āre, -āvī, -ātum *(observe; see)*

wrinkle

witty *adj.* facētus, -a, -um
wolf *n.* lupus, -ī *m.*; *n.* lupa, -ae *f.*
woman *n.* mulier, mulieris *f.*; *n.* fēmina, -ae *f.*; **old ~** *n.* anus, -ūs *f.*
womb *n.* uterus, -ī *m.*
wonder *v.d.i.* mīror, mīrārī, mīrātus sum (*marvel*)
wonderful *adj.* mīrus, -a, -um
wood *n.* lignum, -ī *nt.*
woods *n.* silva, -ae *f.*
wool *n.* lāna, -ae *f.*
woolen *adj.* lāneus, -a, -um
word *n.* verbum, -ī *nt.*; **~ for ~** *adv.* ad verbum
work *n.* opus, -eris *nt.* (*any result of work; employment; workmanship*); *n.* labor, -ōris *m.* (*effort; toil*); *v.i.* laborō, -āre, -āvī, -ātum
worker *n.* operārius, -ī *m.*; *n.* opifex, -ficis *m./f.* (*artisan*); *n.* faber, fabrī *m.* (e.g. *smith, carpenter, engineer*)
workshop *n.* officīna, -ae *f.* (*for all sorts of work*); *n.* fabrica, -ae *f.* (*especially for work in metals or wood*)
world *n.* mundus, -ī *m.* (*universe*); *n.* orbis, orbis *m.* (*planet earth*); *n.* hominēs, -um *m./pl.* (*mankind*); *n.* gentēs, -ium *f./pl.* (*nations*)
worm *n.* vermis, -is *m.*
worn out *adj.* trītus, -a, -um (*exhausted*)
worried *adj.* sollicitus, -a, -um
worry *n.* sollicitūdō, -inis *f.*; *v.i.* sollicitus sum, esse, fuī
worse *adj.* pēior, pēius; *adv.* pēius
worship *n.* cultus, -ūs *m.*; *v.t.* colō, -ere, coluī, cultum; *v.d.t.* veneror, venerārī, venerātus sum
worst *adj.* pessimus, -a, -um; *adv.* pessimē
worth *adj.* dignus, -a, -um (+ abl.)
worthless *adj.* vīlis, -is, -e (*cheap*); *adj.* inūtilis, -is, -e (*useless*)
worthy *adj.* dignus, -a, -um (+ abl.)
wound *n.* vulnus, vulneris *nt.*; *v.t.* vulnerō, -āre, -āvī, -ātum
wrap *v.t.* involvō, -volvere, -volvī, -volūtum
wrath *n.* īra, -ae *f.*
wreath *n.* corōna, -ae *f.*
wreck *n.* ruīna, -ae *f.* (*downfall; ruin of hopes, etc.; in pl., ruins of a building*); *v.t.* frangō, -ere, frēgī, frāctum; **ship~** *n.* naufragium, -ī *nt.*
wrestle *v.d.t.* luctor, luctārī, luctātus sum
wrestler *n.* luctātor, -ōris *m.*
wrinkle *n.* rūga, -ae *f.*

wrinkled *adj.* rūgōsus, -a, -um
write *v.t.* scrībō, -ere, scrīpsī, scrīptum
writer *n.* scrīptor, -ōris *m.*
writing *n.* scrīptiō, -ōnis *f.* (*act of writing*); *n.* scrīptum, -ī *nt.* (*thing written*)
wrong *n.* iniūria, -ae *f.*; *adj.* mendōsus, -a, -um (*incorrect*); *adj.* inīquus, -a, -um (*unjust; unfair; unkind*); *adj.* prāvus, -a, -um (*immoral*); *adj.* iniūstus, -a, -um (*unjust*)

Y

yard *n.* ārea, -ae *f.* (*court*~); *n.* antenna, -ae *f.* (*sail*~)
yarn *n.* filum, -ī *nt.*
yawn *n.* oscitātiō, -ōnis *f.*; *v.i.* oscitō, -citāre, -citāvī, -citātum
year *n.* annus, -ī *m.*
yearly *adj.* annuus, -a, -um; *adv.* quotannīs
yearn *v.i.* dēsīderō, -āre, -āvī, -ātum
yeast *n.* fermentum, -ī *nt.*
yell *n.* ululātus, -ūs *m.*; *v.i.* ululō, -āre, -āvī, -ātum
yellow *adj.* flāvus, -a, -um
yes *adv.* ita
yesterday *adv.* herī; *n.* hesternus diēs, hesternī diēī *m.*
yet *adv.* adhūc; *conj.* tamen; **not** ~ *adv.* nōndum
yield *n.* frūctus, -ūs *m.*; *v.t.* efferō (ecferō), efferre, extulī, ēlātum (*produce*); *v.t.* reddō, -dere, -didī, -ditum (*give up; surrender*); *v.i.* cēdō, -ere, cessī, cessum (+ dat.)
yoke *n.* iugum, -ī *nt.*; *v.t.* iungō, -ere, iūnxī, iūnctum
yolk *n.* lūteum, -ī *nt.*
yonder *adv.* illīc
you *pron.* tū (*sg.*), vōs (*pl.*)
young *n.* partus, -ūs *m.* (*the offspring of any species*); *n.* pullus, -ī *m.* (~ *animal*); *adj.* iuvenis, -is, -e
your *adj.* tuus, -a, -um (*you sg.*), vester, vestra, vestrum (*you pl.*)
yourself/yourselves *refl. pron.* Use forms of tū (*sg.*) or vōs (*pl.*)
youth *n.* iuventus, -ūs *f.* (*age of youth; young men as a social class*); *n.* iuvenis, -is *m./f.*
youthful *adj.* iuvenīlis, -is, -e

Z

zeal *n.* studium, -ī *nt.*
zealous *adj.* studiōsus, -a, -um
zenith *n.* vertex, -icis *m.*
zest *n.* studium, -ī *nt.* (*enthusiasm*); *n.* sapor, -ōris *m.* (*flavor*)
zigzag *n.* anfrāctus, -ūs *m.*
zodiac *n.* orbis signifer, orbis signiferī *m.*
zone *n.* regiō, -ōnis *f.*

Appendix A
Geographical Names (Latin–English)

Aegyptus, -ī *m.* Egypt
Aethiopia, -ae *f.* Ethiopia
Aetna, -ae *f.* Mount Etna
Āfrica, -ae *f.* Africa
Alexandria, -ae *f.* Alexandria
Alpēs, -ium *f./pl.* Alps
Appenīnus, -ī *m.* Appennines
Armenia, -ae *f.* Armenia
Asia, -ae *f.* Asia
Assyria, -ae *f.* Assyria
Athēnae, -ārum *f./pl.* Athens
Britannia, -ae *f.* Britain
Byzantium, -ī *nt.* Constantinople
Calēdonia, -ae *f.* Scotland
Carthāgō, Carthāginis *f.* Carthage
Caucasus, -ī *m.* Caucasus,
Circulus Aequinoctiālis, Circulī Aequinoctiālis *m.* equator
Collis Quirīnālis, Collis Quirīnālis *m.* Quirinal Hill
Collis Vīminālis, Collis Vīminālis *m.* Viminal Hill
Crēta, -ae *f.* Crete
Cyprus, -i *f.* Cyprus
Dānuvius, -ī *m.* the upper Danube River
Eurōpa, -ae *f.* Europe
Forum Rōmānum, Forī Rōmānī *nt.* Roman Forum
Gallia, -ae *f.* France
Gangēs, Gangis *m.* Ganges River
Genāva, -ae *f.* Geneva
Germānia, -ae *f.* Germany
Graecia, -ae *f.* Greece
Helvētia, -ae *f.* Switzerland

Hibernia, -ae *f.* Ireland
Hierosolyma, -ōrum *nt./pl.* Jerusalem
Hister, Histrī *m.* the lower Danube River
India, -ae *f.* India
Ītalia, -ae *f.* Italy
Iūdaea, -ae *f.* Judaea, Palestine
Libya, -ae *f.* Libya
Londinium, -ī *nt.* London
Lūtētia, -ae *f.* Paris
Mare Atlanticum, Maris Atlanticī *nt.* Atlantic Ocean
Mare Caspium, Maris Caspiī *nt.* Caspian Sea
Mare Germānicum, Maris Germānicī *nt.* North Sea
Mare Internum, Maris Internī *nt.* Mediterranean Sea
Melita, -ae *f.* Malta
Mōns Aventīnus, Montis Aventīnī *m.* Aventine Hill
Mōns Caelius, Montis Caeliī *m.* Caelian Hill
Mōns Capitōlīnus, Montis Capitōlīnī *m.* Capitoline Hill
Mōns Esquilīnus, Montis Esquilīnī *m.* Esquiline Hill
Mōns Palātīnus, Montis Palātīnī *m.* Palatine Hill
Nīlus, -ī *m.* Nile River
Pompēiī, -ōrum *m./pl.* Pompeii
Pontus Euxīnus, Pontis Euxīnī *m.* Black Sea
Rhēnus, -ī *m.* Rhine
Rōma, -ae *f.* Rome
Sicilia, -ae *f.* Sicily
Sinus Arabicus, Sinūs Arabicī *m.* Red Sea
Sinus Persicus, Sinūs Persicī *m.* Persian Gulf
Tiberis, -is *m.* Tiber River
Vertex Aquilōnius caelī, Verticis Aquilōniī caelī *m.* North Pole
Vertex Austrālis caelī, Verticis Austrālis caelī *m.* South Pole
Vesuvius, -ī *m.* Mount Vesuvius

Appendix B
Geographical Names (English–Latin)

Africa Āfrica, -ae *f.*
Alexandria Alexandrīa, -ae *f.*
Alps Alpēs, -ium *f./pl.*
Appennines Appenīnus, -ī *m.*
Armenia Armenia, -ae *f.*
Asia Asia, -ae *f.*
Assyria Assyria, -ae *f.*
Athens Athēnae, -ārum *f./pl.*
Atlantic Ocean Mare Atlanticum, Maris Atlanticī *nt.*
Aventine Hill Mōns Aventīnus, Montis Aventīni *m.*
Black Sea Pontus Euxīnus, Pontis Euxīnī *m.*
Britain Britannia, -ae *f.*
Caelian Hill Mōns Caelius, Montis Caeliī *m.*
Capitoline Hill Mōns Capitōlīnus, Montis Capitōlīnī *m.*
Carthage Carthāgō, Carthāginis *f.*
Caspian Sea Mare Caspium, Maris Caspiī *nt.*
Caucasus Caucasus, -ī *m.*
Constantinople Byzantium, -ī *nt.*
Crete Crēta, -ae *f.*
Cyprus Cyprus, -i *f.*
Danube River (lower) Hister, Histrī *m.*
Danube River (upper) Dānuvius, -ī *m.*
Egypt Aegyptus, -ī *m.*
Equator Circulus Aequinoctiālis, Circulī Aequinoctiālis *m.*
Esquiline Hill Mōns Esquilīnus, Montis Esquilīnī *m.*
Ethiopia Aethiopia, -ae *f.*
Etna, Mount Aetna, -ae *f.*
Europe Eurōpa, -ae *f.*
France Gallia, -ae *f.*
Ganges River Gangēs, -is *m.*
Geneva Genāva, -ae *f.*

Germany Germānia, -ae *f.*
Greece Graecia, -ae *f.*
India India, -ae *f.*
Ireland Hibernia, -ae *f.*
Italy Ītalia, -ae *f.*
Jerusalem Hierosolyma, -ōrum *nt./pl.*
Judaea Iūdaea, -ae *f.*
Libya Libya, -ae *f.*
London Londinium, -ī *nt.*
Malta Melita, -ae *f.*
Mediterranean Sea Mare Internum, Maris Internī *nt.*
Nile River Nilus, -ī *m.*
North Pole Vertex Aquilōnius caelī, Verticis Aquilōniī caelī *m.*
North Sea Mare Germānicum, Maris Germānicī *nt.*
Palatine Hill Mōns Palātīnus, Montis Palātīnī *m.*
Palestine Iūdaea, -ae *f.*
Paris Lūtētia, -ae *f.*
Persian Gulf Sinus Persicus, Sinūs Persicī *m.*
Pompeii Pompēiī, -ōrum *m./pl.*
Quirinal Hill Collis Quirīnālis, Collis Quirīnālis *m.*
Red Sea Sinus Arabicus, Sinūs Arabicī *m.*
Rhine River Rhēnus, -ī *m.*
Roman Forum Forum Rōmānum, Forī Rōmānī *nt.*
Rome Rōma, -ae *f.*
Scotland Calēdonia, -ae *f.*
Sicily Sicilia, -ae *f.*
South Pole Vertex Austrālis caelī, Verticis Austrālis caelī *m.*
Switzerland Helvētia, -ae *f.*
Tiber River Tiberis, -is *m.*
Vesuvius, Mount Vesuvius, -ī *m.*
Viminal Hill Collis Vīminālis, Collis Vīminālis *m.*

Appendix C
Names of Peoples (Latin–English)

Aborīginēs, -um *m./pl.* the Aborigines (*a tribe of Italy from whom the Latins were thought to be descended*)

Aegyptī, -ōrum *m./pl.* the Egyptians

Aethiopēs, -um *m./pl.* the Ethiopians

Āfrī, -ōrum *m./pl.* the inhabitants of Africa

Āfricānī, -ōrum *m./pl.* the inhabitants of Africa

Amāzonēs, -um *f./pl.* the Amazons (*the mythical nation of women warriors*)

Arabēs, -um *m./pl.* the Arabs

Athēniēnsēs, -ium *m./pl.* the Athenians

Britannī, -ōrum *m./pl.* the inhabitants of Britain

Celtae, -ārum *m./pl.* the Celts

Christiānī, -ōrum *m./pl.* the Christians

Etrūscī, -ōrum *m./pl.* the Etruscans (*who lived in Tuscany*)

Gallī, -ōrum *m./pl.* the Gauls (*who lived in the area of modern France*)

Germānī, -ōrum *m./pl.* the Germans

Graecī, -ōrum *m./pl.* the Greeks

Hebraeī, -ōrum *m./pl.* the Hebrews

Helvētī, -ōrum *m./pl.* the Helvetii (*a people of the area of modern Switzerland*)

Hispānī, -ōrum *m./pl.* the Hispani (*people of Spain*)

Indī, -ōrum *m./pl.* the inhabitants of India

Ītalī, -ōrum *m./pl.* the inhabitants of Italy

Iūdaeī, -ōrum *m./pl.* the Jews

Lacedaemoniī, -ōrum *m./pl.* the Lacedaemonians or Spartans

Latīnī, -ōrum *m./pl.* the Latins

Libycī, -ōrum *m./pl.* the Libyans (*a people of Libya in north Africa*)

Nomadēs, -um *m./pl.* nomads; the inhabitants of Numidia in North Africa

Parthī, -ōrum *m./pl.* the Parthians (*who lived in an area southeast of the Caspian Sea*)

Persae, -ārum *m./pl.* the Persians

Phoenīcēs, -um *m./pl.* the Phoenicians
Pictī, -ōrum *m./pl.* the Picts (*a British tribe that lived north of Hadrian's Wall*)
Poenī, -ōrum *m./pl.* the Carthaginians
Rōmānī, -ōrum *m./pl.* the Romans
Scythae -ārum *m./pl.* the Scythians
Sērēs, -um *m./pl.* the Chinese
Siculī, -ōrum *m./pl.* the Sicilians
Teutonēs, -um *m./pl.* the Teutoni (*a Germanic tribe*)
Trōiānī, -ōrum *m./pl.* the Trojans

Appendix D
Names of Peoples (English–Latin)

Aborigines (*a tribe of Italy from whom the Latins were thought to be descended*) Aborīginēs, -um *m./pl.*

Africans Åfrī, -ōrum *m./pl.*; Āfricānī, -ōrum *m./pl.*

Amazons (*the mythical nation of women warriors*) Amāzonēs, -um *f./pl.*

Arabs Arabēs, -um *m./pl.*

Athenians Athēniēnsēs, -ium *m./pl.*

Britons Britannī, -ōrum *m./pl.*

Carthaginians Poenī, -ōrum *m./pl.*

Celts Celtae, -ārum *m./pl.*

Chinese Sērēs, -um *m./pl.*

Christians Christiānī, -ōrum *m./pl.*

Egyptians Aegyptī, -ōrum *m./pl.*

Ethiopians Aethiopēs, -um *m./pl.*

Etruscans (*who lived in Tuscany*) Etrūscī, -ōrum *m./pl.*

Gauls (*who lived in the area of modern France*) Gallī, -ōrum *m./pl.*

Germans Germānī, -ōrum *m./pl.*

Greeks Graecī, -ōrum *m./pl.*

Hebrews Hebraeī, -ōrum *m./pl.*

Helvetii (*a people of modern Switzerland*) Helvētiī, -ōrum *m./pl.*

Hispani, or people of Spain Hispānī, -ōrum *m./pl.*

Indians (*inhabitants of India*) Indī, -ōrum *m./pl.*

Italians Ītalī, -ōrum *m./pl.*

Jews Iūdaeī, -ōrum *m./pl.*

Lacedaemonians Lacedaemoniī, -ōrum *m./pl.*

Latins Latīnī, -ōrum *m./pl.*

Libyans (*a people of Libya in North Africa*) Libycī, -ōrum *m./pl.*

Nomads; the inhabitants of Numidia in North Africa Nomadēs, -um *m./pl.*

Numidians of North Africa Nomadēs, -um *m./pl.*

Parthians (*who lived in an area southeast of the Caspian Sea*) Parthī, -ōrum *m./pl.*

Persians Persae, -ārum *m./pl.*
Phoencians Phoenīcēs, -um *m./pl.*
Picts (*a British tribe north of Hadrian's Wall*) Pictī, -ōrum *m./pl.*
Romans Rōmānī, -ōrum *m./pl.*
Scythians Scythae, -ārum *m./pl.*
Sicilians Siculī, -ōrum *m./pl.*
Spartans Lacedaemoniī, -ōrum *m./pl.*
Teutoni (*a Germanic tribe*) Teutonēs, -um *m./pl.*
Trojans Trōiānī, -ōrum *m./pl.*

Other Titles in the Hippocrene
Latin Language Studies Library

Ancient Rome in So Many Words
Christopher Francese

The brief word histories in this book use language as a window into the culture of ancient Rome. The author delves into the hidden story behind some common Latin words, using them not only to illustrate aspects of Roman life but to avoid traditional caricatures of the Romans as uniquely noble or depraved and find out what mattered to the Roman themselves and how they thought about it. *Ancient Rome* includes word histories of almost 100 classical Latin terms spread out across such diverse areas of ancient Roman social life as childhood, status & class, debauchery, and insults.

248 pages · 6 x 9 · 0-7818-1153-8 · $12.95pb

Fairy Tales in Latin: Fabulae Mirables
Victor Barocas, Susan Schearer & Brad Rhodes

Directed toward intermediate and advanced Latin students, these stories, which include "The Three Little Pigs (*Tres Porcelli*)," "Little Red Riding Hood (*Lacernella Rubra*)," and "The Emperor's New Clothes (*Novae Vestes Imperatoris*)" are not as technically difficult as prose excerpts from authors like Livy or Cicero. Each story is about 500-1,000 words in length, and accompanied by a lively illustration. A comprehensive glossary of 900 entries includes the English translation for all words used in the text.

94 pages · 8¾ x 5¾ · 0-7818-0787-5 · $12.50hc

Grammar of the Latin Language
Leonhard Schmitz

This timeless classic for the student of Latin examines such topics as orthography, noun declension, and verb conjugation. A special section on sentence structure helps to put the grammar in context. A unique feature of this book is its analysis of etymologies, particularly the Greek origins of many Latin words. The book focuses on Classical Latin from the "Golden" period (100-14 B.C.), but other variations of the language are also addressed.

318 pages · 5½ x 8½ · 0-7818-1040-X · $14.95pb

Latin Phrasebook
C. Meissner

With 5,000 Latin phrases sensibly organized by subject, this phrasebook is a remarkable reference source for students and scholars of the Latin language. Subjects included are Space and Time, World and Nature, Arts and Science, the Mind and its Functions, Emotions, Religion, War, and many more.

5,000 entries · 338 pages · 4½ x 7 · 0-7818-0666-6 · $14.95pb

Treasury of Roman Love Poems, Quotations & Proverbs in Latin and English
Edited by Richard A. Branyon

This lovely bilingual gift volume contains over 70 poems, along with sonnets, proverbs and aphorisms, in Latin with side-by-side English translations. Major Latin love poems included are: Lucretius, Catullus, Virgil, Horace, Tibullus, Propertius, Ovid, Petronius, Juvenal, Pervigilium Veneris, Carmina Burana, and Joannes Secundus. This is a perfect tool for students of the Latin language.

127 pages · 5 x 7 · 0-7818-0309-8 · $11.95hc

Prices subject to change without prior notice. **To purchase Hippocrene Books** contact your local bookstore, visit www.hippocrenebooks.com, call (718) 454-2366, or write to: HIPPOCRENE BOOKS, 171 Madison Avenue, New York, NY 10016. Please enclose check or money order, adding $5.00 shipping (UPS) for the first book, and $.50 for each additional book.